Dodger
MBIS MBISS
CH AM GCH
Kells Touch Of Fleet Street

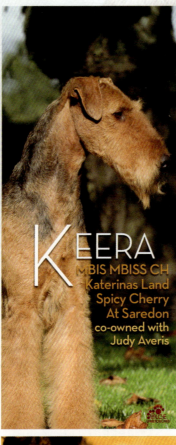

Keera
MBIS MBISS CH
Katerinas Land
Spicy Cherry
At Saredon
co-owned with
Judy Averis

Pippa
CH Ivornhill
Poinsetta

Jonas
Ell-Ell's Just Me
co-owned with
Lisa Croft-Elliott

©advertising & photography Croft-Elliott

Dog World Annual 2014

annual 2014

After a surge of success during the second half of the year the Standard Poodle Ch Afterglow Maverick Sabre became a contender for the Top Dog all breeds award, previously won three times by the Afterglow kennel, and at the time of going to press was just one point behind the Wire Fox Terrier pictured opposite.

He is owned by Jason Lynn and John and Sandra Stone, handled by Jason and bred by him and Mike Gadsby – they also bred the leading gundog of the year.

Ricky's first major success was RBIS at the National, but he moved up a gear with his first BIS at Bournemouth, followed by RBIS at City of Birmingham, then the top spot at Richmond, and at three consecutive shows, Driffield, Belfast and South Wales, and reserve at Midland Counties.

He is a son of BIS winner Ch/Am Ch Del Zarzoso Salvame from Afterglow and a double great-grandson of former Top Dog Ch/Am Ch Afterglow The Big Tease.
photo Alan Walker

Contents

2013 in review
Simon Parsons and Dog World photographers............3-48
Junior stars of the group rings
Victoria Wilkins.. 49-53
Where will we be in five years?
Kennel Club chairman Steve Dean........................ 54-55
The Saxonmill Saga... 56-60
It's the breeders who matter, Sheila Atter..... 62-63
Stockholm's hidden gem
The Dog in Art, Nick Waters.....................................64-67
Ferelith Somerfield's life in the dog world
Simon Parsons...70-79
Rafael de Santiago, the FCI's new president......80-82
The Pouch Cove story, Andrew Brace............... 84-91
Ireland, Joyce Crawford-Manton...........................92-93
United States, Bo Bengtson....................................94-97
Canada, Mike Macbeth..98-99
Norway, Espen Engh..100-101
Finland, Paula Heikkinen-Lehkonen..................102-103
Sweden, Dan Ericsson...104-105
Denmark, Vibeke Knudsen...................................... 106
Poland, Janusz Opara...107
France, Anne-Marie Class..................................108-109
Germany, Wilfried Peper.....................................110-111
Belgium and Luxembourg, Karl Donvil......112-113

Netherlands, Haja van Wessem........................114-115
Spain, Portugal and Gibraltar
Marcelino Pozo...116-117
Italy, Richard Hellman...118-119
Hungary, Gábor Szalánczi..120
The World Show in pictures...............................121
Austria, Maria-Luise Doppelreiter............................122
The European Show in pictures........................123
Russia, Alexey Kalashnikov................................124-125
Israel, Yossi Guy...126
Croatia, Petra Buva..127
Greece, Lila Leventaki...128
South Africa, Greg Eva..129
Australia, Lee Pieterse......................................130-131
Around the dog world.................................... 132-133
New Zealand, Rosemary Hubrich....................134-135
Japan, Mai Ozeki..135-136
Summer show special, Steven Seymour........138-139
Obituaries...140-141
Breeders' advertisements....................................142
The Annual Tradition...151
Forthcoming shows.......................................425-427
Dog-friendly holidays...428
Trade index and juniors' index...........................429
Breeders' index...430-432

2

Eight BIS for Striking Steel

Few dogs can have enjoyed such a sensational show career as Sue Browne-Cole's Wire Fox Terrier Ch Travella Striking Steel, handled by Richard Allen and bred by Sue's husband Bill.

He made his debut at WELKS and won the group, then took BIS at his next two shows, the National and Scottish Kennel Club. The same weekend his sire Ch Travella Starlord, a BIS winner in the UK, was BIS3 at the World Show.

Another group, then BIS at Border Union followed before he could claim his title, which he did at Blackpool with his fourth BIS from six shows. His next BIS came at Leeds and he was reserve at Paignton, BIS at Welsh Kennel Club and a week later he took his seventh BIS at the Scottish KC having thereby been unbeaten in Scotland!

Belfast and South Wales saw him take RBIS and his eighth BIS came at Midland Counties – only the second dog to win eight BIS in one show season. He is the fifth BIS winner for the team.

He, Richard and Sue are pictured at Blackpool with secretary Steve Hall and judge Martin Freeman.
photos Alan Walker

Production

Annual editor: Simon Parsons
Project leader: James Morrissey
Production: Colin Swaffer, John Clement
Editorial: Simon Parsons, Adrian Marett
Advertising: Adrian Marett, Mason Ponti, Gary Doran, Sam Edworthy, Marina Scott, Pam Blay, Alan Walker

Published and distributed by:
The DOG WORLD Ltd
Williamson House, Wotton Road
Ashford, Kent TN23 6LW
Telephone 01233 621877
Fax 01233 645669
Email annual@dogworld.co.uk
Website www.dogworld.co.uk
Subscriptions www.dogworld.co.uk/subscribe-now

Also publishers of DOG WORLD, Britain's top selling weekly canine newspaper
Copyright The Dog World Ltd
Printed by:
Advent Print Group
19 East Portway Industrial Estate, Andover, Hampshire, SP10 3LU
ISBN: 978-0-9567535-3-3

Featured on the front cover is the Jack Russell Terrier Ell-Ell's Just Me, owned by Tony and Jean Barker and Lisa Croft-Elliott.
See also page 1, and for more details of the breed see pages 286-295.
photo Lisa Croft-Elliott

Crufts 2013
Group winners on the move

Reigning Top Dog
Jilly tops Crufts

The Dog World in 2013

AFTER THE public relations disaster that was Crufts 2012, with the heartbreak caused by six of the 15 high-profile best of breed failing their veterinary checks, the 2013 shows was anticipated with some trepidation.

In the event it was almost entirely incident-free, apart from some traffic problems on the first day, and was a thoroughly pleasant experience. The fact that all the BOBs passed this time undoubtedly helped enormously!

The entry in the breed classes, gamekeepers' classes and Obedience Championships was 20,566, a pretty impressive figure compared with all the other UK shows, and as usual the biggest in the world since the previous Crufts.

Nevertheless it was the lowest Crufts figure since 1997, 463 dogs down on 202 in spite of the fact that 145 dogs of 13 imported register breeds were competing for the first time. On the plus side, dogs competing from overseas topped 2,000, covering 41 countries.

Over all the disciplines, more than 25,000 dogs were scheduled to take part. Labradors, with 490, and Golden Retrievers, 454, topped the breed entries.

A new feature of the show was the impressive stand of the Kennel Club Accredited Instructors' Career Zone, providing advice and lectures for those hoping to make a living in the canine world. It attracted an enthusiastic response with 1,300 people visiting.

If relations between the veterinary profession and the breeding world are sometimes awkward, the facts that more veterinary students than ever attended the show and that the International Canine Health Awards were presented there might well have helped bring them together.

An appealing innovation was having the group judges appear alongside their choices before BIS was judged.

A big bonus was that the Sunday TV programme was broadcast on Channel 4, the first time a major channel had shown the event since the BBC withdrew. This was seen by an average of 1.7 million people.

Best in show at Crufts was the Petit Basset Griffon Vendéen Ch Soletrader Peek-A-Boo, handled by Gavin Robertson and pictured with group judge Ben Reynolds-Frost, owners Sara Robertson and Wendy Doherty and BIS judge Geoff Corish. 'Jilly' had comfortably won the Dog World/Arden Grange Top Dog title for 2012, having won six all-breed BIS during the year. She sprang to fame at Crufts 2011 when she won RBIS while still a young junior, and won an all-breeds BIS that year too. After her Crufts success she retired from regular competition, though she will be competing at the Eukanuba World Challenge In December. She – and Gavin – have not, however, been idle during the year – see page 32.
photo Alan Walker

The other evenings' programmes were shown, as before, on More4. Once again we were lucky that popular Clare Balding was the host.

The TV schedule required BIS to be judged an hour earlier than usual. A plan to start Sunday judging at 8am was thankfully abandoned and in the event no one missed the group so all was well.

The event was also live-streamed and 13,000 people took out subscriptions to the Crufts YouTube channel.

It was claimed that the number of people attending the show was 149,500, up on 2012.

At the 2014 show, children under 12 will be admitted free.

> Pictured opposite with Jilly are the other six group winners from Crufts. Clockwise from top right, Bill Moffat and Joyce Robins' King Charles Spaniel Ch Maibee Theo, handled by Tanya Ireland to the breed's first such success at Crufts; David Roberts, Judy Price and Fiona Whitehead's Tibetan Terrier Kybo Pandarama (now a champion); Bernice Mair and Carole Hartley-Mair's Bernese Mountain Dog Ch Meadowpark Whispers Breeze, handled by Gary Dybdall; Neil Allan and Robert Harlow's Australian Shepherd Ch Allmark Fifth Avenue, handled by Angie Allan; Franco Bărberi's Labrador Int/It Ch Loch Mor Romeo, from Italy, who went on to RBIS and has since gained his UK title; and Sue Breeze's Skye Terrier Ch Salena The Special One.

Frenchies leave the the high profile list

THANKFULLY, the veterinary checks on general and group championship show best of breed winners and new champions in the 14 high profile breeds have been mainly positive during 2013. And one of these breeds has now left the list.

Five dogs, the Pug BOB winners at Boston and South Wales, the Bulldog and Mastiff from Midland Counties and the Bulldog from a non-CC entry at East of England, were failed by the show vets, the first Pug because the vet thought she was suffering from pigmentary keratitis in both eyes, and the second because an eyelash was rubbing on the surface of the eye.

Both cases proved controversial as it was hard to know how judges, with the time available to them, were supposed to be able to spot these conditions.

Eyelashes were also the reason for the East of England Bulldog's failure. The Mastiff, the vet said, had a rash under the chin.

At Crufts the checks were carried out this time by the show's own veterinary team which was led by Dr Andreas Schemel, thus bringing the arrangements in line with those at other championship shows.

Everyone welcomed the fact that all the BOB winners there passed though many found it hard to understand why there should have been such a big difference between the test results between 2012 and 2013.

Judges of the high profile breeds and the vets who do the checks had been invited to an education day in February where more than 100 examples of the breeds were on display.

Visible

Observation of the judging of the high-profile breeds at general and group championship shows resumed in 2013, as not enough data was being produced to be able to monitor these breeds' progress.

An article in the December 2013 *Kennel Gazette* hinted that the process might eventually be discontinued 'as judges of the high-profile breeds succeed in demonstrating to, and convincing their critics that they can and do recognise and penalise dogs with clearly visible and detrimental exaggerations of conformation'.

The KC annual meeting received a report from the working party set up the previous year to look at the checks which indicated that they would continue and that confusion over the vet's and judge's roles could be resolved through good communication.

The report recommended that judges could be present at the checks, if the exhibitor and vet agree, as well as a KC appointed person to ensure consistency. At the time of writing, this has not yet been put in place.

It also recommended that 'the KC should ensure it keeps under active review the breeds categorised as high-profile and that as soon as possible a detailed framework through which breeds can work towards removal from the list be devised'.

Other recommendations came to pass later in the year, when the KC announced that championship show judges of any breed which is categorised on its Breed Watch list will have to send in a report to the club with their observations on whether any health and welfare issues were visible during their judging appointment. This already happens for the high profile breeds. Judges of any other breed may also send in a report if they feel the need to.

Breeds can move between the three categories – high profile breeds; those with

One of Britain's leading show dogs of the year is the Australian Shepherd Ch Allmark Fifth Avenue, handled by Angie Allan for her husband Neil and Robert Harlow. She was conceived in the US after her dam was sent there to be mated. During 2012 she was RBIS at Welsh KC and BIS at the Scottish group show; in 2013 she won the group at Crufts, BIS at Welsh Working and Pastoral, WELKS, where she is pictured with judge Jane Lilley and president Maureen Micklethwaite, and Paignton, and RBIS at Three Counties.
photo Alan Walker

Breed Watch listings; and those without – if problems are thought to be emerging, or conversely if conditions are found no longer to be prevalent within the breed.

At first glance we felt this was a welcome initiative, perhaps making the high profile breed people feel less isolated, and certainly helping to highlight any difficulties before they really take hold within a breed. It is more similar to the situation in countries such as Sweden and Holland where a much higher number of breeds are being watched, but without the stigma attached to high profile status in this country.

When one looks at the current Breed Watch list on the KC website, however, it becomes apparent that inclusion on it seems somewhat random. Many breeds, which one might have thought had points worth watching, do not have an entry, whereas in others the items listed are questions of type or presentation, rather than potential welfare problems.

At the end of the October it was announced that the French Bulldog was being removed from the high profile list due to 'improvements in the health

Dog World Annual 2014

The Dog World in 2013

We are used to recording amazing successes for the Afterglow team, but they have excelled themselves in 2012, producing two BIS-winning animals who are likely to top their group for the year, one of them in with a chance of Top Dog, and in addition won both the principal sponsored stakes competitions.

The Pro Plan/Dog World Pup of the Year final, judged by Stuart Mallard, went to the American Cocker Spaniel Afterglow Dragon Quest, owned by Jason Lynn, Gilda Rix and Andy Yau and handled by Mike Gadsby who co-bred him with Jason and Gilda.

This was the third time Mike has won POTY, having previously done so with a Tibetan Terrier and with 'George's' ancestor Sh Ch Boduf Pistols At Dawn with Afterglow who went on to become Top Dog. George had already won two CCs and quickly gained his title, but since then he has been held back as the team has also been campaigning his half-sister, pictured below. Also in Stuart's final six was the Afterglow Standard Poodle who has gone on to a spectacular year.

photo Alan Walker

of the breed and the substantial health programmes put in place by the parent breed club'.

Praising the commitment of owners and exhibitors of what she described as a 'breed pre-disposed to conformational health and welfare concerns', KC secretary Caroline Kisko said: "The KC no longer considers it necessary for French Bulldogs to undergo veterinary health checks at general and group championship shows, as the breed health co-ordinator and breed representatives have been consistently and comprehensively managing visible health concerns within the breed and therefore fulfil the high profile breed removal criteria.

Improvement

"The French Bulldog representatives have demonstrated to the KC an improvement in the visible health of the showing population and provided detailed information of a long and short term health and welfare strategy to ensure they safeguard the future of the breed.

"What we want to see is improvements, which are now clearly visible in the show population, across the breed as a whole. Show dogs are seen as being the leaders in breeding and the improvements we have seen in dogs competing in the show ring will undoubtedly have an effect on the health of non-show dogs.

"Furthermore, due to the hard work of the French Bulldog breed clubs and breeders, puppy buyers are more informed than ever before and are encouraged to join in with health initiatives. Higher numbers of French Bulldogs in the show ring will mean the more we can help make a difference to the health of the breed as a whole."

The 13 remaining high profile breeds are the Basset Hound, Bloodhound, Bulldog, Chow Chow, Clumber Spaniel, Dogue de Bordeaux, German Shepherd Dog, Mastiff, Neapolitan Mastiff, Pekingese, Pug, Shar-Pei and St Bernard.

BIS at Three Counties and Darlington was the American Cocker Spaniel Sh Ch Afterglow Pearl's A Singer, owned by Susan Crummey with Jason Lynn. She also took RBIS awards at WELKS, the May Scottish Kennel Club, Border Union and Welsh Kennel Club. Her dam, the Japanese import Sh Ch/Jap Ch Nereid JP Mele Kalikimaka, was also a BIS winner and her sire Sh Ch Afterglow Trinidad also sired the Pup of the Year winner. Judge at Three Counties was Patsy Hollings and the Countess of Darnley, president of the agricultural society, presented the card.

photo Alan Walker

congratulate our winners, a few of whom are pictured here

www.royalcanin.co.uk

Dog World Annual 2014

Property deal brings Kennel Club a £12m windfall

The Dog World in 2013

AFTER something of a rollercoaster ride, the Kennel Club is richer to the tune of £12 million and by the end of 2015 should be installed in new, purpose-built offices 30 per cent larger that its current home.

Originally, KC members voted in November 2011 for a plan in which Chelsfield Partners would take over the Clarges Street premises as part of a development plan. The company would provide a new home for the club a little further down the street. By May 2012, however, the deal had fallen through.

Next on the scene was another development company, British Land, which came up with another plan to develop the entire Clarges Estate, which covers a prime position off Piccadilly. In return for vacating its current premises, the KC was offer a lump sum of £12m, plus a new freehold property further down Clarges Street. All expenses were once again to be paid but this time the new offices really would be new, rather than refurbished.

Voted

KC members met in January and, needless to say, voted to accept the offer.

The new offices will be spread over six floors, with the main entrance on Clarges Street and rear access form Bolton Street. Facilities for members and staff, including the all-important loos, should be significantly improved.

The development of the whole site will create a mixed-use scheme of offices, retail units and flats.

The £12m is subject to tax, but some or all of this could be offset depending on how it is used. Donations to charities, such as the KC's Charitable Trust and Educational Trust, and property acquisition for the benefit of the world of dogs were two possibilities.

Chairman Steve Dean believes the windfall should be 'invested in projects which leave a lasting legacy for the world of dogs'.

A meeting of members is scheduled for December to discuss proposals about how it should be used.

Contracts were exchanged in March and in September British Land received the go-ahead from Westminster Council.

This special meeting was the first time that proxy voting, a requirement of the KC's new company limited by guarantee status, had been used. In the event, even if everyone present had voted against the proposal, it would still have succeeded thanks to the proxies.

The Redwitch team's triple success at Southern Counties must surely be unprecedented. BIS went to the Akita Ch Redwitch Born This Way, owned by Arlene Clure (handling) and Jenny Killilea while his half-brother, their Redwitch Will I Am, handled by Dave Killilea, was best puppy in show, and Dave also handled the reserve BIS-winning Bouvier! Born This Way is the kennel's fourth BIS winner at this level, two of the others winning at this show, and later took RBIS at East of England. Will I Am took five BPIS awards at all-breeds championship shows and was a group winner while still a puppy.
photo Alan Walker

Assured Breeder Scheme achieves UKAS accreditation

THE KENNEL CLUB Assured Breeder Scheme has achieved its long-awaited accreditation by the UKAS (United Kingdom Accreditation Service) which, it is claimed, increases confidence that those certified within the scheme are operating to agreed standards and are continually monitored to ensure they maintain those standards.

This means that in future every new member will be inspected before being accepted, and existing members will be inspected within three years. The number of inspections will therefore double. Inevitably this will lead to some additional costs; the fees have not changed since 2004.

Earlier in the year the scheme had tightened its rules. Members are now required to put in their sales contract that puppies should be taken to a vet after sale, or have the puppy looked at by a vet before sale. They must also keep more detailed records.

All the scheme's rules are contained in a document called the ABS Standard.

During the year the KC surveyed ABS members to see what they wanted from the scheme.

"Members are now required to put in their sales contract that puppies should be taken to a vet after sale, or have the puppy looked at by a vet before sale"

Fav 5®

Fav 5® CL

Fav 5® CL hybrid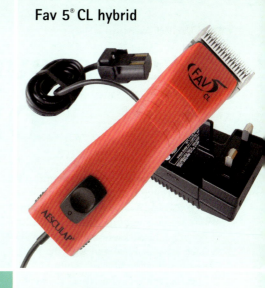

SnapOn blades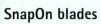

Aesculap®
Tools for the professional groomer

SnapOn blades

Favorita II

Favorita CL

Akkurata / Exacta

Favorita blades

Holder for blades

Akkurata / Exacta blades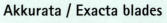
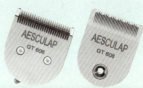

Diamond Edge
Diamond Edge

Aesculap Master Service Centre
Diamond Edge, 126 Gloucester Road, Brighton BN1 4BU
Tel 01273 605922 Fax 01273 625074
diamondedge@btclick.com www.diamondedgeltd.com

B|BRAUN
SHARING EXPERTISE

Dog World Annual 2014

A year around the big shows

The Dog World in 2013

SINCE moving from its home town, Darlington show had spent six years at Newby Hall, near Ripon. It was a beautiful, spacious site in the parkland of this stately home, but the ground surface was not ideal and with inadequate drainage was vulnerable to flooding.

The committee therefore decided to move just a few miles to Ripon Racecourse, where its debut show in September was a great success, the committee expressing its gratitude to the co-operation of the racecourse staff. Certainly the rings were far more level and better drained, and the layout allowed for the popular 'in and out' tents.

Meanwhile the Kennel Club allowed Paignton to go to four days. Many expressed amazement at this as gundog day was immediately before National Gundog, and hound day immediately after the Hound Association.

A number of shows were cancelled over a weekend in mid March when six-inch snowdrifts hit the Midlands and North.

After suffering from the closure of one of the usual NEC car parks in 2012, the Ladies Kennel Association will hold its 2013 show in different halls at the NEC, adjacent to the north car parks. The halls cover a similar area to those we are used to, but are more modern with better acoustics and floor surface.

A total of 2,500 exhibitors completed an online survey run by Birmingham Dog Show Society which asked them what they wanted from the show. Costs proved to be the most emotive subject and the topic of judges created the largest response. The society aims to use the results of the survey to improve this, Britain's oldest show. As a start the classification has been reviewed, catering facilities improved and a practice ring, run by Sue Whitehead, introduced during the show.

Bournemouth has not had the easiest time since the death in 2012 of its long-standing secretary Denise Courtney. In March Wendy King was elected as the new secretary. In May the chairman Mick Howes resigned saying he felt he did not have the support of the full committee – he had earlier applied for the secretary's post. In July Anita Emery retired as treasurer after 20 years. This was followed quickly by the resignation, just two weeks ahead of the show, of the new secretary.

The show, only the second to be held at the society's own showground near Poole, therefore had to go ahead with an acting chairman (John Farrant), secretary (Jenny Stratten, who held the post briefly many years ago) and treasurer (John Appleby). In the event this did not appear to make the slightest difference and the show ran well. Later Bill Short was appointed acting chairman and Kirsten Rotchell acting secretary.

National Gundog offered prize money as a thank you for exhibitors' support. The Scottish Kennel Club's shows' layouts were radically changed and by the August show the whole thing was in the three exhibition halls at the Ingliston venue and the consensus was that the events were greatly improved in every respect.

After twice being abandoned in recent years, Blackpool show survived this time but rain and wind still caused some concern on the final day. The society has now bought 30 acres of grassland 14 miles to the east, through the 2014 show will remain at Crown Fields.

There has been some speculation about the future of East of England, though a spokesman for the agricultural society said that it is solvent and the show will continue. A scheduled 8.30 start did not prove popular with exhibitors, especially when it did not actually materialise on two of the days, and this will not be repeated.

Subsequently Jill Broadberry, who had been secretary of the dog section since her mother Pearl Crocker died in 2007, stepped down, but has since returned, and a new committee has been formed which will include new members. Eight of the original committee were asked to step down. Next year's event will again include Just Dogs Live.

For the first time since 1929, a King Charles Spaniel has won BIS at a UK all-breeds championship show. At East of England Swedish judge Dan Ericsson chose Bill Moffat (standing third right) and Joyce Robins' Ch Maibee Theo, handled by Tanya Ireland. He is the breed's CC record holder and also won the group at Crufts, and was bred by Joyce with Bill's wife, the late Shealagh Waters. With them are dog show chairman John Orbell and secretary Jill Broadberry.
photo Alan Walker

Gordon Setters are one of Britain's oldest show breeds, having been exhibited since the start of dog shows in 1859. Yet amazingly none had won best in show at a UK all-breeds championship show until Sh Ch Hernwood Talladega Racer topped the 2012 Ladies' Kennel Association under Ken Sinclair (left). He is owned by Chris (standing right) and Pete Sandiford and Claire Lewis (handling), and the team also won the show's Pup of the Year heat with another Gordon. Vice-chairman Anne Bliss presented the card.
photo Will Harris

Do you know about our
Breeder Partner Club?
Join us today and enjoy the benefits:

- Preferential prices and FREE delivery on orders over 20kg
- FREE puppy and kitten recommendation packs
- Reward points scheme
- Exclusive promotions
- Dedicated Breeder Team and Nutritional Helpline for ordering and advice
- James Wellbeloved Events Team at national shows and events

Orders and Breeder Team advice: 0845 300 5965

Nutritional Helpline: 0845 603 9095

www.wellbeloved.com

Complete Dog Food
For healthy digestion, skin and coat

The specially selected wholesome ingredients used in James Wellbeloved complete dog food make the recipes naturally healthy, completely satisfying and very tasty for your dog.

With no beef or pork, no wheat or wheat gluten, no dairy products, soya or egg, our complete dog food is hypo-allergenic and free from many of the ingredients which are believed to be the most common causes of food intolerance.

It contains no added artificial colours, flavours or preservatives.

Each of our foods contains a single source of meat protein: turkey, lamb, duck or fish. We then add ingredients such as seaweed, linseed, alfalfa, tomato, chicory and sugar beet, all of which contribute in different ways to producing a naturally healthy food. Each ingredient in all of our recipes is specially selected to provide the nutritional goodness your dog needs for a healthy balanced diet.

We are very proud of the raw materials we use, and list them all on every pack.

Different dogs have different nutritional needs, so we have a range of foods tailored to their unique requirements dependent on their size, life stage and specific needs. We have a range for large and small breed dogs as well as a light range for weight management and no cereal foods for dogs with extra sensitivities.

If you breed healthy happy dogs and agree with our ethos, we'd love to have you on board. Why not join our Breeder Partner Club?*
FREE today, for SPECIAL breeder prices, FREE puppy packs and other great benefits. Just call our dedicated breeder team on 0845 300 5965

Nutritional Advice: 0845 603 9095

www.wellbeloved.com

*terms and conditions apply

© Crown Pet Foods Ltd 2013 - All Rights Reserved.

Dog World Annual 2014

Are there any solutions to declining entries?

The Dog World in 2013

SERIOUS dog people have been increasingly concerned at the declining entries at championship shows, many of which have sunk to the level of more than 30 years ago, but spread over more breeds.

Each of the all-breeds championship shows from LKA 2012 to Midland Counties 2013 drew a lower entry than the previous year, the drops varying from two dogs (May Scottish Kennel Club) to 1,127 (East of England) and averaging at 334 dogs.

Kennel Club chairman Steve Dean, whose views can be found on pages 54-55, felt the economic climate was mainly to blame.

The year has seen considerable debate on what can be done to buck things up, encourage new exhibitors to join the sport and existing ones to stay within it. Indeed DOG WORLD gave exhibitors the chance to express their views though a survey; more than 800 did so and the results are being analysed.

Classes for champions, removing them from competition for the CC, grading and CCs for all eligible breeds at all shows are among the suggestions and judges, of course, are another major factor in exhibitors' decision-making.

What was disappointing is that the Kennel Club, through the *Kennel Gazette* and elsewhere, was only too keen to pour cold water on these ideas, while at the same time not coming up with any viable alternatives, prompting some to suggest that the club is content to preside over a 'managed decline' of dog showing.

At a time when may were thoroughly depressed, amazement was expressed at the KC's decision to cut 78 sets of CCs from 60 breeds in the 2016 allocation. Surely exhibitors should be encouraged to travel and show their dogs, not the reverse, many felt.

To help decide which shows should lose these CCs, the KC set up a consultation with the breed clubs in the breeds concerned, who were asked for their suggestions as to the unlucky shows.

Although welcoming this willingness to involve those who mattered, some wondered if this was altogether a wise move as it would only increase dissent if the clubs' suggestions were not able to be adopted.

In October, however, the KC announced that it had had a change of heart and that there would be no reductions in CCs in 2016; the 2015 allocation would be repeated except that eight breeds would gain an extra 14 sets between them. This was met with much relief though there was irritation that breed clubs had been put to this unnecessary work.

The KC General Committee said that cutting the CCs could be considered detrimental to the current show scene, which was what the rest of us had been saying all along!

A thoroughly positive move was that a working party would be established under the chairmanship of Keith Young, General Committee member who had recently retired as City of Birmingham secretary, to investigate ways to 'repopularise exhibiting at dog shows'.

The other members are General Committee member Mark Cocozza, Staffordshire Bull Terrier exhibitor and judge Karon Jackson, and secretary and organiser of Liskeard CA's premier open show Kevin Burdett-Coutts.

After taking three BIS awards in 2010, John Cullen's imported German Shepherd Dog Ch Elmo vom Hühnegrab returned to the limelight to take his fourth such award at Manchester 2013, handled once again by Steve Cox. With them are chairman Bob Gregory, secretary Paul Harding and judge Ron James. For a high profile breed, it must have been especially satisfying to win under a veterinary surgeon. It was initially thought he had retired after his third Crufts BOB but no, he returned to the ring at Bath and took his fifth BIS.
photo Alan Walker

Its remit is 'To look at ways in which dog shows can be improved upon in order to retain existing exhibitors and to attract new exhibitors to the show scene'.

DOG WORLD's hope is that the working party will not be afraid to look at possibly revolutionary ideas to make our show scene suited to the aspirations of 21st century potential exhibitors.

More big ring success for handler Steve Cox and owners John and Pauline Cullen came at National Working and Pastoral Breeds where Ferelith Somerfield chose their new champion German Shepherd bitch Veneze Ellie as BIS. Also pictured are group judge Terry Munro and secretary Ann Arch.
photo Alan Walker

CaniRep HB

The Swedish Canine Semen Bank

For expert help with fresh chilled and frozen canine semen, international shipping, and AI using non surgical transcervical deposition in the uterus for best results.

More than 35 years' experience

Contact us for Lectures and Courses on Recent Advances in Canine Reproduction and Reproductive Problems for veterinarians, technical staff, breeders and organizations

photo by Liza Kajanus

Our CaniRep Uppsala Chilled Semen Extender may preserve dog spermatozoa of good quality for 1-2 weeks at 5°C. User friendly system. Much easier and cheaper than shipping frozen semen.

Using our **CaniRep extenders** you can now also import/export chilled semen and have it frozen on arrival, which saves you the high freight cost and return shipment of the ordinary liquid nitrogen containers.

Our CaniRep Uppsala Freezing method, and our Uppsala Equex Freezing Extenders have in our own studies and in studies performed by independent international research groups also proved to be among the best in the world, and are used by experts worldwide.

Import and export of dog semen requires meticulous advance planning, therefore, please contact us well ahead of time. **(At least 2-3 months for frozen semen).** For more information, and prices, visit: www.canirep.com.

Prof em Catharina Linde Forsberg, DVM, PhD
Diplomate European College of Animal Reproduction
Specialist in Dog and Cat Reproduction
Honorary and Founding Member of The European Society for Small Animal Reproduction
Honorary and Founding Member of The Swedish Society for Small Animal Reproduction
CaniRep HB, Fjällbo 110, SE-755 97 Uppsala, Sweden
Email: canirephb@gmail.com
Mobile: +46 708 36 36 23
www.canirep.com

Dog World Annual 2014

The Dog World in 2013

Chips for all from 2016

FROM APRIL 6, 2016 all dogs in England will have to be microchipped.

Environment Secretary Owen Paterson said the aim was to tackle the growing problem of stray dogs.

Dogs Trust charity announced that a free microchip would be made available for all unchipped dogs, and they, Battersea and the Blue Cross will chip dogs free at their centres. The Kennel Club, another long-time advocate of compulsory chipping, is to donate a scanner to all local authorities.

It is estimated that 60 per cent of the country's eight million dogs are already chipped; how the new rule will be enforced is not yet clear.

In June the KC hosted a debate at the House of Commons to discuss the implications of the new rules.

In Wales, all dogs must be microchipped by March 2015. A consultation by the Welsh Government showed an overwhelming vote in favour. Scotland has started a consultation on the same issue.

Goodbye to the *Gazette*

THE *Kennel Gazette*, the Kennel Club's official publication, will close in January after being published monthly for 133 years. It will be placed by a monthly digital *Kennel Club Journal* which will include the basic information currently in the *Gazette*, plus a chairman's report, but nothing more than that.

Print copies will be available for those without internet access and the online version may be seen by all via the KC website.

Many expressed disappointment at the decision, upon which KC members have not voted, and were unable to understand why the traditional name should be changed. Some wondered whether affiliate or associate members would find their membership package worth renewing.

The Saredon/Irvonhill team has had two leading terriers in contention and at Windsor Sue Garner awarded BIS to John Averis and Tony and Jean Barker's latest US-imported Irish Terrier Ch/Am Ch Kells Touch Of Fleet St, their second Irish to take a BIS along with a number of other terriers owned by the Averis family. The patron, the Earl of Buchan, presented the trophy.
photo Alan Walker

Registrations stagnate

UNTIL now, Kennel Club registrations have in general bucked the trend which has seen show entries steadily decline. However the 2012 total of 229,230 was six per cent down on the previous year, the lowest since 2002 and the third lowest of the past 20 years.

As usual Labradors were top breed with 36,487 registrations, though nearly 3,500 down, followed by Cockers, English Springers and German Shepherds. The biggest leaps in the table came from two of the currently most fashionable breeds, Pugs which rose from ninth to fifth place and French Bulldogs which came from nowhere to twelfth, with an astonishing number of imports, 483, mainly from Eastern Europe.

Of the total, 13.13 per cent were bred by Assured Breeders.

It looks as if the 2013 total will be down again. The first two quarters of the year showed a continued decline. There was a recovery in the July-September quarter, the figures slightly exceeding those for the same quarter of 2012, but the total for the first nine months of 2013 was 168,652, compared with 174,936 for the equivalent in 2012.

The Airedale Terrier Katherina's Land Spicy Cherry of Saredon could hardly have made a more exciting UK debut than going BIS at National Terrier. Bred in Estonia, she quickly became a champion and won several more groups. She is handled by John Averis for his mother Judy, who bred her sire, and Tony Barker. In the picture are chairman Max King, judge Jane Miller and secretary Jennie Griffiths.
photo Alan Walker

Dog World Annual 2014

AVIFORM — Perfect Health & Condition
For all dogs, from pets to show champions

SUPPLEX — Veterinary Spec Joint Care
PRICES START FROM £21.95

SUPPLEX offers the very best veterinary specification joint mobility formula for dogs at an affordable price.

PROVEN INGREDIENTS - Highest purity Chondroitin Sulphate, Glucosamine HCl, MSM and Hyaluronic Acid at the optimum ratios for maximum effect.

EASY ADMINISTRATION - Available as a convenient capsule or a palatable powder.

ECONOMICAL - 120 capsules offers 2 months maintenance supply for a 25kg dog.

Each 755mg capsule contains:
- 250mg - Glucosamine HCl
- 200mg - Marine Chondroitin
- 300mg - MSM pure
- 5mg   - Hyaluronic Acid

Available as capsules or powder.

120 capsules   £21.95
300 capsules   £41.95
225g powder   £29.95

BUY 2 GET 1 FREE CHEAPEST ITEM FREE

VITAL COAT — Coat & Skin
PRICES START FROM £10.95

Palatable combination of fish and vegetable oils, essential fatty acids, vitamins and starflower oil (highest GLA), in a convenient dispensing pack.

BENEFITS - show winning glossy coat, healthy skin and also maintains mobility in older dogs.

PREVENTS - a greasy coat, scaly or itchy skin and excessive moulting.

250ml pack should last a 20kg (22lb) dog over 8 months!

125ml with pump   £10.95
250ml with pump   £19.95
1000ml (refill)   £39.95

NATURAL CALM
PRICES START FROM £13.95

For stressful periods including shows, fireworks, training and travel. Suitable for long or short term use without side effects.

250ml   £13.95
1000ml   £32.95

MOBILEAZE — Mobility
PRICES START FROM £13.95

100% natural palatable liquid, that maintains mobility and optimum joint function.

Rich in organic silica which helps to protect cartilage and lubricate joints.

250ml   £13.95
1000ml   £32.95

MONTMORILLONITE   £9.95
Far more effective than kaolin.   250ml   £9.95

PREBIOTICS — Digestion
PRICE £14.95

Effective in assisting with digestive problems (persistent loose/jelly motions), recovery after illness/medication.

250g   £14.95

FREE UK DELIVERY* 9/10 CUSTOMERS RE-ORDER†

CALL NOW: **01508 530813** OR VISIT: **www.aviform.co.uk**

†9 out of 10 customers re-order or intend to re-order based on 117 customer product satisfaction questionnaires. *FREE UK delivery if ordered online or over £50. TDP, Aviform Ltd, FREEPOST NATE 944, Long Stratton, NORWICH, NR15 2BR. (no stamp req'd). E&OE DW 13v1

Keep your puppy Clean 'n' Safe

For puppies and dogs of all ages

- Super absorbent gel locks in moisture and odours
- Leak proof pads dry in 30 seconds
- Keeps paws and floors clean and dry

Full range of products for puppies and dogs, now available from your local pet shop.

Johnson's Veterinary Products Ltd, Sutton Coldfield West Midlands B75 7DF

www.jvp.co.uk or call: **0121 378 1684** for more information

No health tests before a dog can be shown

AT THEIR annual meeting, Kennel Club members threw out a proposal to raise membership fees by £15 to £175, and another that increases should be made in line with the consumer price index.

Many felt this would be hard to justify at a time when the club seemed likely to come into a great deal of money. The cynics later wondered whether the decision to reduce the benefits of membership by killing the *Kennel Gazette* was the committee's response to the members' rejection of the fee increase.

On most other topics members had little to say. On the subject of two-tier registration, brought up at the 2012 meeting, the KC had carried out a consultation and decided that it would provide basic three-generation pedigree information as part of the registration document, with limited health data; it will not encourage or require veterinary health tests as a one-off or annual event in order that a dog can be shown; it will offer a voluntary endorsement which a breeder can place requiring a puppy to undergo Assured Breeder Scheme-required health tests before being used for breeding; it will consider reformatting health data and commentary on the website and explore the compilation of a 'health pedigree'; and will consider implementing a new requirement that if breeding on an annual basis – volume of litters to be determined – of whatever breed, the breeder must have a kennel name.

After a number of group wins, Faye and Carol Bevis' Akita Ch Dykebar Revenge Is Sweet at Stecal won her first BIS at Boston under Dianna Spavin. On the left is chairman Phil Kirk. She is the family's second BIS winner and the second in different breeds for breeders John and Lorraine Ritchie.
photo Alan Walker

The Dog World in 2013

Disciplinary chairman disciplined

WILSON Young, Kennel Club General Committee member, chairman of the Kennel Club's Disciplinary Sub-Committee and the Field Trials Sub-Committee, was fined and warned for impugning the decision of a judge, Jean Brown, at an open stake in July 2012. The matter was dealt with by a special ad-hoc sub-committee consisting of General Committee members Mike Townsend, Graham Hill and Tom Mather.

This led to a proposal at the 2013 KC annual meeting by Eleanor Heard that members who have had a complaint against them upheld should not be 'permitted to serve' for ten years afterwards.

Amazingly, the KC in response said that if this was brought in, no fewer than 61 members would have been ineligible for service on KC committees, including six current or past General Committee members!

In the event the proposal was defeated, though it received the support of almost half those who voted. Some who had sympathy for the reasons it was put forward nevertheless felt unable to support it as it was too all-embracing, covering even the most minor complaint.

Mr Young was re-elected to the General Committee and, later, as chairman of the Field Trials Sub-Committee. His is, however, no longer a member of the Disciplinary Sub-Committee of which Steve Croxford is now chairman.

Coat testing saga continues

COAT TESTING is to resume, it was announced at the Kennel Club annual meeting in May, but at the time of going to press it had not yet happened.

The subject came to prominence after Miniature Poodles and West Highland Whites were tested, and failed, at Crufts 2011. This provoked something of a revolution, and at the AGM a few months later it was agreed to suspend coat-testing. A working party was set up and a consultation process received 167 responses.

It was recommended a 'code of practice governing the permitted usage of block white chalk at show be developed' and another 'governing the light use of hairspray to frame topknots in Poodles'.

After that the working party was split in two, one dealing with procedure and regulation, and one looking at the scientific aspects.

At the 2013 AGM Dr Ron James said the working party had come to the conclusion that it was unlikely a position would be reached which would satisfy all parties, so the General Committee had resolved to reinstate coat testing with revisions and guidelines.

Full details were promised in due course but now, five months later, nothing more has been heard of the details although the KC chairman later expressed the hope that more dogs of more breeds would be tested at more shows.

Meanwhile the Poodle Standard has been amended at the breed council's request, removing the recommendation for the lion clip and saying: 'all traditional trims permissible in the show ring and the dogs judged on equal merit, as long as there is sufficient length to demonstrate colour and quality of coat'.

Dog World Annual 2014

Bright Eyes Drops for Pets – IT WORKS!

My dog started to get cataracts over both eyes. The vet told us there was nothing that could be done until his eyes had fully crusted over. A few months down the line he was totally blind & we were told the operation would cost between 4 and 5 Thousand pounds. This was an unaffordable option & in desperation I started to search the internet for another solution. I found this product & decided to try it. I have not yet told the vets I am using it. The dog is on his 4th bottle & can see clearly in daylight & only has problems with steps in darker surroundings. The vets checked him last week & confirmed that the swelling behind his eyes had gone & they were clearing up. I am waiting for his eyes to get a bit better at night before I tell the vet what I am using on his eyes. This way they will hopefully recommend the drops knowing that they work. If I had heard of them before searching the internet then maybe my dog wouldn't have had to go blind before I did something about it!

K Davies, Mersyside, UK and *Slinky*

You'd have to be barking mad to choose any other eye drops!

Put the Sparkle back into your pet's eyes... with Ethos Bright Eyes Drops for Pets

ethos.ag
petdrops.com
Freephone 0800 046 9830   Promo Code DW10%OFF

safedog
crash tested car crates

www.safedog.co.uk   020 8658 0002   info@safedog.co.uk

Showrooms in Kent and Norfolk. Crates shipped to UK and ROI via courier.

Dog World Annual 2014

How secure are Britain's borders?

WORRY remains about the leniency of the pet travel laws, and the possibility that rabies could arrive in Britain. The potential problem is made worse by the lack of checking at the ports of departure, and many believe that considerable numbers of unvaccinated puppies are being smuggled into the UK.

Another problem, according to vets, is that the number of rescued street dogs coming legally to Britain, with their higher risk of rabies. Currently dogs have to wait only 21 days after their rabies vaccination before they may cross borders; the incubation period can go far beyond that.

There has been a 62 per cent rise in the number of people travelling with animals since the regulations were eased.

These fears were exacerbated when two four-month-old puppies, imported legally to the Netherlands from Bulgaria, were found to be rabid.

Closer to home, three puppies unvaccinated against rabies were discovered in Peterborough.

The Dog World in 2013

A passport to travel from Ireland?

THERE IS concern about 'puppy trafficking', especially from the Republic of Ireland to the UK. In December 2012 87 puppies were seized in Greater Manchester.

Subsequently there has been much confusion about whether dogs travelling between the UK and the Republic of Ireland need a pet passport. Strictly speaking, EU rules require that they do; in practice this has not been enforced until recently when some puppies coming from Ireland to England have been seized as they did not have the relevant documentation, presumably in an attempt to stop trafficking.

This caused concern to owners of show and pet dogs wishing to holiday or attend shows across the Irish Sea, and to charities aiming to rehome puppies and which could not afford to have them all passported.

Conflicting advice has been given – the Irish Department of Agriculture said that Ireland does not currently implement border checks on pets travelling to or from the UK, but the Kennel Club reminded us that by law a passport and rabies vaccination are needed.

Sue Smith and Val Freer's Samoyed Ch Nikara Diamond Dancer was best in show at City of Birmingham. He is a former winner of the Junior Warrant Winner of the Year final and already has a group-winning son.
photo Alan Walker

BIS at Hound Association of Scotland under Valerie Foss was Mike Howgate and Yvonne Hull's Whippet Ch Palmik Magical Whispers. Chairman Anne Macdonald presented the trophy.
photo Robin Bryden

At the Houndshow Rachel and Ann Snelgrove's Whippet Huntinghill Jazztastic was BIS after winning his first CC. Brian Cleveley of Dorwest Herbs presented the trophy and also pictured are judge Jenny Startup and secretary Shirley Rawlings.
photo Alan Walker

KC and FCI make progress on judges

THE FEDERATION Canine Internationale (FCI) and the Kennel Club have reached an agreement regarding the mutual recognition of judges, though it is not clear to what extent this is yet set in stone.

FCI international judges will be eligible for automatic approval to award CCs in the UK to breed they have judged for five years in countries other than their own, while UK judges who have awarded award CCs will be allowed to awards CACIBs in that breed. There are also provision regarding the recognition of group judges, and judges on the A2 list who have yet to award their first set of CCs.

Later the KC chairman Steve Dean described this as a 'framework document' and that the two organisations would now attempt to negotiate a 'workable agreement'.

Welcome to the Home of Healthy Pet Food

HAPPY DOG SUPREME
UNIQUE RECIPES AND EXCLUSIVE INGREDIENTS

Trusted feeding. Since 1968.

Developed by our Vets for you

Fit & Well products are optimally suited to the daily activity of your dog. By feeding your dog the recommended amount of the variety that is perfectly tailored to him, you can avoid overfeeding and the resulting problems. Each Fit & Well product has a quite unique recipe in a specially adapted croquette form.

- Exclusive quality raw ingredients, and multi protien such as salmon, chicken, duck, turkey, lamb.
- Optimally suited for allergies and the prevention of lifestyle diseases
- Over 90% digestibility (smaller feeding quantities, smaller stool amounts)
- Natural variety for a balanced diet and the unique Happy Dog LifePlus Concept®

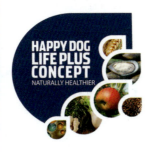

Supreme Fit & Well - Following nature's example!

www.happydoguk.com | 0844 409 5000 | Free next day delivery*

2 Dovecot Workshops, Barnsley Park, Barnsley, Cirencester, Glos, GL7 5EG | 08444095000

* on all orders over £20, terms & conditions apply

Advisory Council recommendations 'disproportionate', says KC

IN DECEMBER 2012 the Advisory Council on the Welfare Issue of Dog Breeding (DAC) identified four more 'priority health problems' in addition to the eight already on its list: glaucoma, breed-specific cancers, hypothyroidism and other breed-related auto-immune disorders. These join ocular and breathing problems, both linked to head conformation, epilepsy, syringomyelia, heart disease with a known or suspected inherited basis, skin problems, limb defects and separation-related behaviours.

The new priorities were revealed a meeting, to which the public were invited, chaired by Professor Sheila Crispin.

Discussion points included the council's desire to work with breed health co-ordinators; it believes data collection is important with regard to the welfare priorities.

The council's breeding standard for dogs was discussed. Prof Sir Patrick Bateson's report stated that fewer than 40 per cent of dogs were registered with the Kennel Club, and that arguably the worst problems were in those not registered.

The council believed there was little point in having both its own breeding standard and that of the Assured Breeder Scheme (ABS), and those at the meeting heard that the KC had carried out a gap analysis and had 'made moves to close some of the gaps'.

This process is still ongoing. From an outside perspective, it is hard to see how agreement could ever be reached on a few sticking points, such as inbreeding levels.

In order to 'make the next step to resolve the differences between the two standards constructively', the council asked Sir Patrick to chair a working group to look at the differences and resolve them, drawing on 'veterinary and extensive breeding knowledge'.

The council agreed to pursue the development of a website on which coefficients of inbreeding could be calculated, and which was available to all. Why the KC's existing Mate Select programme could not be used was not clear.

In September the DAC made its recommendations to the Government.

These include that ANYONE who breeds a dog should be registered with their local authority, be given a registration number and give their address and details to the veterinary practice they use.

Anyone breeding TWO or more litters a year should be licensed. 'Enforcement authorities' should be allowed to remove the breeding licence if the person or establishment fails to comply with improvement or care notices issued under the welfare Acts.

Advertisements for puppies should include the breeder's registration number, and all breeders should comply with the DAC's 'Standard for Breeding Dogs', which should become a statutory code of practice.

This standard, mentioned in last year's ANNUAL, comprised 53 separate suggestions, including that dogs and bitches used at stud must be at least two years old before being bred from, and bitches should have one litter only a year no more than four in a lifetime, and only one caesarean section, and that inbreeding coefficients should be less than 12.5 per cent.

The DAC also recommended that the new regulations should impose new duties of care on those planning a mating of dogs and any organisation exercising public duties with regard to the establishment of breed Standards, and that the Royal College of Veterinary Surgeons should be asked to consider telling its vets to give advice on breeding issues 'and be accountable for that advice'.

Vets should report surgical changes of conformation and caesarean sections; if carried out on KC-registered dogs they should be reported to the KC, and others to the Small Animal Veterinary Surveillance Network or Vet Compass.

No puppy less than eight weeks of age should be sold, supplied or gifted and all dogs and puppies sold should be microchipped. No puppy or dog should be sold or provided unless the breeder's registration number is lodged with the local council, or if there are plans for it to be sold or given to a third party.

Prof Crispin said: "We believe strongly that all dogs, be they crossbred or pedigree, whether bred by, for example, an individual pet owner or a large scale commercial breeder, are entitled to enjoy the good standards of health and welfare which the Animal Welfare Acts were intended to deliver. The sad fact is that the current legislation does not deliver effective protection from negligent care or shoddy breeding practices."

However, the KC, while welcoming some aspects of the recommendations, said that many of the suggested measures were disproportionate and could deter responsible breeders from breeding, leaving puppy buyers in the hands of those with lower standards.

Local authorities are unable to cope with current regulations, it said, so it was hard to see how they would be able to inspect all breeders, keep up a database and enforce the law.

BIS at the 2012 British Utility Breeds Association was the consistent group-winning Dalmatian Ch Offordale Chevalier, one of three champions in a litter bred by Jenny Alexander after she drove to Norway to use a stud dog there. With them are judge Jack Bispham and chairman Sheila Jakeman.
photo Alan Walker

Pat Clayton gave BIS at the Scottish Breeds to Ann Stafford's Shetland Sheepdog Ch Rannerdale Bugsy Malone, handled by daughter Clare who bred him. Chairman Ken Aird presented the trophy.
photo Robin Bryden

ESTAVA RAIN AMERICAN AKITAS
WWW.ESTAVARAIN.NO

ESTAVA RAIN TOUCH THE FLAME
Specialty BIS Winner!
Best In Show J. Montichiari Int. Italy
J.BOB & EJW-13 European Dogs Show Geneva!
Nr. 1 American Akita Bitch in Scandinavia!

GBCH INTCH NORDCH
ESTAVA RAIN HOLD THE NEWS

First none UK/US bred
Am.Akita to become GBCH

Nr.1
American Akita Dog
in Scandinavia 2013

INTCH NORDCH ITCH
ESTAVA RAIN FRONT ROW

Int. BIS winner in 3 countries
Nr.2 All Breeds in Norway 2011

MULTI WINNER, ITCH
ESTAVA RAIN PLAY MAGIC

Winners Dog, res. Winners Dog
National Specialty Week, USA

Int. BIS Winner Sweden &
BOS World Dog Show 2013

Dog World Annual 2014

Why can't everyone work together?

The Dog World in 2013

DISCUSSIONS by the various groups supposed to be looking at the future of dog breeding often seem to be counter-productive with everyone pulling in different directions.

For example the cross-party Environment, Food and Rural Affairs Committee (EFRAcom), which heard evidence from various interested parties, wants anyone breeding more than two litters a year to be licensed and the Dog Advisory Council to be made a regulatory body, to extend the list of banned breeds, and for the Kennel Club to stop registering puppies from breeders who do not comply with Assured Breeder Scheme standards. An annual review of breed Standards should be led by vets.

The committee was highly critical of DEFRA's 'belated, simplistic and woefully inadequate' measures to tackle dog welfare and control.

In reply to the committee's report, published in February, KC chairman Steve Dean said that the Government needs to get tough on principles such as mandatory health testing. "The requirements of our ABS can only be extended when breeders are required by law to breed to the same standards," he said.

The committee also called for a full review of the dangerous dogs legislation. Its recommendations were somewhat contradictory, promoting the ideal of 'deed not breed' but also allowing the Secretary of State to add more breeds to the 'banned' list.

From our point of view Professor Dean summed up what should surely be aimed for when he said at a January meeting of the Associate Parliamentary Group for Animal Welfare (APGAW) that everyone should work together to ensure that people buy from good breeders and not puppy farmers.

For once his views were echoed by British Veterinary Association (BVA) president elect Robin Hargreaves who said that by concentrating on the areas on which they agreed, progress could be made.

Discussing the EFRA select committee's enquiry into dog control and welfare, Prof Dean said that another review of breed Standards would influence only those breeders who show their dogs – no puppy farmer would bother reading them.

Later in the year Prof Dean accused the EFRAcom of 'an astonishing level of bias' against KC-registered dogs. Nor was it just the KC which was arguing with the committee on a regular basis; the Government too, which seems to have little appetite for extra legislation.

However even the Government suggested that the Advisory Council's funding should be provided by those actually involved in dog breeding; DOG WORLD's view was that this is quite unreasonable considering how little dog people and the KC are represented on the council.

Breeding law for Northern Ireland: Wales still consulting

AS FROM April 2013, anyone in Northern Ireland who advertises or supplies three or more litters a year or advertises a business of breeding or selling of puppies must be licensed. All dogs at the premises must be microchipped.

The Welsh Government is still trying to sort out regulations covering breeders and the latest draft also suggests a three-litter rule. Campaigners held a rally outside the National Assembly to try to speed up an end to puppy-farming. The draft regulations were later withdrawn through lack of clarity on some aspects, and yet another consultation was announced in August.

No longer denied at Windsor

THANKS to the bizarre law, it is still illegal for dogs legally docked since April 2007 to compete at shows which charge the public an admission fee. Most of the general championship shows have therefore ceased to charge and another was added to the list in 2013, Windsor. To compensate, there were rises in car parking, catalogue and caravan charges.

Only Leeds, East of England, the LKA and of course Crufts continue to charge the public to come in to their shows.

Dogs docked since January 1, 2013 may not be shown at any event in Northern Ireland.

In spite of the distances involved Franco Barberi from Italy is a regular visitor to UK shows. His Labradors excelled themselves in 2013. It Ch Loch Mor Giulietta won her UK title in ten days with a group, group 2 and BIS at the parent club, and later topped National Gundog where they are seen with judge John Thirlwell and president Rosemary Davies. Litter brother Int/It Ch Loch Mor Romeo was RBIS at Crufts and they gained their UK titles the same day.
photo Alan Walker

For the second time Sergio Amien travelled from Spain to win BIS at UK Toy with a Yorkshire Terrier; he also has a RBIS there. This time the winner was the multi-titled Ch/Int Ch Royal Precious JP's F4 Juliana, whom he campaigns for Yoshiko Obana from Japan. Judge was Di Fry and also pictured are Phil Yeomans from Happy Dog and chairman David Guy.
photo Alan Walker

Dog World Annual 2014

The Dog World in 2013

After winning the Eukanuba champion stakes final, the Standard Poodle Ch Afterglow Maverick Sabre is entitled to compete in the World Challenge in Florida in December. He is seen with judges Steve Hall and Patsy Hollings and owners Jason Lynn and John and Sandra Stone. This could have interesting implications for the battle for Top Dog 2013 where he is one of the two main contenders, as the final show of the year, LKA, is the same weekend as the Challenge…
photo Alan Walker

KC database goes online, at last

MANY OF us have hoped that one day the Kennel Club might put its enormous extensive registration database online and make it publicly available, as has happened in Finland, Sweden and a number of other countries.

There had been little if any indication that this would ever happen so it was a very welcome surprise when MyKC was launched at Crufts.

This free online service enables those who sign up to it to view not only parentage, colour, date of birth and health test details of their own dogs and those they have bred and sold, but also information on every single dog the KC has registered for at least the last 30 years, plus any foreign dogs who appear in their three-generation pedigree.

For one's own dogs, you can also add in various personal details, enabling you to keep the records required of an Assured Breeder.

The site links in with the published details of health test results and with the Mate Select service which calculates coefficients of inbreeding.

For potential buyers MyKC also helps them to find registered puppies, and links to a database of dog-friendly venues.

This wonderful new resource was widely welcomed by breed historians; let us hope that as the site is reviewed it eventually becomes as easy to follow as, for example, the Finnish Kennel Club's online records, where every necessary detail of an individual dog, including titles, a full pedigree and its complete show record, is available on one page, and is linked in with the full results of every show and the full records of what every judge has put up and where.

Canine Alliance calls for grading

THE CANINE Alliance held its first members' meeting in November 2012 and it was agreed that the Kennel Club should be approached with a view to suspending the still controversial veterinary checks and instead adjusting the 'yellow form' which high profile breed judges have to complete after a championship show appointment, extending this to all breeds.

It was also felt that a grading system, as used in Europe, would be particularly advantageous in this country now that health is such an issue, Later two Alliance members, Stuart Mallard and Andrew Brace, met three KC General Committee members, Simon Luxmoore, Anne Macdonald and Ron James, to discuss grading.

In one way the Alliance and KC see eye to eye – like the KC, the alliance is now a company limited by guarantee.

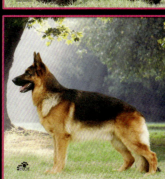

KEEP UP
WITH THE CHALLENGE
http://www.facebook.com/
EukanubaWorldChallenge

Beagle: Ch Annavah Ginny   Dobermann: Ch/Lux Ch Supeta's Ozzy Osbourne JW   Whippet: Ch Supeta's Razzalicious JW, ShCM   Border Terrier: Ch Foxfactor Pied Piper JW, ShCM   Pointer: Sh Ch Kiswahili Martin At Kanix   Tibetan Terrier: Ch Kybo Pandarama   Irish Wolfhound: Ch Moralach The Gambling Man JW   Standard Long Haired Dachshund: Ch Zarcrest Hugo Boss   Gordon Setter: Sh Ch Lochfain An Aus Approach at Glenmaurangi JW   French Bulldog: Ch Jafrak Pistols At Dorn   English Springer: Sh Ch Trimere Tigra   Samoyed: Ch Nikara Diamond Dancer JW   Saluki: Ch Baghdad Karim ShCM   Elkhound: Ch/Ir Ch Kestos Ispy At Graythor JW ShCM   Pointer: Sh Ch Wilchrimane Ice Maiden JW   Whippet: Ch Shalfleet Simply A Lord   American Cocker: Sh Ch Afterglow Pearl's A Singer   Whippet: Ch Collooney Going Dutch   Gordon Setter: Sh Ch Hernwood Diamond Rock JW ShCM   Standard Poodle: Ch Afterglow Maverick Sabre   Shetland Sheepdog: Sh Ch Edglonian Singin' The Blues   Chinese Crested: Ch Mongoshi Gatecrasher   Dobermann: Ch Supeta's Secret Wizard At Dronski JW ShCM   Wire Fox Terrier: Ch Travella Striking Steel   GSP Sh Ch/NL Ch Kavacanne Toff At The Top JW ShCM

Eukanuba Salutes the 2013
Eukanuba Champion Stakes Finalists

Eukanuba Champion Stakes Final
19th October 2013
Chesford Grange Hotel, Kenilworth

The 2013 Eukanuba Champion Stakes Final Overall Winner &
UK Representative to the Eukanuba World Challenge in Orlando

CH Afterglow Maverick Sabre

Top breeders recommend Eukanuba*

* 2012 Winners of Crufts, World Dog & Euro Dog Shows

Why do top breeders recommend Eukanuba?
learn more at our website

BRED BY EXPERTS.
FED BY EXPERTS.

www.Breeders.Eukanuba.co.uk

Dog World Annual 2014

Jaunt raises £49,000 for children's and canine charities

The Dog World in 2013

IN A YEAR in which falling entries made many dog people seem rather depressed, one remarkable effort shone out as something totally positive.

Jilly's Jolly Jaunt was the brainchild of Gavin Robertson, handler of the 2013 Crufts BIS winner and 2012 Top Dog, the Petit Basset Griffon Vendéen Ch Soletrader Peek A Boo, who said: "I wanted to use the profile that our Crufts win gave us to do something for deserving causes."

He therefore set about organising a 130-mile walk from the scene of the Crufts triumph, the National Exhibition Centre near Birmingham, to the centre of London, using the Grand Union Canal towpath as the most pleasant route.

The walk took place in June covering five days, blessed by fine but not excessively hot weather. Gavin was accompanied by Amelia Siddle who has had a great year with her Pointer Sh Ch Wilchrimane Ice Maiden. 'Jilly' and 'Flo' walked most of the way; for short stretches they were relieved by kennelmates.

The plan had struck an immediate chord with dog people who were keen to help by either participating or sponsoring. Owners or handlers of past Crufts BIS winner were invited to join in for stretches of five miles or so, along with this year's Crufts group winners and other leading dogs. The high profile and vulnerable native breeds were also represented, all, even the smallest toy breeds, proving they were fit and healthy.

It was claimed that by the end of the week 248,348 steps were taken, 584 miles walked by the dogs, 17,917 calories burnt, 11 blisters treated and six dogs found themselves in the canal!

DOG WORLD was represented by Stuart Baillie with his Border Terrier, Adrian Marett with his PBGV and Simon Parsons with his Pembroke Corgi.

In total, £49,000 was raised, Great Ormond Street Children's Hospital taking £29,420, DogLost, the charity which helps find missing dogs, £17,150 and the Kennel Club Charitable Trust £2,450.

Flo, Amelia, Jilly and Gavin about to set off on the Jaunt from the NEC. Supporting them are Dianna Spavin, Adrian Marett, Melanie and Marion Spavin and Paul Sparks.
photo Dan Kyprianou

Among the participants were several high-profile breeds and Jilly's main rival for Top Dog 2012, the Toy Poodle Ch Vanitonia You'll See (left). The shirts were sponsored by Royal Canin.
photo Dan Kyprianou

And now for the Pawscars

HOW DO you follow that? Gavin and Stuart Baillie of DOG WORLD have made sure that after the success of the Jaunt, the spirit of goodwill will continue.

Next March will see the launch of the Peek A Boo Trust, which will encourage fundraising throughout the world of pedigree dogs and disburse that cash to children's and canine charities.

And on the night before Crufts 2014 the first 'Pawscars' award ceremony will be held in the Metropole Hotel at the NEC. The awards will recognise success and hard work in all areas of the show world, celebrating all that is good in the UK dog show scene as well as raising more money for good causes.

'Of the Year' awards will go to a championship show, training class, breeder, journalist, exhibitor, junior handler, steward, trade stand, open show, breed note writer, judge, photographer and unsung hero, plus an award for outstanding achievement, each sponsored by a company or organisation involved with the dog world.

The Top Dog, Top Stud Dog, Top Brood Bitch and Pup of the Year will also be honoured.

After reaching the Kennel Club in London on the final day of the walk, Jilly and Gavin pose with the Crufts BIS cup.

SOLE UK & IRELAND DISTRIBUTORS OF PURE PAWS

- Enriched with Silk, Botanical Extracts and Herbs for a Healthy Shiny Coat.
- Custom Formulated for Drop Coat Breeds!
- Silk Basics Line - a Silk Spa for your Dog!

PRODUCT DEMOS AVAILABLE AT SELECTED SHOWS

NEW Retail Outlet and Showroom open to the public! Find us at Bradeley Green, Whitchurch. SY13 4HD (off A49)

Wide range of pet products available.

Secure Online Ordering

Join our mailing list online for news of special offers!

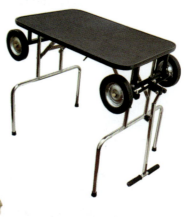

www.petcetera.co.uk
01948 668100

Dog World Annual 2014

DDA to cover private property

The Dog World in 2013

THE DANGEROUS Dogs Act is to be amended to cover incidents which take place on private property. This will close a loophole which was highlighted by the case of Jade Anderson, 14, who was killed by dogs after visiting a friend's house. Their owner could be convicted only of charges of causing unnecessary suffering to the dogs, resulting in a suspended four-month jail term.

The amendments are to be included in the anti-social behaviour legislation.

There has been concern that dogs who bite, for example, a burglar or trespasser could be at risk, and it is hoped that the wording of the law will take account of this.

To the dismay of many, planned changes to the law in Wales have been suspended and the Welsh Government hopes to co-operate with the UK Government to take forward the proposals together.

There also remains concern for the welfare of dogs held for long period under the Act, expressed for example by two vets in a letter to the *Veterinary Record* at the end of 2012.

In August the public were given the chance to take part in an online consultation regarding the length of sentences for irresponsible owners whose dogs cause the death of a person or assistance dog.

John Thirlwell's Welsh Springer Spaniel Sh Ch Ferndel Aeron Magregor won BIS at Gundog Society of Wales under Sandra Marshall. On the left is secretary Richard Stafford.
photo Alan Walker

Colin Reed gave BIS at Working and Pastoral Breeds Association of Scotland to Deborah Weightman's Bearded Collie Debbeacol Harmony In Motion. Secretary Sheena Harkins completes the line-up.
photo Robin Bryden

Gundog Breeds Association of Scotland saw top spot go to the Gordon Setter Sh Ch Hernwood Calypso Goddess, handled by Claire Lewis and co-owned with Christine (second right) and Pete Sandiford. She is by the LKA 2012 winner Talladega Racer, owned by the same team. Secretary Gordon Haran, judge Mike Gadsby and president/chairman Mary McCance are also pictured.
photo Robin Bryden

The top working dog of 2012, Fiona Lambert, Janet Hughes and US breeder Pat Murray's Bouvier des Flandres Ch/Dutch Ch I'm Special Inessence Movado at Kanix, has won two more all-breeds RBIS awards in 2013, at Manchester and Southern Counties, plus the same position at National Working and Pastoral Breeds. He and handler Dave Killilea, whose Akitas won BIS and BPIS at the same show, are pictured at Southern Counties with group judge Richard Kinsey, James Barker and president Lord Watson of Richmond.
photo Alan Walker

Aimee Davies and Jean Day's Smooth Chihuahua Ch Sundowner Play Misty For Me at Dachida's won two RBIS awards while still a junior, at Scottish Kennel Club in August and Richmond, where group judge was Mervyn Evans.
photo Alan Walker

Save 20% on Churchill Pet Insurance

Get 20% off Churchill Pet Insurance if you buy online. Plus save an extra 10% if you have an existing Home or Motor Policy with us.

(Discounts applied consecutively. Introductory discounts applied over first 12 months.)

Visit churchill.com to get a quote

Chat to Churchill
0800 032 4960
churchill.com

The business of life...

Underwritten by U K Insurance Limited

Dog World Annual 2014

How much should the KC support crossbreeds?

The Dog World in 2013

TO WHAT extent should the Kennel Club become involved with crossbreeds? The debate was initiated by a question from Pat Brigden at the club's annual meeting. Chairman Steve Dean said: "If people out there are determined to breed crossbreeds the KC will have to decide whether it will help these people or turn their back on them."

Although there was no suggestion of opening the breed register to these dogs, something Prof Dean stressed later in the year, the possibility was broached at a KC question time of some sort of separate register for 'designer' crossbreeds, if health tested. Crossbreeds can of course already go on the KC's Activity and Companion Dog registers and compete in some disciplines.

Certainly the KC under Prof Dean's leadership is keen to provide a means for ALL dog breeders to access relevant health tests, and he also said: "We must continue to support everybody who has signed up to our high standards aimed at ensuring our world is populated by healthy, well socialised dogs. If this includes responsible owners of crossbreeds then surely we should embrace this too."

Among several major successes for Annette Siddle's Pointer Sh Ch Wilchrimane Ice Maiden, handled by daughter Amelia, was topping the Canine Supporters Charity's Contest of Champions. In the line-up are Gary Gray of Royal Canin, Annette, judges Enrique Maté-Duran and Angel Sotoca Santos, CSC patron Karina Le Mare and judge András Korózs.
photo Colin Waddell

No longer the enemy

THE KENNEL Club is no longer 'the enemy' in the eyes of politicians, veterinary professionals, animal charities and the public, said chairman Steve Dean in his speech at the Welsh Kennel Club dinner.

This perception had been 'successfully altered', and the club was now seen as an important part of any solution designed to address canine health, welfare and behavioural problems.

"We are increasingly seen as an important part of any solution designed to address dog behaviour or health and welfare," he said.

"In fact, this past year has seen a number of examples where we are very much on the front foot on an issue rather than on the back foot trying to defend the pedigree dog against inaccurate perceptions.

"This is not an accidental change and has required a considerable degree of hard work by our staff and many breed clubs."

One significant example, Prof Dean said, was 'the increasing acceptance' that the source of much of the poor health and welfare of recognised breeds lay outside the KC registration system.

Christine and Andrew Macdonald's Ch Bitcon Gold Coast at Northey became the first Hungarian Vizsla dual champion when he also achieved his field trial title.
photo David Tomlinson

Rachel Spencer's Littlethorn Colt at Tobermoray is only the second full champion Border Collie in the UK, and the first to do so via the current show Border Collie working test. His third CC came at WELKS where he was group 4.

36

The Wren Infra Red Heat Lamp

Exclusive to

Diamond Edge
Diamond Edge

www.diamondedgeltd.com

Standard Unit,
as illustrated
£52.50
incl. VAT
+ £3.00 p&p.

Quantity discounts available.

We also offer an extensive range of control options; thermostats, time switches, etc.

Please visit our website for full details and prices.

DIAMOND EDGE LIMITED
126 Gloucester Road, BRIGHTON, BN1 4BU
Tel: 01273 605922 and 683988
Fax: 01273 625074
Email: diamondedge@btclick.com

Lonjevitee.com Advanced Products For Dogs

As featured in Jane Lilley's column "Living with dogs" July 26th 2013

Advanced Eye Drops for Dogs
For treatment of conditions such as Cataracts, Dry Eye and Glaucoma

1 box for £33
3 boxes for £90 saving £9
6 boxes for £165 saving £33

L-Carnosine for Dogs - To prevent illness, slow down ageing and to speed up the healing process

30g for £30
60g for £50
100g for £70
5 x 100g for £280

"We have a Jack Russell called Bert who kept chasing rabbits and then getting lost because his eyes were so clouded he couldn't find his way out of the bushes. So we tried Lonjevitee's eye drops. We used the drops once an hour until his eyes cleared, which took about 10 days. After that Bert didn't get lost until about 6 months later when the cloudy eyes started again. Then we followed the initial advice given to us and also used the drops once a day to keep them clear. Since then he hasn't got lost at all." *Richard and Victoria, Clevedon, UK*

10% DISCOUNT ON YOU FIRST ORDER USE CODE: NC10
www.lonjevitee.com   email: sales@lonjevitee.com
FREEPHONE: 0800 046 9267 or 020 3280 3677

Is the acquisition ...

The Dog World in 2013

The first set of Nova Scotia Duck Tolling Retriever CCs was awarded at Crufts by Frank Whyte. His winners were Elaine Whitehill and Babs Harding's Trevargh The Entertainer at Brizewood, who was BOB and who two shows later was the breed's first UK show champion, and Sally Parr's Danehaven Pelly on Kymin. Entertainer's second CC came at the breed club's first championship show where he was BIS.
photo RBT

First Eurasier to win a championship show best of breed, at WELKS after the breed came of the imported register, was Ruth and Bryan Bickford's Darchen Smokey Quartz.
photo Alan Walker

First Pyrenean Sheepdog (Longhaired) to take a UK championship show group place was Pat Phillips' French import Friponne du Pic d'Espade Kelltara, handled by husband Steve, who was group 3 at Working and Pastoral Breeds Association of Wales under Derek Smith. She won the same award, plus best rare breed, at National W/P which was also the first breed club show. photo Farlap

The Catalan Sheepdog came off the imported register in 2013 and at the breed club's first open show BIS was Angie and Trevor Fieldsend's imported veteran Mei d'Espinavesa at Starwell. At WELKS she won the breed's first championship show best of breed.
photo Andrew Brace

News in brief

A DECISION by the Kennel Club to move the Spanish Water Dog, Lagotto Romagnolo and Kooikerhondje from the gundog to the working group provoked strong protest from the respective breed clubs. The reason for the decision was that a breed-specific working test was not available so how would full champions be crowned?

After appeals from the clubs were received, however, the KC announced that after all the Lagotto and Spanish Water Dog would remain as gundogs, to the relief of breed club members, but the Kooikerhondje would move to the second choice of breed club members, the utility group, in 2014.

THE KENNEL Club will no longer accept registrations from merle Bulldogs. However it rejected a plea by Boston Terrier people to stop registering puppies of 'abnormal' colours.

Another breed making progress is the Canadian Eskimo Dog and Rachel Bailey's Canadian import Napu of Northwinds at Akna, made history with a group 4 at East of England. Bred from dogs used in polar expeditions, he was registered under the Kennel Club's unverified parentage scheme.
photo Alan Walker

Andrew Stewart, Michael Boulcott and Virginia Dowty's Clynymona Hercules Morse at Ingerdorm became the first Bolognese to win a UK championship show group place when Sonya Saxby made him group 4 at WELKS. photo Alan Walker

The Kennel Club has split the Anatolian Shepherd Dog into two, with differing Standards in colour and other aspects. One type is now known as the Turkish Kangal Dog, and only these are currently being shown. First BOB winner under this name was Deely Cumming's Foudland Tatyyibe cum Clanquiach, taking her fourth such win at Welsh Kennel Club as two different breeds! photo Alan Walker

SmartPets International Animal Care College
N Ireland's Only Specialist Accredited Dog Grooming & Pet Care Training Provider

ARE YOU READY to start a business or a new career? Gain Qualifications or improve your skills.

- Tailored grooming tuition to your needs or choose one of our specialist courses.
- Bespoke training and improver grooming at your salon.
- New for 2014 Weekend and pay as you go courses available.

Range of distance learning and attendance pet care courses available including:
Level 2 and 3 Open College Network Accredited courses
Pet dental Hygienist, Canine and Equine massage, Pet Microchipping, Cpr and first-aid courses for pet care professional, cat grooming, kennel and cattery management, pet sitting and dog walking, dog behaviour and much more …
For full details visit:
www.smartpetsgroomingschool.co.uk

CALL US TODAY 02891450585
SmartPets

MAKING DREAMS A REALITY FOR A CAREER IN DOG GROOMING/PET CARE INDUSTRY!

---

dogworld
Exhibitors' Desk Diary

AVAILABLE NOW from the Dog World show stand and www.dogworld.co.uk

2014

of memories.

The Dog World in 2013

Welsh Kennel Club Top Dog competition winner for 2012 was Joan Wonnacott's Danish-bred Sealyham Terrier Ch Whitepeppers Saturday Night Fever at Jacott, pictured with Sue Garner, one of the judges.
photo Charley Barrett

The Scottish Kennel Club's Scottish Dog of the Year competition was won by Christine Wood's Rottweiler Westlodge Dizzee Rascal at Chaila, handled by Isabelle Nicol. With them are Alison Morton from Royal Canin and judges Peter Jolley, Liz Stannard and Robin Newhouse.
photo Ruth Dalrymple

News in brief

CONCERN has been expressed by the Pet Advertising Advisory Group (PAAG) and others about some of the advertisements for puppies which appear on the internet. In response, one site, Gumtree, made a number of changes to its rules in an aim to prevent puppy farmers using the site. Later the PAAG compiled a set of minimum standards for sites offering animals for sale.

A STUDY by the Medical Research Council and Cambridge University Veterinary School found that paralysis in some dogs, caused by spinal injuries, could be reversed by injecting them with cells grown from the lining of their noses. It is hoped that this could have a role in treating human patients too.

THE KENNEL Club has once again approved a number of DNA testing schemes, covering late onset ataxia in Parson Russell Terriers, primary ciliary dyskenesia in Old English Sheepdogs, curly coat dry eye and episodic falling in Cavaliers, neonatal cerebellar cortical degeneration in the Beagle, mucopolysaccharidosis type 111B in the Schipperke, glycogen storage disease type II in Finnish Lapphunds and progressive retinal atrophy 3 in Tibetan Spaniels.

It also approved a DNA control scheme for von Willebrand's disease in German Shorthaired Pointers.

Channel Islands Dog of the Year winner was Peter Walker's Whippet Pipijay Spirit In The Sky, pictured with Kennel Club of Jersey president Steven Edwards.

Jenny Alexander's Dalmatian Ch Offordale Sapphire won the Pets As Therapy Show Dog of the Year final at Crufts. With them are PAT's Lisa Coleman, judge Dr Ruth Barbour and Peter Partkinson of HiLife.
photo RBT

The Dog World/Royal Canin Top Stud Dog and Dog World/Yumega Top Brood Bitch of 2012 were both repeats of the previous year: Eva Ciechonska's Irish Setter Sh Ch Caskeys Concept at Aoibheanne and Dee Hardy, Trish Hallam, Sue Kite and Jeff Gillespie's US-bred CC record-holding Basenji Ch/Am Ch Klassics Million Dollar Baby at Tokaji.
photo Carol Ann Johnson

Overall winner of the gamekeepers' classes at Crufts was Dawn Hall and Brian Twigger's Flat-coated Retriever Ch Blacktoft Stray Cat Strut with Ghilgrange, pictured with judge David Bellamy and sponsor Bill Chudley.
photo Alan Walker

Subscribe to ...
ProGroomer
For all things Grooming

Only £14 per year (4 editions) for the industry's MUST READ publication.

Education and information from the grooming world's leading suppliers as well as advice from award-winning groomers.

Issue 16 available NOW

Easy ways to subscribe ...

1. Telephone
Order via credit card on the phone, just call
01233 616525

2. Online
Order via credit or debit card just visit
www.dogworldshop.com

You can't afford NOT to read ProGroomer!

---

dogworld

We're more than just a newspaper!

Design for print or online
Our in-house studio will professionally typeset and design your artwork at a competitive price and delivered on time.
- Stationery, brochures, leaflets and newsletters.
- Adverts, posters, pop-ups and signage.

Prices from £99

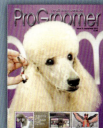

eBooks
Reading eBooks is becoming increasingly popular. Do you want to convert a book that is out of print or maybe you have written a book?
We will produce your ebook and help you market it online.
- Includes iPad and Kindle versions.
- Also works on Android.

Let us help you be part of this exciting new age of digital media.

Prices from £199

For further details please contact the sales department on tel 01233 621877 or email advertising@dogworld.co.uk

---

'DINO' a US multi BIS winner in 2013

2013

✔ UK No 1 all-breeds contender
✔ Top Utility and Top Gundog
✔ Pup of the Year winner
✔ Eukanuba Ch Stakes 1st and 3rd
✔ 100 + owned or bred UK Champions
✔ BOW Poodle Club of America

AFTERGLOW

Michael Gadsby and Jason Lynn

www.afterglowdogs.com

Dog World Annual 2014

The Dog World in 2013

David Latham's Labrador FT Ch Delfleet Neon of Fendawood won the 2012 International Gundog League Retriever Championship, repeating his success from two years earlier.
photo Paul Rawlings

Winner of the Kennel Club English Springer Spaniel Championship was Eddie Scott's FT Ch Broomfield Rosetta.
photo Paul Rawlings

Alison Burgess' Koroyza Candy Dreams at Wheelgates was Road Dog Champion at the National Carriage Dog Trials. Alison, founder of the National Carriage Dog Society, later became the first Kennel Club accredited instructor for this sport.
photo Paul Tester

Will Clulee's Moelfamau Griffon won the Kennel Club Cocker Spaniel Championship.
photo Paul Rawlings

News in brief

FIRST club to achieve listed status for the sport of rally, only recently recognised by the Kennel Club, is Lancashire-based FITdogs.

AT CRUFTS the Kennel Club signed an agreement with the World Union of German Shepherd Associations (WUSV) to work in partnership in all matters related to the breed. This will include working to implement the worldwide application of the Standard, and securing agreed health requirements.

AT THE German Shepherd Dog world's major event, the Sieger show in Germany, no Sieger or Siegerin was declared. The select VA animals, 14 dogs and 14 bitches, were not placed in any order. The concern was that over-use of the top few animals could decrease genetic diversity.

JUDGES awarding CCs for the first time in a breed need no longer be evaluated if they already give CCs in two other breeds in that group. The appeal process against non-approval to award CCs has been tightened up and failing to include all available information on the questionnaire is no longer basis for an appeal.

Tony Lockyer's WT Ch Lawinick Come N Get It at Hartshill won the TD stake at the Kennel Club's Working Trial Championships.
photo Wendy Beasley

For the second year, winner of the PD stake at the Kennel Club Working Trial Championships was Dave Olley's WT Ch Little Raymond, seen performing his test of courage.
photo Wendy Beasley

Dog World Annual 2014

The Dog World in 2013

The Crufts Agility Champions, judged by Graham Partridge: Large, Anthony Clarke and Border Collie Ag Ch Blazing Red of Rujaff; Medium, Sian Illingworth and Border Collie Ag Ch Falconmoor Shadow Dancer; and Small, Bernadette Bay and Shetland Sheepdog Ag Ch Obay Itz Got Pizazz who also won last year.
photo Alan Walker

Winning flyball team at Crufts was 4 Paws Flyers.
photo Alan Walker

The winners of the Crufts Inter-Regional Obedience Competition judged by Sue Garner were the Northern team managed by Pat Wilson and consisting of Paul Tennant and Braysuz Genna, Stewart Kimblin and Schaisla Midnight Storm, Marj Isaac and Genex Blue Eye Tynka, Tina Walker and Raycris Kinda Kool, Barbara Walsh and Schaisla True Star, Rachael Young and Sarkam Mr Daydream at Jarysmystic, Jeny Miller and Foxfold Unexpected Edition and reserve, June Young and Jarysmystic Pure Magic. Vince Hogan represented *Our Dogs*.
photo Charley Barrett

Crufts Obedience Dog Champion was Mary Ray's Ob Ch Colliewood Blue Jeans (left), Mary's fourth Crufts Champion to go with an Agility Champion and her regular appearance in the main ring doing heelwork to music. Winner for bitches, though without the certificate, was Madge Thompson's Ob Ch Forevermagic It's Trendy. They are pictured with judge Jen Jessop and commentator Dave Ray.
photo RBT

Winners of the international freestyle competition at Crufts were Jules O'Dwyer with Fyurdyhoeve Flynn from Belgium performing their 'Dog Catcher' routine.
photo Alan Walker

Overall winner of the freestyle competition was Sue Betteridge with Glenalpine Katie, performing to a Hans Christian Andersen medley.
photo Alan Walker

Heather Smith and Bearded Collie Moonlight Magic Dancer won the heelwork to music final with a routine based on *El Tango del Roxanne* from *Moulin Rouge*.
photo Alan Walker

Dog World Annual 2014

The Dog World in 2013

The Kennel Club Cancer Centre at the Animal Health Trust (AHT) in Suffolk was opened in November 2012 by the Princess Royal. Its existence was facilitated by a £1.5 million interest-free loan from the KC, and the project was started by a donation from a long-time supporter of the AHT, the late Tom Scott.

The Duchess of Cornwall visited Battersea Dogs and Cats Home before Christmas 2012 and is pictured with Beth and Bluebell, the dogs she adopted from Battersea, and TV personality Paul O'Grady who has given so much publicity to the plight of dogs in the home in his award-winning programme *For The Love of Dogs*. In August 2013 Prime Minister David Cameron also visited the home.

News in brief

THE PROBLEM of stolen dogs was again brought into the spotlight when a champion German Shorthaired Pointer, Barleyarch Atora at Tequestra, disappeared, believed stolen, in December 2012. With the support of a huge number of fellow dog people, known as 'Angel's Army', owner Dawn Maw has made every possible effort to find her, including remortgaging her house to be able to provide a £10,000 reward, but with no luck at the time of writing.

THE KENNEL Club has expressed disappointment at the number of vets who report caesarean operations, as they are asked to do. Only 2.7 of the caesars reports submitted came from vets. This is particularly frustrating in view of the fact that puppies will not be registered from bitches who have had more than two caesars – how can one be sure that this is enforceable?

BREEDERS who wish to mate their bitch to two different stud dogs in the same season no longer need to get permission in advance from the Kennel Club. It is felt that the practice, resulting in puppies in the same litter having different fathers, could help improve genetic diversity.

British team members did well at the European Open Agility Championships in Belgium. Sian Illingworth and Maybe (centre) won gold and Natasha Wise and Dizzy silver in the medium individual final, while Matt Goodliffe and Quincy (left) won bronze in the large individual final.

Dog World and Pooch & Mutt introduced a competition to find the best rescue organisations. Breed Rescue of the Year was 4 Paws Rottweiler Rescue – Hughy and Helen Cannon are pictured with DW managing director Stuart Baillie and rescue columnist Geraldine Cove-Print. The General Rescue title went to Large Breed Dog Rescue – seen with Stuart are Sharon Farrington and Tracy Buckingham.

Alison Rogers won the 2012 British Dog Grooming Championships.

Dog World Annual 2014

The Basset Griffon Vendéen Club hosted the breeds' world congress along with its 25th anniversary championship show, won by Jolanda Huisman and Marion Konings' Grand Int Ch Xprezo du Greffier du Roi, from the Netherlands. Judges were Nick Frost (now from the US), Jeff Bunney and Lydia Erhart (Netherlands).
photo Alan Walker

The Dog World in 2013
News in brief

AFTER Russian president Vladimir Putin introduced anti-gay laws including the prohibition of 'homosexual propaganda', many dog people felt concern about attending the 2016 FCI World Show in Moscow.

American Kennel Club chairman and chief executive Alan Kalter and chief executive officer Dennis Sprung wrote a strongly worded letter saying that holding such a prestigious show in these conditions 'flies in the face of the human-canine bond', and said that the AKC 'cannot and will not support participation in the show if it is held in Russia'. Our Kennel Club was more equivocal, and said that it hoped the FCI would listen to the views that dog owners present to them. The FCI General Committee also issued a statement expressing its deep concern and regret at the situation.

FCI president Rafael de Santiago did not rule out the show going ahead but said: "I will make sure that the FCI will stand strong and united against any type of discrimination or abuse against dogs, humans or any living creature."

THE KENNEL Club Educational Trust is funding authors of a new online canine genetics and epidemiology journal, by paying half the costs of processing articles which concern domestic dog health.

AN INCREASING number of people are buying puppies online or from pet shops, rather than from a responsible breeder, the Kennel Club warned.

Its research indicated that a third of the puppies bought online, through social media or in pet shops failed to 'experience overall good health'; nearly one in five puppies bought via social media or the internet die before they reach the age of six months; 12 per cent of them end up with serious health problems which require ongoing veterinary treatment from a young age; and 94 per cent of puppies bought directly from a breeder were reported to have good overall health.

Half those who bought puppies online or via social media said their puppy had shown behavioural problems.

The Kennel Club of Jersey celebrated its 125th birthday with a two-day Canine Festival. Among the attractions was a championship show where BIS was Sarah Cooper's Shih Tzu Debeaux Russia Wiv Love at Forepaws, handled by Lorraine Stewart-Smith.

The Weimaraner Club of Great Britain celebrated its diamond jubilee with a championship show and working events. Pam Edminson and Tricia Grime awarded BIS to Jackie Hawkins' Enryb Party Surprise for Sagunto, without calling on referee Christopher Hill (centre).
photo Lewis Baucutt

BIS at the English Setter Association's diamond jubilee championship show was Rachel Goutorbe's Dyrham Diversity at Redhara, seen with dog judge Fran Grimsdell and referee Ros Croft.
photo Colin Waddell

BIS at the Welsh Corgi League's 75th anniversary championship show was Sarah Matthews' veteran American import Ch/Ir/Int Ch Maplecreek Beach Bunny at Craigycor. BIS judge Mary Winsone is flanked by the dog and bitch judges from the US, Judy Hart and Patty Gailey.
photo Andrew Brace

The Dog World in 2013

DOG WORLD's Award of Excellence went to Margaret Everton who has achieved so much, so graciously as a Great Dane breeder, BIS judge, show organiser and chairman of the Kennel Club Judges Sub-Committee. Andrew Brace made the presentation.
photo Alan Walker

Many aspects of the Scottish Kennel Club have changed and Beth Harrison has taken over from Myra Orr as secretary and office manager, while Stuart Payne is show manager.
photos Alan Walker

Latest in Andrew Brace's 'An Audience with…' series featured the great American professional handler and now judge Frank Sabella. The fascinating interview is available on DVD from DOG WORLD, along with previous Audiences.

The Crookrise Pointers, founded by Walter and Kitty Edmondson and carried on today by their daughter Cicely Robertshaw and granddaughter Helga Edmondson, celebrated their eightieth anniversary at Darlington.
photo Alan Walker

R William Taylor from Canada, known worldwide for the St Aubrey Elsdon Pekingese, was awarded the country's Queen Elizabeth II Diamond Jubilee Medal for his lifetime commitment to purebred dogs. MP Anne Minh Thu Quach made the presentation and the nomination came from Alan Villeneuve (left).
photo Allen

Kerry Williamson would have been delighted at the recipient of her memorial award for an 'unsung hero' as it went to Laura Breen who set up a Facebook group which was instrumental in finding Heather Simper and Liz Scoates' Tibetan Spaniels who were stolen in 2012, and has gone on to help many more who have been in the same difficulties. Kerry's husband Adrian Willson made the presentation.
photo Alan Walker

Keith and June Young have retired as secretary and assistant secretary of City of Birmingham after many years involved with the running of the show. They are seen been presented with gifts by Frances Chapman-King, wife of chairman Bill King. Keith is now to chair a working party looking at ways of revitalising the show scene. David Bell (inset) is interim secretary.
photo Alan Walker

Bill Browne-Cole is now chairman of Bath; Muriel Iles becomes patron.
photo Alan Walker

Petronelle Kitson, founder of the Quinoa English Toy Terriers, celebrated her hundredth birthday in February.

Joyce Collis-Cosme has announced her retirement from judging, as did Clive Davies after doing the gundog group at the Welsh Kennel Club. Betty Flavell awarded her last set of CCs at Darlington.
photo Alan Walker

Dr Mark Vaudin, a genome scientist and geneticist, is new chief executive of the Animal Health Trust.

Martin Wyles has retired after five years as chairman of Birmingham Dog Show Society which runs the National show.
photo Alan Walker

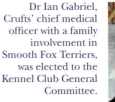

Dr Ian Gabriel, Crufts' chief medical officer with a family involvement in Smooth Fox Terriers, was elected to the Kennel Club General Committee.

Dog World Annual 2014

The Dog World in 2013

Tina Dixon's Chinese Crested Ch Debrita Diaz has broken the breed CC record. Winner of several groups, she is handled by Tina's daughter Dawn. Some years ago the family also held the record with one of her ancestors.
photo Elizabeth Shepherd

Pets As Therapy Dog of the Year is Ann Burrell's Leonberger Scrabble. They make 100 visits to care homes and a hospice each year.
photo Alan Walker

The charity Newfound Friends, through which Newfoundlands and their owners held sick children, has now raised a million pounds.

As part of its ninetieth birthday celebrations the Saluki or Gazelle Hound Club held an 'Arabian Saluki special event' where dogs could be assessed by Hamad Ghanem Shaheen AlGhanem, director of the Saluki of Arabia Club. He presented a canvas to all his winners and is pictured with best special event winner, Vicki-Ann Tompkins' Sivendra Abishai, best puppy, the same owner's Galifa Sivendra Al Djaliibaajah, steward Karen Fisher in Arabian costume, best veteran, Jenny and Steve Macro's Ch Nefisa Jeevun, and Brian Buckley also in costume.
photo Alan Walker

Canine Concern Scotland Trust's Therapet of the Year is Boxer Pepper, seen with owners Alyson and Willie Raworth and (left) chairman George Leslie.

A record number of 222 Golden Retrievers paraded in front of the breed's effective birthplace, Guisachan House near Inverness, for the Golden Retriever Club of Scotland's Gathering there. It was a momentous year for the breed with the parent club celebrating its centenary.
photo Linsey Dunbar

In the Welsh Corgi League's platinum jubilee year the Queen met members of the League's East Anglian Sub-Section and their dogs in the walled garden at Sandringham.
photo Jackie Mann

Dog World Annual 2014

JUNIORS
in the picture

The Dog World in 2013

Will Croxford became the first young man for 14 years to top the Junior Handler of the Year final. He is one of the successful juniors featured on the following pages.
photo Alan Walker

Luke Johnston handled the Whippet Danluke Dicky Bird to win the Young Kennel Club stakes final at Crufts. He too is featured on the next few pages.
photo Alan Walker

Sophie Wing won the Young Kennel Club Groomer of the Year contest at Crufts.
photo Dog World

Naomi van Mourik from the Netherlands won the International Junior Handling final at Crufts. Judge was Bill McFadden from the US and Gerard Jipping of the Dutch Kennel Club and Liz Cartledge presented the trophies. Naomi went on to win the junior handling final at the World Show in Budapest.
photo Alan Walker

Laura Stuart-Cook chose Hollie Kavanagh as Young Kennel Club Handler of the Year at Crufts. Victoria Wilkins represented DOG WORLD.
photo Dog World

Ashley Pace won the Scottish Junior Handler of the Year competition. She is seen with vice-convener Chris Holmes, Alison Morton of Royal Canin and judge Katie Hamilton.
photo Ruth Dalrymple

Welsh Junior Handler of the Year was Melissa Phillips, seen with judge Sarah Gibbons and organiser Phillippa Pearson.
photo Will Harris

Dog World Annual 2014

Juniors stars of the group rings

Imagine you are sitting ringside at a general championship show – best of breeds for the group of your choice file in and quite often you see a handler, a junior, running alongside their charge.

This sight is becoming increasingly frequent and juniors, considered to be the future of our hobby, are challenging the older generation, winning best of breed and in some cases group placings.

VICTORIA WILKINS highlights some successful juniors who are turning up the heat in the breed rings and pushing even their own parents for the top spot.

Luke Johnston

Luke took Ch Jorjenjo Mirzam of Fernlark to a group 3 place at Crufts 2012.
photo Carol Ann Johnson

Luke Johnston has had much success over the past two years handling both Whippets and Salukis, the latter for which many will know him. Luke tells me about his successes and how dogs have now well and truly taken over his life.

Many of us will remember Luke as the youngster with a dicky bow at Crufts 2012 who won a group placing with his winning Saluki. Others will remember him from previous years when he was handling Whippets under the Danluke affix and winning £5 in a Young Kennel Club stakes class was his ultimate pride and joy.

Luke's mum has shown dogs since he was 13 years old and he insists that the bug bit him straight from then. To date, he estimates that he has handled around 30 breeds, but will remain a true hound lover with his roots planted firmly with Whippets and Salukis.

His successes took off in 2011 when he handled the Saluki Ch Jorjenjo Mirzam of Fernlark to his first CC at East of England. The pair went on to get a group 2 at the show under the late Denise Courtney and this set the ball rolling for a truly memorable year for them.

"Rafi and I have the greatest rapport with each other," Luke says.

"He is the dog who has let me achieve the majority of amazing things that I have and he's such an interesting dog; at home he's the alpha male and at shows he's a laid back, well behaved showman who never puts a foot wrong."

Over the course of 2011 and '12, Rafi and Luke amassed 12 CCs, six RCCs, three group 2, three group 3 and a group 4. On the Continent, Rafi won two CACs. The pair's winning streak

ELISE O'CONNOR

Aged 12

Highlights for 2013 include:

Numerous JHA and YKC handling wins including Crufts

Reserve Best Junior in Show – South Coast Handler

Qualifying Khados Dancing Bear (Tibetan Terrier) and Santosha Sandy Storm over Charizgate (Shih Tzu) for Crufts 2014 in their respective breed classes

We would like to wish Elise good luck with her first homebred puppy Charizgate Of Ice And Fire (Tibetan Terrier).

All our dogs are exclusively trained and handled by Elise.

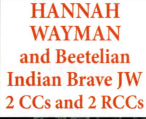

HANNAH WAYMAN and Beetelian Indian Brave JW 2 CCs and 2 RCCs

Third place 12-16 years Hounds, many thanks to all

ABIGAL GOREE and BONARIO BURLESQUE

Abigail has had another successful year showing and handling Gundogs and Terriers
3rd at Richmond Semi-Finals 2013

49

stayed well into 2012 where Rafi was crowned top Saluki and second top hound behind the 2013 Crufts BIS winner, the Petit Basset Griffon Vendéen Jilly.

This wasn't the first time Jilly had pipped the pair to a win; she was also present at their most memorable moment of 2012.

Talking about that day Luke said: "Crufts 2012 has to be the most memorable moment of my dog-showing life; the feeling was indescribable and it was a truly once-in-a-lifetime moment."

Rafi had won his third and crowning CC on hound day at Crufts and group judge Keith Thornton had pulled them into the final ten for a closer look. The crowd had rapturous applause for all finalists, but when Luke and Rafi went around for their own final movement solely, the crowd truly showed their support.

Luke said: "Words can't describe Rafi, he is just perfect."

Keith had those thoughts too and pulled the Saluki in for group 3 at the biggest dog show in the world.

Luke, who says his inspiration is Frank Sabella, has won 23 CCs and 15 RCCs in his seven years in the hobby and out of the ten times he has been in a group ring, he has been placed seven time. Even though he is still a junior, he continues to push the adults.

Luke said: "Juniors are the future of our hobby and without them there would be no future, so it's vital young people get involved and give it a go."

This sentiment is something that Luke firmly believes in and feels that hard work is the root to his success.

He said: "I believe hard work is needed for anything, especially in this game, whether it be practising to become better at handling or taking your dogs out to train them so they show themselves off to the best of their ability – it's all hard work."

Hard work has earned Luke success in Whippets as well, winning RBIS last year at Border Union with Danluke Dance Of Love, who also won the Young Kennel Club members stakes final overall under Stuart Plane at Crufts 2013.

Looking to the future, Luke hopes to try agility and obedience and is currently concentrating on handling an Italian-imported Saluki and Rafi's half-sister, along with his Whippets, and attended the Kortrijk show in Belgium to handle Salukis.

Will Croxford

Will Croxford won the 100th CC for the Whittimere Norwegian Elkhound and Finnish Spitz kennel at Richmond 2013. With his Elkhounds he has become a well-known character both in and out of the group ring, winning junior handling classes and his semi-final age group this year – and since this article was written he has become the UK's Junior Handler of the Year. Will tells me about his wins and why his heart lies firmly with his beloved Elkhounds.

We all talk about 'lucky shows' and 'lucky charms' and as far as lucky shows goes Will certainly has one in Richmond dog show, held annually in September.

Will handled Ch/Ir Ch Ennafort The One And Only to group 3 at Richmond.
photo Alan Walker

SINEAD KERR-MOIR
Rozamie Daysha Too Jansanleis

Toy 6-11 winner 2013
Utility 6-11 winner 2012
Richmond JHA semi-final
Tel: 01968 672883

Isobel Khawaja
Shetland Sheepdog
Smiddyshaw Rumba Carrumba

Congratulations on qualifying for Richmond 2013 at only 6 years old. We are so proud of you. Well done and good luck for future shows.

JESS ANDREWS
1st 12–16 years with
FALLOWFEN FOXY VIXEN OF JEMMATEE
(Toffee)

Many thanks to the Judge Mrs Claire Sharp and thank you to all who have supported me

Will, 16 years old, from Thrapston, Northamptonshire, actively competes in both junior handling and breed rings with Norwegian Elkhounds, with most of his success coming from handling the Elkhound bitch Ch/Ir Ch Ennafort The One And Only whom he describes as 'one hell of a character'.

At Richmond, it was once again 'Pearl' who helped him achieve a landmark success for the Whittimere kennel, owned by Robert Greaves, Will and his mum Nicola. It was here that he won the kennel's 100th CC. Another testament that came at this lucky show was in the Junior Handling Association semi-finals where Will, who took another Elkhound named Odin into the ring, won first place, qualifying for one of the 14 spots at the final in November.

Talking about Richmond, Will says: "I felt over the moon when I won my class and winning the 100th CC was one of the most happy and memorable moments.

"The junior handling class was the first time Odin had ever been used in such a class, so to win was like conquering an ambition."

It wasn't third time lucky for Will, but fourth, as he has previously been placed second, fourth and fifth in the semi-finals.

Juniors, for Will, are extremely important and he believes the sentiment behind 'they are the future'.

He said: "It's very important for the younger generation to get involved as we need new blood coming through to take over and carry the sport on.

"I would like to see, as part of the younger generation, that dog shows continue to maintain the enthusiasm in years to come as they do now."

Will's enthusiasm for Elkhounds is firmly rooted and they are definitively his favourite breed. He has been around both them and Finnish Spitz since the age of six and won his first CC at the age of ten with Ch Bowerhinton Bright Knight at Cakirjo. Over the last year with Pearl, he has gone on to win two group placings, one at Paignton 2012 and the other at SKC this year. He has won 11 other CCs and five group placings for the kennel.

"My secret to success in the big ring is to stay calm and make the dogs presentable and in good condition," he says.

"I have always had to compete against adults since I started as I was always allowed to complete in the breed rings. I believe that you should always show respect, be polite and above all be professional."

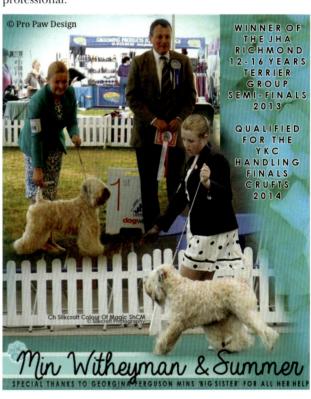

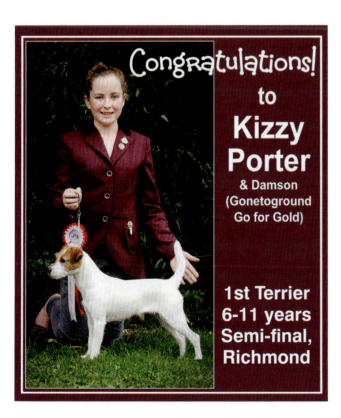

Dog World Annual 2014

His inspiration, Will says, comes from top handlers and breeders Geoff Corish and Michael Coad, whom he regularly shadows and gains experience from and says they have spent much time and patience teaching him about all aspects of the dog showing world. His other inspiration comes from right at home in the Whittimere kennel in the form of Robert Greaves.

For the future, Will continues to focus on his handling abilities; however, after the JHA final he will continue to focus on breed classes and promoting Whittimere.

Michaella Dunhill-Hall

Michaella Dunhill-Hall, at the age of 14, has amassed a grand total of 55 CCs with Rottweilers, Soft-Coated Wheaten Terriers and Japanese Shiba Inu and plenty of group places to boot. Michaella talks to me about her most memorable moments in her dog-showing career and her beliefs for the future of dog showing.

There are few adults let alone youngsters who can claim to match or beat Michaella's current collection of CCs across a variety of breeds. At the age of six she won her first CC, which makes her possibly the youngest person ever to be awarded a CC.

Michaella, from Retford, Nottinghamshire, was well and truly born into the world of dogs as the daughter of Liz Dunhill, a well-known handler, breeder, judge and trainer. She was just four years old when she showed her first dog, a Shiba Inu named Saporro Hollie Hobby, who went on to win the progeny class at a Shiba Inu club show.

At the age of six, Michaella won her first major win at under the late Gail Storie, beating her mum to win BOB at the CC with the Soft-Coated Wheaten Terrier Fantasa Blonde Isabelle.

Her winning continued and now, Michaella has amassed, along with her CCs, three group wins, a group 2 at Crufts, BOB at Crufts two years in a row and runner-up at the Contest of Champions with the Wheaten Ch Fantasa Blonde Lilley, along with many other group placings.

Michaella says: "My most treasured achievement was gaining my first CC along with winning the group with my Rottweiler Ch

Michaella winning a group in 2012 with the Rottweiler Ch Fantasa Smirnoff Ice. Ben Reynolds-Frost was the judge and Sue Roome represented the Boston committee.
photo Carol Ann Johnson

Fantasa Smirnoff Ice at Boston last year."

When talking about competing against adults in the group, she describes the experience as 'daunting'.

She said: "At first it is very daunting, but I am one of the few who has been brought up in an adult world, so mixing with adults has always come naturally to me from a very young age."

Mixing with children her own age is something Michaella also does well and in 2011 she was crowned Junior Handler of the Year at Earls Court, London, on behalf of the Junior Handling Association. This meant that Michaella went on to

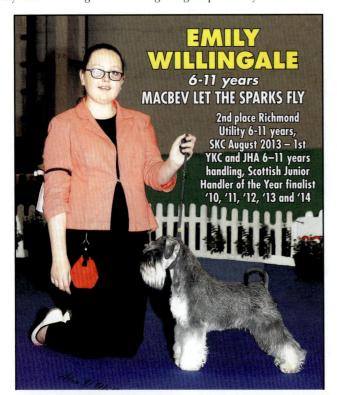

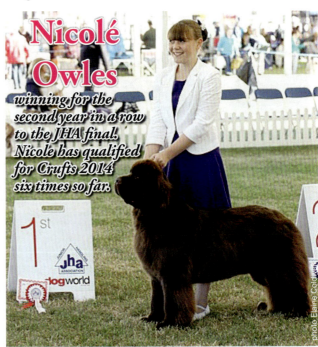

compete against 36 other countries at Crufts 2012 for the title of International Junior Handler of the Year.

Although she was not placed, junior handling and her involvement in dogs has made her speak out and champion the younger generation.

"Juniors are very important – they are the future and without juniors no one can continue dog showing," she says.

"Junior handlers need to remember the importance of breed showing and in the future one thing I would like to see is less bullying of children by adults.

"I feel some adults need to realise young children need their confidence building and not destroying. I have been bullied and so have other juniors and we have all helped each other to move forward."

Michaella's biggest inspiration comes from her mum and her secret of her success, in her eyes, is hard work and dedication to the hobby.

Talking about what it's like having a successful parent in the hobby, she said: "I found it hard work at first as people always expected me to be as good as my mum at handling, and they were very big shoes to fill.

"I had to work twice as hard so I could be as good as her; now I try to think of new ways to get the best out of my dogs, and have my own style of handling, which mum says is very important to be an individual. Mum and I listen to each other and she loves new ideas.

"I find it fascinating to sometimes to spend my free time looking through the old scrapbooks of the Fantasa, Vormund, Poirot and Jagen Rottweilers and through the many boxes of rosettes and old photos of my mum winning groups and BIS with all the old winners such as the Shiba Ch Vormund I'm Smartie and Rottweiler Ch/NZ Ch Rolex Rumour Has It by Fantasa."

In the future, Michaella, who is still at school, loves to get her creative side flowing, taking part in art, cooking, creative media and photography, with her main goal for them to help her in the world of dogs.

JON-PAUL CHURCH & KIAMINOGUES PAINT IT BLACK

Congratulations on your success this year. Good luck in your YKC grooming, handling and stakes classes at Crufts 2014. Love Mum, Dad and family.

HANNAH PEARSON and SAMHAVEN FAIRY DUST AT MONFORTMAGIC 'Lilly' 12-16 Years

Well done Hannah on all your excellent achievements throughout 2013. We are all very proud.

Alice Potter

Congratulations Alice and Monty on an incredible 2013, winning Crufts YKC 6-11 Years Gundog Handling, and another 15 Championship Show wins in YKC/JHA Handling, plus many other wins and placings at all show levels.

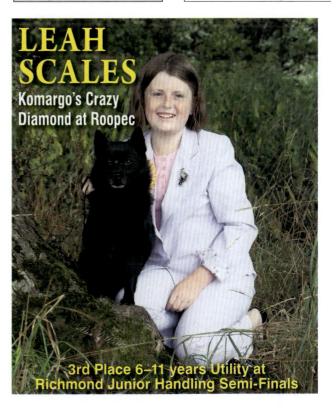

LEAH SCALES
Komargo's Crazy Diamond at Roopec

3rd Place 6–11 years Utility at Richmond Junior Handling Semi-Finals

Dog World Annual 2014

by Kennel Club chairman Steve Dean

Where will we be, five years on?

THE EDITOR asked me to comment on where the world of dogs might be five years from now. After a great deal of thought and gazing into my crystal ball, the most likely answer is where we deserve to be or alternatively where we wish to be, and they may not be the same result.

Following bad publicity around five years ago it could be expected that the pedigree dog would be an unpopular choice with the public and yet that does not seem to have been the effect. The interest in pedigree puppies remains high and even the majority of the high profile breeds have retained their popularity. Perhaps people are right when they say there is no such thing as bad publicity.

In contrast, registrations and entries at dog shows have been on a downward trend and the commentary within the dog community, both in the press and online, has largely been directed at trying to blame either lack of action or various positive initiatives for the reduction.

In some areas this may be true for there have been several actions that contribute towards a reduction in registrations and show entries – banning of close matings; the restriction to two caesareans; docked dogs banned from shows where the public pays; veterinary checks of bests of breed.

Nevertheless the state of the national economy has also had an undeniable effect with the cost of travel being the most significant.

Uproar

Readers will recall the uproar following the introduction of veterinary checks of high profile breeds at Crufts 2012 and the claims it was badly thought through. It has in fact changed very little since its introduction and now we see the breeds concerned positively engaged in reducing the exaggerated features that can lead on to poor health and welfare.

Much of the negative dog press coverage focused on the people involved yet nobody is challenging the intent to improve health. Indeed some sectors have called for far more draconian checks on all breeds. Many dogs presented in the show ring this past year have had less undesirable exaggeration and judges have played their part by rewarding correct conformation.

Jeff Horswell chose the Pointer Sh Ch Wilchrimane Ice Maiden, handled by Amelia Siddle for her mother Annette, to top the Kennel Gazette Junior Warrant Winner of the Year final at Crufts. They have gone on to many successes including reserve BIS at Blackpool.
photo Alan Walker

Comments from dog exhibitors have suggested a wide range of reasons why show entries have declined with the most commonly quoted confirming various actions designed to reduce cost. For example, a reduction in the number of dogs entered at a show; sharing cars for longer journeys (thus reducing space to take dogs); being more selective in supporting specific judges; or going to shows that offer exhibitors the best value for money.

Everyone has their favoured solution for reversing the declining trend and those where the Kennel Club has significant influence involve benching at championship shows, allocation of challenge certificates and the request for champions classes.

Some of the other more frequent comments have mentioned the quality and integrity of some of our UK judges, including the frequency of their appointments, as well as the restrictions on open shows (eg permitted number of classes and the required average entry per class) and the cost of entries at championship shows.

All suggestions are being considered by a working group at the KC and a little more time is needed to consider the merit of each suggestion, its effect on dog showing and for discussion about those selected as possessing the most merit.

The CC and the status of the UK champion are at the very centre of this issue and one thing is certain, any committed dog person will wish to see the standard of champion maintained.

To make up a champion in the UK does require more than just entering a series of dog shows and those who win CCs and go on to see their dog earn its champion title value this award very highly indeed. So in considering how we might make changes to the CC allocation in the UK, we must be certain that it will first do no harm to the status of our homebred champions and secondly that any change will increase the popularity of our dog shows in the longer term.

The same applies to issues such as benching. Not everybody agrees with discontinuing the use of benching although some good points have been made for the smaller shows and perhaps some greater flexibility is sensible.

However, to carry out an extensive trial, as some suggest, could seriously damage the business model for the benching contractor and if they should exit the market pre-emptively, this would not be a

Dog World Annual 2014

Joanna Mayston and Mists of Tawny won the Kennel Club Good Citizen Dogs Scheme Pre-Beginners Obedience final at Crufts. With them are obedience, agility and events director Maurice Cooke and judge Annette Benoiste. photo RBT

Crufts' Friends For Life event was won by Anatolian Shepherd Dog Haatchi, devoted companion of young Owen Howkins who has a muscular disorder. As a youngster Haatchi had been tied to a railway line and had to have a leg and tail amputated.

Noodle, an 11-month-old Cocker/Poodle cross owned by Tory MP Alan Duncan, was declared Westminster Dog of the Year.

reversible decision. In such an event, any trial would become a reality overnight and shows which might have wished to retain benching to any extent, may find they do not have that option.

Similar logic applies to increasing the number of CCs available: it cannot be trialled as once done it is not easily reversible. After all the increased number of CCs already allocated as a result of exhibit numbers increasing over the past decade are proving very difficult to remove without exhibitor rancour when the trend reverses.

Against the background decline in the show world, the contrasting rising popularity of other activities is very noticeable. Agility and field trials are leading the way but increasingly the dog owner is choosing to take part in other canine activities.

Perhaps it is because many of these events are welcoming to the visitor and interested newcomer? Perhaps the friendly atmosphere of a typical agility event is the attraction or maybe the competitors feel they get better value for money? Whatever the reasons the younger competitor is taking part in these events and they are generally very popular.

So five years from now we could develop an inclusive community of dog owners with the ability to compete at a wide variety of dog events as individuals or as a family.

Many pedigree dog exhibitors started out at shows similar to today's companion dog shows, competing simply for fun, and often their first dog was a crossbreed. Many then moved on to a pedigree dog to further their interest.

Bedrock

The pedigree dog will remain the bedrock of our interest as they offer a high degree of predictability in form, function, health and temperament. Registration provides a data resource that helps identify the source of inherited disease and then assists in the research and ability to moderate or eliminate mutations.

Without the pedigree dog there can be no crossbreed, deliberate or otherwise. Surely crossbreeds deserve equal attention paid to their health and welfare as we provide for our pedigree dogs?

So the KC will continue to develop the Assured Breeder Scheme as an aid for the puppy buyer and a quality marker of those who are prepared to act positively to improve and protect the health and welfare of dogs. In five years every reputable dog breeder should want to be part of this scheme and be subjected to a visit to assess their commitment to the standard it represents or something equivalent.

We will also consider investing some of the £12m we have earned from the agreement with British Land in a project to assist breed clubs to identify the health status of their breeds and help focus attention on those areas requiring further research. Such work will also identify differences in disease prevalence in pedigree and non-pedigree populations.

A further investment could be in land in the North dedicated to all forms of canine activity and it is almost certain we will develop a purpose-built premises in Aylesbury to house our registration activities, including Petlog and our online facilities.

Online

Ongoing development of our online capacity should mean registrations and microchip data is increasingly managed online with access to registration data, along with health information, becoming increasingly accessible through the MyKC service, an innovation that will become the central electronic portal between the dog owner and the KC.

Most importantly, the pedigree dog will still be the centre of our interest. However compulsory microchipping will bring the KC into greater contact with an increasing range of dog owners and many will be pet owners of a crossbred dog.

There is no intention of recognising the various crossbreed types as breeds, but surely the KC should be doing all it can to engage with anybody who breeds a dog, or owns a dog, to help ensure they breed with health and welfare in mind, provide good socialisation training for their puppies and use our influence to ensure legislation does not unnecessarily restrict our enjoyment of a dog's company. If this can be expedited by providing access to statistics, health data, health testing and published information then it will be put in place.

Five years from now the pedigree dog will be at least as popular as it is now. If we all play our parts well, the reputation of each breed will be enhanced and we will increasingly demonstrate to the world how the UK dog breeder takes their responsibility very seriously and remains the most reliable source of healthy, well socialised dogs.

Dog World Annual 2014

Quality doesn't have to mean quantity – the Saxonmill Saga

Few breeders have bred as many champions from so few litters as has ROBERTA HALL of the Saxonmill Afghan Hounds. Here she explains what has made her very limited breeding programme so successful down the generations.

The foundation bitch Ch Sacheverell Kanika of Saxonmill, bred by Monica Booth Thomson.

I HAVE been involved in Afghan Hounds since the mid 1960s and bred one litter in 1969 but it is 1976 when the story really starts.

The Sacheverell kennel used one of the Horningsea greats, **Ch Koolaba Horningsea Eboni Earl** and produced a litter to **Zelda** (sister to **Ch Sacheverell Zukwala**) and from this I bought my foundation bitch, a houndy black and tan, **Ch Sacheverell Kanika of Saxonmill**.

I consider myself very fortunate to have had such a lovely bitch to build my Saxonmill kennel on. She was houndy, had a most beautiful head and eye, ring tail, good body and a real quality look with excellent breed type.

I showed her to her title and she produced just one litter to **Ch Karnak Shamrock**. I chose him because I thought his breeding linked to my bitch, common ancestor Eboni Earl who was a real stallion of a dog, very houndy, long legs and a real free mover with excellent breed type. As a young girl I had always admired the Horningsea Afghan Hounds.

Shamrock had the attributes of his heritage and complemented Kanika in all respects. He came from the famous Karnak litter of five champions, a record I would equal in the future!

This produced my first homebred champions **Black Currant** and **Black Iris**, the latter owned by Heather Crossfield (now Andrews) and dam of a champion. The Saxonmill 'type' was starting to be established.

Black Currant was owned by Sandra Weston (Sanstas). As a puppy he injured the end of his tail and I didn't take the risk of keeping him. Sandra gave him a wonderful home, campaigned him to title and many accolades and he became a very prolific and influential sire of the '80s producing 13 champions. He was top stud dog in 1991, '92 and '93.

Black Currant was used on **Ch/Ir Ch Playfere's Petticoat Wag at Harlextan** and it was from here I made a 'real steal'. I was fortunate and grateful to obtain a beautiful black and tan bitch, **Ch Harlextan Piara at Saxonmill** (born in 1988 and top brood in breed 1998 and '99).

Black Currant would have always been my ideal choice as a stud for Petticoat Wag. Both were of a similar look and had common ancestors going back to Shamrock and Eboni Earl. The attributes of both animals complemented each other and this litter produced four champions for the Harlextan kennel.

Piara was a delight in all respects, she had an excellent temperament, beautiful breed type, head and eye, very soundly constructed and a great bitch to breed on with.

It was at this point that I really looked to Ch Saxonmill Black Currant. His litter sister was Ch Saxonmill Black Iris.

Black Currant's daughter Ch Harlextan Piara at Saxonmill, bred by Graham and Christine Parsell. photo John Hope

Ch Karnak Shamrock	Ch Amudarya Shalar	Ch Amudarya The Pagan
		Amudarya Shakila
	Oregano Rosemary of Karnak	Ch Koolaba Horningsea Eboni Earl
		Pandora of Khyber
Ch Sacheverell Kanika of Saxonmill	Ch Koolaba Horningsea Eboni Earl	Horningsea Surivor
		Ch Horningsea Kayacci
	Sacheverell Zelda	Ch Ghuura Khan of Tarril
		Ch Safiya of Scaheverell

56

Dog World Annual 2014

Ch Saxonmill Currant Bun.
photo Carol Ann Johnson

		Karaburan Count Baisey	Ch Viscount Grant
Ch/Ir Ch Karaburan Jelly Roll Morton			Karaburan Raving Red Rita
		Sacheverell Anoushka at Charadelle	Ch Koolaba Alexander of Sacheverell
			Ch Sacheverell Madam Zinnia
Ch Harlextan Piara at Saxonmill		Ch Saxonmill Black Currant	Ch Karnak Shamrock
			Ch Sacheverell Kanika of Saxonmill
		Ch/Ir Ch Playfere's Petticoat Wag at Harlextan	Ch Karnak Shamrock
			Ch Harlextan Mad Miranda

fix my type and look. My preference was for a houndy animal with good conformation, no real exaggerations but with a beautiful head and eye and all the characteristics that make an Afghan what it is.

I studied pedigrees and had the benefit of having been around for 'a while' so knew or had seen most of the dogs in the pedigrees of that particular decade.

I decided that I needed to use a Black Currant son and this would then certainly cement the Saxonmill line and give me a consolidated look to take forward. It would also afford me more scope for the future and perhaps be able to move a little further afield once my gene pool had been 'fixed'.

Piara had two litters, one to the Black Currant son **Ch Karaburan Pretty Boy Floyd at Shirobana**, producing **Ch Saxonmill Currant Bun** and CC and RCC winners.

Piara's second litter was to **Ch/Ir Ch Karaburan Jelly Roll Morton**, a dog I admired for type, angulation and free striding movement. This produced a litter of five of whom three were champions, **Rum Tum Tigger**, **Jennyanydots** and **Bustopher Jones**, and one was a CC and RCC winner, **Rumpleteazer**.

I have never been averse to selling to potential first time owners. Rumpleteazer was owned by Bob and Joy Sanghera and they used him to found their own successful line, Sitana. Similarly Bustopher Jones and **Lucy Locket** (two CCs and litter sister to Currant Bun) were owned by Ross Gilbert and Fiona Grant (now Nisbet) and founded the very successful Firos line and latterly Finix and Affietar.

This fourth generation of Saxonmills was bred with a view of producing a bitch that I could put to the half-brother from the previous litter, further consolidating the

Ch Saxonmill Rum Tum Tigger.
photo Carol Ann Johnson

Ch Saxonmill Jennyanydots.

Ch Karaburan Pretty Boy Floyd at Shirobana	Ch Saxonmill Black Currant	Ch Karnak Shamrock
		Ch Sacheverell Kanika of Saxonmill
	Karaburan Cleopatra	Toptani's Barracuda of Karaburan
		Sacheverell Anoushka of Charadelle
Ch Harlextan Piara at Saxonmill	Ch Saxonmill Black Currant	Ch Karnak Shamrock
		Ch Sacheverell Kanika of Saxonmill
	Ch/Ir Ch Playfere's Petticoat Wag at Harlextan	Ch Karnak Shamrock
		Ch Harlextan Mad Miranda

Ch Saxonmill Bustopher Jones.

57

Ch Saxonmill Jellicle Jett.
photo Carol Ann Johnson

Ch Saxonmill Currant Bun	Ch Karaburan Pretty Boy Floyd at Shirobana	Ch Saxonmill Black Currant
		Karaburan Cleopatra
	Ch Harlextan Piara at Saxonmill	Ch Saxonmill Black Currant
		Ch/Ir Ch Playfere's Petticoat Wag at Harlextan
Ch Saxonmill Jennyanydots	Ch/Ir Ch Karaburan Jelly Roll Morton	Karaburan Count Baisey
		Sacheverell Anoushka at Charadelle
	Ch Harlextan Piara at Saxonmill	Ch Saxonmill Black Currant
		Ch/Ir Ch Playfere's Petticoat Wag at Harlextan

line and type.

Morton was not so close, genetically, as Floyd so I thought that the two offspring together would be suitable in terms of coefficient of inbreeding (COI).

Rum Tum Tigger put the kennel 'on the map'. He acquired 18 CCs, specialty BIS, numerous group placings and was my first homebred hound group winner. He won the dog CC at Crufts three times, in 1997, '98 and '99, but lost to the referees for BOB. He had his critics as all great dogs do. It's interesting that as soon as you appear above the parapet you are swiftly 'shot at' and need a good thick skin!

He was used sparingly but produced around ten champions at home and abroad. He again contributed to some successful kennels of today, including Tulak and Cloudside.

Bustopher Jones also made his mark, particularly at Zareesh, and sired six champions.

On the basis of the two litters Piara achieved a phenomenal accolade as runner-up Top Brood Bitch all breeds in 1999. I was immensely proud as she had only the two litters and we were a small kennel, keeping few dogs and trying to perpetuate a line, not just the numbers game from multiple litters.

With essentially one line I was never able to use Tigger on any of my bitches; in fact at that time I had only one bitch who could be bred from, Jennyanydots – quite a precarious position to be in and one that I vowed not to be in again!

She was a lovely bitch of excellent construction and breed type, a pale masked gold with free striding movement much like Rum Tum Tigger and Bustopher Jones. She was lightly coated with a natural saddle

Ch Saxonmill Rum Tum Rio. photo Michael Trafford

and had 'nothing to hide'.

She produced just one litter to Currant Bun and this culminated in **Ch Jellicle Jett** who had the highest COI I had produced. She was from a half-brother to half-sister mating from a half-brother half-sister mating – perhaps this would be frowned

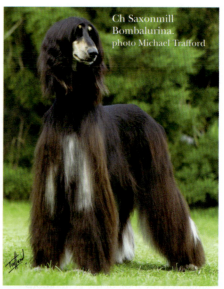

Ch Saxonmill Bombalurina.
photo Michael Trafford

Ch Saxonmill Grizabella.
photo Michael Trafford

Ch/Int/Ir/Dan/ Sw/Bel/Lux Ch Exxos Gameboy at Zharook (imp Denmark)	Int/Nord Ch El Khyrias Zon Of The Master	Int/Dan/Dutch Ch Boxadan Xercise Makes Master
		Sw/Norw Ch El Khyrias Private Collection
	Dan Ch Exxos Escape	Sw/Dan Ch El Khyrias Tell Me A Secret
		Exxos Celeste
Ch Saxonmill Jellicle Jett	Ch Saxonmill Currant Bun	Ch Karaburan Pretty Boy Floyd at Shirobana
		Ch Harlextan Piara at Saxonmill
	Ch Saxonmill Jennyanydots	Ch/Ir Ch Karaburan Jelly Roll Morton
		Ch Harlextan Piara at Saxonmill

Ch Saxonmill Rocket Man. photo Michael Trafford

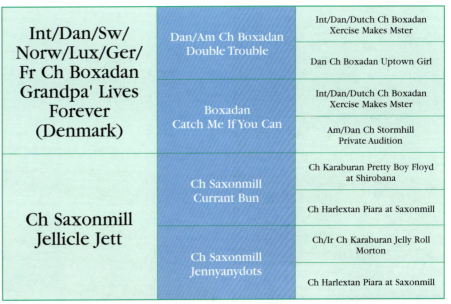

Int/Dan/Sw/ Norw/Lux/Ger/ Fr Ch Boxadan Grandpa' Lives Forever (Denmark)	Dan/Am Ch Boxadan Double Trouble	Int/Dan/Dutch Ch Boxadan Xercise Makes Mster
		Dan Ch Boxadan Uptown Girl
	Boxadan Catch Me If You Can	Int/Dan/Dutch Ch Boxadan Xercise Makes Mster
		Am/Dan Ch Stormhill Private Audition
Ch Saxonmill Jellicle Jett	Ch Saxonmill Currant Bun	Ch Karaburan Pretty Boy Floyd at Shirobana
		Ch Harlextan Piara at Saxonmill
	Ch Saxonmill Jennyanydots	Ch/Ir Ch Karaburan Jelly Roll Morton
		Ch Harlextan Piara at Saxonmill

Ch Saxonmill Rocket Rider. photo Michael Trafford

Ch Saxonmill Star Struck. photo Michael Trafford

Ch/Int/Sp/Port Ch Saxonmill Star Style. photo John Hope

Ch Saxonmill Star Attraction at Karandikar.

upon now?

Jellicle Jett (Dolly) represents for me what Saxonmill is about. She had the temperament, quality, breed type and movement that I had been aspiring to. She maintained the look of the generations before her and had the improvements too!

She acquired 12 CCs plus specialty BIS wins and was my second homebred group winner. She was top brood bitch in breed 2006, '07 and '08 and Top Brood Bitch all breeds on two consecutive years. Her progeny accumulated over 60 CCs with eight UK champions and three CC winners, quite something from just two litters!

By now we are at 2002, a new century and time to preserve and utilise the fixed type from Dolly. I thought she needed an outcross. I wanted to use something that had a similar look but was not related.

The first litter first was to the import from Denmark, **Ch/Int/Multi Ch Exxos Gameboy at Zharook**. He was from old Scandinavian lines and in particular the famous El Khyrias. At Crufts 2002 I gave him the RCC.

He complemented Dolly by being a medium sized dog with all the breed points, excellent movement and I felt the pedigree and the look of the dogs in it would suit my own tightly bred all English lines. So in the offspring I went from a COI of around 24 per cent to 0 per cent!

This litter produced three champions, **Rum Tum Rio**, **Bombalurina** and **Grizabella** (Jayne Edwards and Jill Ohmke) and two RCC winners.

Rum Tum Rio became a very famous dog winning 23 CCs, group placings, specialty BIS, BOB Crufts 2008, three group wins and BIS at Richmond 2007 and Leeds 2009, my third homebred group winner and first general championship show BIS winner.

He was top Afghan in 2007 and '08 and has been top stud dog in the breed for the last three years on very few litters, producing seven champions. He won under all types of judge, breed specialists, hound specialists, all-rounders and overseas judges.

In 2003 Dolly produced a second litter to **Multi Ch Boxadan Grandpa' Lives Forever** – again no genetic link but a similar look and type and a pedigree of very good and influential Scandinavian dogs from El Khyrias and Boxadan. I had judged him in Germany and felt his construction, breed type and movement would complement Dolly.

Again a 0 per cent COI for the offspring but this litter produced five champions, thereby equalling the Karnak litter, and a CC winner.

The champions were **Rocket Man** (seven CCs, group placings and my fourth homebred group winner), **Star Struck** (15 CCs and specialty BIS, top bitch in 2007 beaten by Rio with whom she did the double several times), **Ch/Int/Sp/Port Ch**

Ch Saxonmill Midnight Muse. photo Garamond

Ch Amudarya Shekinah at Terstine	Ch Mandinah Days Of Thunder at Amudarya (imp Sweden)	Int/Nord Ch El Khyrias Zon Of The Master
		Int/Sw Ch Khalibadh Honeysuckle Rose
	Ch Amudarya Shullah	Ch Boxadan Give Me A Break at Benatone (imp Denmark)
		Ch Amudarya Shushila
Ch Saxonmill Star Struck	Int/Dan/Sw/Norw/Lux/Ger/Fr Ch Boxadan Grandpa' Lives Forever (Denmark)	Dan/Am Ch Boxadan Double Trouble
		Boxadan Catch Me If You Can
	Ch Saxonmill Jellicle Jett	Ch Saxonmill Currant Bun
		Ch Saxonmill Jennyanydots

Ch Saxonmill Midnight Majic. photo Palamedees

Ch Saxonmill Midnight Dancer. photo Garamond

Ch Saxonmill Midnight Cowboy. photo Garamond

Star Style (Jayne Edwards and Lyn Appleby), **Star Attraction at Karandikar** (Geoff and Wendy Bastow, four CCs, speciality BIS and foundation bitch for the Karandikar kennel), and **Rocket Rider** (Colleen Witham (now Neilly), three CCs).

CC winner **Star Realta** was Rory Daly and Shona Bettany's first Afghan, produced two champions and formed the foundation for the Cubanba kennel. Star Attraction has produced a CC winner and two RCC winners and Star Style has produced two CC winners and a UK/Irish champion.

And so to the seventh consecutive generation of Saxonmill champions. Star Struck was top bitch in the breed for three years and was campaigned quite actively. I perhaps should have had an earlier litter from her but I didn't and she had the opportunity to have only one litter.

I agonised for quite a while as to where to go – it was getting more difficult and my expectations were perhaps higher too!

Anyhow I was conscious that looking at Jellicle Jett and Star Struck I had maintained and improved the overall conformation. My bitch line is also particularly strong in type and as producers of quality offspring. Movement was really good as were toplines and heads. However I did not want to lose size, legs or croups.

I chose the last Amudarya champion as her mate. I have always admired Anna Paton and her commitment to our breed. She was one of the first to blend the Scandinavian lines into our English pedigrees and had consistently produced generations of champions. I thought the male would complement Star Struck and ensure that I did not lose traits that were recognised as Saxonmill.

Star Struck and **Ch Amudarya Shekinah at Terstine** produced a litter of eight, four of whom are champions, **Midnight Cowboy** (four CCs), **Midnight Muse** (three CCs), **Midnight Majic** (Thomas Devaney, ten CCs, specialty BIS, top bitch 2012) and **Midnight Dancer** (Catherine Barnes, three CCs), plus CC and group 2 winner **Midnight Mayhem** (Chris and Terry O'Neill and Nadine Thompson) and a RCC winner.

Star Struck achieved another accolade in 2012 by becoming runner-up Top Brood Bitch all breeds following in her mother and great-great- grandmother's footsteps.

From 1976 to 2013 there have been 22 champions owned or bred from Saxonmill (19 homebred, and the one I haven't mentioned is the Rum Tum Tigger son **Ch Karnak Jeera at Saxonmill**, bred by Keith and Brenda Thornton), around 150 CCs, four homebred group winners and one BIS winner, and seven consecutive generations of Saxonmill champions, plus top dog, bitch, breeder, stud dog and brood bitch awards. Not a bad record for a small kennel and litters in single figures! Where next?

Roberta and Rum Tum Rio after his Richmond BIS. photo Carol Ann Johnson

SAXONMILL

…producing consistency and quality over seven consecutive generations of Champions, 19 homebred / 22 in total

The present…

Top UK Afghan Hound Breeder 2006/07/08/09 & 2012

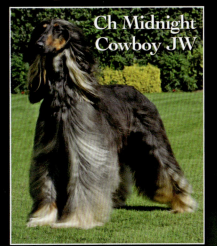

Ch Midnight Cowboy JW

Ch Saxonmill Midnight Majic JW
TOP UK AFGHAN HOUND 2013*
Owned by Thomas Devaney

Ch Saxonmill Rum Tum Rio JW
TOP UK AFGHAN HOUND STUD DOG 2013*

*at time of going to press

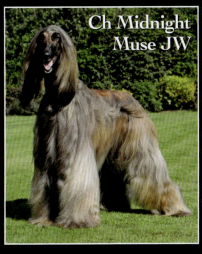

Ch Midnight Muse JW

The future…

Garamond Juniperberry Saxonmill
A Ch Saxonmill Rum Tum Rio JW grand-daughter. (Ch Cloudside Warstrike x Ch Ashahni Azanti at Garamond JW, 23.05.13)

All photos: Garamond

PUPPIES planned in 2014
from Ch Saxonmill Midnight Muse JW

ROBERTA HALL
www.saxonmill.com
+44 (0)1332 780175   roberta@saxonmill.com

Dog World Annual 2014

It's the breeders who matter the most

by Sheila Atter

The Meadowpark Bernese Mountain Dogs bred by Bernice Mair and Carole Hartley-Mair had an amazing Crufts winning not only the working group but the Kennel Club breeders competition final. Their team is pictured with Jonas Derninger of Agria, Vince Hogan of *Our Dogs* and judge Michael Coad.
photo Alan Walker

WHY DO we show our dogs? It used to be claimed that dog shows were a means by which breeders could evaluate the worth of their own stock against that of others, could draw the attention of prospective buyers to puppies that they had for sale and could attract interest in their stud dogs.

Certainly that has always been so, but if we go right back to the origins of the dog show it is evident that for many of the early exhibitors it was all about competition – my dog is better than your dog, and here's the prize card to prove it.

Indeed many of those who were successful exhibitors in the nineteenth century were not breeders at all, but rather 'fanciers'. It's a term that has all but disappeared from modern usage, but maybe it is appropriate to describe many of those who are successful in the show rings of the twenty-first century?

If we are not going to shows in order to, in modern parlance, 'subject our breeding stock to peer review', then why do we go?

There is great emphasis at present on having a good day out, providing all sorts of extras that might attract the whole family, with or without show dogs, and ensuring that every one has an enjoyable time.

Is that really what dog showing is all about – a family day out with prizes for everyone? That seems to be the view from Clarges Street, but what of the ordinary exhibitor? What are their hopes and expectations from a day at a dog show?

Hopes and expectations seem to have become two completely separate entities as far as the average exhibitor is concerned. Most of us who show are by nature fairly competitive, and we all go to every show hoping for success. If we are realistic we weigh up our chances in comparison to the other dogs we think will be there, and our expectations increase as we become more experienced.

While even the very novice exhibitor dreams that their dog might win best in show, most are more realistically hoping for a Crufts qualifying place, maybe a first prize card. In time that is not enough, and a CC becomes the hoped for result, maybe best of breed or even a group place.

But if that is what is hoped for, what are the actual expectations? Speaking to exhibitors about this, I received the same comments time and time again. "Nothing much", "not a lot", "zero", "zilch" – pressing for more information elicited comments such as "it's all sewn up in our breed" and "we all know where the tickets are going today".

Cynics will say that it was always like this, and human nature is such that it always will be. For every judge with integrity, knowledge and a sense of fair play there will always be another who lacks knowledge, is simply following form, feels they have to favour their friends or is just plain corrupt. The trouble is that nowadays these latter seem to outweigh the honest ones. Why should that be?

Solid base

Is it perhaps because dog showing seems to have developed a two-tier system, whereby a minority of dogs, owners and handlers occupy an exalted position, winning the major awards at all the shows, to such an extent that when one of these is knocked it is that, rather than the exciting new prospect that beat the favourite, which becomes the talking point of the show?

Below these well known winners there is a solid base of also-rans. This certainly includes the people who have just come for an enjoyable day out with friends, and with no expectation of anything other than possibly a lower place card; it includes the novices at their first shows, totally in awe of anyone who has achieved even a minor win.

It also includes many of the experienced breeders, who have been establishing a respected kennel type over many years and have achieved at the minimum a modicum of success in the past, but who somehow lack the flair that propels them into the upper echelons of our hobby.

This is, I think, the biggest turnaround that pedigree dog breeding and exhibiting has seen in the last 20 years or so. No longer is the successful breeder regarded with respect, or even awe. It is the handlers and owners who are household names and frequently they did not breed the dog with which they are successful – or if they did there is a co-owner to help pay the bills.

In effect we are back to the fanciers of the earlier days; those with money – and often, it must be said, an excellent eye for a dog – who enjoy the sport of dog showing and can afford to pay someone else to campaign it for them.

As far as the future of pedigree dog breeding is concerned there is nothing wrong with this – in fact it can be regarded as a good thing as it is a means whereby excellent dogs can reach their full potential in the show ring, unencumbered by lack of

Dog World Annual 2014

Over the past year, three immensely distinguished breeders enjoyed their ninetieth birthday, among them Phyllis Wise of the Astrawin Cockers, and a former DOG WORLD breed correspondent, who celebrated by working on a breed club stand at Crufts!
photo RBT

The amazing Marion Spavin, founder of the Dialynne Beagles, was in great form at her big party, particularly appreciating the presence of Jack the Butler!
photo Andrew Brace

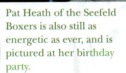

Pat Heath of the Seefeld Boxers is also still as energetic as ever, and is pictured at her birthday party.

finance or an inept handler.

We can look to the great fanciers of the past to see how terriers in particular were brought to new heights in the show ring through the interest and support of the fancier. But the difference now is that group and BIS competition have become so much more important.

We do have to be careful. While there is absolutely no question that the dogs that do reach the very top are in nearly all cases not merely excellent examples of their breeds, but also have that star quality that propels them towards the winner's podium, we have all seen occasions when lesser dogs win awards of which they are not worthy, simply because of who is on the end of the lead.

That is something for which we cannot blame the handler. No-one is going to turn to a judge and say "Sorry, sir, but you shouldn't give me the ticket, as this isn't my big winner, but his vastly inferior half-brother that the owner is struggling to make up so he can be sold overseas for a small fortune."

No, it is up to the judge to be sufficiently well-educated to be able to assess conformation, movement and breed specifics; to be confident in their own ability to recognise both quality and mediocrity; and to have the integrity to judge the dogs in front of him without fear or favour.

I don't think it is by chance that British dog breeders no longer have quite the universal respect they once had. Maybe the fact that here in the UK the breeders competition isn't regarded as important in the way in which it is viewed in the Scandinavian countries, is indicative of the emphasis that we place on the quality of the individual dog as opposed to the merit in breeding generations of dogs with a recognisable kennel type.

Those great dogs have to come from somewhere; occasionally they are a one-off, a flyer from fairly mediocre parents, but more often they are the result of years of hard work by individuals dedicated to the promotion of one particular breed.

The respected breeders of the past are gone or are cutting down, and there are few younger people who have the time, money or facilities – or indeed the inclination – to take their place. It's a situation we need to face and to which we need to find a solution if we are to regain our place in the wider canine world.

Dog World Annual 2014

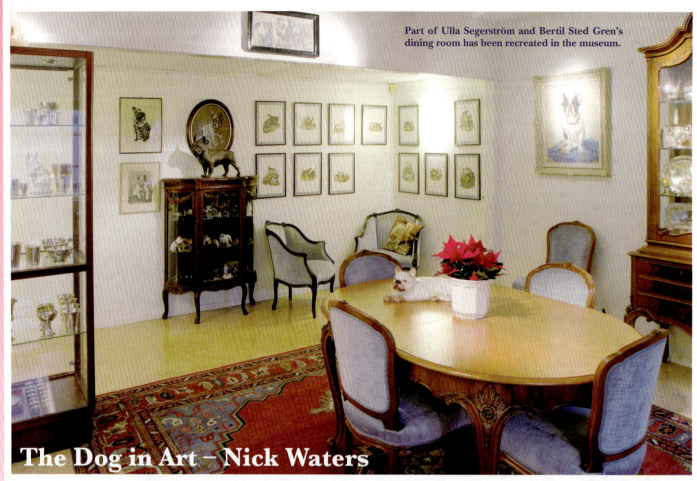

Part of Ulla Segerström and Bertil Sted Gren's dining room has been recreated in the museum.

The Dog in Art – Nick Waters

STOCKHOLM'S HIDDEN GEM
THE SWEDISH KENNEL CLUB MUSEUM

The Swedish Kennel Club's library.

THE SWEDISH Kennel Club museum is one of the hidden gems of the dog art world. It was established in 1992 when rooms were made available in the club's new premises.

It was the idea of a group of enthusiasts, including Renée Sporre-Willes who has helped with this feature and supplied the images of some of their treasures. Renée was curator for two decades and is a member of the Swedish Cynological Academy which now looks after the collection.

The aim of the museum is first and foremost to collect Swedish and Nordic art and in doing so to extend the historical importance of the museum and chart the development of breeds in that part of the world, while introducing Scandinavian artists to a wider public.

The museum has in recent years been able to buy some very important art thanks to generous legacies from judges and breeders of the past. Chief of these were Ulla Segerström and her husband Bertil Sted Gren, who left their assets in a substantial legacy to the Swedish Kennel Club (SKK). They entertained lavishly their many friends in dogs; hence the decision to move part of the dining room to the museum as a show room and a reminder to many of pleasant times past.

Among some of their pictures are two classic contemporary portraits of two of their dogs by Erik O Stövling which Ulla commissioned in 1987 to commemorate their dogs who died in the devastating fire at Ulla and Bertil's home in 1986. One is of the French Bulldog Multi Ch Paling Corinthian, imported from England and who was Dog of the Year in Sweden in 1973. The other is the English-bred Bulldog Ch Tyegarth Lucifer who won best in show at all the major shows in the 1980s.

The SKK was founded in December 1893 by members of the landed families and Swedish nobility interested in shooting over Pointers and setters, with the original purpose to establish a body caring for the purebred dog and nurture and preserve the breeds' original working ability. Its chief founder was Count Adolf Patrik Hamilton and among some of the memorabilia is the Count's personal writing accoutrements donated by the Hamilton family.

The first picture bought by the Academy was a painting of two Bulldogs by the British nineteenth century artist, Joshua J Gibson. Painted in the mid 1870s, it was

64

Dog World Annual 2014

Two Bulldogs, by Joshua J Gibson.

bought to show the breed at the time of the breed's first Standard.

The earliest picture in the museum, the club bought at auction in 1989 as a gift to itself to celebrate the centenary that year. A huntsman resting with three hounds was painted by David Klöcker Ehrenstrahl (1628-1698), one of the most important artists of the period for his depictions of so many breeds and who was the favourite artist of the dog-loving Queen Hedvig Eleonora. The white hound is thought to be King Charles XI's favourite hound, Gallas.

Two historically important pictures from the time of the founding of the SKK were both painted by Bruno Liljefors (1860-1939), Sweden's most influential and commercially successful wildlife and animal painter from the late nineteenth/ early twentieth century who kept what was effectively a private zoo of animals he used as models.

One features the first Swedish champion made up in 1909, the Swedish Hound (renamed in 1920 the Hamiltonstövare) Kling, owned by Captain Torstehn Kroplien and a descendant of Count Hamilton's most famous hounds. This picture was acquired by chance in 2009 when an eagle-eyed observer noticed it coming up at auction in Stockholm.

The other picture is of the two first field trial winners in Sweden, both English Setters. The blue belton is Arthur Wendel's English-bred Ranger of Moors, winner of the first field trial in 1893, and the orange belton is Ranger's daughter Loola, winner of the second trial in 1895 and again in 1896 and 1897.

The museum borrowed it from the Wendel family to feature in an exhibition celebrating the centenary of the first field trial and in 2006 was able to buy it from the family along with two silver cups won by Ranger and Loola.

With setters and Pointers at the very root of the SKK's founding, it is fitting they have an equally impressive picture of Pointers. Painted by zoologist, sportsman and artist Gustaf Swenander (1874-1952), best known for his illustrations of birds in a three-volume work, the dogs have been identified as the artist's own. In the foreground is Lord of Stockholm, born in 1891 and descended from famous stud dogs from Germany and England, and backing him is Pang, born in the mid 1890s.

Ch Rowsley Courtly, by Gustav Muss Arnolt.

Ch Rowsley Betty, by Gustav Muss Arnolt.

This bronze Pointer head is, uniquely for a sculpture, attributed to the famous painter Maud Earl.

Important

Another historically important picture in the museum was painted by Airedale breeder and artist Richardis Sörvik (1893-1975) and features the blue roan Cocker Spaniel Ch Valstar Craftsman, imported from England by Lilian Öhrström in 1947. He was successful in the ring but is remembered for being Sweden's most influential sire of any breed. He also had the distinction of having a working qualification, necessary then for the title of champion.

Another successful import from England painted by Sörvik and on view is the Greyhound Ch Treetops Dusky Maid, bred by Judy de Casembroot and owned by Marianne Fürst-Danielson. Dusky Maid left a string of champions of great importance, a number in the only litter sired by the coursing dog bred by Audrey Dallison, Gosmore Yankee, who was killed by a horse before the litter was born.

Carl Fredrik Kiörboe's (1799-1876) *The Inundation* tugs at the heart-strings of all who see it and is well known to all Newfoundland folk, second only perhaps to Sir Edwin Landseer's *A Distinguished Member of the Humane Society*.

It is a typically tragic mid-nineteenth

Erik O Stövling's portrait of Ch Paling Corinthian.

Ch Tyegarth Lucifer, by Erik O Stövling.

65

Dog World Annual 2014

century sentimental picture of a landseer Newfoundland bitch and her puppies on a raft being swept down a flooded river. Like George Earl, Kiörboe made copies of his own work, one of which is in a museum in Gothenburg and one which is said to have been bought by the French government in 1850. The museum acquired its copy in 2008.

To life one's spirits, there is a much lesser known follow-up picture, not in the museum, where they have all arrived safely at shore. This was sold at auction in Uppsala in 2006 for 20,000 SEK.

While serving as a military attaché in London during the second world war, Carl-Reinhold von Essen bought four paintings by one of America's best known dog artists Gustav Muss Arnolt (1858-1927) who completed 170 cover illustrations for the *American Kennel Club Gazette*. The Wire Fox Terrier Ch Rowsley Courtly and the Irish Terrier Ch Rowsley Betty are two of the dogs featured in the pictures. Von Essen donated the paintings to the SKK in 1946 when he took office as chairman.

Karin Gustavsson of the Annelunds Dalmatians donated a painting of the American import Int Ch Garrets Ice Creame Check Mate and Int Ch Annelunds Bessie who were the foundation of the kennel's successes in the 1970s. It was painted by artist, actor and film director Bror Bügler (1908-1975). Among the artist's commissions was the Pekingese Elise, pet of Sweden's Queen Louise, sister to Lord Mountbatten.

Maud Earl sculpture?

The most important three-dimensional piece of art is a bronze head of a Pointer modelled on the head of Largo who was owned by William Arkwright. It was attributed to Maud Earl (1863-1943) and Arkwright took it with him when he went to judge at Stockholm show in 1906. There are no records of Miss Earl ever having worked in anything other than paint, so this could well be the first known sculpture by her and would rewrite the history books of England's most famous dog artist.

Other three-dimensional art includes a hunting group in porcelain of two riders on white horses with hounds from Italy's best known ceramic factory, Capodimonte; an animalier bronze of a Pointer and setter with a pheasant by Clovis Edmond Masson (1838-1913), a gift from the Finnish Kennel Club to commemorate the SKK's 75th anniversary, and a bronze patinated béton (a fancy name for architectural concrete) of a Leonberger

This was sculpted by Norwegian artist Brit Skajaa and produced in an edition of only 20 (although 50 were planned). It was commissioned by the Norwegian Leonberger Club for a special breed show in 1990 and one of the dogs used as a

This room contains memorabilia of the club's chief founder Count Adolf Patrik Hamilton.

Ranger of Moors and his daughter Loola, by Bruno Liljefors.

Int Ch Garrets Ice Creame Check Mate and Int Ch Annelunds Bessie, by Bror Bügler.

Kling, the first Swedish champion, by Bruno Liljefors.

The Inundation, by Cal Fredrik Kiörboe.

Dog World Annual 2014

model was Ch Arko av Nordenlöwe from the first litter born in Scandinavia.

Also on show in the museum is one of Sweden's most important and impressive trophies. Standing in total nearly two feet high, it is made in 22 carat gold and enamel with a cast Pointer in gold as the finial to the cover and is mounted on a marble base with gold plaques applied. It was made by goldsmith K Andersson in 1927, commissioned by Erik Akerlund and awarded to encourage young promising Pointers at field trials.

Those who would like to learn more about the SKK Museum will soon be able to as a book written by Renée Sporre-Willes will be published in February 2014 to celebrate the club's 125th anniversary. It will be published by MBF Bokförlag, Sweden, email mbab@swipnet.se.

The museum is at the club's premises, Rinkebysvängen 70, Spånga, Stockholm. Opening hours are 9am to noon, 1pm to 4pm weekdays. It is best to make an appointment at the reception (0046 8 795 30 00) and ask for a guided tour. A brochure in English is available at the museum.

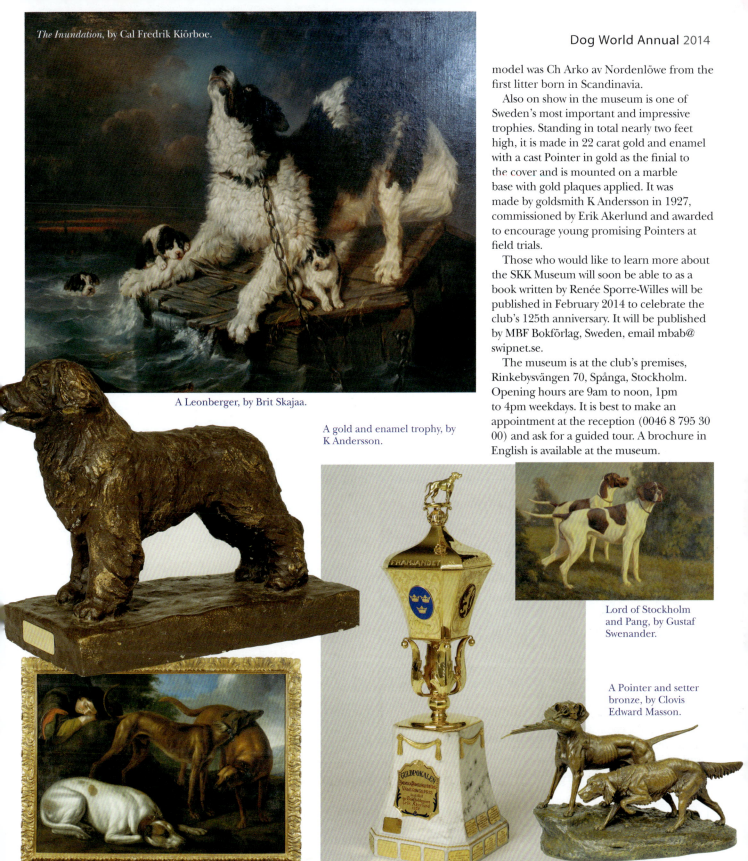

A Leonberger, by Brit Skajaa.

A gold and enamel trophy, by K Andersson.

Lord of Stockholm and Pang, by Gustaf Swenander.

A Pointer and setter bronze, by Clovis Edward Masson.

A huntsman and his hounds, by David Klöcker Ehrenstrahl.

A Capodimonte porcelain hunting group.

Ch Valstar Craftsman, by Richardis Sörvik.

Ch Treetops Dusky Maid, by Richardis Sörvik.

Dog World Annual 2014

Art & Crafts

ESC portraits

Transform photographs of your dogs into realistic pencil portraits.

Suitable as gift ideas, montages (multiple dogs on one portrait) avaliable.

www.facebook.com/
escportraitsretratos
Tel: 07510 067 712
emmastuartcook@hotmail.co.uk

Detail is what I love best
Michelle Martin Professional pet portrait artist

Michelle Martin is a professional artist who will capture every detail of your beloved pet in watercolour or pencil.

Email your photograph to willowmoorart@yahoo.com

It can take Michelle approximately 3 weeks to complete a portrait, so any birthday or occasion presents need to be thought of well in advance ready for you to have framed.

Prices and more information can be found at:-
www.artonboard.co.uk

Julia's Pet Portraits

Detailed watercolour paintings that aim to capture the character and true likeness of your pet, by artist Julia Pewsey.

For details on how to commission a portrait please visit my website

www.jpetportraits.co.uk
tel (01787) 280569 or
email jpetpix@aol.com

Award winning artist Stephen Mckeown presents 2 Staffordshire prints. Signed and Limited to only 500 worldwide

£50 for a A3 mounted unframed
with FREE UK P&P
or
£70 for a A3 framed (not glazed)
with £8 UK delivery

Please make cheques out to Stephen Mckeown

49 South Parade, Belfast BT7 2GL
www.stephenmckeown.com
Tel: 07857125364
stephenmckeownart@gmail.com

This remarkable photograph of two of her own Bull Terriers won its creator, Dutch breeder and photographer Alice van Kempen, a holiday in Africa!

Alice says: "When my eye caught an advert in a advertising brochure 'Be wild and win a holiday to Botswana' I thought 'That's something I really want to win'.

"The photo contest was organised to promote the release of a nature film made in the Netherlands, called *The New Wilderness*. To compete, one had to send in a picture that showed 'anything' wild. I decided to send a photo of two of my Bull Terriers behaving 'wild' at the beach.

"One beautiful summer evening in June we took our Bull Terriers to the beach, actually a relatively new part of the Netherlands, as the photo is taken at the second Maasvlakte which is land that has recently been reclaimed from the North Sea.

"Just 15 minutes before sunset I decided to try to make some silhouette shots of the Bull Terriers running and jumping. The result was a lovely series of photographs of which a couple have been used in a coffee table book published by me. This book contains 200 pages of photographs of Bull Terriers doing what they do best, enjoying life. It was released during the recent International Bull Terrier Weekend.

"One of the forewords was written by Sally Ann Thompson, which is a great honour to me."

Further details of the book, Bull Terriers in Action, can be obtained from http://i51361.wix.com/izimbali#!news/cdwx or info@alicevankempen.com.

CARTERS DOG SHOW MATTING

610 gramme per square metre PVC coated polyester material available in 3 widths, namely 205 cms, 150 cms or 102.5 cms. This can be cut to any required lengths in the colours, green, blue, red or black and rolled on a cardboard centre, which should be used at all times. It should not be folded as this affects the ability of the matting to lay flat.

We are aware of the large part that ladies play in arranging Dog Shows and for that reason, 102.5 cms is the most popular width as it can be transported in a car and easily handled in laying out and rolling up afterwards. The material is best cleaned after use using a wet mop with detergent.

Prices are as follows inc. VAT:
205 cms - £10.55 per lineal metre
150 cms - £8.60 per lineal metre
102.5 cms - £6.00 per lineal metre

Delivery charges may vary according to the size of the order but this can be calculated quickly.

CARTERS
Supplier to over 200 Dog Clubs
Tel: 0118 9575589
Email: Info@carterandsonltd.co.uk

Dog World Annual 2014

A life in the dog world

Simon Parsons talks to Ferelith Somerfield

The founders of the Oudenarde kennel, Margaret Temple (with her husband Montague) and her sister Helen Hamilton.
photo Photopress

AT THE British Utility Breeds Association, held just as this Annual is published, Ferelith Somerfield will judge best in show and best puppy.

After a judging career lasting 57 years, this will be her final appointment. "There comes a point when a life you've known has to change, and you know when it's time to retire," she says.

Over those years she has built up a reputation as one of the world's foremost judges, admired for her integrity, her kindness to dogs and exhibitors and for the care with which she approached every assignment.

But this is just one of many areas in which she has influenced the world of dogs. Few can have matched the breadth of her interests, with family or personal connections with top class dogs in almost all the groups, as chairman of a general championship show society and hard worker for breed clubs, as a Kennel Club sub-committee member and liaison council chairman and, of course, through her connection with DOG WORLD over more than 50 years.

'Feffie' was literally born into the sport. Indeed the Oudenarde affix is ten years older than herself. It was registered in March 1927 by two sisters, Helen and Margaret Hamilton, and derives not from the battle of that name (though there are family connections) but to a contemporary novel whose hero was Roger of Oudenarde.

Helen Hamilton was fascinated by animals of all sorts, and was proud of an ancestor who had bred four Derby winners. The sisters owned Fox Terriers and Pekingese (any puppies they bred were usually bought by the 'Alderbourne' Ashton Crosses), but it was Cairn Terriers in which their serious interests lay.

They did win a CC, pre-war, under Holland Buckley, but it was taken away by the Kennel Club as the Cairn was entered only in special beginners which didn't count in those days. Margaret (later Mrs Montague Temple) was especially interested in Airedales.

While all this was taking shape, a young lady, Diana Sisterson, was gaining a solid apprenticeship in dogs and dog showing. She had been brought up comfortably in North Yorkshire, but family financial difficulties meant that she had to make her own way, and she determined to be fully trained in kennel lore.

She started by working for the famous Cooden Westies and went on to kennels of several other breeds. Among these were Dalmatians, and here she inherited the kennel on the owner's

All knees! Feffie, her brother John and three Oudenarde Dalmatians.

Feffie's mother, Diana Hamilton, and Ch Oudenarde Fair Prospect, her favourite among her many champions.

death. She was able to keep two and remained loyal to the breed for a lifetime.

In the 1930s she joined the Misses Hamilton. Shortly afterwards their brother George, an officer in the Buffs, returned home on leave… and in 1936 he and Diana were married. Ferelith arrived the next year, followed by her brother John.

In those troubled times an army couple had to live a nomadic existence, living in locations as far removed as Sussex and West

As an exhibitor, one of Feffie's happiest moments was winning a third CC with the Boxer Gold Bangle of Panfield at Crufts under Pat Heath.
photo Phil Holley

Stafford Somerfield with Ch Louline Lord Fountleroy.
photo Robert Owen

The American-bred Irish Terrier Ch Trackways Booger Red, imported by Feffie and Stafford and handled by Peter Bell.
photo David Dalton

Early days – late 1960s – at DOG WORLD's Ashford office: Liz Henricson (now Cartledge), Brian Doyle with one of Bryan Mitchell's Japanese Chin, and Feffie.
photo Angela Cavill

Wales. Mrs Hamilton and the children spent most of the war years in her native Yorkshire while Lt Col Hamilton was a prisoner-of-war. Dog activities were inevitably limited but Feffie remembers Jo and Charlie always being there – the former a Dalmatian and the latter a Cairn (officially **The Abbot of Oudenarde**).

Peace restored, the family settled near Uckfield, Sussex, just a few miles from where her aunts were based. All three ladies determined to build up a successful kennel and within a few years Diana's extraordinary talents as a breeder became evident. The partnership proved most rewarding, even in later years when the two establishments were situated further apart.

The Hamiltons were also fortunate in that over the years a number of people helped with the dogs who had a significant impact on the kennel. Notable among these was Sheila Thomas (later Mrs Tarry) who joined the Hamilton sisters in 1943 and was instrumental in transferring Mrs Temple's interest from Airedales to Irish Terriers for which Oudenarde became so famous.

She also started the kennel off with Japanese Chin and Beagles. In later years she made up in her own right a Beagle and an Irish under her Penwarne affix, and Helen Hamilton spent the last years of her long life (she died aged 95, having been regarded in her youth as 'delicate') with the Tarrys.

The remarkable aspect of the Oudenarde kennel is that not only did the partners create one of the greatest strains in the major breed, Cairns, but bred champions or CC winners in all the other breeds they were interested in. For an all-round judge, no better background could be sought, especially as the breeds involved spanned several groups.

From an early age young Feffie was dog-mad, as her school reports habitually pointed out. But neither she nor her brother received any favours – they, like their mother before them, started at the bottom, cleaning out, exercising and so on.

Shows were not allowed to interfere with their boarding school education, so were confined to the holidays; nevertheless Feffie, without even trying, early became familiar with the dog show world. Nor could she help but be a part of the build-up of Oudenarde into one of the most successful affixes of all times. Mrs Hamilton and her sisters-in-law eventually owned or bred 48 British champions.

The majority of these, of course, were Cairn Terriers, starting with **Ch Oudenarde Duskie Belle** (reserve BIS at the only Cambridge championship show) born in 1945. The early stars were all bitches, descending mainly from a Woodthorpe dog, Otford bitches and the original pre-war line, but a mating of **Ch Oudenarde Queen Of Light** to the elderly **Ch Bonfire of Twobees** (son of the famous **Splinters**) got the great Oudenarde male line started, though dogs from other strains were used, when appropriate.

Result

The result, **Firelight**, won a reserve CC and sired **Ch Sandboy**, sire of **Ch Midnight Chimes**, sire of **Ch Midnight Marauder**, sire of the outstanding stud dog **Ch Raiding Light**, sire of **Ch What Next**, sire of **Ch Wot A Lad**, made up by Feffie after her mother's death.

There were far too many other champions to mention, but one can't ignore **Ch Fair Prospect**, Mrs Hamilton's choice as her best ever, **Ch Special Edition** (in the final three of the group at Crufts) or **Ch Sea Hawk** (a great winner and sire for Betty Hyslop in Canada).

In spite of her work commitments, Feffie herself maintained an interest and bred **Ch Oudenarde Light Melody** and later owned her daughter **Ch Oudenarde Fancy Light**.

To summarise, it's enough to say that throughout the '50s, '60s and '70s Oudenarde, by then based in Wiltshire, was one

Dog World Annual 2014

of the Cairn Terrier strongholds, never needing to campaign a champion to huge numbers of CCs as there was always something else to follow.

Second breed, in terms of the champions produced, was Irish Terriers, the concern mainly of Mrs Temple and Miss Hamilton. Mrs Tarry obtained their original bitch from Mr Davey's Farriers kennel in Cornwall and when he became ill they got two males from him, **Oudenarde Farriers Comrade** and his son who became **Ch Oudenarde Farriers Galloper**.

The sisters never handled the dogs, nor judged, and the Irish were shown variously by Sheila, Norah Woodifield, Billy Norman, Georgie Barr and, latterly, Peter Bell. Several champions were bred including the notable dogs **Thunderflash** and **Soldier**.

In the '70s, after Mrs Temple's death, the line nearly came to an end, but was revived when Diana and Feffie obtained, through Edna Howard Jones, **Divine Emerald of Oudenarde**, a descendant of Soldier. In Peter Bell's hands she was top bitch for two years, in between producing an exceptional litter by the **great Ch Redneval Ballinruan Beau** containing three British champions and one in Germany. A repeat mating gave **Oudenarde Ragtrade** who, after several years retirement, re-emerged to become the forty-eighth Oudenarde champion at the age of ten.

Dalmatians were an important part of the Oudenarde tradition. In fact Feffie's first dog of her own was a small liver bitch called Ran who, she says, 'walked like a crab'.

A great friend of the family was Evelyn Barnes of the famous 'of the Wells' Dalmatians and Australian Terriers (and aunt of Margaret Barnes of the Suntop English Setters). After the war she owned a super dog called **Raff of the Wells** whom she wasn't fit enough to exhibit to advantage. So Mrs Hamilton took him over, made him up and reached the last ten in the BIS ring at Crufts.

In much later years the kennel made up two more Dalmatian champions, **Dalpanda Debs Delight** and **Golden May**, while Feffie owned a reserve CC winner, **Shepherdess**.

For many years a line of Beagles was kept. Characteristically Mrs Hamilton always used top-class stud dogs, and bred two reserve CC winners. A third reserve CC winner was bred by Angela Goddard. At the time of her last illness in 1979 there was a good young dog by **Ch Dialynne Gamble** in the kennel; to help out, Catherine Sutton gave him a home and Geoff Corish piloted him to become **Ch Oudenarde Gaffer of Rossut**. As sire of **Ch**

Feffie has been awarding CCs for almost 50 years. Three Counties 1964 saw her second appointment – here she is going over one of Gay Marsh's Toptwig dogs.
photo C M Cooke

Feffie's first Deerhound CC appointment, at LKA 1969. Her winners were Miriam Dickinson's Ch Amoretta of Champflower and Norah Hartley's Ch Furze of Rotherwood (BOB).
photo C M Cooke

Thirty-nine years later Feffie judge the Scottish Deerhound Club of America's national specialty. BOB was Ch Windswift Balmoral, owned by Sheila Matheson and Judith Bowman.
photo Cook

72

Dog World Annual 2014

Dialynne Blue Boy he is behind many subsequent greats.

Japanese Chins were also favourites of Feffie's aunts and here too a champion was bred, **Oudenarde Pikko**, plus several CC winners, and the affix can be found far back in top British and Scandinavian pedigrees.

As an all-rounder Feffie would not admit to have a 'special' group; if anything she is perhaps thought of most as a terrier person. But those who know her well will appreciate her love for a good gundog. Of all the breeds owned by Oudenarde she was most closely involved with the English Setters.

She was responsible for buying the foundation bitch, from the 'Fiveacres' Harrisons, and often handled them in the ring. Eventually a show champion, **Dancing Glory**, was made up (handled by John Oulton), and the successful stud dog **Noyna Suntop Royal Wizard** was actually bred at Oudenarde.

Finally, Border Terriers, a breed Mrs Hamilton had known at home as a child. A foundation bitch came from Sybil Churchill, and a dog co-owned and handled by Ted Hutchinson won a CC.

It is extraordinary how in all these breeds the Oudenardes have bred on and are behind many present day kennels. Indeed in 1988 the Crufts BIS-winning English Setter, **Sh Ch Starlite Express of Valsett**, went back to Royal Wizard and **Ch Brannigan of Brumberhill**, the RBIS-winning Border, was closely line-bred to a bitch bred by Mrs Hamilton.

Manchester 1980, and Feffie's BIS was the German Shepherd Dog Ch Royvon's Red Rum, handled by Roy James. With them are Eric Egerton and president Mumford Smith.
photo Frank Garwood Dog World

While still in her prime as a breeder, Diana Hamilton was taken ill after an overseas judging trip and died in 1979. Regarded as an outstanding judge of Cairns, she awarded BIS at championship show level and did the terrier group at Crufts the year **Ch Dianthus Buttons** the West Highland White won BIS.

What of Feffie herself? School was followed by 'finishing' in France and a year at a London secretarial college. Perhaps this might have led to a life away from dogs, had it not been for the great all-round judge Leo Wilson who in 1955 had, with Fred and Julia Curnow (Tavey Dobermanns and Min Pins and Woodcourt Borzois), Raymond Oppenheimer (Ormandy Bull Terriers) and Stanley McKie (Colvend English Toy Terriers), recently bought a share in DOG WORLD.

That year he judged BIS at Paignton and gave the award to a Cairn, **Ch Redletter McMurran**, the first of only three of the breed to win this. Afterwards Diana Hamilton and McMurran's owner, her great friend and rival Walter Bradshaw, went up to chat with Leo and mentioned his new venture. "I'm looking for a youngster who knows something about the world of dogs, preferably has secretarial training and who wouldn't mind starting at the bottom," he said. Mrs Hamilton kept quiet but Mr

Skirt lengths may rise and fall but classic Shelties don't change: at the Northern Counties Shetland Sheepdog Club in 1974, the CC winners were Felicity and Patience Rogers' Ch Riverhill Rather Special and Ann and Keith Barraclough's Ch Pruneparks Jason Junior (BIS).

English Setter Association 1993: Glenis Williams, Feffie and Jack Bowen with the BIS, Halstead's Westonfields Velvet of Hammoon.
photo David Bull

At Paignton 1984 Marita Rodgers was BIS with the Standard Poodle Ch Montravia Tommy-Gun and Joyce Mitchell reserve with the Pekingese Ch Micklee Roc's Royale.
photo David Dalton

Sadly there does not seem to be a good photograph of Feffie with her Crufts BIS winner Ch Olac Moon Pilot. Perhaps this one of Stafford Somerfield and Bill King presenting Paddy and Joan and Derek Tattersall with the Dog World/Pedigree Top Dog trophy will make do.
photo David Dalton

Dog World Annual 2014

Bradshaw said: "I know just the girl…."

So Feffie travelled to Idle, near Bradford, Yorkshire, for an interview and was accepted.

For an 18-year-old girl 300 miles away from home in a very different environment, earning six guineas a week, life cannot have been easy. But Feffie was determined and despite long hours and an initial degree of homesickness stuck to the job.

She was helped as ever by her interest in dogs and today she still counts many Northern dog people as among her greatest friends. For relaxation she would attend the frequent local match meetings and sanction shows where the many talented breeders in the area would bring out their young stock, whose progress she was able to follow at the championship shows.

She learnt much, too, from Leo Wilson, the brilliant and controversial judge and journalist who could not help but be an inspiration. His dedication was such that, if he were unsure about a breed, he would buy one and show it. It was he, too, who set DOG WORLD on the course which it follows today with its reputation for fearless comment on the day's issues, and as complete a coverage as possible of the show scene.

One form of training, unavailable to today's judges, which Feffie found a great help was the writing of ringside reports, when it was known the judge would not contribute one for that paper. This was done down to third place even at members' shows, and for an apprentice like Feffie was an ideal way of making her actually look at the dogs and marshal her thoughts on them.

Another help was to listen to Leo on a Monday morning after a busy weekend's judging. Great judge that he was, he was never too proud to say that he might have been mistaken, and he would conduct a fascinating 'post mortem' on his classes, admitting, on occasion, that were he to judge this or that class again he might have placed them a different way.

Humility

A valuable lesson in humility, and anyone who knows Feffie today will soon realise that she too never laid claim to that almost papal infallibility which some senior judges seem to adopt. She has always been happy to discuss her placements, especially with those whom she accepts as knowing more about the breed than herself.

For many years the Monday morning tutorials continued as I can testify when Feffie used to tell Kerry Williamson, Elisabeth Matell and myself all about her weekend's judging when we probably ought to have been sub-editing breed notes or designing advertisements!

As for her judging career, it began in the usual way, three classes of Cairns at Hammersmith CS limited show on Sept 22, 1956. Then followed four classes at Beckenham open show where her BOB was a puppy, **Merrymeet Tathwell Therese**, who became a great champion, in fact Diana Hamilton considered her the best Cairn bitch she ever saw.

Feffie's opportunities as a variety judge came in the North, first match meetings then going on to the small shows, making her debut at Manchester Sporting Terrier Club's 20-class sanction show in March 1961. Next was Bury Sporting Terrier Association sanction show, where BIS was a Sealyham, **Jenmist Aureole of Axe**, owned by Bert Lambert – an interesting choice in view of later events.

Her first open show variety appointment was at Corbridge in 1962 and a glance at the show report illustrates another way in which a young judge could gain valuable experience in those days. Among the entrants were at least five current champions including the Bedlington **Ch Northcote Lucky Strike**; the Chows **Chs Rena of Ricksoo** and **Ricky of Kaioko**; the Whippet **Ch Blik's Ringmore Bardoph**; and Biddy Horn's first champion Sealyham, **Mister Woo**, plus other future greats not yet crowned such as the Cocker **Westside Story of Weirdene**.

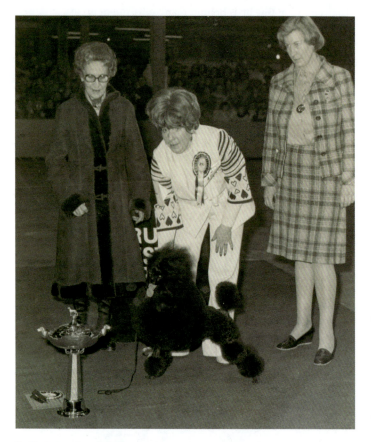

Feffie has, uniquely, judged all seven Crufts groups. The first was the utility, won by Rita Gee's Miniature Poodle Ch Beritas Banacheke. Princess Dolores de Bourbon Orleans presented the trophy.

Today, the showing of champions at open shows is often frowned upon – but what an opportunity for a judge at her first open show. So Feffie is grateful that the policy, prevalent then especially in the North, of bringing out top champions at open shows gave her the chance to go over dogs like the Wire Dachshund **Ch Gisbourne Inca** and the Chow **Ch Ukwong King Solomon**, so helping to set a standard in the young judge's mind.

Gradually more and more engagements came her way. When Feffie eventually came to judge BIS at Crufts she said that this appointment was an honour not only for herself but for those who taught and helped her in the early days – her mother and aunts, Sheila Tarry, Walter Bradshaw, who encouraged her from her earliest days, Phyl and Frank Hayward from Preston, the Pitts from her local society, Shipley, and so many more, not forgetting the great specialists who let her go over their champions or taught her about their own breeds.

In 2000 Feffie's terrier group winner, the Kerry Blue Ch Torum's Scarf Michael, handled by Michael Coad, went on to BIS under Ellis Hulme. NEC chairman Roger Vernon presented the trophies.
photo David Dalton

Chihuahuas are among Feffie's favourite breeds to judge. She is seen awarding the Crufts toy group to **Ch Dachida's Master Angel**, handled by Aimee Davies. Two years earlier she had awarded him his first all-breeds BIS. Susan Burgess presented the trophy.
photo Carol Ann Johnson

For Mr Bradshaw she had particular respect, a man with little money or background who, through sheer talent, became the most successful Cairn exhibitor ever, a top judge and eventually a Kennel Club committee member – 'A real dog man'.

Meanwhile she gained extra responsibilities at DOG WORLD. At the age of 22 she was appointed assistant editor, and within a few weeks Leo Wilson went off on an extended overseas judging trip, leaving her in sole charge…

1966 and '67 brought many changes. DOG WORLD separated from its Yorkshire printers, Watmoughs Ltd, and moved south to Ashford, Kent where it has remained ever since. Leo Wilson died and Feffie was appointed editor.

With a very small editorial staff (Brian Doyle, later editor of *Cats*; two other future Crufts BIS judges in Tom Horner and a young Swedish girl, Liz Henricson, now Mrs Cartledge; joined a year later by Bryan Mitchell) there was plenty of work, but the foundations laid by Leo Wilson and maintained by Feffie paid dividends in the form of an ever-increasing circulation.

Weekends were busy too with more judging appointments. Feffie first awarded CCs to Cairns at Leicester in 1963 (her winners, **Craiglyn Cavalier**, BOB from junior, and **Truelove of Yeendsdale**); followed by Dalmatians at Manchester 1966 (BOB, **Greenmount Grace Darling** from graduate, dog CC **Ch Colonsay April Jest**); Australian Terriers at the National Terrier (never having previously judged a breed class!); Norfolk, Norwich and Irish Terriers, Schipperkes…

Feffie considers her 'big break' came in 1969 when the LKA invited her to do Keeshonds and Deerhounds, breeds she was interested in but in which she had no family connections

Although for so many years based in the far South, she is proud that many of her judging landmarks have come from the North, such as her first group (Manchester 1971, won by the Scottie, **Ch Brio Checkmate**) and her first BIS (Leeds 1979, won by the Smooth Chihuahua, **Ch Belmuriz Brevier**).

She has since given all-breeds BIS awards to **Ch Royvons Red Rum**, GSD; **Ch Apoco Deodar Aristocrat**, Smooth Chihuahua; **Ch Jokyl Gallipants**, Airedale; **Ch Montravia Tommy-Gun**, Standard Poodle; **Ch Gladsomes Harvest Gold**, Basset; **Ch Aedan Twice As Nice**, Toy Poodle; **Ch Snowgoose Kings Ransome**, Maltese; and **Ch Elve The Sorcerer**, Norwich.

Then came Crufts 1990 where at the age of 53 she was, and remains, the youngest person to judge BIS there singlehanded.

Her choice was the West Highland White **Ch Olac Moon Pilot**, 'Paddy' one of the great dogs of the era who had previously, like many such dogs, been very unlucky at the 'show of shows'. Reserve was another all-time great in the Whippet **Ch Nutshell of Nevedith** whom Feffie later gave a BIS.

More recently she has put up **Ch Wildermist Clara**, Scottish Terrier; **Ch Lamedazottel Flamboyant**, Old English Sheepdog; **Ch Bassbarr O'Sullivan**, Basset Hound; **Sh Ch Seashine Periwinkle**, the UK's first German Shorthaired Pointer BIS winner; **Ch Fantasa Bronze Bruin**, Rottweiler; **Ch Bronia Conquistador**, Longhaired Dachshund; **Ch Kanix Zulu**, Bouvier; **Ch Buffrey Arrabelle at Daedalus**, Dalmatian; **Ch Davmar Northern Dancer**, Sealyham Terrier; **Ch Iceglint I'm Alfred**, Bulldog; **Ch Dachida's Master Angel**, Smooth Chihuahua; **Ch Minarets Secret Assignment**, Miniature Poodle; **Ch Dvojica Voodoo**, Dalmatian; and the Pekingese, **Ch Yakee Ooh Aah Cantona**, a pretty good cross-section of great dogs of the era.

She is approved to give CCs in 140 breeds. Uniquely, she has done all seven groups at Crufts, starting with the utility, won by the Miniature Poodle **Ch Beritas Banacheke**, and the old full working group, won by the Samoyed **Ch Zamoyski Lucky Star of Ostyak**, whom she had given his first CC as an unknown junior.

Later she put up the Borzoi **Ch Sholwood Striking Rubies**, the Kerry Blue **Ch Torum's Scarf Michael** when he went on to BIS, the Flatcoat **Sh Ch Gayplume Dream-Maker**, the Smooth Chihuahua **Ch Dachida's Master Angel**, and this year, when she rounded out her Crufts career with her seventh group appointment, the Bernese **Ch Meadowpark Whispers Breeze**.

The most memorable dogs she has seen over the decades? It's a hard thing to ask though she cites her Crufts stars Moon Pilot and Nutshell. Then there was the charismatic Brevier, Lucky Star and her favourite of all time, the Lhasa Apso **Ch Saxonsprings Fresno**, plus the incomparable English Springer **Sh Ch Hawkhill Connaught**.

Greatest breeders

Putting her on the spot I also asked her to name some of the greatest breeders, judges and handlers she has known, as well as those 'mentors' whose example she has tried to follow.

She says: "Many of these people could just as easily appear under other categories and I have not even started on the people and dogs I have met overseas but I would definitely include Anne Rogers Clark from the US and the 'three Finns' in the judges category."

Here goes: Breeders: Judy Averis and Lesley Crawley from the terrier world, Mary Hambleton who rebuilt her great Boxer kennel from scratch; Beagle doyenne Marion Spavin, Anne Knight in Whippets and Judith Hancock in English Springers. Florence Nagle, of course, who bred great show dogs and great working dogs, and two outstanding Cocker people, Richmond Weir and Joan Macmillan with John and Jean Gillespie, plus three kennels that have passed into legend: Mary de Pledge with Pekes, Felicity and Patience Rogers with Shelties and Dorothy Whitwell in Whippets, Greyhounds and gundogs.

Mentors? Her mother, obviously, Walter Bradshaw and Dibbie Somerfield, Beryl and Joan Herbert and Mary Davis from the Sheltie world and one could hardly ignore Nigel Aubrey-Jones!

(She says in the breeders' and judges' categories she has purposely kept to people of the past, but exceptions are Judy Averis, Lesley Crawley and Marion Spavin whose kennels span three generations.)

When we came to her favourite handlers she at first started off very enthusiastically, but the list was becoming alarmingly long and she asked to be excused from answering. This is what she said: "I first started watching the terrier handlers from the days of Billy Mitchell. They all seemed marvellous to me. I later mention the handlers who took on our dogs, but must specially mention Albert Langley who was so very kind and helpful to Angela Smith with her presentation and handling.

"Today's terrier handlers are also extremely skilful and greatly to be admired. But of course I should not leave out those who also handle other breeds, like Geoff Corish, Michael Coad, Marita Rogers, Dave Killilea and the GSD people. Of course there are excellent owner handlers, who often help out the new owners, and many of the handlers have either bred or own, or co-own, their charges. They all enrich our rings."

One who certainly fits in all these categories and was a judge Feffie always looked up to was the great Gwen Broadley, along with Bobby James whom we lost while still in his prime, Bill Taylor and Ellis Hulme. Few around today will have seen Leo Wilson or Enid Nichols in the ring but they too made a big impression on Feffie in her early days.

She has no regrets about not awarding CCs in every breed; that was never her ambition. "I wouldn't want to judge a breed that didn't want me," she says, and is proud to have been invited to do breed club shows in the great majority of the breeds in which she has given CCs, including the Cocker, Old English Sheepdog, Irish Setter and Cairn Terrier centenary events.

Favourite breeds to judge, other than her own? She has always loved doing Shelties and the Collie breeds, Samoyeds too, and she is just crazy about Chihuahuas!

Naturally overseas appointments have followed, including such memorable experiences as Santa Barbara and Chicago in the US and Sydney and other Royals in Australia. Australian visits are combined with a chance to see her niece Caroline and family.

Awarding top spot at the world's great terrier shows, Montgomery County, Great Western and of course National Terrier, was a special privilege. Indeed the UK's group shows are always among her favourites.

Challenging

What she has found particularly challenging have been her Scandinavian appointments, and not only because of the high quality of their dogs.

"At the time of my first appointment there, I had been doing a lot of variety judging in England," she says. "This meant going over large numbers of dogs in a limited time, and perhaps I was tending to become a touch too superficial.

"So to be forced to take one's time over each dog and to write a report on each one was a valuable corrective.

"I also found that they take their breed Standards much more seriously than we do, which again made me stop and think."

Has she any advice for younger judges?

"First, always remember that the exhibitors have spent a lot of money to show under you, not only in entry fees and petrol but in breeding, rearing and conditioning their dogs. So you should try always to be fit, not tired or bored, and to do one's best – you can't do more.

"Another thing, it is important to keep in practice, so take every opportunity to go over dogs – you can learn at a match or an exemption show. Don't turn down appointments merely because they don't count towards a KC questionnaire.

"Don't worry if there is ringside criticism. Thank goodness, Britain is a free country, and it's everyone's right to criticise. It can be hurtful, but sometimes there's a basis in truth."

A major boost for DOG WORLD came in the early '70s when Stafford Somerfield started his *Men, Women and Dogs* column. For ten years editor of the *News of the World* in its mass-circulation days, and previously involved with other national papers, he naturally had an influence on DOG WORLD's already trenchant presentation of the news. Inevitably a friendship developed between Feffie and Stafford and his wife Dibbie, whose Panfield Boxers had been so important since the breed's early days in Britain.

At that time the Somerfields had made a comeback to the Boxer ring with the vibrant **Ch Seefeld Goldsmith**. 'Mr Smith's'

Judging the Contest of Champions final 1982, won by Wyn Lepper's Pembroke Corgi Ch Olantigh Black Diamond. Dai does not seem impressed! Eric Smethurst presented the salver.
photo Frank Garwood Dog World

exceptional personality revived Feffie's long-standing affection for the breed.

The Somerfields had also long been interested in the terrier breeds and with Feffie's help Stafford obtained some top-class dogs who were shown to their titles by John Oulton, Andrew Hunt, Peter Bell and others. These included Sealyhams, Welsh, Wires and a Lakeland, the greatest being the Sealyham **Ch Roderick of Jenmist**, obtained from Mr Lambert's famous Northern kennel. Feffie still considers him one of the best dogs she has seen.

Dibbie (an expert, incidentally, on antiques as well as dogs) died in 1977 and, as had been her wish, Stafford and Feffie were married – so she could look after the dogs! He became chairman and she managing director of DOG WORLD Ltd which at that time published several other magazines and ran a big trade exhibition. For the best part of 50 years she compiled the review of the year for this ANNUAL, an invaluable resource for historians of the dog scene.

She retired as editor in 1986 but continued to be heavily involved as editor-in-chief and, following Stafford's death in 1995, as chairman, until she sold the company in 2007.

During her time as editor she maintained the paper's reputation for full, frank, fearless and fair coverage of the issues of the day, never afraid to be critical of the Kennel Club though at the same time respecting its long history and the difficult situations the governing body had to face.

DOG WORLD played a major part in exposing the horrors of the Japanese export trade and covered fully the judging scandal of the early '80s which lifted the lid on various unpleasantnesses. With such memories in mind, Feffie is still not keen on the idea of exporting to countries with inadequate anti-cruelty laws. She was happy to support the recent attempt led by Bull Terrier people to persuade the KC not to issue export pedigrees to such countries

With Angela Smith's help, she and Stafford had continued to maintain the Oudenarde Cairns and Panfield Boxers on Romney Marsh. In view of the great traditions begun by her mother and aunts in Cairns, and by Dibbie Somerfield in Boxers, perhaps her proudest moments were winning her third CC at Crufts with 'Koochie', **Ch Gold Bangle of Panfield** (Dibbie's last Boxer and bred in partnership with Sue Harvey) and making up the Cairn **Ch Oudenarde Wot A Lad**, the last in the line of Oudenarde champion dogs.

Stafford's trimmed terrier interest was kept on with a number of champions in various breeds, notably the Wire **Ch Louline Lord**

An early Scandinavian appointment. At the West of Sweden Terrier Club where BIS was the British-bred Scottish Terrier Ch Kennelgarth Tiger.

used, especially in a numerically small breed – but produced well, contributing the American movement and showmanship as well as correct colour and coat texture. He can be found in many subsequent pedigrees.

His most famous son was **Ch Tubereasa Beau Venture Ardgabha**, bred by Angela out of My Demererra, who was campaigned to BIS wins by Peter for the Semple family.

A bitch, **Ch Gamekeeper's Fergie**, was also imported and produced a champion.

Eventually the time came to cut down the kennels; the last Irish joined the Saredons, and recently Feffie has transferred the Oudenarde kennel name to Angela Goddard who worked with her aunts and Sheila and has known the dogs since her mother's day.

On retirement Feffie was joined by her old DOG WORLD colleague Bryan Mitchell, who had returned to the UK after two decades near Sydney. They moved to Herefordshire, in an idyllic spot with an extensive view of the Malvern Hills, taking a Boxer, Cairn and Irish as well as Bryan's Cavaliers. Time goes on, and today they no longer have any dogs, but with a beautiful garden in part fashioned from an old quarry and Feffie's continuing commitment to the world of dogs, there is no risk that boredom will set in.

She joined the KC's Ladies' Branch in 1970 and was a strong supporter of the efforts of Florence Nagle and others to attain full membership rights for women. Today it is hard to believe that it took until 1979 for this to be achieved; there can be little doubt that Feffie and Stafford's support in the pages of DOG WORLD must have played a part in Mrs Nagle's eventual triumph.

Mission Accomplished

This led to a firm friendship with this remarkable woman which lasted to the end of her long life. She asked Feffie if she would write her biography; this promise was honoured and copies of *Mission Accomplished*, a full account of Mrs Nagle's astonishing achievements in so many fields, are much sought after.

Some years earlier she had edited a profusely illustrated encyclopaedia of dog breeds.

Many regret that with her rounded views and common sense, Feffie never served on the KC General Committee, to which she would surely have been a major asset. Given her professional obligations, this would have been difficult, but she has been involved with the KC in other ways, and her long membership and valuable service was marked recently with honorary life membership.

With her own expertise as well as her wide knowledge of who was who in the dog world, she was an obvious choice to serve on the Judges' Sub-Committee, including some years as vice-chairman under Margaret Everton whom she credits with making the whole process more transparent and rigorous.

Feffie and Harry Jordan judged at Sydney Royal 1985. She gave BIS to Warren and Carole Goldsworthy's Scottish Terrier Ch Aberdeen Fordyce.
photo Michael Trafford

Fountleroy, who was shown to many CCs by Andrew Hunt and who was bred by Geir Flyckt-Pedersen before he came to Britain.

The Irish Terrier connection also carried on through the Tubereasas owned by Angela who started working with the Oudenardes during Mrs Hamilton's day. Her **Ch Tubereasa My Demererra** was shown by Peter Bell to the top Irish title in 1987.

Feffie had always admired the Irish she had seen in the US and felt that they had qualities the breed needed in the UK. In the early '90s she imported the beautifully bred **Trackways Booger Red**, and in Peter's hands Boog quickly gained his title. It was a great relief when the breed's doyenne, Edna Howard Jones, said she approved of him!

He wasn't used at stud a great deal – not a problem in Feffie's view as she feels it can be dangerous for any stud dog to be over-

She still serves on the breeds liaison council, having been chairman for some years. This has been a satisfying task when ideas put forward via the council have eventually come to fruition, though others were perhaps not taken as seriously as the council might have wished – a bit of a vicious circle as societies then come to feel it's not worth submitting items.

Ideally, she wishes that the whole process could be speeded up a bit, and that there didn't have to be the distinction between the elected breed representatives, and the delegates, elected from among those reps, who actually attend the meetings. Even if it isn't possible for all the delegates to attend, she feels those from any breed which is putting forward a proposal should do so.

Her special interest is the progression of up and coming judges. Today's neophytes, of course, seldom have the luxury of the education at matches, sanction and limited shows which Feffie and those of previous generations enjoyed. Nor, except in the numerically strongest breeds, are there the same opportunities to practise at open shows compared with even 20 years ago. So, "Are we doing enough to help?" she asks.

In her case she has been involved with the KC's judges development programme from its outset, covering several groups though principally the terriers. She is pleased that a number of breed clubs, not least in her own main interest, the Cairns, have given JDP graduates the chance to judge at their open shows.

With declining entries it is inevitable that the general championship shows will be seeking a higher proportion of judges who are capable of doing several breeds, so the JDP's work is crucial to the future. And Feffie feels it important that judges who do groups and best in show have as wide a knowledge of the individual breeds as is possible.

Yet at the same time she appreciates that too high a proportion of non-specialists is not ideal – a sensible balance of all-rounders to specialists is so important for any breed, she feels, with the former sometimes able to notice the trend for a particular fault that the specialists may well have missed.

One change since she started is the proliferation of breeds – when she started all-rounders awarded CCs in only about half the breeds someone of similar status would judge today. This means, too, that today's gradually decreasing number of entries are spread over an ever greater number of breeds.

The 'new' breeds add interest and variety to the scene but Feffie can't help feel sad at the decline in numbers of so many of the traditional British breeds, the terriers in particular.

Just as important for a judge as knowledge is, of course, integrity, sometimes all too obviously missing. In this respect Feffie was fortunate to have Leo Wilson as an exemplar in her youth – no one would ever dream of questioning the honesty of his decision-making in the ring.

Essential

Today she feels it essential that new judges – in whose training, unlike in the old days, so much money and effort has been invested – then demonstrate the same integrity in their turn.

She is also disappointed at some of the behaviour of those at the top of the game who should be setting an example. She appreciates that different members of a partnership may want to judge and exhibit – as indeed was the case when Stafford's terriers were being shown – but feels that some people should consider carefully what may or may not look the right thing to do. The same applies in situations such as that where people enter into temporary partnerships simply to get their name on a dog with a Stud Book number in a breed they want to judge.

Another way in which Feffie tried to help potential judges revealed an unexpected comic talent – she used to give hilarious demonstrations of 'how not to judge'.

Feffie has been concerned about health and basic soundness in the dogs she judges long before the events of recent years. I for one can long remember her saying of the dogs in the ring: "They've got to look as if they will last the day," and that philosophy has certainly prevented me for one from various wrong decisions. It was she, too, who taught me always to run your hand down a dog's tail, especially in the coated breeds, to check for kinks or lumps.

In principle, she has supported the concept of the health checks on certain breeds – "It is important to make judges understand that part of their procedure should be improving the health of the dogs."

She recalls attending, with Ronnie Irving, an excellent Swedish meeting on the subject, and being impressed with their positive approach. Subsequently she presented a paper on the subject at a meeting to which our KC invited many judges, though sadly few attended.

Next came the classification of 15 (now 13) breeds as 'high profile' which may have had its unfairnesses but was at least

A proud moment for any terrier judge, doing BIS at Montgomery County. This was 2005 where Feffie's choice was the eight-year-old Smooth Fox Terrier Ch Pennfox Trackway Wicked Brew, handled by Liz Tobin. With them are Dr Josephine Deubler and Jim McTernan.
photo John Ashbey

In 2012 Feffie gave BIS at National Terrier to the imported Irish Ch/Am Ch Fleet St Fenway Fan. Pictured are chairman Max King, handler John Averis, co-owner Tony Barker and Shannon Thomas of Royal Canin.
photo Alan Walker

a step towards paying greater attention to health and lack of exaggeration, she feels.

And so to Crufts 2012 and the health checks by vets. Like many, Feffie had imagined the main purpose was to stop lame dogs appearing in the group rings – there had been a number of complaints that such dogs had done so in previous years though of course that could easily have had an accidental cause.

In the event, though, it was eyes which appeared to be the vets' chief concern. Anyone who knows the care with which Feffie approaches her judging, and her attitude to the health issues, will surely have shared her horror that one of the several best of breed winners rejected at that fateful show was the magnificent Clumber Spaniel from Croatia, whom she had judged in the breed. This bitch was admired by many experts, beforehand and on the day, for her soundness, character and lack of exaggeration, and none, including Feffie, had felt that her eyes gave cause for concern.

It must have been a heartbreaking moment for all but Feffie, though upset, treated the matter philosophically and with the attitude that there's always something more to learn.

On the positive side she is impressed by the improvements over recent years in many of the high profile breeds – Chows and Shar-Pei for example – and the efforts made by so many breed clubs.

What are the answers to the problems of today's dog world? CCs for every breed, every show, is not the solution (though she finds it hard to understand why a breed like Boxers can not have CCs at some events), not least as many breeds wouldn't have enough judges to go round and the costs and space considerations would be a problem for many societies.

As we know this is the format in many European countries but Feffie is not convinced it is necessarily a good thing – in some breeds there she has noticed a deterioration in quality and a cheapening of the standard of the champions.

If this system did ever come to pass in Britain, it certainly wouldn't work without grading, and here judges would need careful training. From her own experience Feffie knows that grading is easy in high quality entries and/or in breeds you know really well. But in lesser entries it's all too easy to get lazy and grade more kindly than you should. And unless you are able to judge regularly and keep in practice, it's all too easy to slip into bad ways. Not everyone judges every breed equally well and it isn't always easy to be consistent in your gradings.

Feffie is, nevertheless, disappointed that the KC has made cuts to the CC allocation in 2016 which she feels is discouraging for the exhibitors at this difficult time. She would like to see a wholesale new look at the way the CCs are allocated, conducted by the relevant committee members, rather than the staff who may not always be aware of the complete picture.

She appreciates what a difficult balance it is, bearing in mind the numbers in each breed, the location of the shows, the size of each show and their spread through the calendar – and feels a new start would be the best.

She was uneasy about the KC asking breed clubs for their thoughts on which shows should be 'cut' – purely because if it turns out their suggestions can't be implemented, there will be even more dissatisfaction than if they had never been asked in the first place! *(This was written before the KC had a change of heart – at which Feffie is, of course, delighted).*

Supportive

In general though, Feffie feels supportive of the KC and what it is trying to achieve, especially with its liaison with outside bodies and through the Charitable Trust. Most people look only at what affects their own particular interest, whereas the KC has to look at the bigger picture, not just the minutiae of the show scene.

How can we restore people's enthusiasm for the show scene? One way is for clubs to look after their 'pet members' in the hope that some of them will go on to be involved with the show scene. Feffie is always impressed by those clubs which give their members fun days, Christmas parties and so on. The KC's Good Citizen Scheme has helped in this respect, and she feels it is important that where classes for these dogs are scheduled, judges should take them seriously.

At open shows especially, judges need to make an effort to make the newer exhibitors feel welcome. She regrets that so many of Britain's agricultural shows have dropped their dog sections which for many people was their first taste of a dog show. Cannot we persuade some of them to re-consider, even just with a companion show?

For years, Feffie advocated the principle of open membership of the KC. It's still her ideal, though she appreciates the practical difficulties. And how many would take it up?

A week after her final judging appointment at BUBA Feffie will be wearing a different hat as chairman of the Ladies' Kennel Association. She is now the LKA's longest serving committee member – she was originally asked to join as Mrs Nagle, then in the chair, felt that there was someone with links to the other dog paper on the committtee, so there should be someone from DOG WORLD too!

Mrs Nagle was succeeded by Norah Hartley, whose vice-chairman was Molly Collins. On her retirement Feffie took her place, graduating to the chair nearly 25 years ago. With her good friend Sybil Churchill as the association's formidable long-standing secretary, the Cairn breed was well represented at the LKA!

The LKA has long prided itself as being 'the dog person's dog show', especially in comparison with the other extravaganza a few weeks later at the same venue – but even here change is at times inevitable. With a new website, and a move to a different part of the NEC which should make life easier for exhibitors, the LKA is definitely looking to the future.

"I have always tried to welcome change," says Feffie. "This is one thing DOG WORLD taught me. When I became editor, many people would come up to me with ideas. My initial response was often 'We've tried that and it didn't work' but I quickly came to realise that this was a far too negative attitude, and I would start to invite people to sit down and discuss their suggestions.

"Change often means extra work and adjusting to new ideas, but without it there can be no progress."

Feffie maintains her Boxer interest as president of the British Boxer Club. She is also life president of the Portuguese Water Dog Club of GB, and is patron of the Irish Terrier Association, the Greater London and Homes Counties Old English Sheepdog Club, the Bichon Frisé Club of GB and the Samoyed Breeders and Owners League.

She has for many years been on the committee of the Southern Cairn Terrier Club, as was her mother before her. Talk about full circle – she is currently revisiting her editing days and producing a handbook to mark the club's centenary next year, following on from presiding over the joint breed clubs' highly successful world symposium this year.

Spare time sees her take a serious interest in sport, in particular tennis – her barrister uncle Montague Temple was secretary of the All England Club for some years – and her real passion, cricket – some years ago she achieved a long held ambition by becoming an associate member of the MCC, and tries to attend matches at Lord's when she can. I can well remember her excitement when she found that the Leeds hotel where the show judges were staying was also playing host to the England team, captained by her pin-up David Gower, during a Headingley test match!

Even if no longer judging, she hopes to continue attending club shows in a variety of breeds that interest her and in which she has many old friends, as well as helping bring on a new generation of judges to maintain the standards she has set herself over so long.

From DOG WORLD, March 23, 1956: "Daughter of Cairn breeder one of this year's debutantes – Miss Ferelith Anne Hamilton, only daughter of Lieut-Col G F Hamilton and Mrs Hamilton (owner of the Oudenarde Cairns) was presented to Her Majesty the Queen at Buckingham Palace last Wednesday by Mrs Eveleigh Nash. Miss Hamilton joined the editorial staff of DOG WORLD on October 3 of last year."

Dog World Annual 2014

The FCI'S new president

RAFAEL DE SANTIAGO from Puerto Rico was elected president of the Fédération Cynoligique Internationale in 2013, succeeding Hans Müller who had held this post for 27 years. Here he talks to Simon Parsons

photo HotDog

Rafael with his most famous Afghan Hound Ch Blue Boy do Vale Negro, bred by another stalwart of the FCI, Carla Molinari.

S: Do you come from a dog-owning family background? Did dogs and other animals play a significant role while you were growing up?

R: Although my family was not involved in the dog show world, we always had dogs at our home. Having a dog developed my sense of responsibility and influenced me during my life.

S: Please can you give us some idea of your professional background?

R: I have a degree in liberal arts and journalism. At the moment I am the president of Imagen Optima, Inc, a communications agency based in San Juan, Puerto Rico.

S: How did you come to be involved with the world of showing and breeding?

R: I was visiting a dog show in San Juan with a friend. I was amused by the different breeds and how they were presented. I decided to be part of this world and bought my first dog.

I bought my first Afghan Hound in 1970 and I started showing in local dog shows. He became very popular, since he was featured in many advertising campaigns in the national media. He was more famous in the national media than in the dog shows. After much reading and studying about dogs I started my own kennel, named Radesa.

S: Which breeds have you owned over the years?

R: Afghans have been my passion since the beginning but that does not mean that I do not enjoy other breeds. In the past we have owned Whippets, Briards and Lakeland Terriers

S: I know you and Roberto Velez Pico have enjoyed much success with your Afghan Hounds. Which were your most significant dogs and please outline their major achievements? What bloodlines did you work with?

R: Blue Boy do Vale Negro was campaigned by us across the United States, Europe and Latin America. He came from Portugal and was bred by Carla Molinari. My breeding programme was based on Akaba (US) and Do Vale Negro (Portugal).

S: Did you show your dogs beyond Puerto Rico?

R: We always managed to find time to show our dogs abroad. We showed them in the US and Latin America and occasionally we would fly them to Europe.

S: Please could you give us some insight into the dog scene in Puerto Rico. Has it always been linked more with the FCI than with the US? How has the dog world there changed and developed since you first became involved? Do your shows regularly attract exhibitors from other countries?

R: Puerto Rico is a Commonwealth with the USA and our first dog show was organised under the American Kennel Club rules in the 1950s. The Federación Canófila de Puerto Rico (the Kennel Club of Puerto Rico) was created in order to achieve a national championship.

I got involved in the organisation in 1972. In 1977 I was appointed president and sought recognition by the FCI. Since 1979 we have been recognised by the FCI and became federated members in 1981.

With the recognition by the FCI, dog fanciers started showing more in the FCI system dog shows. The most important events are the ones organised by the FCPR under the rules and regulations of the FCI.

Our dog shows are very popular with exhibitors in the US and Latin America. You can come to a dog show and enjoy a relaxing time in the Caribbean. We also attract European exhibitors, especially from Germany, Spain and France. In the past two years we have received exhibitors from Russia, Lithuania and Ukraine.

S: When did you start judging, and which breeds? How many years did it take to reach all-breed status? How much time do you spend judging around the world?

R: I started judging Afghan Hounds and it took me more than ten years to become an all-breed judge. At the moment I am judging three out of four weekends every month, mostly in Europe and Asia.

S: Which have been your most prestigious judging appointments over the years? Of the dogs you have judged, please could you name some of those who impressed you most.

R: I have judged at 20 FCI World Dog Shows, the Supreme FCI Champion of Champions Show in Switzerland, Westminster in New York, the Eukanuba National Championship, the Eukanuba World Challenge, FCI Section Shows in Europe, America and Asia.

Judging best in show in 1997 at the World Dog Show in my country was not only prestigious but emotional as well.

There are a lot of dogs who have captured my eye. Each dog has its stars. To name just one would not be fair to the others.

S: Please outline your involvement over the years with the Federación Canófila de Puerto Rico (Kennel Club of Puerto Rico). Over your time at the head of the club, what innovations have you introduced? Presumably the 1997 World Show was the highlight of the country's canine activities?

R: I became president of the FCPR in 1978. My first achievement was the recognition by the FCI and to become the most important canine organisation in the country and an important member of the section.

The World Dog Show 1997 was a great challenge but at the same time a great accomplishment. Puerto Rico was the

The great moment for Puerto Rico's dog show scene was hosting the FCI World Show in 1997. Rafael is pictured awarding BIS to the American Cocker Spaniel Ch Afton's Absolut, shown by Flavio Werneck, the talented Brazilian handler who died tragically young. Also in the line-up are Roberto Velez Pico and Hans Müller, whom Rafael succeeded in 2013 at FCI president.
photo John Ashbey

centre of the canine world. The WDS 1997 was a cultural event for Puerto Rico and it changed the way Puerto Ricans enjoy and interact with their dogs socially, in sports and in their recreation, education and above all the health of the dog.

S: When did you first become involved with the administration of the FCI? What positions have you held over the years? In which areas do you feel you have been able to improve and extend the work of the organisation?

R: I joined the FCI Standards Commission in 1991 and served for two terms. In 1999 I joined the FCI General Committee during the FCI General Assembly in Mexico City. I was appointed to join the Executive Committee as treasurer.

I served as treasurer of the FCI for 12 years until 2011 when I was elected as vice-president during the FCI General Assembly in Paris. In 2013, I became the FCI president during the General Assembly in Budapest.

During my years as treasurer, the global economy was very weak and we managed to maintain the FCI finances healthy and growing. I also work directly with our communications and public relations efforts.

S: For readers who may not be familiar with the work of the FCI, please could you outline briefly how it is made up and what its principal functions are.

R: The Fédération Cynologique Internationale is the World Canine Organisation. It includes 89 members and contract partners (one member per country) which each issue their own pedigrees and train their own judges. The FCI makes sure that the pedigrees and judges are mutually recognised by all the FCI members.

The FCI recognises 343 breeds. Each of them belongs to a specific country. The countries of the breeds write the Standard of these breeds (description of the ideal type of the breed). The Standards and Scientific Commissions of the FCI revise the Standards submitted by the country of origin, and the translation and updating are carried out by the FCI.

These Standards are in fact the reference on which the judges base themselves when judging in shows held in the FCI member countries; they are THE reference assisting the breeders in their attempt to produce top-quality dogs.

Every member country conducts international shows (conformation shows) as well as working/hunting trials and tests, and races/coursing.

Results are sent to the FCI office where they are processed. When a dog has been awarded a certain number of awards, it is eligible to receive the title of International Beauty, Show or Working Champion. These titles are confirmed by the FCI.

In addition, via the national canine organisation and the FCI, every breeder can ask for international registration of his/her kennel name.

The FCI keeps a list of all the judges appointed by its national organisations.

S: In 2013 you were elected president of the FCI on the retirement of Hans Müller who has occupied that post for so long. What specific aims do you have for the future of the federation and its work?

R: During my speech before the General Assembly I presented my plan for our organisation, The FCI Plan for the Future, which is summarised and focused in three main topics.

· Modernisation, innovation and empowerment
· Dogs' and dog owners' rights
· Growth and globalisation.

In my plan I detailed my vision of what the FCI should represent, for each of our members, for every breeder, for each dog fancier, for every dog owner. I visualise the FCI as an advanced and vanguard organisation, which will set the tone of the canine discussion around the world in a spirit of openness, with an atmosphere of intellectual exchange and as a global brand that seeks the best interests of dogs worldwide.

S: What do you feel will be the major challenges facing the international canine world over the next decade or so? Many countries are experiencing declining show entries and/or registrations. How can this be halted or even reversed?

R: Through the history of the FCI, there have been multiple threats to the dog world. The FCI has survived two world wars and multiple global economic crises. The FCI has survived because of the love for the dog, and because of what the dog represents. Dogs are a common element within cultures and it is an element that unifies the world, which is why we will fight against actual threats to the dog sport and above all the FCI.

Although we stand for dog rights and wellbeing, some groups are pushing for extreme legislation against breeds and breeders around the world that not only jeopardise the sport but the dogs as well. We will always defend responsible dog owners and breeders around the world and we will support, in all ways, our members to fight against nonsensical legislation.

Another challenge affecting the canine world is the rising travelling cost and also the restrictions on pet travel imposed by airlines around the world. I will create a multi-sectorial committee to work with this issue and find a realistic solution to all the parties involved.

S: A vitally important issue is to encourage younger people into becoming involved in pedigree dogs and, even more significantly, to maintain that interest into adulthood. Do you have any views on how this can be done?

R: In The FCI Plan for the Future, I presented the FCI Youth Project, which will be my direct connection with the next generation of the FCI. It will comprise members from each country using an online platform and social media networks like Facebook and Twitter. This commission will give junior handlers and young dog fanciers the opportunity to express their ideas and concerns regarding the FCI and dog-related themes.

S: The United Kingdom is certainly not the only country in which the need to breed and exhibit only sound and healthy dogs has become the very highest priority in recent years. In what ways has the FCI taken this on board and how does it encourage its member countries and their breeders and judges to take these issues even more seriously than they have done in the past?

R: The dogs' health must be the number one priority in a breeding programme and when showing dogs. It is established in our regulations and all judges and breeders must be aware of health issues in dogs.

The FCI is working with an initiative proposal based on dog health, wellbeing and welfare. This novel initiative will create an online network to support canine health, well-being and welfare worldwide and promote international collaboration by initiating partnerships and building on relationships with both members' and non-members' cynological organisations to address common goals through sharing of information, expertise and experience in an atmosphere of collegiality and co-operation. At our last General Committee meeting it was decided that the proposal will be sent to our members for comments.

S: Our own Kennel Club has more than once gone through its breed Standards to change any aspects which it is felt might lead to harmful exaggerations. Is this something the FCI is likely to do, or does it leave its breed Standards in the hands of the country of origin of each breed?

R: Modifications suggested to the Standards and Scientific Commissions are referred to the country of origin for their comments and approval.

S: Another major issue of recent times has been breed-specific legislation, regarding so-called 'dangerous dogs'. How does the FCI help responsible dog people in those countries fight such laws?

R: I am personally against such legislation regarding any specific breeds and so is the FCI. I personally worked against this type of legislation in Puerto Rico.

I learned that we have to fight these nonsensical proposals with scientific and convincing facts.

As president of the FCI I am encouraging our members to fight against these threats to dogs and we will back them on all possible scenarios to save the lives of hundreds of innocent dogs and the right of the owner to choose the breed of their preference.

S: Some of the world's major governing bodies, such as our own KC and the American KC, do not belong to the FCI. In an ideal world, would you like to see that change?

R: All national organisations seek the same goal, the wellbeing of dogs. It will be ideal if we could all agree on the topics related to health issues.

This would benefit all countries and collaborate towards the protection of dogs worldwide.

S: Realistically, though, KC or AKC membership isn't likely to happen in the foreseeable future, so in what ways will the FCI liaise with these bodies on issues of mutual interest?

R: The most important topics on which we should collaborate and converge are canine health, anti-dog legislation and dog cruelty. Collaborating on these topics will benefit dogs worldwide.

We can also collaborate and seek mutual recognition regarding pedigrees, Standards, judges and recognition of championship certificates.

I am looking forward to a meeting with the KC officials and start a proactive and positive collaboration between the FCI and the KC, the American KC and the Canadian KC.

S: One subject which always causes

At the second Eukanuba World Challenge in 2008, Rafael judged one of the heats and sent through the Saluki from Germany Int Ch Dakira Sawahin, handled by Dagmar Hintzenberg-Friesleben, who went on to win overall under Hans Müller. Leif Kopernik represented the German Kennel Club.
photo Sheila Atter

discussion is the mutual recognition of judges. Am I right that judges approved by one FCI member country are automatically approved by all other members, even if the depth and length of their training programmes may differ?

R: Judges training is different from country to country, and we trust our member countries with their educational programmes.

I am a personal believer that the FCI should organise our own education programmes and offer them during World Dog Shows or section shows. For example, the Americas and Caribbean Section organised, since 2000, the FCI congress for judges, hopefuls and breeders.

S: Would you like to see organisations such as the KC and AKC approve automatically judges approved by FCI countries, and vice versa? This has been the subject of talks between the KC and FCI – do you feel progress has been made?

R: As said before it would be ideal to have automatically mutual recognition, but I also respect national policies regarding this matter. I believe that with the correct conversations and discussion we can reach an agreement that will benefit both organisations.

During the World Dog Show 2013 in Budapest the KC and the FCI reached an agreement to study ways in order to achieve mutual recognition of dog show judges. This is an example of how we can collaborate for the benefit of the sport.

At the moment we have appointed a committee to work with the KC to further develop the mentioned concept.

S: A number of British dog people would like to see grading of the exhibits introduced at our shows, as at FCI events. And if time permitted, some feel that critiques on all dogs, not just the winners, would be ideal. What do you feel are the advantages of these procedures?

R: I personally like writing critiques at dog shows. It gives us the opportunity to really evaluate the dogs and for dog owners and breeders it is an important tool to use in their breeding programmes. On the other hand sometimes the number of dogs at some events makes it very difficult for the organisers to manage the schedule and the costs of such a big show.

S: The FCI recognises far more breeds than does, say, the KC or AKC. Is there a point where 'enough is enough', especially as some breeds are numerically very small so maintaining a healthy gene pool is hard? What would be the FCI's attitude to possible registration of 'designer crossbreeds' which exist around the world?

R: Our Standards and Scientific Commissions are constantly monitoring breeds and their health. It is up to the General Assembly to decide whether or not to accept a new breed and that decision is based on the recommendation of our Commissions.

About the possibility of accepting 'designer breeds' I am personally against. It is my belief that a new breed responds to a specific circumstance (cultural, ethnical, the need for assistance) and acceptance should take into consideration genetic and health information and not be based on looks.

S: The first major controversy of your presidency has been Russia's attitude to gay people and its new legislation, which has caused concern to many people in the dog-showing community in regard to that country hosting the 2016 World Show. Can the dog world, in its small way, join with others in making an effective international protest against these laws? If the laws are still in place by 2016, will the FCI still be prepared to allow the show 'World' status?

R: Two years ago, during the FCI General Assembly in Paris, Moscow was voted (by a majority of votes) to hold the 2016 World Dog Show. Nobody thought that two years later anti-LGBT legislation would be approved by the Russian Government, taking a step back in the pursuit of equality.

Although I am personally against the mentioned Russian law, I have to make sure that the FCI follows our statutes and procedures as established. We must guarantee our member countries' rights, but as a global organisation we should stand not only for dogs but for dog owners as well.

S: To end on a more optimistic note, what are your hopes for the future of the pedigree dog scene around the world?

R: Dogs unite people, and we should encourage people around the world to celebrate dogs, to respect dogs and include dogs in our society. We should encourage people to become responsible dog owners and get involved in activities where the whole family can share and enjoy the greatness of dogs.

S: Thank you.

The Club Français du Bullmastiff et du Mastiff,
and the Club Français du Bulldog Anglais

would like to welcome you
to some major french events

The French Championship Show on June 7th & 8th
in Angers
entries on www.cedia.fr

The Bulldog "Nationale"
the biggest Bulldog Club Show
on the continent in Chicamour Château (Orleans area)
on April 26th & 27th
information Heldenis@aol.com
entries on line www.cedia.fr

The Mastiff and Bullmastiff "Nationale",
the biggest Club show devoted to these two breeds
on the continent in Montagny-les-Beaune (Burgundy)
on September 13th & 14th
information Amclass@aol.com
entries online www.cynoprint.com

The Metz International meeting with a seminar
and 2 specialty shows
on November 1st and 2nd
(CAC on Saturday, CAC and CACIB on Sunday)
www.caninelorraine.fr

Welcome to France!

Dog World Annual 2014

The Pouch Cove story

Andrew Brace is FACE TO FACE with PEGGY and DAVID HELMING

THE CITATION for the American Kennel Club's Breeder of the Year Award reads "AKC Breeder of the Year Awards honor those who have worked to uphold Standards of Excellence in producing quality pure bred dogs and shared their knowledge with newcomers, creating the next generation of breeders".

It is quite an accolade but in 2005 a couple were honoured with the overall Breeder of the Year Award by the AKC, having three years previously received a similar award in the working group. In 2006 they further received the 'Winkie' Award for Breeder of the Year, presented at the Purina Show Dog of the Year Dinner.

I write of Peggy and Dave Helming whose Pouch Cove kennel has had immeasurable influence on the Newfoundland breed worldwide, has subsequently achieved unrivalled success with Portuguese Water Dogs and has now turned its attention to Norwich Terriers.

Mention the name Pouch Cove to any Newfoundland person, anywhere in the world, and they will respectfully touch their forelock, but they will also – if they know the Helmings personally – speak of a down-to-earth, approachable couple who have to a rare degree managed to combine huge success with universal popularity.

Both Peggy and David grew up with animals which included dogs. David lived on a farm where his father raised Black Angus cattle, so breeding livestock was familiar to him. Peggy was raised with a German Shepherd and Collies who were family pets. She was also known for bringing home any stray dog who roamed into the stable where she rode horses as a child! However neither Peggy nor David was involved with showing dogs as youngsters.

They both attended colleges in Worcester, Massachusetts and first met, via a blind date arrangement at a fraternity party, in 1963. They completed their degrees in June 1965, married the following September, and have now enjoyed almost 50 years of marriage.

Once married they obviously decided to have a dog and a Newfoundland was the eventual choice. Peggy recalls: "We both like large dogs and originally set our sights on a St Bernard. We were living in Connecticut at the time, and discovered the Little Bear Newfoundland kennel was also located in CT. We decided to take a ride to see their Newfoundlands and that magical trip ended our search.

"We obtained our first Newf from Little Bear, a nice

Dave and Peggy Helming with two of their Norwich Terriers.

Ch Pouch Cove's Goliath.
photo Ashbey

Ch Pouch Cove Gref of Newton-Ark (right) started the kennel's distinctive 'look'. On the left is his son Ch Amity's Bearfoot of Pouch Cove.
photo Ashbey

The Hungarian-bred Goliath son Ch Skipper's Eminence King of Helluland, three times BIS at the national specialty.
photo Nutting

Dog World Annual 2014

Ch Pouch Cove's Favorite Son, national specialty winner and the top sire in US breed history.

"The following year, we purchased another Sibyl daughter from a different stud dog. **Ch Kilyka's Becky Jo of Pouch Cove** (ROM) was of the same type as Jessica and these two girls became the foundation on which Pouch Cove was built. Both of these girls produced beautifully but when their children were line-bred, things really began to fall into place.

"In 1976, Jessica was bred to **Am/Can Ch The Sleeper of Newton Ark** and produced a small but very correct bitch, **Ch Pouch Cove Kasha of Newton Ark**. Kasha was bred to Sleeper's top producing brother **Ch Kuhaia's Rego** (ROM) which produced **Ch Pouch Cove Gref of Newton Ark** (ROM) who was the all-time top producing sire in the breed for approximately two decades.

"Gref was also a top winning Newf with many specialty and group wins along the way, including a breed win at Westminster in 1972 and he was number one Newf for the year. Gref still holds a spot as one of the top ten all time producing sires. In retrospect, it was Gref who really started the Pouch Cove 'look'.

"We developed a passion for the breed that has not wavered some 45 years later. Newfoundlands were our entrance into the world of purebred dogs and the many avenues of the sport. We met so many fine people, joined breed and all-breed clubs, participated in a host of dog related activities and subsequently began showing our dogs. Everything really just evolved so, in actuality, there is really no one reason why we began to breed Newfoundlands.

bitch who unfortunately developed a severe case of crippling hip dysplasia. That heartbreaking experience taught us the value of completing more research on potential health issues in advance of obtaining and breeding future Newfoundlands.

"In the late 1960s we purchased a granddaughter of the famous **Int Ch Newton**, and **Ch Katrina of Newton Ark** became our first champion, handled by Alan Levine. Kate was also the dam of our first litter which arrived in January 1968, the same day David was deployed to Vietnam for 13 months.

"From this litter we kept a male, **Ch Waldo of Pouch Cove CD**, who was our first homebred champion and a specialty and Westminster Kennel Club best of breed winner.

"Despite these successes, we sought to change the style of our Newfoundlands in certain ways. In the early 1970s we were able to acquire two quality bitches from Betty McDonnell's Kilyka kennel. The first bitch was **Am/Can Ch Kilyka's Jessica of Pouch Cove CD** (ROM). Her background was based on Kitty Drury's Dryad kennel. Jessica's dam, **Ch Shipshape's Sibyl UDT** (ROM), became the top producing dam in Newfoundland history for many years.

Ch Pouch Cove's Head Of State, BIS winner, national specialty winner and a top sire.
photo Ashbey

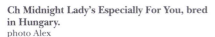

Ch Midnight Lady's Especially For You, bred in Hungary.
photo Alex

Especially For You's son Ch Darbydale's All Rise Pouch Cove, the all-time top winner with 46 all-breed BIS and three national specialty wins, handled by Michelle Scott to BIS at Westminster 2004 under Burt Yamada.
photo Ashbey

85

Dog World Annual 2014

"As we grew to really know the breed from those early years, our desire to breed dogs that better conform to the breed Standard and our attempt to correct some of the health problems in the breed also grew. Along with the help of other conscientious breeders, progress has been made in certain areas. Our goals have always been to strengthen the gene pool with each generation. However, one must realise that this type of journey is never over and there is always something to accomplish."

Whenever I speak to either Peggy or Dave I am aware of an overwhelming sense of both affection and responsibility for the Newfoundland breed. I asked them if they had identified problem areas in the breed, and also what really constituted the very distinctive Pouch Cove 'look'.

"In addressing this particular question, let's articulate how we interpret key dimensions of the Newfoundland breed Standard, which has hopefully been manifested into the Pouch Cove breeding programme.

"First and foremost, a Newfoundland must LOOK like a Newfoundland. Not a Chessie, not a Flat-Coated Retriever, not a Bloodhound.

"On balance (a loaded term) we prefer a massive animal with an impressive head and an outline that includes length of neck, a solid topline, a strong loin, bend of stifle and a well let down hock. We then add in details including dark eyes and pigment, correct ear set and bite, strong bones and pasterns, tight feet, a thick and properly set base of tail, luxurious coat, a regal carriage, sound movement and importantly a classic Newfoundland temperament… best interpreted as being extremely patient with the three-year-old child who is doing way too much tugging and pulling!

Balanced perspective

"It is challenging to boil down 40 years of breeding into a few sentences, but the above captures the essence of the Pouch Cove look. Handsome boys and pretty girls, who look the part, carry themselves with pride and exude the classic Newfoundland temperament.

"That said, producing this look does require a balanced perspective and compromise along the way, and there are tough questions to address in trying to stay within reasonable limits of the breed Standard. Should we use the very handsome dog that isn't just quite right in topline? Should we breed the female who is beautiful in type, but longer in body? Should we use the very sound and well-constructed male that is correct, but not exciting? And of course, how about the big, typy, sound dog who carries himself

Ch John's Big Ben of Pouch Cove.

Ch Pouch Cove's Matter Of Fact, sire of more than 50 champions.
photo Phillips

beautifully but has one hip that may not clear?

"These are examples (and there are many more) of reasonable questions that successful breeders face and address every day.

"That said, over the years we have learned through what are at times disappointing results, more straight-forward answers to certain things that we are very reluctant to touch. Should we use the dog with the straight stifle and close rear movement? How about the one with long hocks? The gay tail? The pretty headed dog with a shallow body and yellow eyes? The sound and extremely handsome dog with the temperament that isn't bad yet isn't entirely stable?

"Cautionary note – some undesirable characteristics, when introduced into a breeding programme, are there to stay for many generations."

For the most part the Helmings have line-bred their dogs, but they will go outside the line to capture traits that they feel would be beneficial to their programme. In those cases, they tend to look for a dog that is line-bred on dogs that possess those desirable traits. But Peggy comments: "Easier said than done in many cases, but we try to weigh both genotype and phenotype in our deliberations.

"We believe in being objective about the dogs in our breeding programme. The sport of breeding and showing purebred dogs rests almost exclusively on the agreement of breeders, judges

Ch Pouch Cove's Seabrook Enough Said was BIS at the 2013 national specialty under Bill Shelton.

Dog World Annual 2014

Dave and Peggy have twice been honoured with awards for 'Breeder of the Year'.

Newfoundlands and a Portuguese Water Dog – naturally!

and exhibitors to be guided by the official breed Standard. Interpretations may differ, but we are aware of the boundaries and the extent of how far we can go with our interpretations of what our breed is or is not.

"We have a clear understanding of what we are trying to produce and we make our decisions and selections accordingly. We look at the total picture and have a strong commitment to raising the bar along the way. I think, I feel and I believe all are part of a clever breeder's fantasy. A little luck doesn't hurt either!"

I asked Peggy and Dave about their most significant Newfoundlands and what made them so great.

"We have been blessed through the years to have had so many fine Newfoundlands. Pouch Cove has bred, owned or co-owned over 400 champions since our first litter in 1968 and 11 of these dogs have amassed over 100 best in show awards.

"At the Newfoundland Club of America national specialty shows, Pouch Cove dogs have been fortunate enough to have been awarded BOB 12 times, best of opposite sex 11 times and winners dog and winners bitch on ten occasions each.

"To name only a few of the most significant is not an easy task. That said, **Ch Darbydale's All Rise Pouch Cove** ROM ('Josh') is the all-time top winning Newfoundland in breed history, culminated by going BIS at Westminster in 2004, presented by his handler and friend, Michelle Scott. Josh accumulated 46 all-breed bests, and he was also OB at the NCA's national specialty in 2001, 2002 and 2003.

"Josh's nephew **Ch Skipper's Eminence King of Helluland** ROM ('Lincoln') repeated Josh's National triple header by going BOB at the 2009, 2010 and 2011 national specialties. Lincoln's sire is the incomparable BISS **Ch Pouch Cove's Goliath** ROM. Goliath was one of our all-time favorite Newfs who produced many champions and two national specialty BOB winners. He believed that the world revolved around him and for the most part he was correct – a truly great Newfoundland.

"Two of the boys who really did it all in and out of the show ring were BIS BISS **Ch Pouch Cove's Favorite Son** ROM ('Jake') and a Josh son BIS BISS **Ch Pouch Cove's Head Of State** ROM ('Jefferson'). Both of them were multi-all-breed BIS winners and both won NCA national specialties. Coupled with these accomplishments, they were both exceptional producers, as Jake is the all-time top producing sire in breed history and Jefferson is number two producer in breed history based on the number of offspring who obtain their championships.

"Some dogs excel only as producers and others only as show dogs but few can do both to the extent of Gref, Jake and Jefferson. And this is the ultimate accomplishment by these gentlemen. Moreover, Jake remains to this day the epitome of breed type for many Newf enthusiasts.

"Another top producing champion was the very typy **Ch Amity's Bearfoot of Pouch Cove** ROM. A Gref son, Bearfoot had much more breed type than his sire, plus the substance to go with it. Bearfoot was the unusual combination – well constructed and enormous – and he produced real quality that impacted the breed decade after decade.

"**Ch John's Big Ben of Pouch Cove** was another big boy and more stretched out all over than what we were accustomed to. That said, he had remarkable substance and perhaps the most beautiful Newf head that we have ever experienced. Ben was one of the greatest for producing consistently beautiful pups that excelled at the national specialty level.

"**Ch Schooner Yosef of Newton Ark** was a popular stud dog that we used several times. He is the sire of Favorite Son and Motion Carried. He stamped his puppies with strong rears, overall breed type and beautiful coats.

"**Ch Jubilee You're The Top** was a Jake son who had a fantastic outline with length of leg, neck, strong topline and deep front and rear angles, and a top producer in the early 1990s.

"**Ch Midnight Lady's Especially For You**, was a Jake grandson that, incorporated with some beautiful European dogs, helped with the gene pool. He was a huge dog that could also readily make his way around the ring. He was the sire of Josh who accumulated 46 all-breed BIS as well as BIS **Ch Pouch Cove's Politician** who was the winner of 19 all-breed BIS.

"**Ch Pouch Cove's Matter Of Fact** ROM, is the number five top producing sire in breed history with more than 50 champions produced, many of whom were NCA regional and national specialty show winners. Matthew was a dog with good leg length, an excellent topline and effortless movement.

Top producing

"**Ch Sunvalley's Petitions Pouch Cove** ROM, a Jefferson son, was once again named the NCA's top producing sire in 2012, a feat he first accomplished in 2009. Christopher is a NCA national specialty BOB winner and a multi all-breed BIS winner.

"**Gr Ch Seabrook's Best Man at Pouch Cove** ROM, a Christopher son, was winners dog at ten months of age at the 2007 NCA national specialty and was also a BIS winner at the Connecticut River Working Dog shows in both 2010 and 2011. Bradley is currently residing with Riccardo Quartiglia at Cayuga Newfoundlands in Italy where he has been successfully bred to several European ladies. **Ch Pouch Cove's Seabrook Enough Said**, a Bradley daughter out of a Lincoln daughter, was selected BOB at the 2013 NCA national specialty.

"**Ch Ad Lib of Pouch Cove** ROM was the type of bitch that breeders would be extremely fortunate to have in their programme. While quite pretty, Ad Lib wasn't the heaviest type girl, but she was to this day one of the best constructed bitches that we have ever seen. With a neck, an iron back, angles and carriage, Ad Lib produced quality males and females, regardless of whom she was bred to.

"**Ch Motion Carried of Pouch Cove** ROM started her show career at the national specialty as a six-month-old puppy. Breeder judge Ron Pemberton awarded her winners bitch over a field of 140 girls, and Anthony Hodges called her 'the Brook Shields of the national' when he had her in for BOB. She also was a producer of national apecialty winners which was the icing on the cake.

"**Ch Pouch Cove's American Maid** was a heavy duty Ben daughter that could multi-task in the show ring and in the whelping box. She was BOS at the national at almost nine years of age and out of the veterans class, after producing four litters of exceptional puppies.

"Then there was **Souvenir of Pouch Cove** ('Sue Sue'). This girl provided a great lesson to even well-established and experienced breeders regarding not so easy choices. A bitch of beautiful type who was also extremely sound in character and construction, Sue Sue had the misfortune of an incorrect bite as she was severely undershot. That said, given her other qualities we just could not bring ourselves to eliminate her from the programme without at least giving her a try in the whelping box. Across three litters she produced good bites overall and, more importantly, beautiful dogs including three all-breed BIS winners and two national specialty BOB winners. Sue Sue was the dam of Favorite Son.

"Many more could be mentioned, but those are the highlights without going too long!"

Peggy and Dave have over the years developed close friendships with various Newfoundland breeders around the world with whom they have co-operated closely, notably in Scandinavia in Europe. Many years ago I remember travelling to Pouch Cove with Phyllis Colgan to look at two litter brothers, the Helmings having agreed to let a male come to the Karazan kennel here in the UK. Phyllis preferred the smaller of the two, **Pouch Cove's Repeat After Me**, but what he may have lacked in size he more than made up for in type and he fitted in well with the Karazan bitches.

Changes for the better

His sire was the all-time top producing Favorite Son and his dam was **Ch Pouch Cove's On All Fours** who herself was a terrific producer. Peter had excellent breed type, great balance and a wonderful way of carrying himself. He was taken full advantage of by British breeders and became a phenomenal sire, stamping his type on all his progeny.

I asked the Helmings what changes they have seen in the breed since they first became involved?

"From our perspective, and not surprisingly, the changes have been for the better. When we first became involved in Newfoundlands there were two primary and distinct lines in the US, Dryad and Little Bear, and they both had their unique characteristics. Generally speaking, the Dryad dogs were of heavy breed type with big heads, lots of bone, good size and were impressive at a glance. For the most part, but not exclusively, the Little Bear dogs were of nice type, yet correct and balanced with strong toplines and appealing angles.

"A couple of breeders such as Jane Thibault at Nashau-Auke took the steps in crossing the Dryad and Little Bear lines with impressive results.

"We did that as well through both direct crosses as well as through Jane's dogs, and what follows are highlights of what we have improved upon on a more consistent basis: significant variation in head type to much greater consistency in appealing heads, stuffier front assemblies to greater length of neck and better lay back, toplines that dropped behind the shoulders to a more level back, straighter and shorter stifles to long stifles with more angle, longer hocks to shorter well let down hocks, close and weak rear movement to wider rears with better drive, coats with curl to straighter coats, and importantly, we now have an overall sounder breed both in movement and on x-ray, in addition to general health improvements given better nutrition and health testing."

Today wherever you see Newfoundlands shown you will see much

Ch Cartmel Sea Master, imported from Pat Jones in England.
photo Reed

more grooming paraphernalia than was ever dreamt of when I first watched the breed in the UK. I dared to broach the subject of elaborate grooming and presentation with Peggy and suggested that it may have taken over the basics.

"Not at all! In fact, we appreciate a well presented exhibit, and on the whole 'presentation' has improved significantly over time, in both handling and grooming. We find the fascination with 'over-grooming' ill-placed, given REAL structural issues endemic to giant breeds.

"Of all the things that breeders and judges should be concerned about, a dog that is inappropriately or over-groomed (whatever that means) falls way behind faulty fronts, rears, toplines, breed type and yes, temperament.

"That said, some people do go a step too far in grooming but, frankly, others do not go far enough, though we see less of this today than we did 30 years ago. Grooming appropriately executed should not be extreme, nor should it stand out as the key feature of a good specimen.

"Moreover, all the expert grooming in the world will not make an average dog a good dog, unless a judge doesn't really know the breed all that well. One step off the stack and reality hits. And most importantly, unlike faulty structure, poor breed type and inappropriate temperament, rest assured that grooming, good or not so good, will not pass from one generation of Newfs to the next!" Wise words indeed.

It is well known that Newfoundland bitches can be rather clumsy mothers, so I asked Peggy how they deal with bitches and newborns.

Watched 24/7

"Our pups are all born in a room off of our country kitchen. We watch them 24/7 for the first several weeks as Newf moms are large and when they set themselves down in the whelping box, it is important to count quickly to be sure no one is under their massive bodies. They love their whelps, but without supervision it can be difficult to keep some of the babies from being compromised.

"After three weeks, the size of the pups and their ability to send out a loud yelp helps the mom to know when she has one underneath and she can then respond appropriately."

Co-ownerships are widespread these days, in the US and beyond, so I wondered how these work and if they are always successful.

"Co-ownerships work best when the parties involved comprehend what the commitment entails and share similar goals with the individuals involved. Much can be accomplished with collaboration with others sharing the highs and lows and how to accept them as

Gr Ch Claircreek Impression De Matisse, currently number two all breeds in the US for 2013, handled by Michael Scott.

Ch Pouch Cove's Monkey Business (left), national specialty BIS, and her brother, BIS winner Ch Pouch Cove's Monkey See Monkey Do.
photo Sombach
photo Nutting

you grow in the sport.

"Our co-ownerships have been a plus for everyone involved and the process has worked well. They are based on a simple and clear understanding of what we jointly expect to accomplish. Principles we follow include: providing mutual support, exchanging ideas, being good listeners, sharing responsibilities, thinking BIG, working hard and respecting each other's positions.

"The use of a contract is necessary so each party can refer back to the original agreement if questions arise. If necessary, contractual changes can be made along the way subject to mutual agreement.

"Our experience with co-ownerships has proven that even in a highly competitive arena you can accomplish great things in a breed by working together toward a common goal which, in reality, brought us together in the first place. If situations arise in a co-ownership that cannot be resolved, both parties should agree to disagree and jointly work towards a settlement that is amicable to each party. It is best not to waste time on the negatives, as there is work to be done."

The Helmings' kennel facility is essentially a section of their home, as you enter it by going through a kitchen door. They have ten runs in the kennel and seven of these tie directly into the house for the indoor portion of the run. The other three runs have insulated dog houses and are used during the day time hours for exercise with the dogs coming in at night. The property consists of 12 fenced acres used as exercise paddocks for daily outings.

"Peggy and Dave are able to rotate the Newfs in and out of 'their portion' of the house where they can mingle with Busy, the senior Portuguese Water Dog (Matisse's grandmother, of whom more later…), and of course the five Norwich Terriers who presently dominate the residence. They have a large grooming, feeding and puppy room which is used by them and the staff for the daily routines.

The kennel is manned around the clock on those occasions when the Helmings are away by one of the four women who work on a part-time basis. Training of the dogs is partially done by staff members with the preparation for shows done by Dave and Peggy. Peggy notes, "We are fortunate to have had our two main staffers here for 28 years. They are family and we are so grateful for their presence in our lives."

We now come to Chapter Two in the Pouch Cove success story following the introduction of Portuguese Water Dogs, and a major part of this adventure has been Milan Lint.

"Dave and I first met Milan at the 1979 Newfoundland national specialty held in Ann Arbor, Michigan. At that time Milan was a teenager who was just getting started, and his Newfs were down line from Pouch Cove dogs. Milan did limited breedings, but he had some nice dogs with good success in the show ring.

Working together

"Interestingly, I judged puppy sweepstakes at the NCA national specialty in the mid-1980s held in California. In my first class, six to nine month dogs, in walks a puppy handled by Gerlinde Hockla – without question an appealing and high quality youngster. The puppy won his class and I ultimately selected him for best in sweeps over 120 pups, and I was, of course, very curious as to his breeding. Turns out it was a singleton puppy that Milan bred (out of a Pouch Cove bitch bred to a Newton-Ark dog), kept, flew to CA and hired Gerlinde to handle. It worked!

"Once Milan began his university studies, he became increasingly interested in the PWDs due to space constraints that would not accommodate the big breeds. Dave and I ultimately got our first PWD from Milan in the early 1990s and that worked out especially well, as Milan had completed his graduate schooling and relocated to New York providing the opportunity for us to work closely on the PWD breeding programme.

"Through the years we incorporated four or so bitches from other breeders then selectively bred them to males we found especially worthy in type, temperament and soundness. One of those bitches, 'Grrrilla' (**Ch Akire Supa Chunky Monkey**) really brought things to life. She was a bitch of extraordinary type and a real producer.

"In addition to winning BOS at the PWDCA national specialty under Michelle Billings, Grrrilla when bred to 'Nick' (**Ch Pouch Cove's Patriot**), produced ten champions across two litters. Those pups included the multiple all-breed BIS male 'Digit' (**Ch Pouch Cove's Monkey See Monkey Do**), the national specialty BOB bitch 'Busy' (**Ch Pouch Cove's Monkey Business**), under breeder/judge Joyce Vanek, sister 'Jane' (**Ch Pouch Cove's Monkey Woman**) BOS

Dog World Annual 2014

PWD national specialty under breeder/judge Carla Molinari, and 'Chloe' (**Ch Pouch Cove's Every Sailors Dream**) who was best of winners at the national specialty from the six to nine puppy bitch class.

"The next major step for the program was the incorporation of 'Carlo' (**Ch Cartmel Sea Master**) who was imported as a youngster from the UK's famous Cartmel kennel of Miss Pat Jones. Visiting with Pat on several occasions, talking dogs and ultimately acquiring Carlo and his kennelmate 'Bess' was one of the most fascinating and rewarding experiences we have had in dogs.

"It also turned out to be a big boost to PWDs in the US and Canada. For example, Carlo when bred to the Grrrilla daughters have in short order produced a long list of specialty and all breed winners, including the Busy son 'Caribe' (best in sweeps and best of winners at the 2009 National) and Caribe's son Matisse who has recently shattered all existing PWD show records.

"In summary, having bred over 50 American champions including many working group, BIS and national specialty winners, Milan and I feel that our approach to producing healthy, happy and handsome PWDs has worked to date. The PWD parent club in the US has been extremely active regarding health issues and related testing, and we have taken full advantage of using identified gene markers which has been a real plus in improving the chances of producing extremely healthy dogs.

"That said, it is a real balance, as our breedings consist of much more than mixing one pile of health certificates with another. For us, in addition to the health clearances, the potential parents must also have the structure, carriage, demeanor and overall breed type that we prefer to look at and interact with each day. Making all of that come to fruition isn't so easy, but we keep on trying and hopefully succeeding!"

Gr Ch Claircreek Impression de Matisse I saw winning a BIS under Ron Menaker earlier this year. Handled by Michael Scott, he is owned by Milan Lint, Peggy Helming and Donna Gottdenker and is having a remarkable year. So what makes him so special?

"There is much that we could discuss regarding Matisse, but simply put, he is the unique combination of looks, personality, and charisma that rarely coalesces in one entity. But when it happens, rare as it is, dogs like this are destined for greatness.

Producer of quality

"Briefly, Donna Gottdenker contacted us about breeding the lovely 'Apolina' (**Ch Claircreek Femme Fatale**) to Carlo, our UK import from Miss Pat Jones. Milan and I had always admired Apolina, and we were not the only ones who found her exceptional, as breed expert Carla Molinari had awarded her group 1 at the World Show in Mexico a few years earlier.

"Carlo had been a strong producer of quality, but we encouraged Donna to consider Carlo's son Caribe, as he is higher on leg and has Busy as his dam. Donna did just that and on June 6, 2011 the Apolina ex Caribe kids were born, including a standout black curly male ultimately named Matisse.

"Since that time, it has been a whirlwind for Matisse. He completed his Canadian championship at age six months and his American title came aged eight months, all breeder/owner-handled by Donna. We were monitoring his progress closely and without question we could tell through each and every photo that this pup exuded that magic charisma that said 'Here I am, come take a closer look'! A stand-up youngster indeed.

"Given that things were going as hoped for, we made plans to have our long-time handler, Michael Scott, further assess Matisse at the 2012 national specialty. The goal was to better understand whether Matisse had what it takes to be a top special, something Milan and I keep an eye out for given our desire to have the breed well represented in top tier competition.

"Our previous special, Matisse's uncle Digit, was the top PWD in 2008 and up to this point we didn't have an obvious follow-up to Digit's impressive record.

Wheatley Wentzell's Ch Pouch Cove's Which Witch Is Which, winning the sweepstakes at Montgomery County and six and a half months.
photo Ashbey

Ch Pouch Cove's Almost An Heir, handled by Andrew Green.
photo Clark

"While watching Matisse handily win best in sweepstakes with Donna at the helm, we also noticed every professional handler at the show watching this boy with keen interest. However, Michael had already identified Matisse as having the potential to be not just a good special, but a great special. Sensing Michael's enthusiasm, we knew there was no way that he was heading home without that 15-month-old pup!

"Michael and Matisse practised throughout the remainder of 2012, winning several groups and their first best in early December. After a holiday rest, Team Matisse entered 2013 by storm.

"As of this writing and in seven months of showing the two-year-old Matisse has garnered an amazing 60 BIS, 14 reserve BIS, and 90 group firsts, including the Westminster group win. Within the US, this has propelled him to number two dog all breeds, number one PWD and the top winning PWD of all time. He attended the PWDCA national specialty just this past week and was awarded BOB and also won the Top Twenty competition. In his spare time, he managed to pass all of his health clearances and sired three litters of pups. What a guy!

"It would be mostly accurate to say that this boy has exceeded our wildest expectations."

At the present time David Helming judges Newfoundlands and Peggy Newfoundlands and Portuguese Water Dogs. Do they intend expanding their judging portfolio?

With refreshing but typical candour Peggy says: "Since we are still actively breeding and exhibiting three breeds, we will not be applying for other breeds at this time. Perhaps we will add a few breeds in the future. We certainly both enjoy judging, but it is difficult to do both."

Having smashed all kinds of records with the Pouch Cove Newfoundlands and Portuguese Water Dogs, there are now new kids on the block chez Helming… Norwich Terriers. I was keen to know how such a smaller breed attracted Peggy and Dave.

"We fell in love with these little guys many years ago when we watched our friends Jim and Marjorie McTernan having some very good runs with their Norfolks. We also liked the Norwich Terriers and decided we might like to have one for our own.

"The Green team started to search for a little girl for us and several months later Andrew called to tell us about a nice litter born nearby that was sired by his top winning special, **Ch Sandina Sorcerer**. Peter and Beth liked all three girls in the litter, so it was all falling into place for us to acquire our first Norwich bitch.

"We were not disappointed when we picked up **Fentondale's Good Witch**, better known as Kate. She has been a delightful addition to our family and was raised by our PWD, Busy (Matisse's grandmother) and took her puppy naps in Josh the Newfoundland's furry tail. She has never admitted to being smaller!

"When it came time to consider a mating with Kate, we again had the opportunity to use a son of Willum (**Ch Chidley Willum The Conqueror**) out of a lovely Cobby bitch that Beth had here for breeding from the UK. The young male from this combination, **Ch Yarrow Venerie Old King Cold** (a cute name as he was produced from Willum's frozen semen!) and Kate made some lovely babies and so far three of the four are finished champions with the fourth pointed and hopefully will finish this year.

"Her black and tan pup **Ch Pouch Cove Which Witch Is Which** attended her first Montgomery County show at just six and a half months and took best in sweepstakes at the national held in conjunction with the show. She finished easily as a young adult with a group first to her credit, owner-handled by Wheatley Wentzell.

"Another sister, **Ch Pouch Cove's Almost An Heir**, finished her championship with five major wins, and was winners bitch and BOS over four specials at the 2013 Westminster KC show.

"We also imported a female from the Cobby kennel of Renee Sporre Willes and hope to incorporate some of the Ragus and Cobby blood with what we have here. We purchased a male pup from the Littlefield kennel and he has some promising pups coming along as well.

"We very much enjoy the breed and our ability to 'pick them up'. Their gregarious nature and size makes it easy to ignore some bad habits, so at times we are more like pet owners than experienced dog fanciers when it comes to discipline. We are excited to hopefully make some exciting combinations in the future. Stay tuned!"

I have every confidence that in the not too distant future Pouch Cove Norwich will be making a huge impression on their breed, given the Helmings' track record.

The Helmings are true role models when it comes to 'putting something back' into the sport. Apart from their demanding schedule as breeders and exhibitors Dave is board director and co-ordinator of the North Branch Cluster Somerset Hills KC of which he is a former president (six years) and show chairman, vice president and show grounds co-chairman of the Morris and Essex KC, board director and treasurer of the KC of Philadelphia and show chairman of the Westchester KC. Deeply involved with the Newfoundland Club of America, he is its delegate to the American Kennel Club and vice-chairman of the NCA Charitable Trust, has been NCA president (three years) and board director (five years). He is also a member of the AKC's Political Action Committee.

Take The Lead

Peggy is Somerset Hills Kennel Club's hospitality chair and a member of its Scholarship Committee, she serves on the Morris and Essex KC's Show Hospitality Committee, is hospitality chair of Westchester KC, was corresponding secretary of Delaware Water Gap KC, sits on the Judges and Breeders Education Committees of the Newfoundland Club of America for whom she also acts as national specialty co-ordinator, and was chair of the AKC video committee for the Newfoundland production.

She has been a NCA board director for 16 years and vice-president for six years. She has been the AKC delegate for the Erie KC since 1993 and also sits on the board of directors for the admirable Take The Lead charity. It would be hard to talk to the Helmings about 'spare time'!

Pouch Cove is the name of a small picturesque fishing town of about 2,000 residents in Newfoundland, Canada. When they came to register their first litter of Newfoundlands Peggy and Dave felt it would be an appropriate kennel name.

In 2004, when Ch Darbydale's All Rise Pouch Cove ('Josh') won BIS at the Westminster KC show, the Helmings received a congratulatory letter from the Town of Pouch Cove and a request for a picture of Josh which would be framed and hung in the Township's headquarters building – they proudly sent them one and this surely was well deserved recognition from the little Canadian township that has become a household name thanks to two of the most dedicated, yet unassuming, dog people I have ever met.

Fentondale's Good Witch (Kate, second left) with her daughters Sydney, Salem and Pippa.

Dog World Annual 2014

IRELAND

Report and photographs by Joyce Crawford-Manton

Getting the finances back on track

AT THE risk of repeating myself a year after writing that the recession had not really manifested itself in the dog show scene, it still seems that the Irish exhibitors have continued to find the money for their entries and travel.

Their enthusiasm has meant that entries still remained steady throughout 2013, the few shows affected being those which would usually see a fair number of exhibitors from Great Britain, and even those saw a very small drop on the previous year.

The Irish Kennel Club Green Star and Judges Committee has been working on education and has set up some further requirements for up and coming judges, also requiring full critiques for their first time judging at championship level. These debuting judges also are assessed. Some people still believe that the current criteria do not go far enough.

Although the General Purposes Committee (GPC) held meetings last year with the representatives from affiliated clubs regarding the restructuring of the way clubs are represented at An Ard Chomhairle (the General Council), sadly, the GPC has not come back to anyone,

Winner of Pup of the Year 2012, hosted by the Combined Canine Club, was Noel Beggs and wife June Wall's Rottweiler Alldenria Eveready.

A first in Ireland for the breed when Kelly Lawless handled her, Kevin Sharp-Dixon and Jude Reyes' Finnish-bred Australian Silky Terrier Ch Curiosity Love Affair to take BIS at Kilkenny under Carmel O'Riordan.

Ahead until the end of October, and close up in second spot at the time of writing, is Harold Quigg and Ron Ramsay's Kerry Blue Terrier Ch/UK Ch Torums Calico Jack, with BIS at Swords and Bray, pictured at the latter where judge was Chris Cathcart, and a RBIS. 'Harry' won his UK crown at three breed club shows. Harold and wife Helena's Ch/UK/Am Gr/Can Ch Saredon Shock Waves of Irisblu was BOB at Montgomery County.

The Irish Kennel Club Dog of the Year is based on points won for all breed BIS and reserves and, for the first time in many years, still has several dogs in contention, with two shows to go. Out in front at time of writing is Ashling Connolly's Bichon Frisé Ch/UK Ch Ashmair Double Trouble. 'Beau' was BIS at Fermoy international, Cork and All Ireland Bull Breeds, and won both the IKC Top Showdog contest in January '12, representing Ireland at the Eukanuba final last December, and the Pup of the Year '11.

so the situation remains. This means that many clubs affiliated to the IKC, having paid their fee, have no representation, while others have. Some clubs that barely exist, and some that seem to have disappeared altogether, send their rep each year to vote at the AGM and the monthly AAC meetings! So democracy is no longer, it seems, as our forbears intended, the order of the day and the council is rather a closed shop.

Since Tony O'Neill, long-time secretary of the IKC, retired last September, there was quite a gap before the GPC appointed a new chief executive officer, in the shape of Pat Kiely, former managing director of the Automobile Association, Ireland.

Pat got his feet under the table at the start of March, and hopefully will, with his expertise and business acumen, steer the IKC back onto a more prosperous financial road. At the AGM in January it was made clear that the IKC's finances had taken a turn for the worse, and with falling registrations, doubtless due in part to the poor puppy sales in the country since the death of the Celtic Tiger, other means of income needed to be sought.

We do of course have our National Show Centre, a most marketable asset, which Tony worked hard in promoting, and with its close proximity to the airport is surely hireable for a vast array of uses to provide a good income. It is hoped that Pat will give the answer to all these woes, though it is a big ask.

So far there have been increases in the

Dog World Annual 2014

Having won the IKC Top Showdog 2012 final under Latvian judge Ligita Zake, Gerry and Pauline Clarke's Irish Wolfhound Ch Roxanne of Shantamon will be Ireland's representative at the Eukanuba World Challenge in Florida.

The Irish Champion of Champions, hosted by Dublin Dog Show Society, was judged by Dutchman Hans van den Berg who crowned the Boxer Ch Walkend Boy at Bessbox, owned by Paul Keenan and Darren Griffin.

David and Jacqui Benson's Spanish-bred Bernese Mountain Dog Ch/UK/Int Patrick de la Galea at Bernervalley became the first Irish-owned Bernese to take an all-breed BIS. In fact he has won two, South Tipperary and Irish Ladies KA, thus joining the other dogs in third place.

Billy Henderson and son Josh's Dobermann Ch/UK Ch Tu-wos Halestorm took two BIS in five days to put him joint third in the running for DOTY, at Clonmel and Limerick. He is a son of the late Ch /UK Ch Aritaur Hypnotique, the UK bitch CC record holder, and the breed record holder UK/Lux Ch Supeta's Ozzy Osbourne; two other littermates are BIS winners too. 'Storm' won the group at Belfast.

Several dogs are tied in third place for Dog of the Year, one of whom is the Pembroke Corgi, Alan and Sarah Matthews' Ch/UK Ch Craigycor Viva La Diva who was BIS at Combined Canine Club international under Harry O'Donoghue (pictured) and at Monkstown, and was a UK group winner.

With one BIS, at Deise, and two RBIS is the German Shorthaired Pointer, Tom and Annie Mervyn's Sh Ch/UK Sh Ch Karlivar Dusky Rose at Tomanipoint.

Top Irish junior handler was Nadine Bermingham, seen here winning at Swords under Fiona Robertson, herself a previous top junior. Also pictured is Mary Davidson of Royal Canin, which has sponsored Swords for many years.

cost of IKC services with clubs finding it more expensive to make use of the NSC; championship certificates now are charged for, as are Celtic Winner certs etc; this practice is standard in some FCI countries, but the Irish are still getting their heads around it.

The IKC run its St Patrick's Celtic Winner championship show the day before the Saint's Day, using our traditional date to hold an event for the general public to encourage them to register their dogs, health-test and microchip them. Many breed clubs took stands and, backed by IKC main sponsor Gain Pet Foods, it was a roaring success and I gather will be repeated.

One benefit was that the NSC was a bit less crowded for the dog show on the 16th. On St Patrick's Day, the crowds from the traditional parade in central Dublin used to flock out to the show; this year, they left the show alone and flocked instead to the 'Discover Dogs' type day.

In October we had the two back-to-back international shows so opportunities for two CACIBs over two days. Both drew good entries, enhanced by a strong band of agility and obedience exhibitors. With Combined Canine and Fermoy at Easter and the May bank holiday weekend respectively, we had four international shows in Ireland in 2013.

In 2004 there will be a 'one off' extra, when Newtownards CC hosts an international to celebrate its ten-year affiliation with the IKC. Other clubs which held shows at this level, gave up in the end and reverted to national events; many reasons were given, expense being one, also the shortage of stewards. However, with the FCI rules regarding judges' payments, the former should not make much of a difference, especially for clubs which traditionally employ judges from abroad, as there are standard expenses which clubs are expected to pay anyhow.

BIS at the second of the IKC international shows was the Golden Retriever, Dan/Int Ch Abinvale Traguardo, owned by Janette Filskov from Denmark and now home in Co Antrim for a while and being campaigned by co-breeder Emma Archibald. He also has a RBIS.

Two ex-junior handlers, Lorna Bermingham and Brendan Beattie, decided to give something back to the sport by raising money for the IKC's chosen charity for 2013, Autism Assistant Dogs Ireland. They 'Cycled the Circuit' during the Munster Circuit week in August and they covered over 550km, up hills and down dales on the country roads of Ireland from Clonmel, via Killarney, Limerick and eventually, saddle-sore and leg-weary, to Tralee, raising over €2,500 with the help of other ex and current members of the Junior Handlers Association of Ireland who had their collecting boxes at every show.

Dog World Annual 2014

UNITED STATES

Bo Bengtson

Easily in the lead as America's number one dog of 2013, the Wire Fox Terrier Gr Ch Afterall Painting The Sky, owned by Victor Malzoni, Torie Steele, Scott and Mary Olund and Diane Ryan.
photo Miguel

Kennel Club focuses on families

Among Sky's successes was BIS at Montgomery County terrier show, the second consecutive victory there, and sixth in all, for handler Gabriel Rangel. Roberta Campbell was the judge and on the right is vice-president Ken Kauffman. Another prestigious win (left) was the 2012 American Kennel Club/Eukanuba National Championship where BIS judge was Edd Embry Bivin.   photos RBT, Andrew Brace

IN SOME ways it was a good year for purebred dogs in America. Year-end figures aren't in yet, of course: there are a couple of months left of 2013 as this is being written, and it also takes several months for the American Kennel Club to add up all the numbers from the vast number of organised activities.

That means we have to rely on 2012 records for exact figures, but it's pretty clear that although the huge entries and massive registration figures of the past are just a memory, at least it seems we're not losing speed as much as some people have feared.

It's difficult not to be impressed by the sheer mass of it all when you look at the most recent AKC year-end figures. There were 1,437 all-breed shows with more than 1.15 million entries, 167 group shows with over 36,000 entries, and 2,432 specialty shows that catered to just one breed with a total of over 121,000 entries.

More than 20,000 regular show champion titles were awarded, with an additional 6,766 grand champion, 201 dual champion and ten triple champion titles. There's no question that dog shows are a popular activity in America.

Of course, simple arithmetic tells you that most shows were pretty small. The average AKC all-breed show now has an entry of just over 800 dogs competing, the average group show has 218 dogs and the average single-breed specialty show just 56 dogs.

All-breed shows were down just over 14,000 entries from the previous year, specialty entries dropped by nearly 3,000, while group shows increased by more than 1,600 entries.

In spite of the lower show figures, the total number of AKC event entries increased from 2,699,339 to 2,793,061, indicating a move from conformation competition towards especially agility trials, which saw a big increase of more than 100,000 entries in just a year. If I have counted right this means that every 15 seconds or so somebody is sending in an entry for some AKC activity...

The 'average' figures don't mean much when the shows vary as

Dog World Annual 2014

In second place among all breeds, and top working dog, Portuguese Water Dog Gr Ch Claircreek Impression De Matisse, handled by Michael Scott to BIS at Farmington Valley under Dr John Ioia. Among his successes was the group at Westminster. He is owned by Milan Lint, Peggy Helming and Donna Gottdecker and you can read more about him in Andrew Brace's feature on the Helmings' Pouch Cove kennel.
photo Ashbey/Dogs in Review

One of the top dogs of all breeds 2013, Robin Greenslade, Luke Norton and Doug Hill's Giant Schnauzer Gr Ch Kenro's Witching Hour, handled by Amy Booth to BIS on the first day of the so-called 'Woofstock' weekend, hosted by Contra Costa KC. Judge Michele Billings, long revered as one of America's top all-rounders, suffered a stroke later in the year and died at the end of October.
photo Holloway/Dogs in Review

In the lead for top sporting dog of 2013, Clumber Spaniel Gr Ch Clussexx Collaboration with Traddles, is US bred but was earlier a top winner in South America. Owners are Wayne Holbrook, Beth Dowd, Missy Capone, Jeane Haverick and Adriana and Patricia Jaramillo.
photo Kayla Bertagnolli

Top toy dog and one of the contenders for number one of all breeds, Miniature Pinscher Gr Ch Marlex Classic Red Glare with owner-handler Armando Angelbello, BIS on the first day of the Ann Arbor KC weekend shows under Patti Widick Neale. Co-owner is Leah Monte.
photo Booth/Dogs in Review

Top hound for the second year in a row, American Foxhound Gr Ch Kiarry's Pandora's Box, bred and owned by handler Lisa Miller, BIS at Macomb KC under Thomas Feneis. Co-owner is Ellen Charles who had two group winners at Westminster, this and the Bichon.
photo Booth/Dogs in Review

much in size as they do, of course. Although dog shows in America aren't nearly as big as they are in Great Britain, we do have some well-supported shows.

The AKC Eukanuba National Championship, held in Orlando, Florida last December, was the biggest show in the US last year, with 3,443 dogs competing. The March shows in Louisville always get good entries: Evansville KC was in second place only to AKC Eukanuba last year with 3,066 dogs at their show, and the previous day's Louisville KC was the year's fourth-largest show with 2,947 dogs.

The New Year's weekend in California ranked high also, with the first of the two KC of Palm Springs shows squeezing into third place with 3,048 dogs, and the Sunday show hosted by the same club followed two steps behind with 2,814 dogs.

Others in list of the top ten shows included the weekend hosted by the Dog Fanciers Association of Oregon in January, with 2,599 and 2,435 dogs at the two shows, respectively, and a couple of Florida shows leading up to the AKC Eukanuba event. All the top 20 shows had more than 2,000 dogs.

Please note that the above numbers indicate dogs present and competing in the official conformation classes only; absentees usually add at least a couple of hundred entries for most shows. The number of absentees must have been particularly high at AKC Eukanuba, as the catalogue lists 4,181 dogs, and the KC of Palm Springs catalogue for its January 2013 show includes 3,499 dogs.

95

Dog World Annual 2014

As we go to press the news is that one of the best shows on the West Coast, Del Valle Dog Club of Livermore in late October, received its highest entry in five years, well over 2,800 dogs. This was in spite of a reshuffle that necessitated cutting the weekend from five to three days. Could it be that fewer shows will result in larger entries at those that remain?

The largest specialty show in America was, as usual, hosted by the amazing Labrador Retriever Club of the Potomac, which had a total of 762 dogs present and competing in the official conformation classes at theiApril show in Maryland.

The Golden Retriever Club of America had 661 dogs at its national specialty, the Collie Club of America 633, followed by Poodle Club of America (459), American Whippet Club (439), American Shetland Sheepdog Association (435), Flat-coated Retriever Club of America and American Boxer Club (430 dogs each), Vizsla Club of America (427) and Bernese Mountain Dog Club of America (408). A large number of other breed clubs had entries in the 200s and 300s.

A specialty show's size isn't necessarily related to the registration figures. Several breeds that are not among the most popular, registration-wise, consistently attract huge entries at their national specialty shows. Again, it's worth pointing out that as the figures above indicate only dogs present in the regular conformation

Top non-sporting dog for the second time (as in 2011) was Toni and Martin Sosnoff's Standard Poodle Gr Ch Brighton Lakeridge Encore, one of several to take her 100th all-breed BIS during 2013.
photo Holloway

The competition for 'best foreign bred' at Santa Barbara KC was won by the British-born Standard Poodle UK Ch/Am Gr Ch Del Zarzoso Salvame from Afterglow, handled by Amy Rutherford under judges Larry Cornelius and Marcelo Veras, both normally active as professional handlers. He is owned by Sloan Barnett and George Lindemann with Mike Gadsby and Jason Lynn.
photo Rodwell

Number one all breeds in 2012, and a top contender in 2013 as well, German Wirehaired Pointer Gr Ch Mt View's Ripsnorter Silvercharm, shown by Phil Booth to BIS at Mount Pleasant Michigan KC, judge Denny Mounce. He won his group at Westminster. Like the probable 2013 Top Dog, he is owned by Victor Malzoni from Brazil.
photo Booth/Dogs in Review

The Swedish import Jack Russell Terrier (in the US known simply as Russell Terrier) Gr Ch Goldsand's Columbus, one of the year's top ten all breeds contenders in the US., shown winning BIS at Kettle Moraine KC under Anne Bolus, handled by Allison Sunderman. Owners are Mark Ulrich and Christina Areskough.
photo Alyssia/Dogs in Review

The first Great Dane to break into the top ten all-breeds rankings in many years, Gr Ch Longo Miller N Lore's Diamond Lil, handled by Laura Coomes to BIS at the second of the two Ann Arbor KC in July. Judge was Debra Thornton. Owners are Tootie Longo, Jay Miller, Lorraine Matherly and Chuck Crawford.
photo Booth/Dogs in Review

classes, the total number of entries received by each club is always much higher.

It's not official, but I'm told the Rhodesian Ridgeback Club of the US has nearly 1,000 entries at its national specialty, which will take place a couple of weeks after this is written. There are reportedly 170 champions entered just in the specials class for best of breed, which may be an all-time record for any breed.

The total number of AKC registrations last year is not known, as those figures are no longer made public. At the peak year in 1992 they exceeded 1.5 million; the last year for which official figures are available was 2010, when 563,611 dogs were registered.

Last year's registration total has been estimated by my press colleagues to around 400,000 dogs, but as far as I understand that's just an educated guess.

There has been a lot of speculation about the reasons for the drop, and suggestions for how to stop it, but no far there have been no conclusive answers. AKC plans on a concerted 2014 media effort to destigmatise responsible breeders and make ownership of purebreds more popular, with special focus on families with kids of eight to 12 years of age and 'empty nesters' – ie those most likely to

In the lead as top herding dog 2013, the Old English Sheepdog Gr Ch Bugaboo's Picture Perfect, started the year with reserve BIS at Westminster while not yet a champion at under two years old. He is shown winning BIS on the second day of 'Woofstoock', Contra Costa KC, under James Reynolds of Canada, shown by breeder and owner Colton Johnson. The youngest Johnson generation, Taylor, Cameron and Dawson, are in front. Co-owners with the family are Ron Scott and Debbie Burke.
photo Holloway/Dogs in Review

Best in Breeders' Showcase at Santa Barbara Kennel Club, the Pembroke Corgis Gr Ch Coventry Allure at Wyndstar and Gr Ch Coventry Swinging On A Star, bred by Bill Shelton, Steve Leyerly, Beckie Williams and Kerry Kirtley. Judges were Augusto Benedicto Santos of the Philippines and Geir Flyckt-Pedersen, previously of Norway and the UK.
photo Holloway

Dog World Annual 2014

BIS at Westminster was the Affenpinscher who had been among the top dogs for two years, Gr Ch Banana Joe v Tani Kazari owned by his Dutch breeder Mieke Cooijmans and Tina Truesdale, and handled by Ernesto Lara. He thereupon retired from the ring. With them are show chairman Tom Bradley, judge Michael Dougherty and president Sean McCarthy.
photo Ashbey

In 2011 the Standard Poodle Ch JaSet's Satisfaction won BIS at the American Kennel Club/Eukanuba National Challenge. A year later he returned to Florida for the Eukanuba World Challenge and won this too. Owned by Beth Harris, Michael Molnar and Jamie Danburg, he was handled by Ann Rairigh. In the line-up are section judge Ramon Podesta, show chairman Ron Menaker, Rafael de Santiago who has since become FCI president, judge Luis Pinto Teixeira and Hounaida Lasry representing the sponsor.
photo Lisa Croft-Elliott

Terrier group winner at Westminster for the second time was the Smooth Fox Gr Ch Slyfox Sneak's A Peek, owned by James Smith and handled by Eddie Boyes – they are co-owners of Britain's top Smooth 2013. Judge was Jay Richardson and Charlton Reynders presented the trophy.
photo Ashbey

Florence Males gave the non-sporting group at Westminster to Ellen Charles, Matt and Paula Abbott, Lori Kornfeld and Mary and Kathie Vogel's Bichon Gr Ch Vogelflight's Honor to Pillowtalk shown by Lisa Bettis. He is a son of former UK Top Dog Ch/UK Ch Paray's I Told You So.
photo Ashbey

add a dog to their family – as well as legislators, breeders, vets and the 700,000 dog lovers who follow AKC on Facebook.

The annual Top Dog competition has, as usual, been the subject of much debate, but it's a little bit like the weather – everybody complains about it but nobody does anything about it, and sometimes it seems the effort would be equally futile.

Suggestions for introducing some kind of limitation on the campaigns have been floated, but I wonder if American exhibitors could accept any system that is different than the current, simple 'one point per defeated competitor'.

That basic premise is the reason the top dogs must be campaigned so relentlessly, often competing at 150–200 shows in a year. It's clearly impossible for a dog to get even close to the top spot without heavy sponsorship. The fact that both the dogs and their handlers still manage to come up smiling is a wonder. Just what it costs to special a dog at top level is seldom made public, but the annual cost is certainly in the hundreds of thousands of dollars.

There are still a couple of hundred shows to go before the year is over, but it looks pretty certain that the same owner will take home the Top Dog spot again, with a different dog. Victor Malzoni of Brazil is the man who made possible the outstanding show career of 2012's number one all breeds winner, and he is also one of the owners of the clear favourite for 2013.

Last year's winner was the German Wirehaired Pointer **Gr Ch Mt View's Ripsnorter Silvercharm**, and this year the Wire Fox Terrier **Gr Ch Afterall Painting The Sky** is already more than 10,000 points ahead of anyone else, which means something really drastic would have to happen for her not to win. Sky's many wins in October have not been counted yet, but they include BIS at the Montgomery Terrier classic, by far the country's top group show with nearly 2,000 terriers entered, as well as at two of the preceding all-breed shows.

Sky, who started out in 2012 as top terrier and was BIS at AKC Eukanuba last December, was bred in the US by Betty Seaton and Al Pertuit, whose Fyrewyre kennel bred both parents. In fact, Sky is, as far as I can see, all American-bred for several generations. Further back in her pedigree there are some imports from France and Belgium, and even further back you will find some Blackdale and Louline dogs as well as Ch Galsul Excellence, Ch Sylair Special Edition and Ch Forchlas Cariad.

Incidentally, Sky's handler Gabriel Rangel has also taken the number one all breeds award before, with the Scottish Terrier Ch Roundtown Mercedes of Maryscot in 2009. They followed that up with BIS at Westminster the next year, and I'm sure the pressure is on to see if Sky is going to be able to match that achievement.

Incidentally, as BIS at Westminster 2013 went to the Affenpinscher **Ch Banana Joe v Tani Kazari**, handled by Ernesto Lara, it should be clear that there are strong influences in the American dog sport these days both from the 'old world' (Joe was born in the Netherlands) and 'south of the border': both Gabriel and Ernesto moved to the US from their native Mexico.

Speaking of imports, although the British influence isn't as strong as it once was, at least two British-born dogs have done extremely well. The Pekingese **Gr Ch Yakee Easily Persuaded** and the Standard Poodle **UK Ch/Gr Ch Del Zarzoso Salvame from Afterglow** are both among the top dogs in their respective groups. The Pekingese has won ten BIS and 43 groups, the Standard six BIS and 21 groups – and the year is far from over yet.

Finally, what are the odds that there would be a direct link between the last two BIS winners at AKC Eukanuba? Not much of a chance. The former was the black Standard Poodle **Gr Ch JaSet's Satisfaction** ('London', who also won the World Challenge at the 2012 show), and the latter was the previously mentioned Wire Fox Terrier, Sky. Well, London's dam was bred by Mary and Scott Olund, Poodle breeders who also got a Wire Fox Terrier as a birthday co-ownership gift from Diane Ryan as a potential show dog and then house dog – and that Wire Fox Terrier is now well on her way to being number one all breeds in the US for 2013!

It's nice to know that when her high-profile show career is over, Sky will go back to a quiet life as the Olund/Ryan house dog.

Dog World Annual 2014

CANADA
A bright beacon of hope

Mike Macbeth

FINALLY! There is light at the end of tunnel, and that bright beacon of hope is named Lance Novak, the new executive director of the Canadian Kennel Club.

For the past decade, the membership had lost faith in the organisation due to a myriad of problems and conflicts. After the resignation of a secretive chief executive officer; after the hiring and subsequent firing within the year of yet another administrator (the lofty title of CEO having been downgraded to ED) the CKC's board of directors finally found the right man to put the club back on track.

It has been a long time coming. But the initiatives put in place by the new ED and the new, excellent communication between the staff and the membership bodes well for the future. The financial situation has improved immensely and staff morale is revitalised.

Along with several other innovations, Mr Novak quickly instituted a toll-free telephone line, an important service in a country that is 6,000 miles wide, and one that the membership had been craving. His priority is service, and many small but vital changes are being made to improve client relations. Among his many talents – he listens. And he understands that the membership is the life force of the club.

The CKC website is being revamped. When completed it is expected to be more efficient, more user-friendly and of more interest to the general public. Breeders are already using the website for litter and puppy registrations in greater numbers. Online registrations have increased from 30 per cent in 2009 to over 50 per cent today, demonstrating the need for electronic commerce. The CKC is committed to a greater reliance on the website for all services, including the costly referendums.

Although Mr Novak is able to make significant internal changes, he is still hampered by the peculiar relationship

Almost unbeatable in the Top Dog list is the West Highland White Terrier NZ/Can/Am Ch Whitebriar Jaw Dropper. An import from the famous Whitebriar kennel in New Zealand, 'JD' arrived in Canada in the midst of the 2012 show season. Although that was only meant to be a warm-up year, within six months he skyrocketed into the top terrier and number five all breed standings.

For 2013 the decision was made to show him all over Canada, an immense country spanning more than 9,000km, so people could see him. To date, in 2013 he has 56 BIS, 97 groups and four specialty BIS. He has already defeated 15,790 dogs.

Originally the goal was to break the Canadian record for BIS for a Westie. That record of 35 was obliterated in May. JD also shattered the Canadian record for most points accumulated by a Westie in a single year.

Owner June Fraser and professional handler David Gignac then set their sights on the world BIS record for a Westie, which is 82. JD currently has 72.

A highlight was attending Crufts 2013, at the suggestion of breeder Maureen Murphy. "Little did we know how complex and expensive it was to get a dog from Canada into the UK," says David. "The entry was one of the most cosmopolitan in years. I am always nervous each time I go into the ring, but I do not ever recall being that nervous before."

Specialist Dot Britten awarded him the CC and BOB and he was shortlisted in the group. "It's a memory I shall never forget", declares David.

Judge pictured is Deb Graffman.
photo Cathy French

Currently number two is the Affenpinscher Can/Am/Int/Dutch/Cro Ch Champagne Charly v Tani Kazari. 'Charly', a winner in Amsterdam and at the Bundessieger in Germany, was bred in Holland by Mieke Coojimans, breeder of the 2013 Westminster winner, Banana Joe. They share the same sire.

Charly came to Canada at the end of 2012 to be co-owned by Dr Michael Tipple and shown by professional handler Allison Foley. He made his 2013 debut by winning two groups and a RBIS on his first weekend out. Since then he has amassed 25 BIS, a specialty best and 64 groups.

Among his most memorable awards was BIS at Canada's largest and most prestigious dog show, the Purina National, which included a cheque for $10,000! They are pictured with judge Juan Naveda Carrero. Once his career in Canada is completed, he will return to Viruch Phrukwattanakul, his co-owner in Thailand.
photo Cathy French

The Yorkshire Terrier Gr ChEx Am/Can Ch NicNak's Second To None (pictured in the garden at St Aubrey Elsdon) is currently third top dog. In Canada, to date, he has 17 BIS (13 this year), four RBIS, 95 groups (77 in 2013) and four toy dog BIS.

'Newt' also won the national specialty in 2012 and is closing in on the Canadian breed BIS record.

Newt finished his American championship in two weekends, winning three groups from the classes.

Owned by Gail Webster, he is shown by professional handler Lynda Torrance.

Newt has become good friends with the Westie, the runaway Top Dog in Canada. When the Westie ventures east into Newt's territory, they can be seen together, walking side by side at the end of the show, the Yorkie in his wrappers and pyjamas. They are not always particularly polite together in the ring, however. On one occasion, both dogs took an immediate dislike to a certain Chow, and embarrassed their handlers by barking incessantly and misbehaving uncontrollably. Neither won BIS that day!

between the salaried executive director and the 12-member board of directors, who are not remunerated but wield the ultimate power. Ideally the board sets policy and the ED implements those policies.

The 20,000 members who had lost respect for their club can only hope that this charismatic, bright and thoughtful new energy will be given enough responsibility to set in motion those significant initiatives that will bring renewed pride in the organisation.

However, there still are glitches to deal with. After several years in hiatus, the CKC made an arrangement with Canada's national newspaper, the *Globe and Mail*, to produce and print the once revered Dogs in Canada magazine and Annual.

Although the first edition was not produced by dog experts and was not widely praised by the membership, it is hoped that this new joint venture will lure advertisements by breeders and exhibitors back from other dog publications.

The board has approved several new dog show initiatives designed to increase revenues. The baby puppy class is one of three new classes the CKC is encouraging show giving clubs to offer. This class for three to six-month-old puppies is optional, and unofficial, as are the new veterans and altered classes.

Also, effective January 1, 2013 the CKC introduced the select dog and select bitch award, mirroring the American KC's initiative to entice more champions back into the ring for a grand championship title. The CKC now has two higher championship designations available: grand champion and grand champion excellent, the latter of which requires a best in show or best in specialty plus a performance title.

There is still much confusion among the membership over all these new, constantly changing rules and revamped systems.

Canadians had cause to celebrate when the Petit Basset Griffon Vendeen **Ch Soletrader Peek A Boo** won BIS at Crufts, as 'Jilly' is co-owned with Sara Robertson by Wendy Doherty of Auriga PBGVs from Ontario, Canada. The Robertsons and Dohertys have co-operated for several years.

Jilly's grandsire **Am/Can Ch Soletrader Bjorn Borg** was number ten all breeds in Canada in 2010 and also won BOB at the American National that year; he is currently doing well in Europe.

Another successful dog of note was the 2013 Westminster working group winner, **Ch Claircreek Impression De Matisse**,

Currently fourth is the Standard Poodle Am Gr Ch/Can Gr ChEx Vetset Kate Winsit CGN. Kate has been Canada's top Poodle all varieties for three years. In 2011 she was top non-sporting dog and in 2012 she was number ten all breeds. She won the variety at Westminster, twice was award of merit at the Poodle Club of America and took BOB at the Poodle Club of Canada. So far she has 42 BIS (19 in 2013), 224 groups (82 this year) and five specialty BIS. She is now among the top all-breed BIS-winning bitches in Canadian history.

Kate is owned and bred by Dr Elly Holowaychuk of Vetset Poodles and handled by Allison Foley, who is particularly known for Poodles.

Campaigning two dogs in the top five can be a nerve-wracking situation for a professional handler. What does she do when both dogs win their groups? "I try to take the dog into the BIS ring that I feel has the best chance of winning. But when showing two dogs that between them have already won more than 150 groups this year it is really difficult to guess which one that might be."

She is fortunate to have two excellent young assistants. When both the Affenpinscher and the Standard Poodle win their groups, Kate is often piloted by Canada's top junior handler, 17-year-old Colton O'Shea, who represented Canada in the international final at Crufts in 2013 and will be returning in 2014.

In addition, Allison is mentoring 15-year-old Katie McGinn who went reserve to Colton at the zone finals, and is regularly winning BIS for the Foley team. In a pinch Allison relies on her husband Todd, who successfully shows their own dogs.
photo Todd Foley

whose breeder is Donna Gottdecker, also of Ontario, Canada. The Portuguese Water Dog has been awarded more than 50 BIS.

Right now Canada's Top Dog competition echoes last year with one dog dominating. The 2013 leader, a New Zealand-bred West Highland White Terrier is almost unable to be caught, having twice the number of points as the second place Affenpinscher.

Last year, the black American Cocker Spaniel defeated a total of 16,208 dogs, more than half again that of Karelian Bear Dog Ch TsarShadows I Speak Of War who was second with 9,534 points.

But the race for third, fourth and fifth this year is considerably more fluid, as less than 200 points separate those three contenders. One BIS can change the order.

Currently in fifth place, the Afghan Hound Am/Can Gr Ch Polo's Air Force is the only dog in the top five handled by his breeder/owner. Although he had a successful puppy career in both the US and Canada, owner Lorianne Amadeo kept him home to mature while she showed another of her well known dogs, Am Gr/Can Sup Ch Polo's The Aviator.

In 2012 she entered 'Captain' at two specialties, both of which he won. He began being shown regularly at the beginning of 2013 in both the US and Canada, winning and placing in groups in both countries. But by early summer, when the decision was made to campaign exclusively in Canada, Captain's career blossomed. At the time of writing, in his first full year of showing, he has won 19 BIS and 53 groups.

His first son took winners dog at the US Afghan Hound National, completing his title. Although very young, his offspring have earned several US and Canadian championships.

Am Ch/Can Gr Ch Mario N Beechwood's Midnight Express CGC, CGN was Canada's Top Dog for 2012. 'Ace' won a record 57 BIS and 112 groups.

Bred and owned by Mark and Pam Ragusa and shown by Marlene Ness, Ace broke every record in Canada that had previously been set by an American Cocker Spaniel. He finished the year by defeating 16,208 dogs, and is the first of his breed to achieve Top Dog status in Canada.

In the US, he has won eight specialties and a BIS to make him currently America's number one Black Cocker in both breed and all-breed systems. He is pictured winning BIS under Frank Sabella.

Dog World Annual 2014

NORWAY

Espen Engh

Restrictions on the way out?

Ch Jet's Just Take Me Home Tonight, owned by Espen Engh and Åge Gjetnes, is currently in the lead for Dog of the Year in Norway and will represent Norway in the 2013 Eukanuba World Challenge in Florida. The Greyhound is the 36th championship show BIS winner bred over ten generations by Espen and his late mother Kari Engh.
photo Ove Larsen

PUREBRED dogs are very popular in Norway and have been for decades. Compared to a human population of just five million people, the almost 100,000 members under the umbrella of the Norwegian Kennel Club (NKK) is quite an impressive figure, as are entries of close to 6,000 dogs at our Oslo international winter show. There are many internationally famous Norwegian breeders, too numerous to mention.

However, and perhaps less fortunately, Norway as a dog country may be even more famous for our expatriates, including many well known breeders and judges. Most remarkably, half the all-breeds judges approved by the NKK reside abroad.

The ban on certain breeds has been

Helge Kvivesen won Dog of the Year 2012 with his homebred Kerry Blue Terrier Int Ch Shyloch Navigator to Edrus. In 2013 his half-brother Ch Shyloch Obama, both ex the great brood bitch Int Ch Shyloch Karaoke, is in with a chance to become Dog of the Year and is currently in third position. Obama has won BIS at international championship shows in both Norway and Denmark.

Ch Antudor Accidentally In Love is co-owned by Rita Wilberg with breeder Debbie Neilson in Australia. The natural bobtailed Pembroke Corgi won his Australian Grand Championship with two BIS at a young age and has continued his winning ways in Scandinavia and on the Continent, including winning BIS at Liege, Belgium. He is currently runner-up on the Dog of the Year list in Norway and is pictured winning the group at Rogaland under Per Kristian Andersen with handler Julie Wilberg.
photo Roger Sjølstad

strongly opposed by the Norwegian dog community. Currently it includes American Staffordshire Terriers, Dogos Argentinos, Czech Wolfdogs and Fila Brasileiros, the rather undefined Pit Bull Terriers and all dogs that can be suspected of being a mix of any of these. A regulation makes it possible for the authorities to add new breeds in a rather cursory way.

It is up to the police to detect and retain suspected dogs, and the police also have the authority to put them down.

Since its introduction to the Norwegian Dog Act some ten years ago, the NKK has consistently fought the ban, including supporting the owner of a suspected dog practically and financially during a court case. However the case was lost, and the dog was put down. So until recently the fight against the breed ban has met with little success. However during 2013, some positive signals have been noted.

First, the Ministry of Justice, in charge of the Act, asked the NKK to report on the issue, highlighting the consequences of the breed ban and some other paragraphs. A factual report was published in 2013 and covered most aspects, including the measures in other countries. Perhaps not surprisingly it concludes that the breed ban should be lifted.

On the same theme, the Ministry finally gave official permission for the otherwise banned breeds to be temporarily imported in conjunction with the FCI European show near Oslo in September 2015. So for this one event only Amstaffs, Dogos, Czech Wolfdogs and Filas are welcome to be imported and shown, but under quite strict restrictions and on the proviso that they are re-exported immediately after the show.

The show expects entries of up to 200 dogs of these breeds combined. Hopefully all will go well, and if so, the resulting positive experience may pave the way for permanently lifting the breed ban.

During 2013 the NKK was also granted a dispensation from our Animal Welfare Act to allow dogs who have been legally docked and cropped in their home country to be shown at this 2015 event only. This was in many ways a groundbreaker as showing docked and cropped dogs has been illegal in Norway for decades.

Consequently for the first time in more than 60 years all dogs of all FCI recognised breeds may be shown. This has not met with universal approval, however, as some exhibitors fear that the docked and cropped guests may have an unfair advantage.

As for travelling with dogs to and from Norway, the requirement for a rabies antibody test was abolished a couple of years ago. However, treatment against echinococcus remains and now has to be administered and attested by a vet. From 2013 this also includes dogs from Sweden.

It was expected that this would markedly reduce the number of Swedish and Finnish dogs who enter shows in Norway, but that

Dog World Annual 2014

The Lhasa Apso Int Ch Stings Velour In Black To Matrix, owned by Birgitte Sperle and bred in Sweden, has dominated the hotly contested veteran finals at the international shows and is likely to become top veteran all breeds.
photo Roger Sjølstad

The Larhjelm Wire Dachshunds, bred by Lars Hjelmtvedt (left), are in a comfortable lead for Breeder of the Year in Norway. One of his breeders groups, consisting of champions who at have also been successful at hunting tests, is pictured winning best breeders group at the Oslo international summer show.
photo Roger Sjølstad

The American Cocker Spaniel Statesman Miss Divine, owned by Vibeke Paulsen, is pictured winning BIS at the Oslo international summer show under breeder-judge Annika Ulltveit-Moe. Miss Divine is among Norway's Top Dogs of 2013.
photo Roger Sjølstad

The Newfoundland Ch Ohoi's Jolly Good Fellow, owned by Sølvi and Ståle Nordtveit, qualified for his champion title with his 13th CC and has won consistently throughout 2013, including three groups at Norwegian Kennel Club international shows.

The Portuguese Water Dog Int Ch Isostar's St Snoopdogg has been a consistent winner over many years and sports a long list of winner titles, including World Winnern. He is one of several highly successful PWDs owned by Runi Kristiansen who won BIS with another at Dogs4All 2012. Snoopdog is pictured winning under senior all-rounder Marit Sunde. He is co-owned with Terje Kristiansen and with breeder Laila Erlandsen.
photo Roger Sjølstad

At less than two years old, Ukkonen av Vintervidda is too young to become a champion in Norway, but has already won more than any Finnish Lapphund outside Finland and is among Norway's Top Dogs for 2013. Owned and bred by Christian Lauluten, he has won several breed club shows as well as BOB at the FCI European Show.

does not seem to have been the case so far. Scandinavian dog people are likely to travel whatever obstacles they may face, and dog shows in Norway seem to be almost immune to the recession.

The NKK arranges 11 annual big international shows, all over the country. Entries have held up or increased slightly at most of them. **Norway covering vast distances,** there are a number of multi-group, multi-breed or single breed club championship shows somewhere in the country every weekend.

The first woman chairman of the NKK, Siv Sandø, was re-elected at the November 2012 annual general meeting. For the second time she defeated an opposing candidate from within her own board.

NKK is a club of clubs, consisting of member clubs as opposed to individual members. Within its umbrella are 225 clubs with a total membership of almost 100,000 making NKK one of the largest voluntary organisations in Norway.

The most important political changes within the sport during recent years include increased democracy and involvement of the member clubs in the decision-making processes. New rules and regulations, or any major changes, as well as all strategies are sent out to hearings throughout the organisation. These receive feedback and inspire suggestions for improvement.

The down side can be that the processes may sometimes be rather drawn out and inconclusive. An example is the much awaited and much needed revision of our show system, aiming to regulate the number of CCs available in individual breeds. After a couple of years of discussions within a fast-track working group, its report was published in 2012. The working group proposed marked changes with a significant reduction in the number of CCs available per breed and breed classes without CCs at championship shows, much like the British system.

The proposals met with a very mixed response. More than a year later they are still being discussed.

A new strategy for the NKK's information technology has also been sent out on a hearing. This follows a rather confusing decision at the 2012 AGM to spend practically all the saved-up funds of the club over a period of three years on improving our computer services. Both clubs and individuals expect continuously updated and improved services, and not all requirements can be met at a reasonable cost. The board has asked for input from all member clubs to help prioritising among vastly different needs while making sure that the resources are well spent.

Plans for the FCI European show at the Norwegian Trade Fair Centre in Lillestrøm, between Oslo International airport and the city centre, on September 4-6, 2015 seem to be well on their way. There are quite a few British judges, rather unusual for a top FCI event, but the Norwegian dog sport has always been inspired by the UK, and breed type in many breeds is closer to the UK than to Continental Europe.

The list is composed of famous breeders and top judges, but not of as many FCI dignitaries as usual, which has not met with their approval, but possibly the approval of the exhibitors.

This will no doubt be the largest show ever in Norway with an estimated entry of 13,000 dogs, half of whom are expected to be local. The venue already hosts our final show of the year, the annual Dogs4All extravaganza in November.

To train for the 2015 event, the 2014 Dogs4All show will include two FCI international shows in one weekend.

The Kerry Blue Terrier **Int Ch Shylock Navigator to Edrus** was Norway's Dog of the Year in 2012, bred and shown by Helge Kvivesen.

Top breeder in 2012 was the internationally famous **Tangetoppen** Pugs owned by Elisabeth Olsen. Top Stud dog was the Dwarf Poodle **Int Ch Sjarmtrollet's Elleville Drømmer** and top veteran the Pharaoh Hound **Int Ch Antefa's Q-Lahn**.

Dog World Annual 2014

FINLAND

Report and photographs by Paula Heikkinen-Lehkonen

Urban Finns lose interest in hunting

ALTHOUGH registration and entry figures have gone down in many countries, Finland seems to be an exception. The interest in pedigree dogs and shows is very strong and doesn't look like weakening.

More and more families have two or three dogs instead of just one, and they like to do something with them. Most of our show dogs live as members of the family, and many of them also compete in agility, obedience or field trials.

However, the emphasis in the dog sports is changing. Traditionally hunting and hunting dogs have played a major role in our pedigree dog scene, but now other dog sports are becoming more and more popular, and hunting clubs are worried because their hobby doesn't seem to attract young people any more.

Most people live in the cities nowadays, and the majority of dog people are women – especially young women. Hunting is just not their thing. The Finnish Hound, which has always been the most popular breed in the country, has lost its leading position to the Labrador Retriever and German Shepherd Dog.

Junior handling competitions are very popular. Hundreds of teenagers, most of them girls, take part in this. There can be over a hundred very skilful competitors at the big shows. The most successful has been **Sanna Mari Martikainen**, who won the European Championship at Geneva in August with her Havanese.

About 50,000 dogs are registered yearly, which is a lot for a nation of five million people. However, the demand for puppies, especially small companion dogs, is greater than the good breeders can produce. Smuggling and importing rescued street dogs is a big problem, which worries the Kennel Club, the vets and customs officers.

Puppies from good breeders are quite expensive. Some misled credulous people think that they can get a similar puppy but pay less when they buy elsewhere. Usually they wake up too late, when it appears that the puppy has faked papers, may be ill, full of worms and other parasites.

It is also understandable that an animal lover will feel sorry

At the time of writing, the final results of the Top Dog list haven't been decided. There are still some big important shows to come. So far the situation looks like that the top dogs of 2012 have continued their winning ways and dominate the scene. This is no wonder, because they are quite young and there is no reason to retire them yet. The Afghan Hound Int Ch Agha Djari's Blue Blood, owned by Mikko Ylitalo, Michaela Ståhlberg and Anita Hirvelä, is in the lead, but only just.

The Smooth Fox Terrier Int Ch Texforrier Get Off My Cloud, owned by Molli Nyman, Sari Laitinen and Janice Campbell, and the Lhasa Apso Int Ch Chic Choix Cleopatra Eurydice, owned by Piia Laurila-Helistölä and handled by Sanna Kopola-Hirsimäki, are not far behind the Afghan and pushing hard.

Currently in fourth place is the American Cocker Spaniel Very Vigie Freezing-in-Finland, owned by Sanna Vartiainen and Tanja Elo.

Among the breeders Tanja Elo's Fabeslfee American Cockers have been extremely successful. This is amazing, because this young breeder has so far had only two litters old enough to be shown, but with enthusiasm and good co-operation with the puppy owners she has managed to show good and even breeders' groups at many shows. Outi Lius with her Wave Seeker's Newfoundlands and Teija Salmi-Aalto with her Edendane Great Danes have also been placed in the breeders' finals on many occasions.

New names in the top dog list are are the Petit Basset Griffon Vendéen Int Ch Nightdream Ricky Martin, owned by Kristiina Bergström, and the Grand Int Ch Minskuhoff's Grand Olivier, Eija Kunnari. Other contenders include the young Keeshond Ch Eerondaali Nightwish, the Pembroke Corgi Ch Haywire's Don't Say A Word and the Rottweiler Int Ch Rexlean Nox.

Outi Lius and Erkki Selin's Newfoundland Int Ch Wave Seeker's Fly Me To The Moon and Riikka and Ulla Björkman's Smooth Dachshund Int Ch Unita's The King have had another good year.

The top veteran list is topped by the Flat-coated Retriever Int Ch Toffedreams Scuff'n Puff, owners Viveca Lahokoski and Riitta Niemelä, and the Finnish Lapphund Int Ch Lecibsin Macce, Taina Miettinen. The Saluki Int Ch El-Ubaid's Kalimantan has done well, not only as a veteran but also in the group finals.

Winner of the European Championship in junior handling, judged by Catarina Molinari at the European Show in Geneva, was Finland's Sanna Mari Martikainen with her Havanese who was also second in the group.

for the abandoned dogs in other countries and wants to give a loving home to at least one or two miserable creatures. However, importing these rescued street dogs from Romania or Spain becomes quite expensive and they are usually unpredictable and unsocialised and cause problems. The vets fear that they might bring illnesses and parasites which have been unknown over here.

Finland will host the FCI World Show in 2014. There is no doubt that it will be a great show.

The last shows of 2013, the three days of Helsinki Winner Shows in December, will serve as a dress rehearsal to the World Show. On the first day the titles of Helsinki Winner are available, the next day the Nordic Winner titles and the last day Finnish Winner. The whole mammoth event is called Dog2013. It looks as if these shows will be bigger than ever. So the World Show will be a piece of cake after this!

Dog World Annual 2014

SWEDEN
Dan Ericsson

Continued focus on health

To say that focus has been on increased health in pedigree dogs in Sweden, and indeed most of the canine world, over the last years, is by no means an exaggeration.

Big steps have been taken by many kennel clubs to lessen the effects of indiscriminate breeding and judging of certain breeds, and Sweden has been one of the forerunners to improve this situation. This work has been monitored skilfully by Dr Göran Bodegård and his committee at the Swedish Kennel Club (SKK) and has attracted interest internationally.

We would like to believe that this increased focus on exaggerations has created an awareness of possible problems in certain breeds, but also sounder dogs overall now that the scheme has been in use over some time.

Late this autumn, the SKK's strategy and document pertaining to this important issue was also largely adopted by the other Scandinavian kennel clubs – a large step forward for pedigree dogs in the Nordic countries and one of which Sweden is very proud.

A well attended annual meeting of the SKK in September saw some changes on the General Committee and consequently also on some of the sub-committees, most noticeably of the Judges' Committee, now chaired by Mats Stenmark who has replaced Carl-Gunnar Stafberg of Bombax Border Terrier fame, a long-standing committee member of the SKK. Chairman Nils-Erik Åhmansson has been on the woolsack for a long time, and he was once again re-elected unanimously.

It is heartening to see that the AGMs of the SKK are calm and sensible meetings reflected in the positive role of the club, which is making its presence felt to a large extent with government issues and other official matters where dogs and dog ownership are involved.

On a sadder note, registrations are down somewhat. There has been no drastic decline, luckily, and one can only hope that this trend will be broken soon. Entries at most shows have also dropped somewhat, most noticeably at some of our largest and most established all-breed championship shows. This does seem to be a trend in many other European countries and is possibly the result of a leaner budget for most people.

Every effort is made by our various clubs to attract large entries at future shows and we welcome every suggestion to achieve this goal. For the future of pedigree dogs, it is invaluable to see and assess the result of previous matings and generations but also to assess the present state of each breed – dog shows' true and most important function, sometimes forgotten amid glitz and glamour which may be appealing at times, but nonetheless are of inferior importance to each breed's continued progress which is helped by dogs being shown to prospective breeders and custodians of pedigree dogs.

Some would undoubtedly argue that all is well in the dogdom of Sweden; there are aspects that could possibly be improved, but overall I believe that we have more to be proud of in the Swedish dog world than the opposite. The SKK, Swedish dogs and their breeders are a major force in dogs all over the world, and one can only hope that this trend will continue.

Each year, the celebrated 'Big' Stockholm show in December attracts thousands of dogs and many enthusiasts from all over Scandinavia, but now also from many other parts of the world. The overall entry for the 2012 show had dropped a little from previous years, but the quality of the BIS line-up was extraordinary.

The honour of selecting BIS was given to the popular Spanish all-rounder Carlos Fernanadez-Renau and there had been much speculation as to whether he would approve of the big winning black Standard Poodle Ch Aleph's American Idol, bred in the USA, owned by Elizabeth Brown but campaigned in Sweden by Charlotte Sandell of Huffish Poodle fame, should he be in the line-up for BIS. This proved to be the case and yes, Carlos did approve and made the internationally acclaimed dog BIS to thunderous applause.

Idol later also won BIS at the Poodle Club of America show thus emphasising his outstanding quality also showing that great dogs can win on both sides of the pond.

His win at Stockholm also made him Sweden's Top Dog 2012, beating the big winning Wire Fox Terrier Ch Crispy Legacy, owned, bred and shown by Agneta Åström, by a small margin. He is now enjoying great success in the US handled by Ernesto Lara, but will eventually return to Sweden.

The final competition of the year for the breeders stakes also proved to be a nail-biting battle between two of Sweden's renowned kennels, Badavie and Almanza, with the former ending the year as Top Breeder 2012, heartily congratulated by the breeders and owners of the Almanzas.
photo Lillemor Böös

Dog World Annual 2014

Each year Sweden's many regional kennel clubs hold many all-breed championship shows all over our oblong country. Some argue that the sport would benefit from fewer shows, but this is a debate which has been ongoing for a long time and no changes have been noted so far.

Therefore, we also have a fairly large number of BIS-winners to report at the end of the year, and more individual dogs have won the supreme dog show award this year than in a long time.

The most consistent winner has so far been the Australian Shepherd Ch Northbay's Rock On Summit, bred in the US and owned by Gisli Omarsson. He has been at the top throughout the year, but as we come to the end of the year he is closely challenged for the top spot by the Affenpinscher Ch Velvet Dandy's D'Artagnan, owned and bred by Veronica Lange. This enchanting breed has really made its mark with remarkable success almost everywhere in the world. The two remaining shows of the year, Växjö and Stockholm, will decide the eventual outcome.
photos Lillemor Böös

No reader of this column in previous years can have failed to notice the kennel name Almanza, synonymous with top quality Flat-coated Retrievers, bred and owned by Ragnhild Uhlin and Susanne Karlström. Once again, their dogs are in the lead for top breeders in Sweden, a feat which they have achieved for more years than I can remember!

To be top breeder once in any country is a wonderful achievement but to repeat this several times over a relatively long period is something most breeders could only dream of. The success of the Almanzas is therefore outstanding and their dogs have also had a major influence on the breed worldwide.

A close second at the time of writing in this prestigious competition are the famous Badavie Salukis of Marie Brandén and Maria Nordin, another internationally renowned kennel which shares the fame and repeated success of the Almanzas in the very hotly contested breeders' stakes in Sweden over a long period.
photo Lillemor Böös

This parkland is the beautiful site for Osterby show.
photo Lillemor Böös

Dog World Annual 2014

DENMARK

Vibeke Knudsen, the Danish Kennel Club

The Standard Poodle Ch Abica's Miles Ahead, owned by Mikael Nilsson, Kirsten Nielsen and Kathy Arnold, was Denmark's Top Dog of 2012 and in the lead for 2013. At Crufts he was BOB and group 3.
photo C Barrett

Here I come... Int Ch Bubbleton Feel The Spirit, owned by Jesper Ravn and Klaus Andersen, is – apart from being a top show dog – also spreading joy at a nursing home. She is currently number two all breeds in Denmark.
photo Mediehuset Wiegaarden

2012 was a really good show year in Denmark and 2013's shows appear to be even better attended.
At this year's last show date on November 3 more than 4,000 dogs have been entered. This is a record number of participants at an ordinary international show in Denmark without special titles. Nice to end the year this way!

The Dog of the Year 2012 in Denmark, the Standard Poodle **Abica's Miles Ahead**, is again leading the annual competition. As Miles is not registered with the Danish Kennel Club (DKK), but in Sweden (he is Swedish/American owned), he cannot – due to new rules – represent Denmark in the Eukanuba World Challenge in Orlando. It will therefore be an excellent Danish-bred dog, the Hungarian Puli **Bubbleton Feel The Spirit**, who will be showing the Danish colours in Orlando.

The positive co-operation with the DKK's main sponsor, Eukanuba, has been extended for a new three-year period. The co-operation with the Swedish pet insurance company Agria is also progressing favourably.

Sponsorships become well run when the parties can make use of each other's knowledge and competence for the benefit of the dog owners, the dog sport – and not least the dogs. "We think that this is the case with these two top professional companies," declares the DKK president for many years, Jørgen Hindse.

Many rumours have circulated about Danish dog legislation. The presentation in certain parts of the media – and not least certain parts of the social media – has given the impression that there is a risk that the police could for no particular reason take one's dog and require it to be put down for a small bite or just because it is a mixed breed. This is fortunately not the case!

Only in cases where a dog assaults and savages another dog or a human does the law comes into effect. And only in cases where a dog looks like one of the 13 forbidden breeds, or it appears that there are other things that connect the dog in question with a forbidden breed, can the police require documentation of legitimate ancestry from the owner.

At the time of writing the law is being revised in the Danish Parliament. The DKK wants the prohibition of FCI-recognised breeds removed, but maintained only when it concerns pit bulls and dogs that may contain pit bull – not least out of consideration for the safety of other dogs.

Moreover, we wish that no legal dog can be put down after a biting incident without the circumstances of the episode having been evaluated by a special dog expert. This way one can make sure that a dog that has bitten in self-defence – eg because a loose dog has approached the dog while it was kept on a leash – will not be put down.

In the Parliament there seems to be wide support for the idea of having a special dog expert to evaluate the incidents, whereas discussion of the extent of the prohibition against breeds is still going on. It is not suggested that any new breeds are forbidden.

But the conclusion is that if you have a legal, well behaved dog, Denmark is a fantastic dog country with wonderful possibilities to run unleashed – not least at our splendid beaches in the winter half of the year. So the DKK is looking forward to welcoming many foreign dog guests in 2014.

POLAND

Janusz Opara

New faces take over

2013 has been a year of some significant changes. The General Assembly held every fourth year turned out to be quite tempestuous. Our chairman of 20 years decided not to stand for re-election which triggered substantial changes not only in the main board of the Polish Kennel Club but also in satellite bodies like the Breeding Committee, Disciplinary Committee and Auditing Commission with many new faces taking over.

Andrzej Mania, our retiring chairman, was unanimously created honorary chairman, the first time this title has been awarded. During his service the club hosted the FCI European Show in 2000 and the World Show in 2006, both perfectly organised and putting our country in a much higher position within the FCI.

Our newly elected chairman, Jan Gajewski, is a vet who has been involved in our organisation over many decades. Formerly a breeder of Great Danes and Bulldogs, he has served as a member and leader of many canine bodies. He is a multi-group judge with molosser breeds being his specialty.

We will watch him and his team with great expectations and anticipate their abilities will meet and match the challenges of today's dog world.

Our show calendar has been overcrowded with shows to the extent one wonders who might be still tempted into entering and picking up all these titles on offer. As predicted by those longer in the fancy, the result is a significant fall in entries but the established shows managed very well. Smaller and newer clubs which can hardly break even with their far too moderate entries will have adjust to the new economic situation.

The hot issue has been the idea of allowing neutered dogs a show career, though separate from entire exhibits, with their own classes and titles.

While well travelled judges and exhibitors support the idea, those less ubiquitous have many objections, the main being that neuters are of no use for breeding.

As our show system has always been instrumental in achieving breeding rights, many people cannot see the two aspects of the dog scene separately. There are however more and more dog lovers whose conditions do not enable them to start breeding or have no interest in becoming breeders. These days when responsible ownership and attitude to dogs has become a priority we surely have to appreciate and support those who stick to what they find suitable and affordable.

We had a similar dispute before finally we allowed veterans to compete on equal terms with younger dogs.

We look forward to seeing all purebred dogs, entire or otherwise, and their owners enjoying events with no limitations based on prejudice.

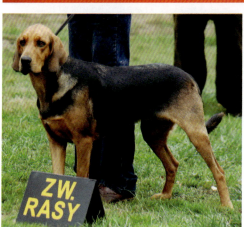

Poland's exhibitors and their dogs have been very successful abroad. At the World Show our well known Aleksandra Szydlowska took part in the junior handling for the last time. Liz Cartledge placed her second in this fiercest of competition and what made us even more proud was her dog, the Polish Hunting Dog (Gonczy Polski) Ch Brylant Klusujaca Sfora was himself World Winner and BOB.
photo Monika Milian

Our national breeds seem to attract more and more dedicated breeders. Polish Lowlands and our new star the Polish Hunting Dogs seem stronger than ever in their homeland and there are no worries about their future.

The Polish Tatra Dog (Polski Owczarek Podhalanski) and Polish Sighthound (Chart Polski) both display reasonable numbers and quality but still have a long way to achieve the highest standards and the Polish Hound (Ogar Polski) seemed in pretty low water over the last decade. This year's specialty brought some consolation in higher entries and more very typical, sound Ogars bred by relatively new breeders who have skilfully incorporated lesser known bloodlines. BIS was Wojciech Pospiech's Rawa z Huculskiej Laki.
photo Monika Milian

At the World Show Beata Klawinska's Polish Lowland Sheepdog Ch Fiakier Prolog Poland was fourth in the group, a first success of such calibre for the breed at this level. Judge was Rafael de Santiago. He was also BIS at Warsaw international show under Jean-Jacques Dupas.

This show has been moved into the picturesque surroundings of Stara Milosna. A vast parkland with beautiful old trees combined with international judges and hard organisational work resulted in a very successful show.
photo Monika Milian

Dog World Annual 2014

FRANCE

Anne-Marie Class

Health becomes a priority

DOG SHOWS are just one aspect of the French dog scene. Many other activities and events are involved, like education and continuing training for judges and breeders, selection for fit and healthy dogs and scientific research on various topics.

A big change came at the beginning of 2013: the creation of ICAD, a new entity which is in charge of the identification files for dogs, cats and domestic carnivores. ICAD is managed by the French Kennel Club (SCC) and the vets. Half the SCC clerks are now working for ICAD. This resulted in some small changes for breeders and some trouble for the management of the SCC, but now everything is running efficiently.

A club 'Dog and Society' was founded to improve relations between the political world and the dog world. It organises events and meetings on all topics concerning dogs and society at the French Senate. The Senate, the upper house of the French Parliament, sits in the Palais du Luxembourg in Paris. Twice a year, the club publishes a magazine to inform the authorities about the work done at the SCC to improve the quality of purebred dogs.

The SCC wishes to exchange view with other countries which are also concerned with research, selection criteria to produce fit dogs, genetic traceability, health topics in each breed, behavioural stability that is necessary for dogs to live in harmony with family and society and all aspects of FCI ethics and rules.

A conference 'Strategy and prospective 2020' was organised in April with the participation of several kennel clubs:

Climax of the 2013 show calendar was the French Championship show in Marseille; 5,287 dogs were entered which was not a good figure. An international panel of judges officiated over two days.

Jean-Paul Kerihuel gave BIS To the Braque d'Auvergne E'Jazz du Ruisseaude Montbrun, representative of an old French gundog breed, owned by Gérard and Elizabeth Fantgauthier and handled by Delphine Domerac. E'Jazz is not only a show dog; he is a French champion which means that he has passed the health tests required in the breed and has also field titles.

Winner of the Eukanuba Challenge, chosen by Christian Eymar-Dauphin, was the Australian Shepherd Fabulous Fiston des Dolmen d'An Arvor, shown by Anne-Emilie Tilly.

France has 52 national breeds and a best dog of the French breeds was awarded each day. On Saturday, winner was the Pyrenean Mountain Dog Floyd de la Plaine d'Astrée, on Sunday the Bichon Frisé Gentilhomme des Portes du Hanau.

The next French Championship Show will be held in Angers in a completely renovated hall on June 7 and 8. France hopes to welcome many foreign exhibitors.

More than 30 CACIB shows were organised all around France during 2012. One of the most successful is the Paris Dog Show. BIS was the American Cocker Spaniel David Beckham New Emeny, owned by Monika Volkmar and shown by Hugues Schuh.

Germany, Belgium, Sweden, Italy, Russia and the UK. The purpose was to make a link between the first international workshop in Sweden in 2012 and the next one which will be held in 2014 in Dusseldorf. The final talk of the day was given by the president of the German KC (VDH), Professor Dr Peter Friedrich.

For the UK, Aimée Llewellyn presented a report on the progress of her English colleagues with regard to breeding and health, and the use of new resources, in particular the collection of information. Bill Lambert spoke about the innovations at the Kennel Club to ensure the promotion and well-being of pedigree dogs in the UK.

Dog World Annual 2014

BIS at Bordeaux was Inge van Englene's Old English Sheepdog Youandi Grand Cru, seen winning the group under Des Manton.
photo Sanchez

BIS at Orléans 2012 was Jocelyne Hauroigne's Peruvian Hairless Duncan Mac Leod de l'Orchidée de Lune.
photo Sanchez

At Troyes BIS under Boris Chapiro was Pascale and André Kolly-Badan's Tibetan Spaniel Booboo of Lollipop, handled by Jean-François Lallemand.
photo Sanchez

BIS at Nice was Barbara Moreschi's Samoyed Cabaka's Bobbie of Storm Cat.
photo Sanchez

At the Cavalier Nationale d'Elevage, BIS was Yvette Rausis-Steffens' Hopkins Royaume des Cavaliers Valaisans.
photo courtesy Sanchez

BIS at Chateauroux under Niksa Lemo was Daniel and Françoise Creton's Bloodhound Eastwood de la Voix des Ardennes. Also pictured is breed judge René Favre.

President Christian Eymar-Dauphin underlined the importance of these links and the help he always finds at the FCI. He added: "The discussion was friendly and constructive, a real meeting of minds between the two workshops on the subject of canine health. After hiding for a long time behind our own convictions, the SCC wishes once again to participate actively in the united efforts of dog breeders everywhere to improve the health and well-being of dogs."

Another concern for the SCC is to keep links with those in the agricultural world who are in charge of research concerning domestic species. The relationship with the vets is also considered of great importance. Test results such as hip or elbow scores are are put on pedigrees as well as other genetic tests, working tests or simple behaviour tests that are compulsory for titles or points in the cotation scale.

In each breed, the climax of the show calendar is the club show, Nationale d'Elevage. The CAC from the club show has the same value as the CAC at the French championship show.

The SCC undertakes a lot of work with breed clubs, of which there is only one for each breed. The breeding policy for each breed is driven by the club in line with the SCC instructions.

Registration figures in most popular breeds stay stable. The total increased in 2012 to 207,987 and we can hope that this will continue. An interesting breed is the Bulldog with more than 1,800 registrations, a success which is credit to the club's dynamism.

Most popular breeds are: German Shepherds 11,205 registrations, Golden Retrievers 8,877; Belgian Shepherds 8,415; Cavaliers 7,680; and Australian Shepherds 7,047.

Best Brittany at the Nationale d'Elevage in St Lô from 357 entries was Gilles Pasty's Gyl de La Plaine Marat. The breed rergistered 4,943 puppies in 2012; the number has been decreasing slightly for five years but the Brittany remains a very popular breed especially for hunters.
photo Haymann

At the Nationale d'Elevage for the Beauceron in Gien, 567 were entered. BOB was Jacques Munilla's bitch Elka des Habits de Feu.
photo Haymann

Dog World Annual 2014

GERMANY

New titles and support for breeders

Dr Wilfried Peper
photographs by Roberto

The two big shows in Dortmund, the Europasieger in May and the Bundessieger in October, were both won the Samoyed Cabaka's Robbie of Cool Cat, owned by Nana Qvist from Denmark.

Germany's representative at the Eukanuba World Challenge will be the Australian Shepherd Energie's Paparazzi Energie des Costys du Tomberg owned by Viktoria Patzold, seen winning BIS at Erfurt under Nemanja Jovanovic. Other BIS wins include Leipzig international.

A constantly developing show scene, a new record low of registration figures, several promising innovations and some surprises are the characteristics of an overall satisfying year for the dog game in Germany.

In January the member clubs of the German Kennel Club (VDH) voted for a modification of the show regulations proposed by the board. As a result, the three events directly organised by the VDH (Dortmund in May and October and Leipzig) are privileged to provide two international shows instead of the traditional national/international combination, and Leipzig is upgraded as 'German Winner Show'.

The titles VDH-Europasieger, German Winner and Bundessieger can be registered in the pedigree; in combination with one more CC awarded at another show, the winning dog can be entered in the champion class.

Finally a new type of title was created – really difficult to win but an attractive incentive for exhibitors to enter their dogs at the international shows of the regional organisations of the VDH too – thus giving them a chance to take some profit from big brother's economic cleverness at least: it's the 'VDH-Jahressieger'.

To gain this title a dog has to win four CACIBs in a calendar year, two of them

BIS at Nürnberg and Karlsruhe was Bilo and Svetlana Azdeniz's Bullmastiff Aspen Ridge Restarting Golden Uelsi.

The Pharaoh Hound Reedly Road Enjoy The Silence, owners Ekaterina Voloshina and Thomas Wastiaux from Slovakia, topped the German Winner Show at Leipzig.

At the May international show in Dortmund, held alongside the Europasieger, BIS was the Petit Basset Griffon Vendéen Carmel Apple van Tum-Tum's Vriendjes, owned by Gwen Huikeshoven from the Netherlands.

at two of the three different title shows or their affiliated international shows, and the other two at different German international shows run by the regional organisations of our kennel club.

Our show scene is really interested to see how many dogs will pass the hurdles to became VDH-Jahressieger 2013 and from which countries they come.

Of course this title can be registered in the pedigree too, the dog may be entered in the champion class and last but not least the winners of this prestigious title will be published in the kennel club gazette *UR*.

No wonder that Germany's show managers are quite happy and contented.

Saarbrücken's BIS was the Weimaraner Gray Clssic's I Kick Azz, owned by Edwin and Kristina Lenaerts and Mike and Tamara Peetermans.

Daniel Huberty's Large Peruvian Hairless Gaius de l'Orchidee de Lune was BIS at Offenburg.

Karin Hessling and Stefan Boieck's Afghan Hound Agha Djari's Clean The Scene was BIS at Neumünster.

Another Samoyed from Denmark, Gitte Morell and Nana Qvist's Cabaka's Kiss The Rain, topped the Bremen show.

Rostock show was won by Rogér Schielke's Greyhound Sobers Svea.

At Dortmund's October international show, held with the Bundessieger, Hans Grüttner gave BIS to the Whippet Gloss And Lipstick of Swala Pala, owned by Dominique Delabelle from Belgium. On the left is VDH president Prof Dr Peter Friedrich.

Nevertheless, there were two surprises: In 2014 – after all – Berlin will be back in the international show scene at a new show venue, and Dresden, after quarrels with the management of the fair centre, will switch over to the neighbouring Chemnitz.

The German representative for the next Eukanuba World Challenge, traditionally chosen at the Bundessieger Show, is the charismatic Australian Shepherd **D'Energies Paparazzi Energie des Costys du Tomberg**, a multiple BIS winner, BOB at Crufts 2012 and FCI World Winner 2013, owned and handled to perfection by Viktoria Patzold.

The record low of 79,934 registrations in 2012 and the fact that too many of our powerful breed clubs – powerful as far as their rights are concerned – are not able to organise skilled education for their breeders, encouraged the VDH to develop and offer an appropriate programme.

In four modules containing all relevant items – from rules and regulations to genetics, anatomy and movement, from breed strategies and programmes with the focus on health to practical problems from mating to birth and rearing of the puppies – participants are instructed by experienced lecturers.

The two-day seminars, held in different regions in order to keep the costs low, pulled just over 100 breeders willing to learn and to be able to do an honest job.

Unlike many 'old crocodiles', at least the participants in this promising approach will be capable to understand the sentence "Every exaggeration is faulty".

The VDH Dog Day, which has now become an institution, was celebrated on June 9. The large variety of canine services, information, sporting activities and entertainment was once again a helpful public relations excercise to promote the aims of the German kennel club and its members.

Dog World Annual 2014

BELGIUM AND LUXEMBOURG

Forgetting our daily problems

Report and photographs by Karl Donvil

In the last few years Belgium has lost several shows, some permanently, others temporarily.

A few years ago, La Louvière in Wallony had a cosy CAC show. Namur held an international show as did Charleroi. In Flanders there was a CAC show in Wieze. Except for La Louvière they are all trying to make a comeback, and Charleroi and Wieze have made a start with a CAC show.

Two shows had to move to an earlier date, Lovanium Trophy and Brussels. That is why you will find them mentioned twice in this report. Other shows have grown like the Ambiorix Trophy and Lommel. LKV Genk made big progress ending up in the top three.

It looks sometimes as if dog shows are invulnerable. I think that people are willing to sacrifice a lot before they cut the budget for their hobby. Probably it is our hobbies that keep us from giving up and getting depressed. And certainly in the canine world the joy and pleasure we get from our pets encourages us not to give up taking care of them. The amount of toys, food in all shapes and varieties, clothes and fancy stuff one can buy is amazing. We dive into a fantasy world to forget the daily problems we have to face due to the economic crisis.

Dog shows are pretty expensive, but the number of entries doesn't seem to drop drastically and exhibitors don't mind travelling thousands of kilometres, notwithstanding the high fuel prices.

Brussels is usually the biggest show in Belgium when it comes to entries though Kortrijk has more participants when you count all the competitions. Brussels is the national show, a collaboration of all the Belgian clubs. In 2012 Miroslav Zidar gave BIS from 3,875 dogs to the Pekingese Billi Boy Iz Sunrise Dragon, owned by Natalia Romanyuk from Russia.

It took Brabo a long time to recover from its lows of the past years but now it is in the top four shows, with an 18 per cent increase to a record 2,057 dogs. Monique van Brempt gave BIS to Edwin and Kristina Lenaerts' Weimaraner Grey Classics I Kick Azz who also won at Hoogstraten which was celebrating 40 years and invited long-serving member, secretary Walter van den Broek, to judge BIS.

Kortrijk show is celebrating its diamond jubilee in 2014. It is the most famous show in Belgium, perhaps in Europe, and sets an example to many others. It has often been copied for its dog-festival aspect, bringing the positive relations between man and dog into the spotlight. At the 2012 show, from 2,987 entries, one of the 173 British dogs was BIS under Javier Sanchez, Claire Millward and Dudley and Glenys Chadwick's Afghan Hound Afterglow Jumping Rainbows of Sofico.

Two weeks before the Ambiorix Trophy show just 600 dogs were entered. Thankfully by the closing date the figure had reached 1,369, but this shows the problems show committees face in the digital age. BIS under Anatoli Zhuk was the American Cocker Spaniel Galaksi Another One Bites the Dust, owned by Jessica van den Boom from Holland.

Dog World Annual 2014

Luxembourg spring show broke its own record with 5,529 entries. Amazing how a little country like Luxembourg can beat a lot of bigger countries in the neighborhood. Its success lies in the fact that the title of Luxembourg champion can be won in the open, champion and working classes. If you win a class twice at this show your dog can be a Luxembourg champion. Junior and veteran champion titles are also available. As you can compete twice in the year, becoming a Luxembourg champion is in many people's reach. Yolanda Nagler's BIS was a British-bred Bichon from Spain, Regina Belstad and Oddvar Havelin's Pamplona Just Magic.

I will never understand why Luxembourg's autumn show is less popular than the spring event but a lot of kennel clubs envy the Luxembourg KC for its two successful shows every year. This one had 3,798 entries. New and even revolutionary was the QR code on the ring numbers. Before the dogs entered the main ring the code was scanned and immediately the breed and other details showed up on a laptop in front of the commentator.

Again a UK-bred dog won BIS when Rafael Malo Alcrudo Rafael chose the seven-year-old year old Petit Basset Griffon Vendéen Soletrader Bjorn Borg. He lives in Holland and is owned by Gwen Huiskeshoven, Wendy and Martin Doherty and Sara Robertson.

While the Brussels show was riding high in 2012, the following year they were forced to leave their regular mid-December date because the venue was not available. As CACIB shows have to be at least two weeks apart it was held at the end of the busy summer period. The result was a loss of almost 1,000 dogs but still a good entry of 2,879. New this year was that everyone with a pedigree dog could come to show him to an all-rounder judge without participating in the show, thus bringing down barriers for aspirant owners to show in the future. Almost 200 showed up.

Hans van den Berg gave BIS to Otto Rinus' Bearded Collie Beardie Connections Kenji, from the Netherlands but Belgian-bred. He had also won the 2012 Lovanium Trophy show under August de Wilde. The Brussels show will organise the European Show in 2016.

Lommel's 2012 show drew a record entry which was a little too much for one day, so in 2013 it went to two days and drew almost as many dogs, 1,342. Liliane de Ridder-Onghena gave BIS to Fonie de Vadder's Bloodhound (known as Chien de Saint Hubert in Belgium, named after the monastery in the Ardennes where this breed was created in the ninth century) Hector of Lufon Royal Pride, who also won at Wieze on the same day as the World Show.

At Mechelen from 1,542 entries Jochen Eberhardt was the best in show judge. The trophy went to a UK-bred American Cocker Spaniel from Holland, Sundust Somethin To Declare, owned by Jessica van den Boom.

Genk's entry has grown dramatically to 2,133 dogs of 14 nationalities. In spite of this success, the Belgian Kennel Club decided that from 2013 the CACIB title must be shared with the Ambiorix Trophy every other year. The club is far from happy. Rony Doedjins from Holland gave BIS to the French Bulldog A'vigdors Ramasseur Des Compliments owned by Aleksandra Nikulina from Russia.

Liège had a bright new hall for its main ring. The show also hosts grooming and handling competitions and an art exhibition, while sighthounds who compete on the track can take part in the 'Beauty and Performance Trophy'. Petru Muntean gave the Golden Dog Trophy for BIS to the Pembroke Corgi Antudor Accidentally In Love owned by Rita Tilley Wilberg from Norway and handled by Christine Sonberg.

In spite of the many shows being held in Belgium during the summer the Lovanium Club's 2013 show drew 50 entries more than the previous year, 1,621. Dominique Delabelle, probably our most famous Whippet breeder in Belgium, won BIS under Zsuzsanna Vaczi-Balogh with Gloss And Lipstick of Swala Pala, bred in France but from the bloodlines of Mr Delabelle's di Mahana kennel.

Mouscron's 40th show drew 1,808 dogs. Agnes Ganami gave BIS to the Pekingese from France, Pascal Lassero and Erick Richard's Vannjty Guillaume The Conqueror.

113

Dog World Annual 2014

THE NETHERLANDS

Haja van Wessem

The ladies take the initiative

AS EARLY as 2006 the Raad van Beheer (Dutch Kennel Club) started preparing for a quality mark for responsible breeders of purebred dogs. The RvB would be the organisation giving the quality mark to breed clubs and the breed clubs would accredit the members/breeders of the club. Criteria would be specified for both parties.

The aim of the quality mark was to improve the welfare of purebred dogs, to promote the careful and responsible breeding of purebred dogs, to improve the public image of purebred dogs and to promote the distinction between responsible breeders and other breeders for the prospective buyer of a puppy, aims that are more than valid in these times.

Several meetings between the RvB and breed clubs took place in 2007 and in December 2008 a final proposal was put on the agenda of the general meeting of the RvB and all the breed clubs and canine societies. A general consensus was achieved.

What happened next was very disappointing and put the Dutch world of dogs several steps backwards. The whole scheme was abandoned without any clear reasons.

Since then, as we all know, criticism of dog breeders was accelerated by among other things the documentary *Pedigree Dogs Exposed* in Britain and television interviews in Belgium and the Netherlands. A new foundation, called Animal and Rights, published on the internet a list of all the dog breeds condemning them all under the heading "Don't buy a disaster dog".

In the meantime the Government has decided to take measures and will choose each year two breeds which will be closely monitored. In 2012 it was the Chihuahua and French Bulldog and in 2013 the Labrador Retriever and the Cavalier King Charles Spaniel.

It was obvious to breeders that with a quality mark they would have had an answer to all the criticism and a negative public image could have been prevented. Only by taking up joint responsibility in order to come to a quality mark can the tide be turned.

Kunogonda is a ladies' club founded 50 years ago by women

Current top winner of 2013 is the Miniature Smooth Dachshund Grandgables Mr Wee Smartly Does It, bred in Canada and owned by Philippe Meier. He won several groups, was World Winner 2013 and BIS at two shows in the Netherlands. However, as he had not been registered with the Dutch Kennel Club on January 1 he did not comply with the rules for the Eukanuba Top Dog competition and he lost his leading position As the runner-up has returned to his breeder in Hungary, the competition for 2013 is still open.
photo Haja van Wessem

Winner of the Dutch Dog of the Year Show was Italian Greyhound Fiefoerniek's Fille De Filante, owned by Sandra de Graaf and handled by partner Lucien Sahuleka. Their Fiefoerniek's Femme Formidable won several groups.
photo Alice van Kempen

Management of the Raad van Beheer office is divided between Ingeborg de Wolf and Rony Doedjins.
photo Haja van Wessem

Dutch Top Dog 2012 was the Deerhound Cairnesund's Pearly Prince, owned by Jasper and Ineke de Vos and bred in Denmark.
photo Haja van Wessem

Joop Reerink (left) died in November 2012. He was a well known commentator speaker at most Dutch shows and one of the instigators of junior handling in the Netherlands, organising the Pedigree junior handling competition for over 25 years.
photo Haja van Wessem

Dog World Annual 2014

At the 2012 Winner Show in Amsterdam, BIS was the German-bred Afghan Hound Agha Djari's Blue Blood, owned by Mikko Ylitalo, Arja Hirvela and Michaela Ståhlberg from Finland. BIS judge was John Wauben and Hugo Stempher represented the RvB.
photo RBT

The RvB organised a party for well known judge and former secretary Martin van de Weijer (left) who retired from judging. His last appointment was best in show at the first CAC show for Dutch breeds. At the reception many dog people took the opportunity to shake hands with one of the most knowledgeable people in Dutch dog history. The royal honour that was presented to him by the Mayor of Haarlem, the city where Martin has lived the greater part of his life, came as a total surprise to him.
photo Haja van Wessem

The first ever CAC show for for 11 Dutch breeds was held in June and 574 were entered. Some breeds had a spectacular entry, such as the Drentsch Patridge Dog with 68. BIS, judged by retiring judge Martin van de Weijer, was the Saarloos Wolfhond Joscha van de Wolfsdreuvnik, owned by Marijke and Jan Verbeeck.
photo Alice van Kempen

Jolanda Huisman's Grand Basset Griffon Vendéen Xpresso du Greffier du Roi was BIS at the 25th anniversary show of the BGV Club in the UK, held with the world congress. He was also RBIS at the Dutch Dog of the Year Show.
photo Haja van Wessem

The Petit Basset Griffon Vendéen Soletrader Bjorn Borg, bred in the UK and living with Gwen Huikeshoven, continued his internationally successful career with a RBIS and several group wins, briefly returning home to gain his UK title. He is grandsire of the Crufts BIS winner.
photo Haja van Wessem

Runner-up in the Top Dog 2013 list is the Welsh Terrier Nagant from Michel, owned by Bob Krautscheid and bred in Hungary. He was World Winner 2012 and World Winner, BOB and fourth in the group at the World Show in Hungary 2013.
photo Haja van Wessem

At Eindhoven the Foxhound Dazzleby Dandelion, owned by Rosemary Griffiths from England, made history by winning the group and ending up BIS4. He was BOB at the Winner Show and is now a Dutch champion.
photo Ria van Middelaar

who were all active in the world of dogs, by being a breeder and/or a judge or in other capacities, united in their aim to improve the health of purebred dogs.

This same club has now taken the initiative and one of the members, Anne-Greet Bonefaas, breeder of Newfoundlands, has, together with lawyer husband Frenk, developed a scheme for breeders through which they can distinguish themselves as dedicated and responsible breeders. The scheme is mainly based on the principle that the breeders are members of a breed club, that the breed club has breeding rules relevant to the breed in question and that the breeders will adhere to these rules.

This scheme will have been presented at a symposium in November and will hopefully be embraced by all Dutch breeders as it is the only answer we can give to all the – so often unreasonable and unfounded – attacks on our dogs.

News from the RvB is that as from April 2013 all dogs, be it purebred or not, have to be microchipped within seven weeks after birth and be registered by the breeder at a databank appointed by the Ministry of Economic Affairs. This measure hopes to put an end to illegal dog trading and puppy farming.

The discussions about the proposed DNA identification testing are still ongoing. Although the RvB would like to introduce DNA testing for identification purposes as soon as possible, breeders still have quite a few issues that have to be cleared first, such as who is the owner of the DNA material, the breeder, the laboratory or the RvB, and what acceptable costs for the testing are.

The office of the RvB has always been headed by one manager, but since March 2013 the management consists of two people. Well known judge Rony Doedijns will be responsible for educational, judges and show affairs. His colleague Ingeborg de Wolf will handle health and welfare, the stud book and IT affairs.

An important step forward in the monitoring of health issues was made by the RvB by making all official test results available online. At the same time the pedigrees of dogs born after Jan 1, 1997 have also been made available online.

For Nova Scotia Duck Tolling Retrievers two DNA tests have become available: one for Addison's disease and one for cleft palate. The tests are not obligatory but many breeders have already made use of it.

Dog World Annual 2014

IBERIA

Report and photos by Marcelino Pozo

Spain
Tribute to an icon

SPAIN AND the dog world lost in 2013 a great icon as judge and breeder, when we said goodbye to Javier Sanchez, known to many as Uncle Javier. These lines serve as a small tribute. Farewell Javier.

The Spanish Kennel Club (RCSE) licensed 30 international shows and 26 national. To these we must add the national specialties of the breed clubs.

There was a remarkable decrease in registrations, maybe due to the economic crisis.

The late Javier Sanchez with the Chow Warrior Legend de la Yakka, a big winner of 2013, who is owned by Jose Carmelo Tolosana.

At the time of writing, well in the lead in the Dog of the Year rankings is the Neapolitan Mastiff Yaromon de Azzurra owned by Carlos Mateo.

The most important event for Spanish dog shows was the presence of Queen Sofia at the spring Madrid international show. Over several hours she visited the pavilion and stands, saluting the exhibitors and watching the groups and BIS with the members of the RSCE. She presented the His Majesty the King Trophy to the BIS winning Pug Ch Didiel Andes Mucho Con Demasiado, owned by Enrique Cid, Alberto Claveria and Diana Restrepo.

A big winner of 2012 has continued at the top in 2013, the Pomeranian Sunterra Sizzling Hot, owned by Julio Martinez de Marigorta.

Yet again a Bearded Collie from Visitación Echeverria's kennel is well up in Spain's Top Dog list: Groucho de Gianvie.

Completing the list of Spain's top winners is Alberto Abajo's English Springer Spaniel Sieger's Match Point, seen winning under Meriel Hathaway.

Portugal

The 2013 calendar of the Club Portuguesse de Canicultura included 12 international shows and 14 national, two of them with qualification for Crufts, two with qualification points for the Portuguese championship all breeds and two for Portuguese breeds. And we must include the breed specialties too. At Lisbon international show the heat caused serious problems and indeed some casualties among participating dogs.

Current Top Dog in Portugal is Luis Graça's Irish-bred Whippet Barnesmore Celtic Tiger, seen winning under Per Iversen.

Among Portugal's main winners of 2013 is João and Rute Soares' Weimaraner Casa de Juno Queen Of Pinups.

Another of Portugal's successful show dogs is Pedro Brito and Claudia Lucas' Samoyed Cabaka's Valiant of Gucci.

Pedro Café's Basset Artésien Normand Fricassee de Lapin da Terra Quente is among Portugal's big winners of 2013.

Gibraltar

At first it was thought that Gibraltar's shows might be affected by the international situation but despite the difficulties, the City of the Rock celebrated with resounding success during the weekend of September 21 and 22. The 38th and 39th international show as usual proved to be a meeting point for the southern European exhibitors because every year offers different attractive opportunities for them.

This time the winners of the CACIBs on the Sunday also obtained a CAC towards the Morocco champion title. For the title of Gibraltar champion a dog must win two Gibraltar CCs regardless of whether it is a champion from another country. The winners of the junior and veteran classes if graded excellent automatically became Gibraltar champions in these categories, while the puppy class winners obtain the title Gibraltar Puppy Winner 2013.

With this in mind many exhibitors crossed the border hoping to take advantage of these opportunities, and among them were the two best in show winners.

BIS at Gibraltar's Saturday show went to a Basset Hound from Spain, Marta Lucena's Bombay de Wila-damar.

At Gibraltar's Sunday show top spot under American judge Edd Bivin went to the Yorkshire Terrier Royal Precious JP F4 Juliana, owned by Yoshiko Obana from Japan and shown by Sergio Amien from Spain, who is pictured winning at Granada. She has been highly successful in the UK with BIS at UK Toy and a group placing at Crufts.

Dog World Annual 2014

ITALY
CACIB shows galore

Richard Hellman

There has been an incredible number of international dog shows in 2013 in Italy, 63 to be precise! When I started showing in this country 30 years ago there were only 18. That number has gradually climbed to an average of 40 CACIB shows but with the hopes of getting as many delegates possible at the Italian Kennel Club (ENCI) elections, just about every show-giving club was granted the possibility to put on an international event this year.

This has unfortunately decreased the number of entries at many events to embarrassingly low numbers and some inexperienced clubs have put on poorly organised shows.

Some kennel clubs, however, have put on some wonderful shows, with great venues and well qualified judging panels attracting a significant number of entries with impressive BIS line-ups. Let's speak about those most prestigious and the dogs that are currently in the top ten.

The top eight are featured pictorially. Number nine, after his BIS at Pescara, is the Miniature Wire Dachshund Amaonoraerispetta del Wanhelsing, usually shown by his breeder/owners, a successful mother and son team. When Francesca and Gabriel Friggione can't make it to the show, this little dog with the long name which translates to Love, Honour and Respect has occasionally been shown by Francesco Vasanella.

Number ten spot is divided by three dogs, Ch Sobers Marmaduke the Greyhound, another Maltese Ch Funny Ladies Rising Sun, who has won two BIS, handled by Pasquale Romanelli for Laura Chialastri, and the US-bred Australian Shepherd Ch Propwash Know How, piloted by me and my partner Roberta Semenzato, and owned by Leslie Frank and Judy Harrington. He is a member of the team sponsored by Lorella Vismara and Massimo Scotti as are the Clumber, Karelian and Greyhound bitch, currently numbers two, three, four and joint tenth all breeds!

With another seven international shows, the only sure thing is that the Maltese is so far ahead that the title of Dog of the Year is already his.

The Maltese Ch Cinecitta' Sasha Baron, bred and owned by Franco Prosperi and Stefano Paolantoni who have been bringing us world class dogs for three decades, has broken all records in Italy this year and will be representing Italy at the Eukanuba World Challenge. His wins put him way out of reach for any other contenders for the top all-breed spot including 11 BIS and six RBIS. And he is merely 27 months of age!

He started his winning streak with a RBIS and BIS at the double CACIB show in Alghero on the island of Sardinia. Those with small dogs can go quickly by plane, but most take an overnight ferry.

The Insubria show, expertly run by Bremadog, is one of the best in Italy, in a beautiful venue, known for its spectacular main ring. On the Friday there is a national show during the day and a banquet in the evening with a Contest of Champions for this year's BIS winners. Saturday and Sunday saw a CACIB show and some specialties. Every Italian exhibitor should feel proud of such a show, one of the best in Europe in my opinion. It drew nearly 3,000 entries, many from abroad.

The Friday evening was spectacular, with professional singers and dancers between the knockout rounds. Winner was the Danish-bred Samoyed imported by Giuseppi Saccane and Barbara Moreschi, Ch Cabaka's Bobbie of Stormcat, who was BIS here two years ago. Norman Kenney from the US placed him RBIS on Sunday; they are pictured above along with group judge Jussi Liimatainen. His BIS3 was the Basset pictured on the next page who was also runner-up at the Invitational while the Maltese took yet another BIS.

The music and laser light show with the dogs beaming under spotlights and the confetti-shooting cannon make this one of the most excitingly choreographed finals in Europe.

BIS at the first of the Eboli double shows under Guiseppe Alessandra was the Akita from Norway, Estava Rain Hold The News, owned by Friedrich Birkmar. A breed not normally so successful in BIS competition, Marina Baskova's Caucasian Ovcharka Baskoy Zver Ezhik Grey, debuted by winning RBIS on Saturday and BIS on Sunday. Later he won another BIS, moving him up to number six spot.
photo Deya

photo Guillermo

Dog World Annual 2014

Making his debut at Milan and winning his first group was Ch Clussexx Kangaroo Jack, a 14-month-old Clumber Spaniel who has dominated the gundog group in Italy winning two BIS and two RBIS. He is currently number two all breeds, owned by Douglas Johnson and Lorella Vismara and shown by Richard Hellman.
photo EB

Milano in January attracted an entry of over 3,500 dogs. This show is in a beautiful venue, easily accessible, with excellent facilities and a wonderful main ring. The show superintendent Bremadog does such a wonderful job organising the show that they were asked to choreograph the European Winner Show in Geneva. President Jolanda Vandoni and her staff welcome you all to the World Show 2015 in the same venue on June 11-14.

Also held are agility, flyball and dog dancing plus the final of the the junior handling competition; 14-year-old Monica Bonifacio represented Italy at Crufts. She had already graced the big ring there having won BOB with her Giant Schnauzer in 2011.

BIS under Hiroshi Kamisato from Japan was the eight-year-old Karelian Bear Dog from Canada, Multi Ch Tsarshadow's I Speak Of War who had just returned to Italy after finishing the year number two all breeds having won 48 BIS in Canada with his handler and co-owner Doug Belter for his breeder Dawne Deeley. He had spent three years as a youngster in Europe with me.

He is currently number three all breeds in Italy having won two BIS and three RBIS as well as RBIS recently at the European Winner Show. He is pictured jumping for joy at winning the group at the European Winner Show under Lisbeth Mach. Handler is Richard Hellman.
photo HotDog

Two other dogs currently in the top ten from Francesco Vasanella's team are the Basset Hound Ch Bassjoy Night Of Love, imported from Malta, co-owned by Francesco's assistant Federica Vicarini and her father Alberto, and Ch Ludstar Don Miguel, a Gordon Setter owned by Gabriella Segato. They are currently ranked numbers five and seven. The Basset, a BIS winner from 2012, won another in 2013 and a RBIS, while the Gordon also has a 2013 BIS and reserve, plus second in the group at Geneva.

photos Deya/Paula Heikkinen-Lehkonen

A Greyhound bred in the famous kennel of Bitte Ahrens and Luigi Primavera, Sobers Marmaduke, owned by Dario and Francesca Purpura and often handled by Federico Sanguinetti, started off the year strongly, taking a BIS, but was put on hold to make way for Sobers Portia Grandcru (pictured), shown occasionally by her breeder/owner but almost always by Francesco Vasanella who has piloted three of the top ten dogs so far. She stands neck and neck with the Karelian at fourth place all breeds, has won two BIS and two RBIS in Italy and was second in the group at Geneva.

Arezzo is one of the better shows, with a great venue in southern Tuscany, well organised with a great BIS ring, and this year it was a double show. Saturday's BIS was the Saluki Del Borghino Oscar de la Renta, owned by Leonardo Galliano, Italy's dog of the year in 2011. On Sunday the dog currently in number eight spot was BIS. Many of you are familiar with this happy-go-lucky dog with his happy-go-lucky owner who won RBIS at Crufts, Franco Barberi's Labrador Ch Loch Mor Romeo.

He has had an incredible career winning at many important club shows in the UK as well as winning the group at the World Show in Budapest and G2 at Geneva. Shown sparingly in Italy this year, he also won top honours at San Remo.

He is pictured winning at the UK's Yellow Labrador Club with referee Sussie Wiles and judges Mark Rawlinson and Per Iversen.
photo John Jackson

119

Dog World Annual 2014

HUNGARY

Report and photographs by Gábor Szalánczi

Kennel Club becomes a union

TWO HISTORIC events took place in Hungary this year, the World Dog Show and a new form of organisation for the kennel club (MEOE).

The World Show in Budapest was a great success, with exhibitors from 70 countries and about 18,000 entries. The main problems of the 2008 European Show were corrected – parking and access – and nearly all the judges, exhibitors and press spoke in flattering terms about the event. The final winner was a Hungarian dog with a huge winning record including a group at Crufts. Apart from him, few Hungarians were successful in the main ring, only best junior or veteran of the day.

There were more successful events in parallel with the show and held 30km away: the World Championship of Obedience, Eurosighthound, Interra, Frisbee Europe Cup etc.

Before the show was the FCI general meeting where a new president, Rafael de Santiago, was elected. Among those elected to the General Committee was Hungary's Tamas Jakkel.

In 2013 the MEOE organised 15 international shows, and about 20 nationals. For the first time in Hungary, one national show was cancelled because of a big drop in entries. There were again fewer shows than in previous years, thanks to the world economic crisis and the ambiguous legal status of the MEOE.

At the end of September the MEOE took the most important step in its history. At its general meeting it became a union rather than an association. Now, the members can be legal entities only, not individuals.

The new members are 110 independent breed clubs and local clubs and the new official name is Magyar Ebtenyésztők Országos Egyesülete Szövetség. The former president was elected again, so Andras will serve for the next five years. Now, the Hungarian Kennel Club is a union, with 110 independent, legal entities.

Apart from those pictured, BIS or best of day winners at international shows included the Maltese **Suzy Ulath Ina Jimido**, Chow **Daydream of Dreams del Fiume Gallo**, and Lhasa Apso **Sayonara Thinker of Golden Sprite**.

BIS at one of the Fehova shows and at the Champion Show Hungary was the Old English Sheepdog bitch Bottom Shaker So Easy To Love, like the World Show BIS owned by József Koroknai and handled by Zsolt Hano.

At the World Show best Hungarian hunting dog was Zsofia Miczek's Wirehaired Vizsla Zöldmáli Irisz. Judge was Zsuzsanna Balogh.

Best Hungarian Shepherd Dog at the World Show was Jozsef Ballai's Komondor Ráró Óhungarikum, seen with Janos Simicsko, a member of the Hungarian Parliament, Andras Korozs, president of the MEOE, and Gabor Korozs.

Heavensway Forever After with Afterglow, a UK-bred American Cocker Spaniel owned by Andy Yau and handled by Javier Mendikote, was BIS at one of the Fehova shows under Blaz Kavcic.

Hodmez Vásarhely's Saturday BIS was Marianna Királyné Némedy's Bloodhound Star-Mountain Strong Angel. Judge was Jaroslav Matyas.

Sunday BIS at Hodmez vásarhely was Dóra Nagyné Csapoda's Briard Cognac Vesely Dvor.

At Szekesfehervar, Saturday's BIS was Anita Anda-Marócsek's Komondor Pasa von Thüringen. Judge was Attila Czegledi, a new Hungarian all-rounder.

Szekesfehervar's Sunday BIS under Peter Harsanyi was Ko Bo's Prometheus, Szegedi Szilárd and Norbert Tibay's American Staffordshire Terrier.

Dog World Annual 2014

WORLD SHOW

Photographs Paula Heikkinen-Lehkonen

Hungarian Bobtail tops 18,000 dogs at Budapest

RBIS was the Lhasa Apso Chic Choix Cleopatra Eurydice, handled by Sanna Kopola-Hirsinmäki, who also won the Grand Prix one-day show. Owner is Piia Helistölä-Laurila, Finland.

The Hungarian Kennel Club (MEOE) did not have the easiest of times in the run-up to the 2013 Fédération Cynologigue Internationale World Show, but its conflicts with the Government were resolved sufficiently that the show was a great success, drawing 18,000 dogs over four days, representing 70 nationalities and 371 breeds.

BIS was judged by Tamás Jakkel (left) and he chose a Hungarian-owned dog in Jószef Koroknai's Old English Sheepdog Bottom Shaker My Secret, handled by Zsolt Hano. Among his many titles is one from the UK and he won the group at Crufts 2012. Also pictured are the new FCI president Rafael de Santiago, MP Istvan Simicszo, MEOE president András Korózs, and finance minister Mihaly Varga.

BIS4: the Kaninchen Smooth Dachshund Formula Uspeha Colibri, seen with group judge Luis Pinto Teixeira. Owner is Irina Hapaeva, Russia.

BIS3 was the UK-bred Wire Fox Terrier Travella Starlord, handled by Divoney Rasera, and seen with group judge András Korózs. Now owned by Victor Malzoni from Brazil, he was a dual BIS winner in the UK and is sire of the top-winning Ch Travella Striking Steel who took his second BIS back home the same weekend.

Group winner under Kari Järvinen: the Samoyed Cabaka's Pretty Good Ideal, owned by Gitte Morell, Denmark.

Group winner: the Leonberger Skjaergaardens Valentine Rua Soleil, owned by Natalia Romanova, Russia.

Group winner under Rui Oliveira: the Rhodesian Ridgeback Faira Arif Kamifilu, for Angelina Evmenova, Russia.

Group winner: the Azawakh Azamour Wahid, owned by Jari-Pekka Kahelin and Jussi Lindholm, Finland.

Group winner under Hans van den Berg: the Gordon Setter Goango Black Booms, owner Minna Malo, Finland. Breed judge was Guy Spagnolo.

Group winner under Carla Molinari: the Crufts RBIS-winning Labrador Retriever Loch Mor Romeo, owned by Franco Barberi from Italy.

121

AUSTRIA
Maria-Luise Doppelreiter

The year after the World Show

2012 was a rather unspectacular year for the Austrian dog show scene. After the big event in Salzburg everything got back to normal, with all the usual shows scheduled.

The Austrian Kennel Club (ÖKV) has a new vice-president, Margit Brenner, who has been on the committee for many years as the 'boss of Austrian judges', and surely one of the most popular cynologists of our country. New general secretary is Andreas Huschka.

Wieselburg's best of day winners were the Italian Greyhound **Lux Loral Jolie Jasmina** and the White Swiss Shepherd **Waroggi Maitreya**.

At Salzburg best on Saturday was the Cocker Spaniel **California Dream z Vejminku**, and on Sunday the Groenendael **Atos von Calruna**.

The Oberwart show is held in connection with Szombathelyi (Hungary); dogs can win a combined title if they get a CACIB at both events. Best of days were the Whippet **Absolute Mann Im Lovin 'It** and the Rough Collie **Dennisay's Day Dreamer**.

The last show of the year is held in Wels, where the Austrian Superchamp competition has been held. In 2013 the rules have been changed, and the event is now called Austrian Champion of Champions.

By a point system the most successful dogs from each group become 'Austrian Show Winner'. For 2012 they were:

Berger de Picardie **Figo de L'Avocat de la Tour**; Dobermann **Promise von der Treuen Seele**; Glen of Imaal Terrier **Spirit of Ireland Beautiful**; Wire Dachshund **Ella von der Zirbenleiten**; Siberian Husky **Venus De Milo of Nordica**.

Beagle **Ob-La-Di's Flying Jacob Elleh Ammer**; Irish Setter **Castello All Day Sunshine**; Flat-coated Retriever **Almanza Sweet Home Alabama**; Lhasa Apso **Ekajati's Baha**; and Whippet **Legend of the Goldenrain Mary Countess**.

The year's first show in Austria takes place in Graz. The Styrian Dog Club has organised it for many years. This time it was the first show for a new team, led by Guenter Wonisch and Iris Urschitz, and they made a great job. With many exhibitors, visitors and trade stands this show is a highlight for all dog fanciers. At this two-day show we have a 'real' BIS as the group winners are invited to come back on Sunday and compete for the overall win. BIS was the Affenpinscher Taonga v Tani Kazari, owner Klaus Leutermann.

Klagenfurt Saturday show started in the afternoon, to give exhibitors the possibility to enjoy the lovely lake before 'duty'. This is a double show with all groups judged each day. Saturday's winner was the Samoyed Cabaka's Bobbie of Storm Cat, owned by Barbara Moreschi; Sunday, Freddy Dhondt's Shiba Fallscreek's Kumo Bear.

Innsbruck welcomed us to a new showground for another double show. On Saturday the winner was the Scottish Terrier who won BIS at the European Show, Filisite Brash Koh-I-Noor, owner Valentina Popova; on Sunday the Flat-coated Retriever Almanza Sweet Home Alabama, Gabriela Baumgartner.

The Tulln Bundessieger Show is very popular with visitors and exhibitors; dogs can run on grass and there are many trade stands as well as delicious food for dogs and humans. BIS was the Newfoundland King of Helluland Feel The Win owned by Sonia and Vlado Krockova.

Dog World Annual 2014

THE EUROPEAN SHOW

photographs by Paula Heikkinen-Lehkonen

Russian Scottie shines in Switzerland

Geneva, Switzerland, was the venue for the Fédération Cynologique Internationale European Winner Show. The entry of around 8,000 dogs might have been higher without the Swiss ban on showing cropped or docked dogs.

Best in show was the Scottish Terrier Filisite Brash Koh-I-Noor, owned by Valentina Popova from Russia, pictured with judge Hans Müller, who retired this year after a long stint as president of the FCI, and Swiss Kennel Club president Peter Rub.

Runner-up was the Karelian Bear Dog Tsarshadow I Speak Of War, owned by Dawne Deeley and Doug Belter, Canada, and shown by Richard Hellman. On the left are show committee members Barbara Müller and Laurent Pichard.

The Whippet Sobresalto Quann Tramonta o´Sole won the group under Tamas Jakkel, and also took best junior in show. Owner is Massimo Fiorillo, Italy.

Group winner under Barbara Müller: the English Springer Spaniel Hollivera's Question Of Quality, Birgitta Pettersson, Sweden.

Group winner under Christian Eymar-Dauphin: the Weimaraner Ch Grey Classic Kick Azz, Kristina and Edwin Lenaerts, Belgium.

BIS3: the Basset Artésien Normand Fricassee de Lapin da Terra Quente, owner Pedro Ribeiro Café, Portugal.

Group winner under Stefan Sinko: the Newfoundland Ch King of Helluland Just In Time, Fantur Oton, Slovenia.

Group winner under Petru Muntean: the Kaninchen Wire Dachshund Goloubet de Rouet del Wanhelsing, Gabriel Pascarella, Italy.

Group winner under Laurent Pichard: the Pug Ch Rose's Knock Down Eight Count, Theerawut Praphasirisulee, Thailand.

Group winner under Carla Molinari: the White Swiss Shepherd Ch Heart Sylver Majestic du Bois des Terres, Adeline Joly, France.

Dog World Annual 2014

RUSSIA
Even closer links with Europe

Alexey Kalashnikov

EVERY author wants to convey objective information about the events taking place around him or her, but for understandable reasons accomplishing this is virtually impossible and often one needs to take a step back to see what is really significant.

Russian and European dog breeding continue to become closer in every way from simple friendship between those who think alike to common projects in breeding, up to tying the knot in marriage. The internet, of course, is a prime factor in bringing people closer together, as are the international dog shows, in which Russian dog breeders are active participants.

For this reason, there are several companies in Russia which specialise in providing bus tours to shows all over Europe. Especially popular is the so-called 'Balkan Tour' to the Mediterranean countries which many professional handlers love to take. The luckiest handlers manage to have all the dogs entrusted to them become international champions, while they themselves have a European vacation. Of course their job is extremely difficult as they travel from country to country by bus and never sleep in the same hotel twice.

More and more Russian dog breeders are participating at Crufts and Westminster. Even those who can't make the shows watch them on television. Of course, Crufts is valued more by Russian dog fanciers, who may criticise the show but advertise any success there for their own dogs.

The World Show in Budapest was an important event for Russia. Breeders from these two countries have traditionally had close business ties, and at the beginning of the 1990s a large number of dogs found their way to Russia from Hungary. Today this process is reciprocal and it is not surprising that the number of dogs from Russia at the show was 1,575; only Hungary had more. Russian dogs scored many victories for kennels such as Rua Soleil Leonbergers, Formula Uspeha Dachshunds, Sunrise Dragon Pekingese (with a UK import) and Simonaland Beagles (with a Hungarian import). The significant number of imported dogs among the Russian winners here points more to the international character of dog breeding in general. The efforts of Mrs Romanova with her Leonbergers and Helen Artemenko in Pekingese have brought these breeds to a significantly higher level in Russia.

For obvious reasons, summer is long awaited by Russian dog lovers. Warm weather is especially appreciated for canine sports and hunting. Every weekend agility, IPO, obedience, mondioring and other popular competitions take place. Hunters regularly take their dogs to training sites

The 'Golden Collar' was the last show of 2012. Two titles are awarded: Best Dog of the year – the winner of the show – and Top Dog of the year, who scored the most points at other shows. The former award, and the prize that came with it, a Citroen C3, went to a Siberian Husky Kristari's Hot Shot From The USA, owned by Nikolay Shushpanov, bred in a famous American kennel.
photo Kalashnikov

Top Dog of the year went to the Giant Schnauzer Gently Born Check Mate, owners Nataliya Barbashova and Anna Vlasova. He was World Winner in 2008 and European Winner in 2010. Gently Born Domingo (pictured left), who was also BOB at the World Show, was runner-up to Best Dog of the year and the team was runner-up to top kennel, having won this trophy from 2006 to '10. Mrs Vlasova and her dogs are pictured in Red Square, Moscow.
photo Kalashnikov

A top kennel award was also presented at the Golden Collar show. The winner was A'Vigdors, owned by Revaz Khomasuridze (top left). Thanks to good sponsorship, Mr Khomasuridze was able to acquire many French Bulldogs from various kennels in Europe, and especially from the Belgian kennel de la Parure and the Danish kennel Daulokke. Standing right is Russian Kennel Club president Alexander Inshakov.
photo Kalashnikov

where poor wild animals are kept as bait to train terriers. Shows are many and the breed specialties tend to be more interesting and less commericalised than the general shows unless the latter have a particularly well qualified judge.

Boredom is not a problem in the Russian dog world. The American Kennel Club unexpectedly came to the aid of sexual minorities in Russia and sent a letter to the president of the FCI requesting it to cancel the World Show in Moscow in 2016 because of anti-gay legislation in Russia. Every club has the right to bring its interests to forefront, but in this case one cannot be surprised. In the Russian dog world there

Dog World Annual 2014

The main event in Russia after the long winter hibernation is the Eurasia show, where all dog fanciers meet up. The 2013 show was an exact repetition of the 2012 event and even the number of dogs entered was only seven fewer! At the first day show there were 6,633 entries from more than 200 breeds. Ten years ago, the show attracted 2,952 entries.

Miniature Schnauzers drew the top entry, 172 dogs. With rare exceptions, the popularity of breeds at the show reflects the popularity of breeds in the country as a whole. Unfortunately, we do not have exact data because the Russian Kennel Club keeps it secret. A second organisation, the Union of Russian Kennels Organisations, has no relationship to the FCI, but is very powerful.

The winner of the Eurasia show over both days, having taken BIS first day, was the Labrador Etu Asti Mondoro, owned by Elena Akimova from Ukraine, pictured with judge Karl Reisinger and president Alexander Inshakov.
photo Kalashnikov

Second day BIS at Eurasia, judged by Horst Kliebenstein, was the US-bred Scottish Terrier Terrier McVan's To Russia With Love, owned by Mariana Khenkina, who shortly beforehand had been BOB at Crufts.
photo Kalashnikov

The Moscow Hunting Club show was celebrating its 120th anniversary. Here are some of the competing spaniels, and one of the hounds.
photos Kalashnikov

Yvonne McGrath from Ireland judged at the Collie specialty in Moscow and her BIS was Olga Saame's Alheniul That's Person Which Knows Her Way.
photo Kalashnikov

are more serious problems, including terrible conditions at some kennels and even incompetent judging. Russia has yet to tackle adequately the problem of homeless animals, as well as legal and illegal dog fighting.

I must also mention the 'dog hunters', a loosely knit group of dog haters who will use any means to kill or cripple any dog. The internet has played a key role in this phenomenon as they have used the social media to organise.

Dog lovers have organised meetings and tried to fight these people, but their efforts have not been very effective. Government organisations, including the police, have not responded to this problem and thus the dog hunters have virtually been given the OK to kill dogs and other pets.

The European Show in Switzerland attracted a large number of Russian entries. While generally Russia did not do well, BIS was taken by Valentina Popova's young Scotch Terrier **Filisite Brash Koh-i-Noor**. Her breeding programme has met with great success and the most famous dog from the kennel is **Filisite Brash Celebration**, RBIS at Crufts 2010.

In conclusion the processes which are taking place in the Russian dog world are extremely contradictory. On the one hand, handlers make large numbers of trips and are becoming more and more influential in the show process. Private parties for judges and private airplanes bringing certain dogs to the show are part of the Russian scene. In addition, Russia has some excellent kennels that are world class.

So the Russian dog world is a strange mix of elements from many countries, but, unfortunately, the best examples are not always chosen for imitation.

The Borzoi national specialty was judged by Bo Bengtson from the US on this second visit to Russia. BOB was Elenea Balakireva's Lunnaya Raduga Afrodita, handled by her daughter.

Dog World Annual 2014

ISRAEL

Report and photographs by Yossi Guy

Kennel Club loses its figurehead

The Israeli Kennel Club ended 2012 on a sad note with the death of its powerful president, Eitan Etinger, aged 60. He started in the dog sport about 40 years ago and among other things took part in establishing Israel's search and rescue unit, military K9 unit and other aspects of dog training. He also had a brilliant mind for organising shows and put together events that brought in 20,000 paying visitors.

In December 2012, the annual Dog of the Year competition was judged by three Israeli all-rounders. The winner was a Cairn Terrier, Ch Happy Beit Dembin, owned by Dorit Dembin. One of the most successful dogs of 2013, Happy is pictured winning BIS at a two-day show in Kibbutz Givat Haim where Leni Finne, Annika Ulltveit-Moe and Harri Lehkonen judged 500 dogs. RBIS was Dr Estella Schindler and daughter Danielle's American Cocker Spaniel Ch Fairies Cockers Christian Dior. Although the Schindler family lives in Israel, their dogs spend most of the time in Spain with handler Felix Duque Cordoba, achieving excellent results.

Dr Lazar Gerassi's Cane Corso Ch Dorian Grey Gerassi Corso has done well at home and in Europe, including a specialty in Italy. His daughter was World Winner in Hungary. In March, the IKC organised three CACIB shows during Passover week. This project was the final initiative taken by Eitan Etinger. It took place in the first Hebrew-speaking agricultural school established in the 1880s, Mikveh Israel. The shows attracted a nice entry and thousands of spectators. The Cane Corso went BIS on the first day under Rony Doedjins, and the American Cocker on the third day.

In October, the IKC held its annual CACIB show in the desert town of Arad. The day before, the Israeli Herding Dog Club organised an all-breed show with two of the judges, Richard Paquette from Canada and Juan Naveda of Spain. The American Cocker came in second on both days while a black Medium Poodle Ch Delight Expression Farouk, owned by Iris Paz and handled by Paz Davidovitch, was BIS on the first day and won the group on the second day.

On the second day, the Groenendael Ch Revloch Could It Be Magic, bred in Ireland and owned by Avishag Morgenstern, was BIS.

At the CACIB show in memory of Eitan Etinger, Yochai Barak put up a Pomeranian from Russia, multiple BIS winner Ch Dan Star Kom Gamlet, owned by Lyudmila Komyakova. He is an American and Canadian champion in addition to many European titles, and did well at the Eukanuba World Challenge.

The author, chairman of the Israel Kennel Club education committee, was invited to give a presentation about dogs at the Israeli parliament, the Knesset, for the police K9 unit. This marked another milestone in the relationship between the club and security forces units that use dogs.

In August, the KC held a show in the community of Savion, whose municipality provided tan air-conditioned gymnasium. BIS was Jacob Lazslau's Japanese-bred Papillon, Ch Queen Bless JP New Star OB.

CROATIA

Dog World Annual 2014

Petra Buva, Croatian Kennel Club

A small country for big dog shows

THE tourism slogan of Croatia is: 'A small country for a great holiday!' Its canine equivalent could be 'a small country for big dog shows'.

The tradition of show organisation dates back to 1932, when the first international show in Zagreb was held. In the past year the Croatian Kennel Club has organised 16 international shows.

The 2012 show season finished with the two Zagreb international shows in November with record entries and exhibitors from 37 countries. A double CACIB event was followed by Friday afternoon's specialty shows and club championships for almost all breeds.

The Samoyed Cabaka's Bobbie of Storm Cat was BIS on the first day and the Petit Basset Griffon Vendéen Kan Trace All I Do Is Win on the second day.

At these shows we choose a supreme BIS winner from these and the specialty shows' winner. This time it was the latter, the Black Medium Poodle Jasenak Back To The Future owned by Dragana and Ivan Vasiljevic (Serbia).

We open the show season in Zagreb with double CACIB shows. The number of entries is a bit more modest than in November but they gave us an absolute winner of both days, the Lhasa Apso Chic Choix Adrenalin Rush owned by Jasna Matejcic, Nikola Smolic, Juha Kares and Nina Tiitinen.

At the beginning of June we had two shows in Umag in a city park with lots of shade which is always more then welcome. Both were won by the Saluki Del Borghino Oscardelarente owned by Leonardo Galliano from Italy.

In July we had two international dog shows followed by two nationals in Split, known by the brand name '4 Summer Night Shows'. These are the second biggest shows in Croatia and winners included the Petit Basset Griffon Vendéen Soletrader Bjorn Borg and the American Cocker Spaniel PBJ's Back In Black. Supreme BIS was the Clumber Spaniel Big Boom's Banditos Dex owned by Lana Levai from Croatia.

The most amusing shows are those in Zadar which at the beginning of May hosted four international shows, with a unique venue, a caravan and bungalow resort on the coast of our beautiful sea near the huge hotel complex. We had four winners: Maltese Cinecitta Diana Lane, Affenpinscher Tamarin Ticket To Ride, Pharaoh Hound Reedly Road Enjoy The Silence and Bullmastiff Full House Limited Edition. Supreme BIS was the Affenpinscher owned by Andrew Bizin and Irina Stepina from Russia.

At the end of May, double CACIB shows were held in Varaždin. Shows have been held for over 30 years on this beautiful showground with grass short enough for golf. Winners were the Bernese Mountain Dog Edelweiss degli Antici Mulini owned by Laura Bernetti from Italy and Rhodesian Ridgeback Amber Grand Star Qwandoya owned by Hana Pankova from the Czech Republic.

In September international shows are held in the east at Osijek, by the river Drava, overlooking the bridges, forts and city. This double CACIB show brought us two winners, the Pomeranian The Best Models Without Doubt owned by Mirko Matkovic from Croatia and Australian Shepherd Silver Dream Aussie's Brigitte Bardot, Katalin Zrupkone Harmat from Hungary.

GREECE
Breeders face tax threat

Lila Leventaki

THE GREEK Kennel Club has major problems to deal with and is trying to find solutions, but it's not easy. The difficulties involve the threat of taxes on breeders. At present non-professional breeders, the vast majority who keep just a few dogs at home, are able to breed two litters a year, while professional breeders with kennels and lots of space have to be licensed, and this licence is hard to obtain.

A successful show was that organised by Athens Canine Society (OKA) in March. The society's new board succeeded in running a perfect show just two and a half months after its election. It is a pity that these people are no longer involved in the society club after such a well organised event.

In between all the problems a double CACIB show was organised successfully in October very close to Athens city centre so it was easily accessible by public transport and attracted a lot of visitors. It was an indoor show and one of the best shows the kennel club has organised in the last eight years.

BIS on the first day was the UK-bred Akita Gr Ch Mynyddhaf's King Of The Ring, owned by Vasilios Panopoulos Vasilios, who was Top Dog of 2012 in Greece. Second day BIS was the Yorkshire Terrier Ch Qoccle's Charlote, owned by Nikoletta Pollini.
photo Lila Leventaki

The Greek Shar-Pei Club held a 'mega-specialty' judged by Viera Staviarska, the breed's saviour Matgo Law and Claire Davies Riahi. In the champion of champions class best dog was Int Ch Brekkukots Roman'Cin The Stone, owned by Chrysanthi Leventaki, who also won the RCC at Crufts, and best bitch Lila Leventaki's Ch Khambaliq Chipria Hug Me.

The Brittany Gr Ch Kris of Amazon Land, owned by Ioannis Papadopoulos, was European Winner 2013 and may well be Greek Top Dog for the year.
photo Lila Leventaki

At the World Show in the Greek breed Hellinikos Ichnilatis, Ilias Iliadis' Ector was World Veteran Winner and Team-Iliadis Ariadni was World Winner and they went on to runner-up best brace in the group.
photo Deya

SOUTH AFRICA

Greg Eva

KUSA hosts the Agility Gala

QUITE A few changes have taken place this year which will affect the Kennel Union of Southern Africa in years to come.

The one which will be very evident is that of splitting the present position of president, chief executive and chairman of the Federal Council into two positions, namely a president and a separate chairman of the Federal Council.

It is believed that this will relieve the pressure as the work undertaken is very heavy indeed and should result in more efficiency in the running of the Union. The necessary alterations to the constitution have been circulated to the clubs who will have the final say on this matter.

The highlight of the 2013 year will have been the holding of the FCI Agility World Championships in October here in South Africa – the first time this has ever been held outside Europe. KUSA has put its best foot forward to ensure that everything runs smoothly and at the same time it will be an event worth remembering in the future.

It has not been an easy task to get everything in line, but the committee involved has done a sterling job and we can look forward to some interesting internet views of the event as a whole.

The clubs are managing to hold their shows, provide experienced judges and use local expertise to the benefit of the exhibitors despite the economic problems. The recession experienced in the world in general has had its bearing on South Africa and is affecting the number of dogs entered at the various shows, with particular reference to the increased petrol price, which, due to our large distances, is already being felt by the clubs who operate outside the main centres.

Various aspects have been investigated with regard to KUSA and its involvement with its members and a careful look at the systems in place is envisaged.

All is not doom and gloom by any means as the enthusiasm abounds, although a few more young faces would make the future brighter.

KUSA National Dog of 2013 was the Afghan Hound Ch Agha Djari's Question Of Honour of Accolades, owned by Ria Wessels, and National Puppy was Joy McFarland and Elrena Stadler's Saluki Elamir Classic Design for Fleetwind, handled by Helen Theron, pictured with president Greg Eva and judges Zoran Brankovic, Monique van Brempt and Jack Peden.
photo Bellstone

KUSA's FCI show was held in Johannesburg and BIS was Rossana Joubert's Siberian Husky Ch Nanook Pvt Svk Kajun Sky of Kamchatka, seen with Greg Eva and judge Jack Peden.
photo Bellstone

Guy Jeavons awarded BIS at Walmer to Roenel Swart's Toy Poodle Ch Cherylu Phoenix Fire. On the right is Connie Jarman.
photo Bellstone

Goldfields Dog of the Year is Ron and Venessa Juckes' Border Collie Ch Linbrie Return T Sender of Venron. With them are judge Bo Skalin, the sponsor's representative and chairman Rob Forsythe.
photo Bellstone

At Breede Rivier Vallei FCI show in Cape Town, Michael Forte's BIS was Lorette Gray-Smith, Jenni Gray and Jacoline Botha's Australian Shepherd Ch Rosemere I'm A Firefly for Stavros.
photo Bellstone

Dog World Annual 2014

AUSTRALIA

Lee Pieterse

In the lead for Australia's Top Dog competition is the Standard Poodle Sup Ch Huffish Dynamite Street 'Lex', owned by Camilla Tell-Collinge and Brett Hamilton, who has won 26 BIS all breeds since January. Lex was exported to Australia from Camilla's Swedish home and was bred by Charlotte Sandell, breeder of some of the top Poodles in Sweden. His kennelmate was Sweden's Top Dog for 2010 and his grandsire was Sweden's number two all-breeds 2006. Among Lex's wins have been three Royal Show victories: Canberra under James Reynolds from 1,701 entries, Brisbane (pictured) under Paula Heikkinen-Lehkonen, 2,418, and Melbourne, Denys Janssen, 3,441.
photo Ingrid Matschke

Celebrating 150 years of dog showing

AUSTRALIA'S first dog show was held in Hobart, the capital of the island state of Tasmania, on November 12, 1862, apparently the first recorded dog show in the English speaking world outside the UK.

Early days in the Hobart Town colony were hard and quite often supplies sent were ruined, inadequate or of very poor quality. Hunting dogs were very useful as on occasion the colony was put on short rations and only the ability to supplement the meat supply with kangaroo fed the people.

In September 1849 it is reported that in Melbourne (Victoria), 1,200 wandering dogs were destroyed by the city's police with apparently little improvement to the harassment of the locals by roaming street dogs. Every household seemingly had loose claim to one or more dogs – mostly large breeds like Newfoundlands, Mastiffs and 'kangaroo' dogs.

By a strange quirk of fate it was this situation which brought about the first recorded Australian dog show in Hobart Town. The impetus was the report from Victoria of a 'non descript and worthless cur' that sallied out from a hole, attacked the heels of a gallant soldier's horse, causing said gentleman to fall off and be killed. The inference was that if people could be encouraged to keep purebred dogs the nuisance of crossbred animals would be lessened!

Thus the grandly named 'Society for the Improvement in the Breed of Dogs' was formed with the intention of conducting an exhibition which would 'educate the populace in the useful varieties, inducing people

Darwin Royal BIS under Marie Merchant was the Affenpinscher Sup Ch Strongfort Que Será Será, owned by Ashley Reid and Kerry McKinnon. The entry was 198 dogs.

Kenneth Edh's choice as BIS at Adelaide Royal from 2,619 entries was Avril Stoffels' Deerhound Ch Anduril Robbie Burns.
photo Ingrid Matschke

to keep a good dog to lessen, as far as possible, the number of useless curs with which the city is at present infested'.

The society's name was changed to The Canine Society and its first president was the barrister/solicitor John Woodcock Graves (the younger).

Now to current times. For 2012 the Canine Exhibition Committee was set up by Dogs Tasmania – the state of Tasmania's controlling body, as each state in Australia runs its own affairs, by and large – to conduct a show to celebrate 150 years since Australia's first dog show.

BIS at Sydney Royal from 3,227 dogs under Barbara Müller was the US-bred Old English Sheepdog Sup Ch To-Jo's If I Could Beam Back Time for Maree Aitchison and Joy Kelley.
photo Ffire

At the 2012 Launceston Royal Show in Tasmania BIS under Nina Karlsdotter was the Border Collie Sup Ch Khayoz All The Kings Men CDX owned by Khayoz Kennels John and Kate Valk). Total entry was 650. He was also RBIS at Melbourne.
photo Trafford

Perth Royal's BIS, chosen by Sergio Pizzorno from an entry of 1,161, was Emma and Christine Luxford's Shetland Sheepdog Sup Ch Ambermoon Sweet Georgia ET.

Dogzonline Show Dog of the Year 2012 was the Dalmatian Sup Ch Paceaway at Rosemount, owned by Fran Matthews, Glen Vernon and Ron and Diane Besoff. At the time of writing he is second in the 2013 rankings, followed by the UK-bred Lhasa Apso Sup Ch Chethang Nathaniel (Paul and Kay York, Jenny Longmire and Michael Camac); Petit Basset Griffon Vendéen Sup Ch/NZ Gr Rokeena Garcon Reveur (Robyn and Russell Wallis, Robyn Hay and Shellie Marshall); and New Zealand-bred Siberian Husky Sup Ch/NZ Gr Ch Alyeshka Little Miss Perfect (Sarah Halliday, Tamzin Letele and Cherie Bryson-Karam).
photo Mayfoto

Dog World Annual 2014

In line with the nature of this 'Australian' celebration both exhibits and judges came from each state. The official opening was performed by Hon Peter Underwood, the Governor of Tasmania, during which he made presentations to the junior handler class winners for the 2012 State Final.

The final of the 'Made in Tasmania' competition was won by German Shepherd **Ch Karraine Blazing Upa Storm**, owned by Patricia and Kevin Eaves-Tennant and handled by Sue Charlton.

BIS was judged by Richard Watson (Tasmania) and he selected an Akita, **Sup Ch Daykene Care Factor Zero**, owned by Tabatha Buckley, Julia Hamill and Tracey Walker.

The (UK) Kennel Club sent a trophy for best Australian bred in show. This was hotly contested and won by by Gaye Walters' Maltese **Sup Ch Merimalt Back Door Phantasy**, co-owned with breeders Peter and Trish Cutler. Thank you to Kaye Klapp for this information.

Meanwhile the tragedy of puppy farming is gaining notoriety in Australia with work by numbers of groups, most notably Oscar's Law based in Victoria, and RSPCA South Australia who have made some spectacularly successful raids on puppy farmers and rescued dogs from the most appalling conditions.

Photographs taken at the scenes of these raids demonstrate the unspeakable suffering these animals have to endure so that their breeders can make an easy tax-free profit.

Increasingly, through media exposure, the general puppy buying public is tending NOT to buy their puppy from a shop, usually supplied by puppy farmers, but rather a kennel control-registered breeder. Not only does such a breeder provide the protection of the strict rules of the kennel control for responsible breeding, the buyer can also meet the parents of their puppy and see how they live.

There is also growing pressure in Australia to join the worldwide move towards legislation to restrict incompetent and irresponsible breeders and to root out unscrupulous puppy farmers.

At the special show held in Hobart, Tasmania, to mark 150 years of dog shows in Australia, BIS was the Akita Sup Ch Daykene Care Factor Zero, owned by Tabatha Buckley, Julia Hamill and Tracey Walker.
photo Trafford

Dog World Annual 2014

Around the DOG WORLD in 2013

BIS winner at Barbados' November 2012 show under Paul Harding was Andy Taylor's UK-bred Japanese Shiba Inu Ch Calicelesti The One N'Only. In March 2013 Peter Jolley put up the Moores' UK-bred Irish Setter Sh Ch Fearnley Fire Storm of Moorlands.
photos Barbara Greenidge

At the Mediterranean Winner Show in Slovenia BIS under Stefan Sinko was Ilze Fraimane's Phalene Magic Sunrise Great Gentleman. The previous day BIS at Koper show was Franco Properi's Maltese Cinecitta' Diane Lane, handled by Javier Mendikote. Judge was Carlos Saevich.
photos Karl Donvil

Four shows were held on consecutive days in Buenos Aires, Argentina, in March. BIS winners were: Ilaria Biondi de Ciabatti's Standard Poodle Ricmart Live Now Pay Later, judge Tamas Jakkel (above), Lilian Colantonio's Dogo Argentino Monika de Don Eloy, Petru Muntean (below right), Ana Beatriz and Mario Knoll's Pomeranian Excalibur Quest Rapture, Paula Heikkinen-Lehkonen (below) and Ricardo Oppenhein's Spanish Water Dog Dalicandyb de Ubrique, Jean-Jacques Dupas (right).
photos Paula Heikkinen-Lehkonen

Winner of Estonia's champion of champions competition in 2012 was Anu-Sirje's American-bred Lakeland Terrier Int Ch Shaireab's Bayleigh Ticket To Ride. Judges were Paula Heikkinen-Lehkonen and Ligita Zake.
photo Kristine Zake

132

Dog World Annual 2014

At Lithuania's main shows of 2012, the BIS winners were Marina Dorokhina's Border Collie Jimjam at Real Pearl and Inguna Grava-Thurman and Kristine GravaBardina's Italian Greyhound Int Ch Lux Loral Innocenzo. Judges were Lisbeth Mach and Paula Heikkinen-Lehkonen.
photos Paula Heikkinen-Lehkonen

BIS winners at Brno in the Czech Republic were Lenka Fjkusova's Schnauzer Ave Concorde Magnifique (judge Miroslav Vaclavik) and Eva Vendlerová Jiroutová's Continental Landseer Arun Z Laderova (judge Gabriella Ridarcikova).
photos Gabor Scalanczi

At Nitra's spring shows in Slovakia the BIS winners (above) were Jószef Koroknai's Old English Sheepdog Bottom Shaker So Easy To Love, handled by Zsolt Hano, and Iva Raic's Petit Basset Griffon Vendéen Around No Problems, who also won supreme BIS at the country's June shows. Judges were Ramuné Kazlauskaité and Tino Pehar.
photos Gabor Scalanczi

At the Timisaora shows in Romania, Andrew Brace's BIS was Natalija Kale ak Radovanovi's Petit Basset Griffon Vendéen Kan Trace All I Do Is Win, while Gabriel Valdez put up Attilio Vaccari's Weimaraner Bentley del Grandi Grigi.
photos Andrew Brace

Dog World Annual 2014

NEW ZEALAND

Rosemary Hubrich

Will democracy revive the sport?

THE NEW Zealand Kennel Club plans to become a more democratic institution, with a view to increasing members' engagement in the administration process.

The first of the constitutional changes was approved at the NZKC conference of delegates, with the decision to adopt 'one club, one vote'. This will mean a great increase in the number of votes for Executive Council positions and a move to postal voting. Voting by member clubs will be compulsory.

The Executive Council elected in 2014 will serve a two-year term, rather than the traditional one year. Unfortunately this has been one reason why the current president, Owen Dance, has indicated that he will not seek re-election. He said that he took on the position with a view to spending about three years mending rifts and sorting out problems. With that mission virtually complete, he now needs more time for his own career.

NZKC finances made a great recovery in the past year, and the Auckland Exhibition Centre is now thriving under local management.

The commitment to a more democratic future seeks to enhance members' involvement and to retain and revitalise interest in the sport of dogs. Participation continues to decline, particularly at shows. There are various factors, not least the participants themselves who too often are unkind to new exhibitors and discourage competition. An NZKC survey indicated this was a major reason for non-renewal of NZKC membership.

There is a growing trend for breeders to sell only unregistered puppies or puppies registered with endorsements so that they cannot be shown or bred from. Breeders who don't want to sell to show homes so that they do not generate competition for themselves, limit the gene pool and any incentive to improve a breed, thus helping to ensure the demise of a breed and of shows.

At the conference the New Zealand Dog Judges Association was officially recognised. It will handle the training and examination of judges. NZKC has final approval of judges' qualifications gained through training schemes administered by the NZDJA.

Eukanuba continues as a generous major sponsor of NZKC. There are NZKC Eukanuba awards for Canine Heroes and Canine Good Citizens, but the main event continues to be the NZKC Eukanuba National Show which features breed competition (where dogs can qualify for Crufts), obedience and Rally-O, plus junior handling with a trip to Crufts for the winner. There is also the Eukanuba Sevens Challenge where seven nominated group shows receive generous sponsorship for cash BIS prizes.

The ultimate Eukanuba prize goes to the year's Eukanuba Challenge winner – the top winning dog in NZ, according to the Dogzonline point score. The winner is funded to travel and compete in the Eukanuba World Challenge in the US. The past two years, the winners have been imports, destined to return to overseas owners, NZKC has approved changes to the rules so that our winners will in future be more truly a NZ representative.

A lot of NZKC energy has been focused on our stance regarding the Animal Welfare Amendment Bill being placed before Parliament. Docking was back in the spotlight and an NZKC survey produced a majority response in favour of our opposition to those parts of the Bill that will limit our freedom to manage our dogs as we chose. NZKC has made submissions to defend our right to be consulted before any regulations or guidelines are created that may impact on our sport.

It is imperative that NZKC can be seen to be an organisation

BIS at the NZKC Eukanuba National Show was the Pointer Chesterhope The Game, owned by Diane, Jordyn and Cara O'Neill.
photo Supashots

New Zealand's number one all breeds and 2013 Eukanuba Challenge Winner is the Kerry Blue Terrier Am Gr Ch/NZ Gr Ch Hayton's Talizman, owned by Denise Clark (NZ) and Balkrishna Setty (India).
photo Supashots

Winner of the 2013 Eukanuba Junior Dog Handling Contest was Gemma Rushton who has been competing in handling contests for years, has attended dog shows since she was a baby and exhibits Pekingese. She will represent NZ in the international final at Crufts.
photo Supashots

Winner of the 2013 Supreme Dog Contest, held in Christchurch was Teresa Lawrence's American-bred Bouvier des Flandres Gr Ch Vanleighofs Kiss The Girls who was also runner-up in the Eukanuba Challenge. In the contest, runner-up was the Longhaired Dachshund Aus Gr/NZ Gr Ch Keaton Kosciosko, owned by Beth Warman and Jim and Lyndall Black.
photo Supashots

of ethical dog enthusiasts. However a significant minority of breeders do significant harm to NZKC by their disreputable treatment of buyers. Damage control by NZKC favours the option of promoting 'Accredited Breeders', then distinguishing breeders who sign up for a set of voluntary code of breeders' ethics.

NZKC is working with NZ's leading online trading forum to develop protocols that will improve the integrity of claims made by people advertising puppies for sale.

The Groomalong contest in Christchurch was a triumph for the NZ team who won the Trans Tasman Trophy, The team was encouraged to compete in the World Team Championship in Barcelona and is currently fund-raising to achieve that goal.

Christchurch is still recovering from devastating earthquakes several years ago and a book has been published about dogs who were heroes and victims of those quakes. Many dogs are still traumatised by their shaky environment.

JAPAN
How can we reverse declining entries?

Mai Ozeki

ALTHOUGH I have stated repeatedly that entries are dropping, 2013 must have been the worst in Japan dog show history.

Average entry for local shows – 90 per cent of shows in Japan are local shows run by local clubs – has been somewhere from 150 to 250. My club has been known to get the biggest entries among local clubs but even this one was affected. Usually we get somewhere around 500 entries but we had only around 300 this year.

The Japan Kennel Club has taken action

It was like a Cinderella story - a Borzoi named Day Day (GoLightly's Big Day), who was born, raised and had been shown for the past six years in the US, came to Japan early in 2013. The FCI Japan International Show in April, the biggest annual show in Japan with over 2,500 entries, was her debut. No one knew who she was except for her owners, myself and her breeder Marcella Harris Zobel, and handlers but after the two days of the show, she had become a superstar.

She won BIS under Heliane Maissen-Jarisch from Australia, having taken BOB and the group under Carla Molinari from Portugal.

The BIS winner here gets the invitation to compete in the Eukanuba World Challenge in December.

She is among the top ranked dogs in Japan for 2013, along with the other dogs pictured on the next page.
photo Mari Nakashima

135

Dog World Annual 2014

and has attempted to allow fewer clubs to run their shows at the same time but the drop has not happened because there are several different shows on the same weekends in Japan, it is because people are simply losing interest in showing dogs.

Some local clubs have attempted to attract breeders and new exhibitors into the show scene, by organising breeder's stakes, owner-handlers competitions, costume contests, and handling/grooming seminars for owner-handlers. Hopefully those attempts will attract more people into the show world.

The Giant Schnauzer Montesol JP's Evelyn's Star, owned by Yuka Isaka, seen winning BIS under Frank Sabella.
photo Mari Nakashima

The Pyrenean Mountain Dog Tiberius of Space Tamura JP, owned by Hitomi Shibata and shown by Miki Tamura.

The Shih Tzu Oh My God of Pierrot Castle FCI, owned by Keiko Fujigasaki.
photo Nakamura

The Standard Poodle Traid Wind JP Wild Flower, owned by Yumiko Sato and shown by Shota Hirai.

The Pembroke Corgi Balmy Winds JP Jake, owned by Toshiko Maeda, seen winning under James Reynolds.

The Toy Poodle Smash JP Winner Take It All, owned by Toshinori Omura.

Daisy Brook
BOARDING KENNELS.

A boarding kennel that is truly a home from home.
- Day & Overnight Boarding
- Training facilities
- Cooked diets catered for
- Customer built facility
- Secure & heated kennels
- Over 3 1/2 acres

Owned & run by Matt & Sally Hunt
Woodland Road
Stanton
Burton-upon-Trent
DE15 9TH
- A444 Stanton
- Main road into Burton
Near to East Midlands & Birmingham International Airport

Luxury Boarding Kennels | Boarding Daycare | Training Facilities

T: 01283 480 248   M: 07860 643 217
E: daisybrookboardingkennels@gmail.com

We are proud suppliers of Challenge Dog Food & Mariners Choice Fish Treats

Dog World Annual 2014

Summertime...
and the living is easy

Steven Seymour reviews the elite of Europe's summer shows

WHAT IS it about the summer shows which are so appealing? We all know that the really big shows are mostly held in the winter. Crufts and the big Scandinavian Winner Shows such as Stockholm and Helsinki are wonderful but it is the summer shows which really lift our spirits.

I thought I would look at my choice for the best summer shows in Europe. I am sure there are plenty which come to mind but my choices are mainly from shows at which I have judged or shown. They all have a certain flavour which makes them beautiful and a treat to be part of.

WINDSOR

What dog person doesn't know Windsor dog show? It is iconic the world over. It represents everything British, held in Home Park with the backdrop of Windsor Castle on one side and the River Thames on the other.

Windsor says summer in so many ways and who doesn't want to bring out their new puppy when the weather is usually at its best?

What makes Windsor so special is the international flavour. This must be in part because of the great location, just a short train trip from central London and only ten minutes from Heathrow Airport.

The ever popular overseas visitors' tent sits at the heart of this. It provides more than a cold drink or a welcome cup of tea. It is the meeting place for people from all over the world to chat and catch up while they take in the very best of British dog shows. Who hasn't been to Windsor and had a Pimm's and lemonade or a few strawberries with cream?

Irene Terry and her hard working team always make judges and visitors welcome. The trademark pink jackets are worn by the committee and they can be seen about the show all day.

Windsor is a show which many always associate with the late Catherine Sutton, a larger than life figure who was known the world over. I have my own fond memories of Windsor from my first visit to the UK in the late 1970s; indeed I was a ring steward for two days and still have the steward's rosette in my box of doggy things. It's lovely to think that Patricia Sutton is still part of the Windsor team keeping that connection alive.

Windsor has always been a great show and part of its fame and reputation must be due to the long list of great names and personalities associated with the club:

FINNISH TOY DOG CLUB

Number one by a mile for me is the Finnish Toy Dog Club show in Helsinki. This is the largest toy show in Europe with well over 1,000 toy dogs every year.

It scores top points for many reasons. First is the beautiful setting. Right in the heart of Helsinki is Kaivopuisto Park with the harbour on one side and backed by a row of embassy houses on the other.

The show is held at the end of August and the weather as a rule is almost perfect, sunny and warm with a lovely sea breeze across the verdant grass.

The show is regarded as the club specialty for many breeds and so many specialist judges are used, which ensures a good breed entry.

As it is just five minutes' walk from the main streets of Helsinki there is always a steady flow of public watching the judging and this gives the whole show a relaxed friendly feeling that not many shows can manage.

The other reason why it takes top billing from me is the stylish and professional way the whole event is run. The late Kirsti Lummelampi was a master of style and class in everything she did. I have it on very good authority that the new team steered by Elizabeth Schauman carried on Kirsti's good work in every way.

Below right: Windsor's covered main ring, situated below the castle, home of the royal family for centuries, and just a short walk from the River Thames.

Judges are accommodated in one of Helsinki's best boutique hotels just a short walk from the showground.

This club wins not only for setting and location but also for its style and flair. This really is a show that toy people want to show, win and judge at.

The club also has a great website which is not only kept up to date but is full of breed information and history of the show and its judges and much more.

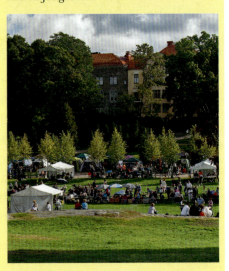

The Finnish Toy Dog Club show held in Helsinki's Kaivopuisto Park.

Molly Garrish, Ken Rawlings, Sir Dudley Forwood, Terry Thorn, Leonard Pagliero OBE, Oonagh Gore and Liz Cartledge just to list a few. Great shows are more than just a good setting, it's the people at their heart and this show proves that fact.

ESTORIL

Once again we have a great show with a big personality at its heart. Carla Molinari knows how to run a show from top to bottom which is no surprise as this show has been run by her since 1983. When you set the show in a tropical park looking out to sea, it becomes a winning combination.

Lisbon in summer can be hot, sometimes too hot, but Estoril Park is lined with cool shady palm trees and served with a good dose of sea breeze to keep everyone happy. The backdrop of the famous Estoril Casino, the largest in Europe, really sets the scene for a bit of glamour.

Carla is certainly no prima donna when it comes to organising things. On the Friday while judges were enjoying a stroll along the sea front or a swim in the hotel pool, Carla was in her best working clothes, hands-on, turning the park into a truly beautiful setting.

The Friday evening has a host of small club shows which help boost entries, followed by two one-day all-breed shows.

One of the lovely features of this show is the BIS ring with hospitality for the judges. The final judging can take several hours but judges are treated to a spread of delicious snacks and drinks all served in style under a huge marquee. Anyone who has been to Portugal knows what fun people they are and this atmosphere is felt the whole weekend. Huge crowds of public made their way to see the show and the final judging was three deep with people all afternoon.

Another nice touch about this show is that Carla lives locally and works well with the local tourist board to promote the show and always tries hard to make use of as many local businesses as possible. The trophies this year were all bought from a local pottery maker. Judges' lunches are taken in one of the many restaurants around the park and ground security is done by local companies.

This is a show with a big international flavour yet the local community is kept firmly in mind at all times.

Estoril show – sea breezes and sun in Portugal.

SOFIERO

Another show with a castle as the backdrop is Sofiero in Sweden.

This is an absolute favourite of mine. It is held early in September and is usually regarded as the last of the outdoor shows in Sweden. I have judged here in glorious sunshine and also pelting rain but if the sun shines this is one of the loveliest settings for any Scandinavian show.

The backdrop of the castle is the highlight with the lush green grass rings. The showground has some beautiful gardens between the two ring areas and it's lovely to take a stroll through them. The other rings which don't face the castle are positioned facing the sea looking out towards Denmark.

Maybe because it's the last show of summer, but there is always a busy atmosphere with trade stands and food vendors occupied the whole day. Judges are treated to lunch in the summer house of the castle with a typical Swedish lunch looking out towards the sea. The judging panel is always very international with all regions of Europe represented alongside many Scandinavian judges, of course. The main ring is always a picture with large floral displays. The trophy table is overflowing with tall cups and rosettes to be won.

What is always nice about Scandinavian shows is that lots of exhibitors stay for the final judging. The picture of the breeders' groups lined up on the lush green grass with the ring assistants all dressed in traditional Swedish costumes makes for a truly special summer show.

SPLIT

This is a four-day cluster of shows in Croatia which has become legendary across Europe. What makes Split shows unique is they want exhibitors to bring along their families and make a real summer holiday of the event.

Judging is held during the night, which is great for the dogs in the hot summer weather, but it also means that people can make the best of a beach holiday while showing their dogs with lazy days on the beach or exploring the history that Split offers. Then at night, after the heat and crowds have gone, the dogs can come out and the shows begin.

It can be a very late night but from what I am told it really is the most fun ever to be had while winning a CACIB.

Ante Lučin really stretches his team to make the shows not only well run, but also a really fun family event. It's no wonder that people travel such huge distances to make Split shows a must for a summer holiday with the dogs.

Once again the judging panel is international so exhibitors have four different judges from near and far. I was amazed looking at the results from past years that some of the winning dogs had travelled huge distances, including from Scandinavia, Russia and Japan. So there is little doubt that exhibitors will travel for a good judge at a well-run show, especially if there is more than just one chance at winning.

Another feature of these shows is the focus on the junior handling events. The many young handlers are given equal billing in the show timetable and a win at this show is highly sought after.

It is interesting that Split shows make good use of social media tools with Facebook to promote the shows and advertise the judges. They also have a very good website packed with information to help exhibitors in every way with information on accommodation, road maps, showground details and a little history of the area. This is certainly the way to get real exposure for a show. Facebook reaches everybody who is involved with dogs and its effect has really worked for this hard working clever team.

I have not been to the Split shows but keep hearing from judges and exhibitors alike that they are the best fun ever to be had at a dog show.

Some of the scenes which make the Summer Nights shows in Split unique.

Obituaries

Over the past year the world of dogs has lost many significant personalities. It is remarkable how many of those we mention were not only clever breeders or exhibitors, but also put so much work into running breed clubs, general societies or welfare organisations. How can we possibly replace them? To the families of all 'dog people' we have lost go our thoughts and sympathy.

In recent times few dog people have been as widely mourned as **Ellis Hulme**. As an exhibitor he started as a boy with King Charles and progressed to Papillons in which his many Tongemoor champions included the breed's first BIS winner and first Crufts group winner. As a judge he was renowned for his knowledge, flair and kindness of manner, and reached the heights of BIS at Crufts. He served on several Kennel Club committees, including the General, and was chairman and later patron of UK Toy. A true 'all-rounder'.

Bill Hardaway was one of the Kennel Club's loyallest supporters, serving on the General Committee for 19 years and as vice-chairman through Ronnie Irving's chairmanship until he reached retirement age in 2010. His calmness, fairness, kind manner and common sense gained him universal respect. His own background was in working trials, mainly with German Shepherds. He was the inspiration behind the highly successful Good Citizen Dog Scheme and earlier in the year the KC gave him an award to acknowledge his work with the scheme. Crufts, the Young Kennel Club and the Accredited Instructors scheme also benefited greatly from his work with them.

Hazel Arris bred some super Afghan Hounds under the Sharazah affix and was a popular chairman of Leeds show. **Shirley Carr** (Bozwood) worked hard for the Afghan, especially for breed rescue; **Chris Greenwood** was partner with Domenico Traversari in the famous Altsides; **Linda Saunders-Bishop** (Lindabeas) was involved in both Afghans and Min Pins, while **Tony van Schaick** (Vanathan) was well known in Beagles, Afghans and Borzois.

Doreen Gilberthorpe (Blaby) showed some exceptional Basset Hounds. **Pam Evans**' Amberleigh Miniature Smooth Dachshunds were a major force in Scotland and **Joan Voaden**'s Berrycourts appear in many pedigrees. **Vivienne Croxford MBE** had the Arbroath Min Longs and **Chris Leyshon** the Picklescotts. **Mary Bearne**, who was 109, had the Tanglewood Wires and was an early breeder of Min Wires. **Ruth Spong**'s Peredurs were of fundamental importance to Min Wires and she had some good Smooths too.

Julie Stevens-Smith of the Redbanner Borzois died tragically when she was hit by a train at a level crossing.

In Deerhounds **Blaze Harris** (Drissaig) was an unforgettable personality. **Roly Cross** (Sallidene) was best known for this breed and English Springers and as a show official. **Sue Rathbone-Scott** bred the Tullygirvan Wolfhounds in Northern Ireland.

Barbara Parsons was the official owner of the world-famous RP Greyhounds, campaigned from Cornwall by her late husband Ralph.

Janet Wiginton (Trevereux) was known for Briards and Affenpinschers but will perhaps best be remembered for her charismatic Otterhound Cypher.

Peter Jones did much for Rhodesian Ridgebacks and for the Justice For Dogs charity.

David Waters died in New Zealand, aged 103. With his wife Hope, who bred the world-famous Burydown Salukis, he wrote an acclaimed book on the breed. **Sonja Lambrinudi** did very well with the Geldaras. Whippets lost **Frances Charles** of the Chatwigs.

One of the gentlemen of

the dog world was **Ed Simpson**, known with his late wife Joan for the Coltrim Cockers, as a group judge, breed club and Kennel Club Committee man and vice-president of the National.

Two veteran English Setter breeders were **Philip Gardiner-Swann** (Silbury) who with his wife bred the 1964 Crufts BIS winner and **Doug Patterson** (Scardale). **Bettie Town** enjoyed amazing success with the Sharnberrys at field trials, and was the first woman to serve on the KC Field Trials Sub-Committee.

Jackie Perkins' Gardenway dogs had a big impact on the Hungarian Vizsla.

Dr June Squire owned some important Flatcoat males and worked hard for the breed and Windsor Gundog Society. With their families **Jean Allen** bred the Allenie Labradors and **Peggy Edwards** the Lasgarns. **Frank Whitbread** (Lathkil/Lathbern) was a long-time Labrador enthusiast and in more recent years had been involved with Bernese Mountain Dogs; in both breeds he did tremendous work for the breed clubs. **Gordon Howells** (Brynseion) did a great deal for the Labrador in Wales. **Doreen Climpson** had the Othamcourts and **Betty Lamming** (Lowna) died at 97. **Frank 'Gaffer' Truslove**, husband of Gwen Broadley, played his part in the story of the great Sandylands kennel.

Pat Holmes bred the Beaconholm Goldens and **Thelma Theed** (Squirrelsmead) was for many years secretary of the parent club. Later in the year Goldens lost three famous names, group judge **Peggy Robertson** of the Stolford kennel, **Jean Bursnett** (Rossbourne) and **Heather Morris** (Sandusky).

One of the most important kennels in Cocker Spaniels history was Weirdene, owned by **Richmond Weir** from Scotland. There were many top winning champions in both solids and particolours and he established a true, distinctive strain. In the same breed **John Tyson** showed the Browsters, **Pamela Gibson** the Meldykes and **Les and Freda Curran**, who died within a few days of each other at a great age, the Curagowries. **Lilian Whiteley** (Snowgate) bred Cockers and Americans.

Many years ago **Alex Roskell**'s Cuerden Clumbers produced some influential dogs, as did **Mary Harris**' Sunreef Sussex. **Keith Payne** bred the Verulam English Springers.

Fred Musselwhite was a highly successful field trialler with his Friuli German Shorthaired Pointers.

Henry Hall had the Caerhayes Pointers and Boxers and was well known as a steward at many big shows. Pointers also lost, at just 41, **Karen Klein-Woolthuis** (Haxalgate).

DOG WORLD had special reason to mourn **Frank Jones** as he was our

representative at the championship shows for many years, as well as writing the *Northern Topics* column. He had been a successful Smooth Fox Terrier exhibitor with the Jonwyre affix and professionally handled a number of other terrier breeds such as Lakelands and Irish. He progressed to group and BIS judging, wrote a history of the Lakeland and did his utmost to get the Northern Dog Centre started.

Monica Shuttleworth (Monary) was a successful Cairn exhibitor and more widely known as secretary for many years of National Terrier.

Fiona Cameron had many successes with her Stryveling Cairn Terriers but will be best remembered for her administrative and editing work for the benefit of the breed. Border Terriers lost **Peter Thompson**, clever breeder of the Thoraldbys, **Joyce Fagan** (whose Elandmead affix was also known in Bichons) and **John Fulton** (Woodneuk) who did much for the breed in Scotland. **Ross Liddell** had the Tebross Airedales.

Jean Halliwell owned the Wigmore Lakeland and Welsh Terriers, achieving RBIS at Crufts with the latter. **Kevin Hall** had the Gosel Lakeland and Smooth Fox Terriers. He left us far too soon as did **Michael Gray** who made a mark with his Graylag Kerry Blue and Smooth Fox Terriers and Boxers. **Sue Holroyd** (Ballroyd) showed Lakelands, Welsh and Griffons.

Flo Stubbington (Calot) was one of the characters of the Manchester Terrier scene. **Eileen Herderson** had the Gundagi Australian Terriers, **Lily Taylor** the Crossmatch Bull Terriers and **Sheila Harding** the Hardras. **Dr David Harris** had lived in the US for many years but started his Brummagem kennel in the UK. His breed books were classics, especially the latest, surely the most comprehensive breed history ever written.

Di Collis' Riplington Parson Russells had a significant impact on the breed.

Shirley Hooper (Yorsar) was a tireless worker for West Highland White Terrier breed clubs as was **Ken Corri** (Inverglen). **Jean Mottram** (Whitewells) was a senior Scottie enthusiast. **Gerry Holmes** had the Holmestaff Staffords.

Brian Daws was a familiar figure on the Bulldog scene with the Outdoors dogs which he and his wife Judith took over from her parents. **Pauline Hayes** was an early Akita breeder with the Brandeezis.

Bob Wine was a long-time Chow enthusiast and an enthusiastic worker for both breed and general clubs, serving as show manager and later vice-president of Paignton championship show. Paignton had a strong Chow connection and **Joan Dimond** was secretary for 20 years and president when she died at 93. **Ida Bishop** bred the Penangwun Chows.

Mary Greening (Tollcross) was successful in

Dog World Annual 2014

both Dalmatians and West Highland Whites and a hard worker for breed clubs who did much to research deafness in Dalmatians. **Janet Tierney** had the Kinkeesha Keeshonds and **Chris Moore**, who was 103, the Gelderlands.

Vivien Watkins was the first lady of French Bulldogs in the UK, having been devoted wholeheartedly to

the breed since 1947. Her Bomlitz dogs left an indelible mark on the breed, She was the figurehead of the breed's parent club, maintained an amazing archive of breed history and set standards of behaviour seldom seen today. For 50 years she wrote breed notes for DOG WORLD.

No one around in the '70s will forget extrovert **Vicky Marshall** with the Vicmars

Standard and Toy Poodles. The former had a profound impact on the breed. She had lived in Australia for many years after passing the affix to Sharon Pine-Haynes.

Jim Outterside's Florontie Miniature Poodles included a BIS winner and he had been chairman of Leeds championship show. **Gwen Holbourn** bred the Shanpave apricot Poodles but was best known as secretary of Coulsdon CS since its foundation, and of the Standard Poodle Club. **Les Harwood** (Nairda) also did much for the Poodle world as well as supporting his wife's showing activities. **Chris Onions** was the senior of three generations with the Chrisalette Poodles and **Arthur Jellings** was yet another breed stalwart.

Dave Johnson (Khados) was successful in Tibetan Terriers and, earlier, Afghans. **Jill White** showed the Gulgates TTs. **Bob Bradley** was partner in the famous Botolph Lhasa Apsos.

Deirdre Jenkins was one half of the phenomenally successful and influential Amcross Tibetan Spaniels; the kennel, at the top for nearly 50 years, continues

with partner MC Hourihane. They bred some super Pomeranians too.

Louise Harrington bred the Ardenbridge Bernese but will have been more widely known as official vet for many of the championship shows.

Eleanor Oliver (Amberglen) was a senior figure in the Bouvier world and had been involved in Rough Collies for many years before that. **Mary Reardon**, **Phyllis Teversham**, **Graham Hicks** (Jilgrajon), **Kim Dodd-Utting** (Heffalump, who died in a car accident) and **Jackie Critoph** (Famrise) were all stalwarts of the Mastiff breed and the latter was also keen on Neapolitans. **Barbara Brookes** was involved in every aspect of the Newfoundland world.

Boxers lost **Moray Bell** (Melvich), one of the great characters of the Scottish scene, **Mary Buswell** (Wanderobo), **Arthur Ainsworth** (Parthanes) and **Charles Walker** (Lynpine), a long-term advocate of the Continental style of dog. The same could be said of **John Hull** (Gaindyke), one of the most popular Dobermann enthusiasts, whose imports have had a big influence on today's breed. **Di Patience**'s Dizown breeding made a big impact, as did the Findjans of **Alma Page Owen**, for other breeders as well as themselves, while **Christine Lamb** bred the Highroyds Dobes and **Peter Clark** the Carrickgreens.

Sue Bown, who died sadly young, had the Sundabish Boxers and, latterly, Bullmastiffs, in which breed **Dorothy Massey** made many Todomas champions and **Joyce James** showed the successful Morejoys in Wales. Her son Ron is a well known judge, secretary and KC committee man.

Jennie Roberts' Arondyke kennel of Great Danes was one of the breed's most influential. **Jack Taylor** (Enydelet) and **Brian Edmonds** (Sherain) also contributed much to that breed while **John Evans** did a lot for the Siberian Husky as both show dog and racer. **Ann Bryant** bred the Attila Rottweilers.

Ann Allen (Shepherdsway) was a well known personality in the Alaskan Malamute world and latterly was best known for her Canadian Eskimo Dogs in which she was for many years the principal UK breeder and importer.

It's hard to know under what breed heading to mention **Barbara Simpson-Collins** (Leircote) for her interests were indeed wide. Pehaps she will be best remembered for her influential Belgian Shepherds, but she also showed Chows, Schipperkes and Manchester Terriers, perhaps one of those people who should have been more widely used as a judge.

Marion Simpson-Wyeth (Ranpura) was one of the founders of the Australian Cattle Dog Society. **Yvonne Westley** had been involved in Belgian Shepherds for over 40 years. **Ian Burgoyne** (Beardievale), well known in both Bearded Collies and Pulis, died sadly young. **Liz Williams**' Rockisland Pulis enjoyed much success and she wrote breed notes in DOG WORLD.

The Dancerwood Smooth Collies of **Judith White** had a significant impact on the breed. In Roughs **Jimmy Tait** (Aberthorne) was both a clever breeder and a considerable character as were **Dick Oliver** (Rixown), **Joan Sykes** (Sykeslaw), **Joan Vaughan** (Laughan) and **Rob McDowall** (Birkmyre). **Terry Dennis** showed the Delaird Briards. **Joan Sanderson** (Colthurst) had been involved with German Shepherds for 50 years.

Joan Real (Tynycoed) bred some superb Old English Sheepdogs and **Bob Cass** was a distinctive personality in the breed. **Clarice Masterson**, too had been involved in Bobtails for many years.

Jackie Harrison showed the successful Glaysdale Shetland Sheepdogs. **Rosemary Seys** (Inchmery), who was almost 100, was probably the last person living to have made up champions before the second world war. Since returning from many years in Kenya she had concentrated on encouraging Sheltie people to get involved in working activities.

Another of Britain's most senior dog people was also involved in Shelties as well as Rough Collies, **Peggy McAdam** of the Helengowans who died at 98. **Mona McConnell** (Shelverne) was successful in both Shelties and Finnish Spitz.

Ray Taylor (Naduska) is a great loss to the Samoyed breed for which he worked so hard, including founding the Samoyed of the Year event. His wife Pam contributes breed notes to DOG WORLD. **Roly Miller** was a popular and successful Samoyed exhibitor.

Doreen Paige bred some excellent Cardigan Corgis, including one-time CC record holder Deb's Delight, under her Grangefield affix. A colourful character, she also founded the natural grooming products company which bears her name. **Annette Finney** bred the Kuanza Cardis. In Pembrokes **Brian Warner** showed the Brisams. **Freda Taylor** (Taymil) had a long standing interest in both breeds. **Elsie Montgomerie**

of the Maldwyn Pembrokes in Scotland died just short of her hundredth birthday. Known for her immaculate appearance, she served as vice-convener of the Scottish Kennel Club of which her daughter Anne Macdonald later became convener.

Tessa Gaines was one of the best known personalities of the Griffon world, continuing the Gaystock kennel founded by her mother. She cared passionately for the breed and for the Japanese Chin, and for many years wrote breed notes in DOG WORLD.

Pekingese lost several famous figures in a short period, notably **Joyce Mitchell** who along with husband Jack made up one of the great partnerships of the dog world. They produced many champions

under the Micklee affix, including a Crufts RBIS winner, as well as a French Bulldog champion. She 'was' the British Pekingese Club, and worked hard for others, and was a group judge.

Dorothy Dearn produced a number of distinguished Dorodea champions, served well several breed, group and general clubs and will best be remembered as secretary for many years of UK Toy, and as a group judge.

Derek Hill had the Derronills Pomeranians, including a Crufts group winner, and earlier had been partner in the Cygals.

Sylvia Brady was successful with the Sylchis Chihuahuas as was **Tony Minoli** with the Marytons and **Chris Belcher** with the Melsel Bichons, in which breed **Paddy Holbrook O'Hara** (Appleacres) was one of the characters. **David Williams** (Huntsbank) was an authority on the Cavalier as was **Betty Dowd** (Tregarron). **Joyce Barton** founded the famous Lorankas now continued by her daughter. **Miriam Tomlinson** showed the Mirroys Griffons and Rottweilers.

Elaine Barnes of the Norleybank Min Pins died sadly young. With his late wife Pauline, **David Abbott** bred the Lordsrake Papillons, while **Gwen Edmed** with the Silverstreaks was a breed veteran. **John Hayes** was partner with his wife Mary in the famous Chantmarles Yorkshire Terriers, in which **Muriel Jackson** bred the Foxcloses.

Overseas, many British judges will have known the ever-stylish **Kirsti Lummelampi**, a Lhasa Apso enthusiast who ran the spectacular shows of the Finnish Toy Dog Club. Spanish all-rounder **Javier Sanchez** was famous for Giant Schnauzers and French Bulldogs.

From Australia, **David Roche** had links to the British dog scene going back more than 60 years. He enjoyed spectacular success with imports, notably in Afghans and

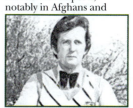

Kerry Blues, and in the '90s brought a homebred Kerry Blue back to the UK and won BIS awards. In 1969, the last year the award was made by a pair of judges, he was the first overseas judge to do BIS at Crufts and still by far the youngest person ever to do so. His art collection is legendary.

In the US, **Walter Goodman** was famous for the immortal Glamoor Skye Terriers, including a Westminster BIS, and latterly as a judge, administrator and benefactor, serving notably the American Kennel Club and Montgomery County on whose show date he died.

Few US all-breed judges were held in such respect as **Michele Billings**, always immaculate and the consummate professional.

141

WE WANT TO THANK THE JUDGES FOR
THEIR APPRECIATION
OF OUR BELOVED DOGS AND
TO ALL PEOPLE AND WORKING TEAM
WHO MADE ALL THIS POSSIBLE!

Team della Golden Era

LORELLA VISMARA, RICHARD HELLMAN, ROBERTA SEMENZATO, FRANCESCO VASANELLA & FEDERICA VICARINI

ad design & photo by Jovana Danilovic © 2013

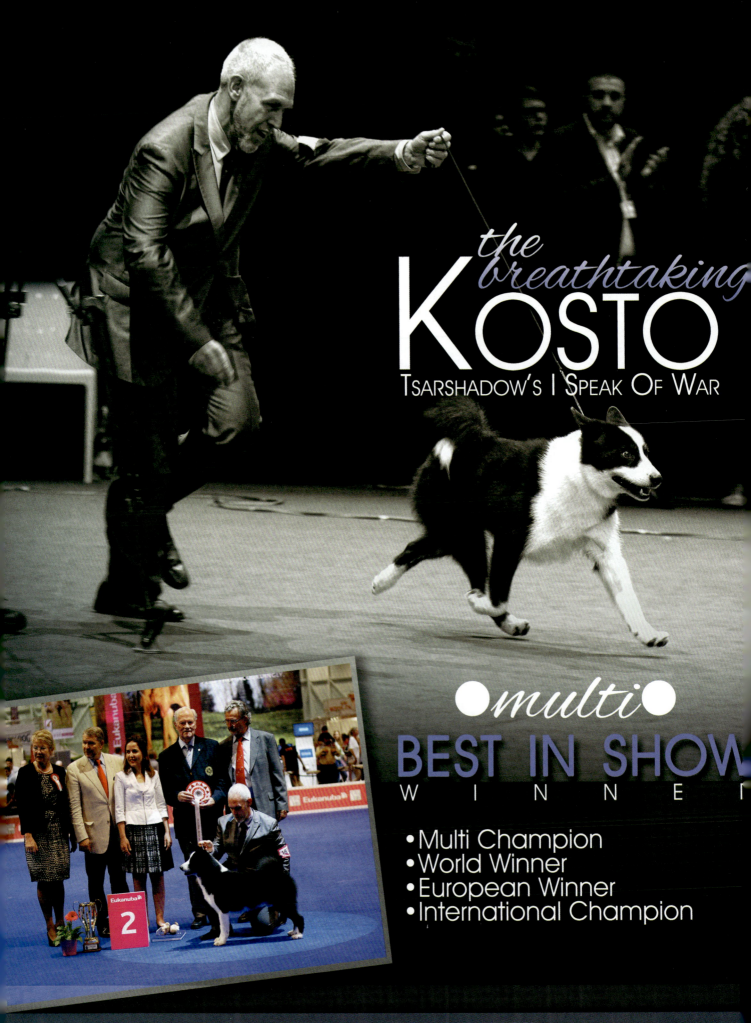

the
one and only
HOWIE
PROPWASH KNOW HOW

●multi●
BEST IN SHOW
P L A C E M E N T
- Multi Champion
- International Champion

GÁBOR

HANDLED BY RICHARD HELLMAN, ASSISTED BY ROBERTA SEMENZATO
OWNED BY LESLIE FRANK & LORELLA VISMARA

ad design by Jovana Danilovic © 2013 · Background photo by Andrea Gaviraghi · Small photo by Gabor Szalanczi

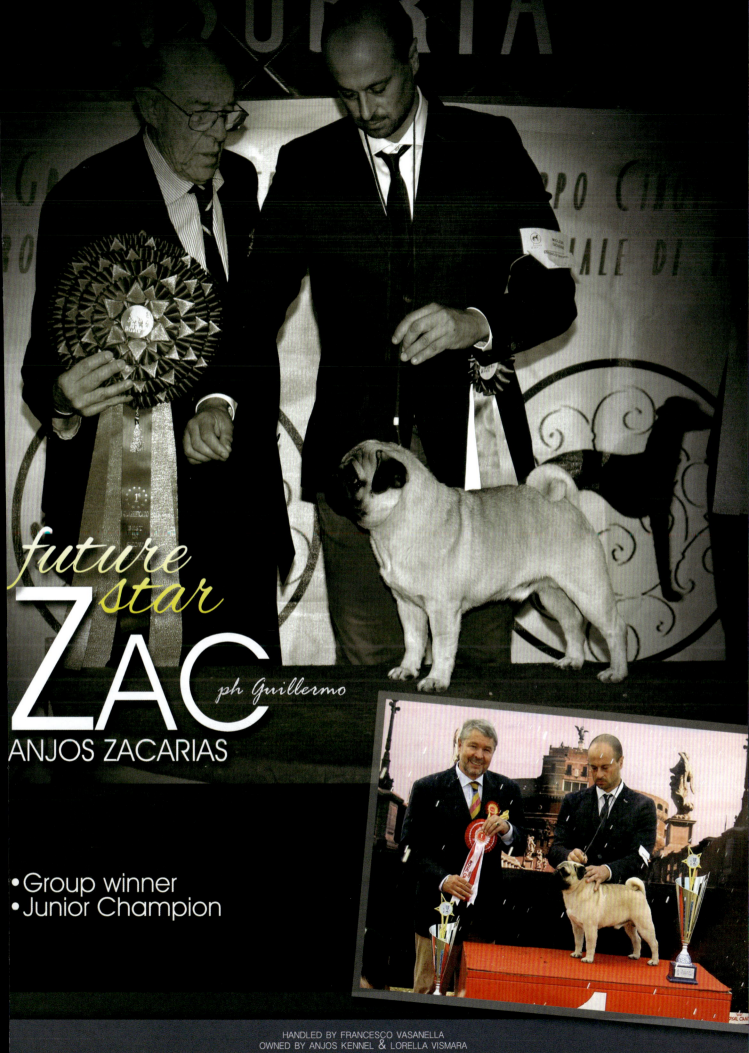

CLEO
WYMESWOLD CRÈME BRULEE

- World Jr. winner
- European winner

OWNED BY
LORELLA VISMARA & SERGE AND SANDRA BAKKER

TRUUS
WYMESWOLD MISS PEBBLES FROM TEXAS

- Multi Champion
- Multi Group winner & placements

OWNED BY
LORELLA VISMARA

BUCK
MOONSTRUCK ST JARNGROSSE

- Multi Champion
- Multi Group placements

OWNED BY
LORELLA VISMARA

ALL DOGS ARE HANDLED BY RICHARD HELLMAN,
AND ASSISTED BY ROBERTA SEMENZATO

ad design by Jovana Danilovic © 2013

The 20 Year Club

As always, we would like to thank the Annual's advertisers for their continued support. Those on pages 152 to 247 and 249 to 251 are members of the 20 Year Club, having first advertised here in 1994 or earlier.

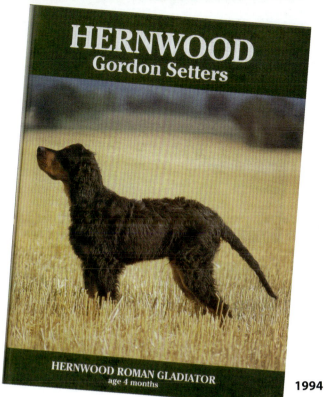

1994

1984

1954

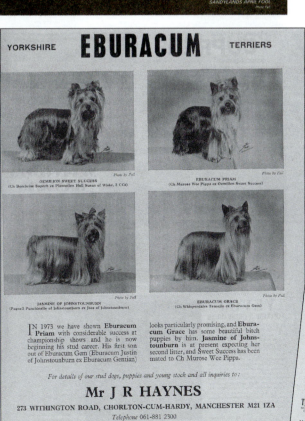

1974

1964

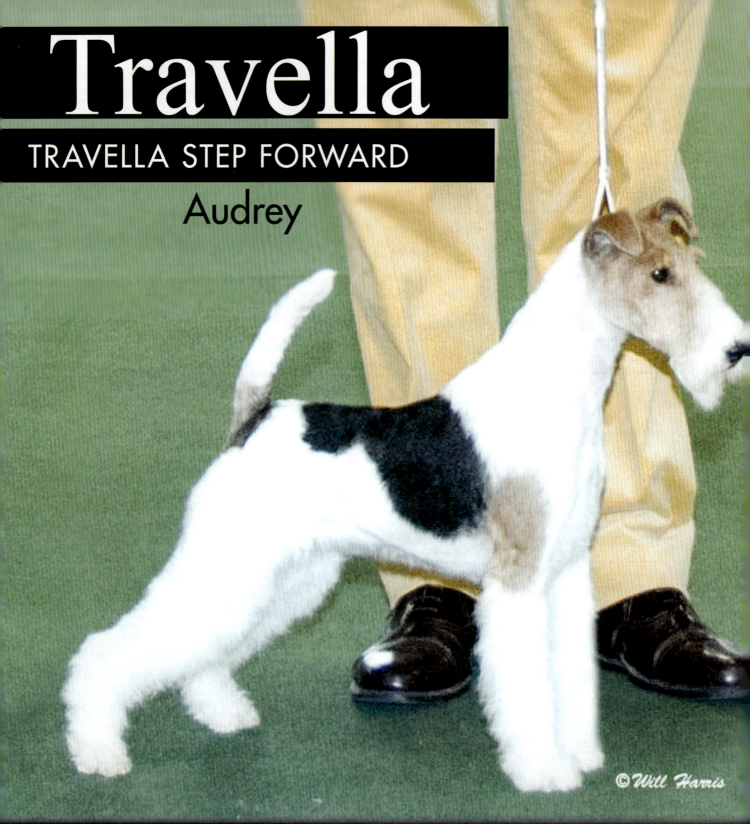

Travella
TRAVELLA STEP FORWARD
Audrey

Untouched photo by Will Harris

Seen here winning BEST PUPPY IN SHOW
at South Wales Kennel Association on her first and only show to date

We look forward to showing her next year.

Owners Geoffrey A Davies and Sue Browne-Cole

Breeder Bill Browne-Cole Handler Richard Allen

Crookrise Agathis
Sh Ch Crookrise Rhum ex Crookrise Rushlight

Crookrise Dom
Crookrise Forest ex Crookrise Free and Easy

Our latest youngster, showing correct balance and construction, tight skin and muscular development

The Kennel celebrated their 80th year in November 2013

Still breeding true to type with a combination of show and working bloodlines

Mrs CICELY A ROBERTSHAW
Thorns Lane, Sedbergh
Cumbria LA10 5LD
Telephone 01539 620316
email crookrise@tesco.net

HELGA EDMONDSON
Mosside Boarding Kennels, Sandyforth Lane
Cowling, Keighley, Yorkshire BD22 0NB
Telephone 01535 637043
email helga@edmondson1361.freeserve.co.uk

www.crookrise.com

The world famous **Crookrise Pointers** EST 1933

JAFRAK
CH JAFRAK PISTOLS AT DORN

PERCY

Proud to be Top-Breeder 2013
jafrak@btopenworld.com
www.jafrak.com

FRENCH BY DESIGN
BULLY BY NATURE

PERCY AND THE YOUNGSTERS

JAFRAK DORAMAAR
&
JAFRAK FRIENDLY PERSUASION

Kanix

20 Year Club

Sh Ch Kiswahili Martin at Kanix

UK's most consistent winner during the last five years – 26 CCs
Sire of 2 UK and 5 North American Champions

Kanix have made up 57 UK Champions
won 53 Groups and 13 BIS

Kari and Sigurd Wilberg
T: 01793 751115 – Sigurd@kanix.cc

Pointers

Coralwood Kanix Mr T

Top Pointer Puppy 2013

Sh Ch Kiswahill Martin at Kanix ex Am Ch Coralwood Yellowleaf Fall Classic

We breed for type and soundness,
but for us temperament is paramount!

Joanne and Heather Blackburn-Bennett

Joanne@kanix.cc

STARGANG Dachshunds & KANIX Pointers 2013

CH SONDEBAR BILLIE JEAN AT STARGANG
(IMP AUS) bred by W Hardie

NEW BITCH CC RECORD HOLDER
25 CCs, 19 with BOB, Top Miniature Smooth 2013

CH STARGANG CZARINA
CC and BOB and Hound Group 3 Crufts

Top CC winning Miniature Wire Bitch 2013

CH STARGANG AVENGER
The 1st UK Male Brindle Miniature Smooth Champion, Top CC winning male 2013

The son of Ch Stargang Lotus Elite, the 1st UK bred Brindle Champion

Owned and loved by
Ellen Blackburn, Joanne and Heather Blackburn-Bennett
Contact: Ellen@stargang.org.uk or shardagang@sky.com

*at time of going to press

STARGANG Dachshunds
2014 HOPEFULS

STARGANG EVORA

2 CCs

Litter sister to
Ch Stargang Avenger

SANDANCA SILVER LADY AT STARGANG

SILVER DAPPLE 2 CCs

As far as records show, the only Dapple Bitch ever to win a CC in the UK

STARGANG MORNING GLOW

Daughter of Ch Sonderbar Billie Jean at Stargang

Miniature Wire/Smooth/Pointer babies will also be making an appearance in the ring in 2014

ASHGATE & HILLCLOUD
West Highland White Terriers

Our boys at stud have produced these wonderful dogs...congratulations to you all

AM GCH ASHGATE US GREAT EXPECTATIONS

(GCh Ashgate McTavish J.E. ex Ashgate US Making Memories at Storybrook)
Owned by Lisa Pacheco and Naomi Brown
2 Owner Handler BIS,1BISS, Number 6 In Breed, Number 5 in All Breed Points as of September 30 in the US

AUST CH YORSAR GOING DOWN UNDER FROM ASHGATE

(Ch Ashgate US Patriot ex Yorsar Penny Borg)
Owned by Tracey Boughen
1 RBIS, 7 Group 1, 10 Group 2. Currently 814 challenge points, Breed leader Queensland

GCH RUSSIA/CH BELARUS HILLCLOUD ICE GLAZE WITH ASHGATE

(Int Ch Ashgate Scots Progress ex Int Ch Hillcloud Drizzle)
Owned by Irina Kharisova handled by Natalya Samoznaeva
BOB at Club Winner Show '13, BOB at specialty show '13, Club Winner '13, 2 CACIB

GCH GREECE/JNR CH TURKEY HILLCLOUD ICEBURG WITH ASHGATE

(Int Ch Ashgate Scots Progress ex Int Ch Hillcloud Drizzle)
Owned by: Theodore Politis, handled by Mitsi Kalaitzidaki
1 BIS, 1 RBIS Brace, 3 Group 1, 3 Group 2, 8 BOB, 2 BOB Specialty Terrier Show

Currently being campaigned and at stud in the UK
Ashgate US Apollo
(Ch Ashgate Aros ex Ashgate US It's All About Meme)

Sue Thomson, Jacky Ash and Kath Berry
email: ashgatewesties@btinternet.com/Hillcloudwesties@btinternet.com
or find us on Facebook. See full stud team at www.ashgate-westies.co.uk

HERNWOOD

TWO GENERATIONS OF BEST IN SHOW WINNERS

HISTORY WAS MADE IN THE UK BY

Sh Ch Hernwood Talladega Racer JW ShCM

THE FIRST GORDON SETTER TO WIN
BEST IN SHOW
AT AN ALL-BREEDS CHAMPIONSHIP SHOW
'DAVE' MADE HISTORY AT LKA 2012

Gordon Setters

Three generations of Group Winners

Top Gordon Setter 2013

Sh Ch Hernwood Calypso Goddess JW ShCM

Best in Show
Gundog Breeds Association of Scotland
2013
Top Puppy 2012
9 CCs, 5 BOBs, Group 3, 4 RCCs

HERNWOOD

The 3rd Gordon Setter to qualify for 'Pup of the Year' final - all from Hernwood

Hernwood Storm Rider

Top Breeder 2013

Runner-up Breeders Competition Grand Final - Crufts 2013

Pete and Chris Sandiford and Claire Lewis

Gordon Setters
20 Year Club

We made another appearance at Eukanuba Champion Stakes Final 2013

Sh Ch Hernwood Diamond Rock JW ShCM

& made history in the USA too...

Only British bred Gordon Setter to win an Award of Merit at the National Specialty

Am Grand Ch Hernwood Magic Formula

Tel: 01582 842242   Email: sandiford@btconnect.com

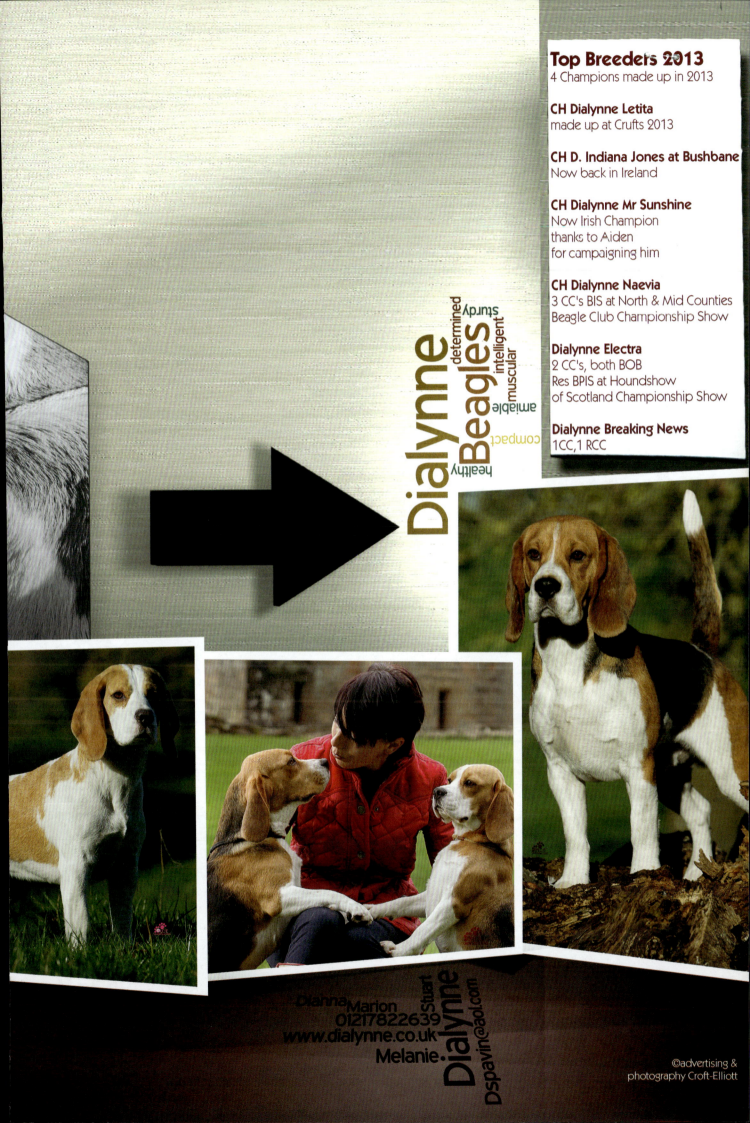

DRAKESLEAT
MINIATURE WIREHAIRED DACHSHUNDS

Another exciting year for the team! 24 CCs up to November and 4 new Champions

DRAKESLEAT MAY CONTAIN NUTS
2 CCs 7 Reserve CCs
Pup of the Year Stakes Runner-up overall
Her brother is Ch Drakesleat Win Tin Tin ..
13 CCs, 15 Best Dog all won in 2013
Top Min Wire to date

CH DRAKESLEAT SCENT SYBIL (7 CCs)
at 14 mths, Pup of the Year Stakes Runner-up overall, Several Best Puppy in Show, and Res Best Puppy in Shows plus Best in Show at the Lancs & Cheshire Dachs Club, Top Puppy 2013
Her brother Drakesleat Fifty Scents (Res CC)
Best Puppy in Show at the Northern Dachs
Dachshund of the Year for the second year in succession: Ch Drakesleat Win Alot
(sire of Tin Tin and Nutty)
Also titles for Ch Noddy Doff
and Ch Ott Favourite

CH DRAKESLEAT WIN TIN TIN

DRAKESLEAT FIFTY SCENTS

Zena Thorn-Andrews
Tel 01905 820720

www.drakesleat.co.uk

Jeff Horswell
Tel 01509 674059

Supreme Ch Statuesque Mudgee Mud

33 Championship BIS
at 6 years, SM grade 0a, PL 0/0, ACES clear (current)

Owner/handler, Gemcourt

~ Puppies planned ~

Frank & Lee Pieterse
Australia

www.statuesquedogs.com

Ballybroke Chihuahuas

AM CH BRAMVERS ETUDE

The pups below have been sired by him since his arrival in the UK

Etude has been MRI Scanned and is clear of SM, he is currently at stud in the UK but will be returning with his owners to Japan after Crufts

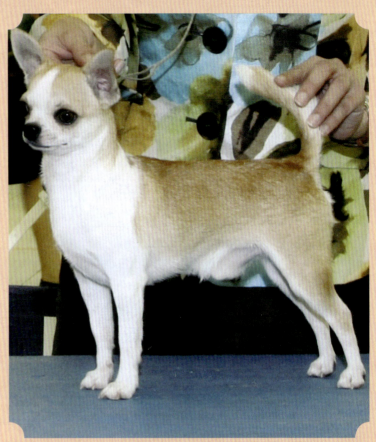

Stud enquiries to **Graham and Margaret Foote,** Hunters Moon, Pease Pottage
Phone 01444 400384

Norw.Dan.Ch.Jet's Just Take Me Home Tonight
Owners: Espen Engh & Åge Gjetnes, Norway,
espenjet@online.no

Jet's Greyhounds

Photo: Ove Larsen

Jet's Griffons

Eng.Ch.Jet's Moulin Rouge
Owners:
Espen Engh & Åge Gjetnes, Norway,
co-owned with David Guy
espenjet@online.no

MELFIELD SECRET AGENT

2 CCs with BOB
2 RCCs
BIS Lowchen Club
Show August

Both boys eye tested clear low hip scores and patella tested sound

ROYAL GROWL LOUIS VUITTON VIA MELFIELD (IMP FIN)

2 CCs with BOB Qualifier for
Top Dog of East Anglia competition

JOCELYN CREFFIELD
KC ASSURED BREEDER
Tel 01449 744250   email melfieldk9@btinternet.com

CHAMPION MELFIELD RUBY TUESDAY

Many thanks to Mr J Bispham Mr T Johnston for her 1st and 2nd CCs and Mr A Stevens for Ruby's 3rd and BIS at the Club Show, also for BPIS with her daughter **MELFIELD SAUCY SAPPHIRE** owned in partnership with Mr Shaun Dring. Ruby PRA clear and low hip score

DONZEATA

Ch Donzeata Royal Vintage

Vintage continues to be the leading living sire in the breed having ten champion offspring to date. His daughters ex **Ch Donzeata Royal Thread, Donzeata Royal Gem** (smooth) and **Donzeata Royal Jewel** (rough) have amassed 2 CCs and several RCCs in limited showing this year.

Congratulations to **Donzeata Royal Secret for Fleetgold** on winning her **first CC** adding to her tally of **RCCs.**

Ch Donzeata Royal Tweed sired **Ch Jets Moulin Rouge** owned in partnership with Espen Engh and Åge Gjetnes before leaving our shores to live in Australia. **Moulin Rouge** has 4 CCs, 3 with BOB to become the first imported smooth to gain her title in the UK.

David Guy (Donzeata) and Stuart Plane (Stuane)
Tel 01915 812200
david.donzeata@virgin.net
stuart.plane@virgin.net

STUANE

Ch Stuane Florette

Appeared once in the ring this year and brought her total to 24 CCs with 8 groups. She has been busy in the nursery along with her sister Floral Tribute. We welcomed home Stuane Floral Design at Millbone who restarted her show career to win 2 CCs.

Stuane Black Velvet with Dechine

Owned by Angela Corish with several RCCs and BIS win to her credit

photos Sarah Oldfield

Ch Stuane Burnt Oak

Siring 3 different CC winners in 2013

RINGLANDS International Papillons *Est 1944*
119 Champions, 15 International Champions. Consistent for Type and Quality
Home of the Papillon (Butterfly Dog) for over 60 years

**INT & BALT/EST/LV/UK/JAP/IR CH
SMILE LINE COVER GIRL IMMORTAL GENE**
A big thank you to Kersti Paju for campaigning Gene to his International Ticket and Baltic Championships in 2013. The only Papillon residing in the UK to have acquired these titles

CH MAD ABOUT SAFFRON FOR RINGLANDS
Winner of 6 CCs, 2 BIS and 6 BOB
Acquiring 2 Bests in Show and 3 CCs in 2013, judges Glenn Robb, Carolyn Roe, Zena Thorn-Andrews and Albert Wight

RINGLANDS SPECIAL GIFT
Last daughter of late Ch Ringlands Hologram. Winner of RBIS and Bitch CC. Consistent Championship Show and Crufts first prize winner during 2013

RINGLANDS SAFFRONS LACE
Daughter of Ch Mad About Saffron for Ringlands by Ch/Aus Ch Rozamie Moulin Rouge. Championship Show first prize winner 2013

RINGLANDS YOKO
Her wins include Best Bitch Puppy, Reserve Best Puppy in Show at Championship Show also consistent first prize winner and qualifier for Crufts. Lightly shown due to maternal duties

Exported to Kersti Paju, Estonia
HARRY PARRY AT RINGLANDS
Full brother to Ch Mad About Saffron for Ringlands Consistent first prize winner at Crufts and Championship Shows 2013

Import: Japan, Smile Line Silenzo Sunshine Garsiv winner BIS at South of Wales Papillon Club Show 2 RCCs and qualifying for Crufts 2013. Congratulates his daughter Ringlands Summer Sun Shine in Blackpark and his son Ringlands Hello Sun Shine at Blackpark for Championship Show wins 2013.

Export: Harry Parry at Ringlands Looking forward to showing his progeny in 2014.

Due to family commitments sadly very few Championship Shows attended in 2013, looking forward to campaigning in 2014

Enquiries Mrs Pat Munn
Tel/Fax +44 (0)2392 632573   email patmunnstmartins@yahoo.co.uk   www.ringlands-int.freeserve.co.uk

Top Clumber Spaniel
Top Toy Poodle Breeder
Top Toy Poodle Brood Bitch
Top Clumber Spaniel Stud Dog

TOP 2013

vanitonia

Lee Cox & Tom Isherwood
Vanitoniapoodles@aol.com
01278 760210
www.vanitonia.co.uk

Star
Vanitonia As You Wish
co-owned with Ann Evans
2 rCC

Trudy
co-owned with Susan Crummey

3 New Toy Poodle Champions
CH Vanitonia life's too short   aka Trudy
CH Vanitonia if the shoe fits seldoop   aka Twix
CH Smash Jp golden sunset over Vanitonia   aka Roger

New Clumber Champion
ShCH Vanitonia Save Me A Spot aka Samantha
Number One Clumber
Sh CH Vanitonia If The Buck Stops Ere

Roger
Group 2 Darlington 2013

co-owned with
Lisa Croft-Elliott

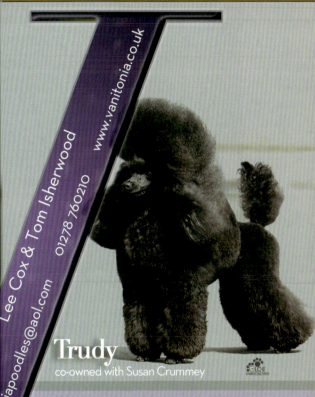

Top Clumber
Group winner
The youngest male
Sh Ch clumber
BIS Cs Club CH show
BPIS National gundog
Edward

Bitch CC Crufts
Group 2 winner
Samantha

©advertising & photography Croft-Elliott

Suki
Pekehuis Temptress
1 rCC, BIS Ventura Open Show

Sebi
Pekehuis Spellbinder
3 rCCs   Best Puppy Crufts

©advertising & photography Croft-Elliott

BOUGHTON
Home of Champion dogs since the 1930s

Ch Bellezza di Boughton

Clare Boggia
01795 535719 / 07912038891
cboggia@fsmail.net

Bayard Beagles

CH BAYARD MAKE AMENDS JW

Sire: Ch Bayard Grafter
Dam: Bayard Daytrip

21 CCs, 3 RCCs,
2 Group 1 and
other group placings

Retires from the show ring to take up her maternal duties after winning her 21st CC at Driffield under breed specialist Penny Carmichael, then the HOUND GROUP and RBIS under Robin Searle

BAYARD HAZEL'S BEANY JW

Sire: Bayard Meant To Be
Dam: Bayard Hazelnut

Still just a junior, has a RCC and many Puppy and Junior wins to start his career

JILL PEAK and SARAH JACKSON
Marcliff Kennels, Marsh Road, Banks
Southport, Lancs PR9 8DZ

Tel 01772 813232
Mobile 0751 5674482
email jill@bayardbeagles.co.uk
www.bayardbeagles.co.uk

The World Famous *Top breeders continually producing Top Dogs*

Wildax Boston Terriers

20 Year Club

Margaret Wildman with SKIN-DEEP'S JACKMAN

Liz Rankin with CH WILDAX AUGUSTUS BROWN Top Boston 2013

Katherine Rankin with WILDAX JUSTICE PREVAILS 1 CC

CH WILDAX SCARAMOUCHE 26 CCs, 27 RCCs

Anna Spencer with WILDAX QUEEN OF SHEBA 1 CC

Liz Rankin with WILDAX SEA SKIPPER 2 CCs, 5 RCCs

Wildax are used to taking top awards and once again are the UK's Top Breeders, Top Boston and Top Puppy. We have an excellent record of selling top class puppies to others that then go on to become champions for their discerning owners. Wildax is synonymous with excellence and we are acknowledged the world over for our recognisable stamp and we are known for letting top class dogs go to others; we are thrilled when they do well with many becoming champions, CC winners, reserve CC winners and also attaining the much sought after Stud Book qualification. We have a top team of Boston and French Bulldog stud dogs that are health tested and offered at stud to approved bitches. We have puppies for sale both for show and companion and visitors are always welcome.

For puppy, stud or export enquiries please contact

Ann, Margaret or Frank Wildman

Wildax Kennels, Aintree Lodge, Croxteth Park, West Derby, Liverpool L12 0HA
Tel 0151 256 7153   email wildax2000@aol.com   www.wildax.co.uk

20 Year Club

The World Famous

Wildax French Bulldogs

Top breeders continually producing Top Dogs

CH WILDAX MISS MONEYPENNY
Top Frenchie 2009, 2010, 2011, 2012,
Top Bitch 2013

WILDAX DUSTY SPRINGFIELD
1 CC

WILDAX DIANA ROSS

AM CH WILDAX PERCY SLEDGE

Ch Wildax Miss Moneypenny's record speaks for itself and surely she will go down in the annals of the breed and be referred to, and held up, as one of the breed's all time greats. She was the UK's Top Frenchie 2009, 2010, 2011, 2012 and Top Bitch 2013. We were delighted when her beautiful daughter **Wildax Dusty Springfield** won the CC and not forgetting our precocious youngster **Wildax Diana Ross** who, although lightly shown, is making her presence felt in the show ring too. **Wildax Smokey Robinson** is a son of the illustrious Ch Wildax Miss Moneypenny and this beautifully bred boy with the stunning head is maturing nicely. His pedigree is second to none and he is producing beautiful puppies. Smokey is now offered at stud with every confidence to approved bitches. Congratulations to Dave Berry on his many successes with his stunning boy **Am Ch Wildax Percy Sledge** and we wish you lots more success in 2014.

For puppy, stud or export enquiries contact:

Ann, Margaret or Frank Wildman

Wildax Kennels, Aintree Lodge, Croxteth Park, West Derby, Liverpool L12 0HA
Tel 0151 256 7153   email wildax2000@aol.com   www.wildax.co.uk

Fallowfield Beagles

20 Year Club

Winning dogs at stud:

Ch Fallowfield Royal Richard
Ch Fallowfield Bartholomew
Ch Fallowfield Barney
Fallowfield Addie (1 CC)

Ch Fallowfield Diamonte

CHRISTINE LEWIS
Ashfield, Tarn Lane, Yealand Redmayne LA5 9RX
Tel: 01524 781284   Mobile: 07507 473098
Email: christinelewis@ic24.net

TIRKANE

CO OWNERS LISA NELSON
MARLIES MORZIK
LEANNE BRYANT
TIRKANE@HOTMAIL.COM

© Will Harris

TIRKANE OPRAH WINFREY

OPRAH IS THE WINNER OF 1 CC 1 RCC
SHOWN LIGHTLY IN 2013

THE BIG ISSUE IS CURRENTLY
TOP TOY POODLE IRELAND & ENGLAND
BEST IN SHOW SLIGO CHAMPIONSHIP SHOW
JOINT 4TH TOP OF GROUP 9 IN IRELAND
MULTIPLE GROUP PLACEMENTS
7 CC'S 6 GREEN STAR'S 10 BEST OF BREEDS

CH TIRKANE THE BIG ISSUE

AD BY L BRYANT

TUSSALUD

Breeding and showing top Papillons since 1972, including Ch Tussalud Story Teller (28 CCs, 6 groups, Top Papillon 1995/96, Top Toy 1996/97, Crufts BOB 1995/96/97). Below is his offspring and the future chapter of Tussalud.

Ch & Fin Ch Siljans Ragge JR Connection At Tussalud (Imp Swed)

15 CCs (14 BOB), multiple group placings, 5 Bests in Shows club championship shows.
Bred by Mrs U Hanis (Siljans), combining top Swedish and English blood lines.
Sire of Several Champions including Ch & Ir Ch Denemore Ragge Sensation (BCC Crufts 2013).

Ch Denemore Story's Echo at Tussalud

9 CCs
Multiple group placings.
Story Teller's granddaughter, bred by Mr S Carroll and Mr J Newman (Denemore/Belliver).
Currently away from the show ring for maternal duties.

Owned and handled by Grandmother and Granddaughter showteam
Kay Stewart and Kirsten Stewart-Knight : 01582 881 223
kirstenstewartknight@hotmail.com

PITSWARREN

21 SHOW CHAMPIONS — *Breeding for quality not quantity* — **OVER 160 CCs**
WINNING BEST OF BREED AND CCs WITH THREE HOMEBRED MALES IN 2013

SH CH PITSWARREN PLANET JW, ShCM 40 CCs
PLANET is the top winning owner bred and handled Vizsla ever in the UK
We are immensely proud of all he has achieved

PITSWARREN SIROCCO
At 20 months Rocco has won
Best in Show at the HWVA 2013
CC, RCC and multiple Best Dog awards
Puppy stakes winner

SH CH PITSWARREN DARWINIAN
Pitswarren's 21st Show Champion
All CCs won with Best of Breed

PETER and LIZ HARPER
pitswarren@btinternet.com
www.pitswarren.co.uk

Switherland-Montravia
Phil Freer and Marita Rodgers

2013 proves to be another great year
Top Basset Hound Breeder 2013

This follows: #1 Basset Hound Kennel UK 2012, 2011, 2010, 2009, 2008, 2007, 2006, 2005, 2004, 2003, 2002, 2000, 1999, 1998, 1997, 1996, 1995

SWITHERLAND ROYAL IMAGE 2 CCs, 4 RCCs and litter sister CH SWITHERLAND RED IMAGE Currently #1 Basset Hound UK 2013, owned by Marita Rodgers and Lauren Armstrong, doing the double at Southern Counties 2013

RUS/RUM/LUX CH IRMA PODKOLDERNIK JADOWITY CC and BOB Darkington 2013 at her first show in UK in the partnership of Irena Antipova, Marita Rodgers & Phil Freer. Breeder Dorota Gorgolewska (Poland)

CH SWITHERLAND TOUCH N THE DARK WITH SASILASY Best of Breed Crufts 2013, owned by Marita Rodgers, Danna Grace and Calum Twaddle

Phil Freer and Marita Rodgers www.switherland-montravia.co.uk
email switherlandphil@aol.com Montraviamarita@aol.com tel 01636 706970

Switherland-Montravia
Phil Freer and Marita Rodgers
7 individual Basset Hounds Take CC's
Breeder of Current #1 Basset Hound UK
Best of Breed Crufts 2013

CH SWITHERLAND STAGE STRUCK
Group 3 Blackpool 2013

SWITHERLAND CLASSIC DESIGN
Res CC Basset Hound Club 2013
Photo taken using the ramp for the first time

SWITHERLAND THE PRETENDER
1 CC and 2 Res CCs

**SWITHERLAND DREAM EDITION 1 CC
and 6 Res CCs and SWITHERLAND CLASSIC
DESIGN 1 CC and 2 Res CCs doing the double
at WKC 2013**

Phil Freer and Marita Rodgers www.switherland-montravia.co.uk
email switherlandphil@aol.com Montraviamarita@aol.com tel 01636 706970

LIREVA

20 Year Club

Averil Cawthera-Purdy and Sean Gwynne

TOP BREEDER, TOP POM*, RUNNER-UP TOP POM*, TOP CC WINNER and 3 NEW CHAMPS IN '13

Ch Lireva's Short Sir Kit
8 CCs 5 BOBs

Made-up in May
Ch Lireva's Flower Of Scotland
3 CCs 1 BOB
Thanks to Eve Smail of Toybox
for the use of her lovely sire

Our latest Champion and Top Pom*
Ch Lireva's Cast An Net
4 CCs, 2 BOB, 1 TG3, 2 TG4

Only just 'Out' but already with BPIB and stakes wins
Lireva's Sir Tan Lee Giggles

Ch Lireva's To Hell An Black
6 CCs 3 BOBs inc BIS NPC and TG4 and Runner-up Top Pom
Thanks to Fay Matthews her handler

TOP PUPPY - BELLIVER UNEXPECTED DESTINY (3 CCs)
RUNNER UP TOP PUPPY - BELLIVER UNEXPECTEDLY AT LIREVA (2 RCCs)
Many thanks to breeders Sean Carroll and James Newman

*at the time of going to press

Life's a Beach

20 Year Club

Gemson Rabelias
in the show ring 2 CCs 2 RCCs
but he knows where he'd rather be

20 Year Club

Gemson Symphony among Auldhelm

1 CC and 7 RCCs 6 Green Stars with a Group 2 and a Group 4

'Maggie Mae'
Hips 4:4 = 8
PRA - Optigen Clear by Parents

Sire: Champion Gemson Orpheus at Proform
Hips: 6:6 = 12
PRA - Optigen Clear

Dam: Champion Gemson Florentina among Auldhelm
Hips: 7:6 = 13
PRA - Optigen Clear

Maggie is owned loved and indulged
by **Doreen and John Barton (Auldhelm)**
Bred, co-owned and handled in the ring by **Jayne Johns (Gemson)**

MOCHRAS
BASSET FAUVE DE BRETAGNE

2013 results include

Ch Mochras Mahogany (Annie)

5CCs, 2 res.CCs

Ch Mochras Melchior (Tid)

3CCs, res CC & res CC Crufts

Harmonie de L'Echo de L'Aulne

Irish Junior Champion

Liz Thornton, Andover, Hampshire

01264 790720   mochrashounds@gmail.com

www.mochrashounds.co.uk

One of the World's Oldest, Smallest and most Successful Kennels

After more than 50 years we're surprised to still be here. No more breedings are planned, and there are few Bohem Whippets anywhere in the world, but they continue to exert an influence way out of proportion to their small numbers.

GCh. Counterpoint Painted by Bohem, SC
(co-owned with Scott Mazer, sired by Ch. Bohem Bon Vivant ex a granddaughter of Ch Bohem Three Ring Circus) was only shown once in 2013, taking BIS at the AWC Western Specialty in Long Beach. His young champion sons and daughters have done well in the US and Europe, with big wins at specialty shows, all-breed BIS etc.

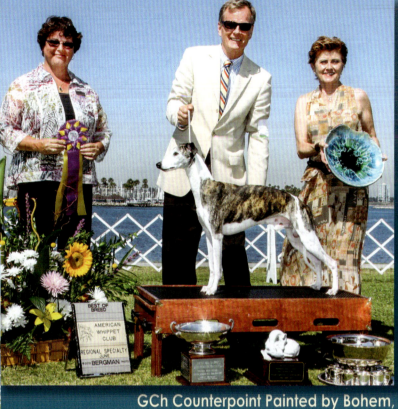

Winning the Stud Dog class at the AWC specialty with son Ch Nysa Hill Timeless Tempo of Bohem (center) and daughter Nysa Hill Timeless Affair.

GCh Counterpoint Painted by Bohem, owner handled to BIS at the American Whippet Club specialty in California 2013. Judge Wendy Paquette.

A daughter, **GCh Bohem Swan Song**, the only bitch from our last homebred litter, is not yet 2 years old but already a Group winner. On the East Coast her young black half brother, **Ch Shamasan Bohem Breezing Up** (co-owned with breeder Phoebe Booth) was Winners Dog at the 2013 AWC National Specialty and is a multiple BOB winner. The offspring of **Ch Bohem Just In Time, CR** (owned by Nancy Doucette but bred here) have won big in the U.S., Canada, Europe and Russia, including many all-breed and specialty BIS. A son from his A.I. litter in Italy was just Best Puppy in Show. There's also a "frozen" litter by the late top sire **Int Ch Bohem Flight Time** (born 1992). One of the puppies is coming to California and will be shown by us.

It looks like we'll be around a little longer…

GCh Bohem Swan Song

Ch Shamasan Bohem Breezing Up

Ch Bohem Just In Time at 9 years of age

Bo Bengtson
PO Box 10, Ojai, CA 93024, USA
email bobengtson@impulse.net
www.bohemwhippets.com

AMANTRA

KING CHARLES, CAVALIERS and JAPANESE CHINS

CHAMPION AMANTRA CHEERS

'NIGEL'

26 CCs 10 RCCs

Best Veteran in Show KCSC Championship Show

Winner of Veteran Stakes at Birmingham National, Windsor and Richmond Championship Shows

Owned, bred and loved by:
DI FRY AND TRACY JACKSON
01934 824828
tracy@amantra.co.uk

Ch. Shalfleet Simply A Lord

TROY

UK's No.1 Whippet
20 CC's

Photos & Artwork Paulinesoliverphotos

BREEDER/OWNER/HANDLER
Jane Wilton Clark
www.shalfleetwhippets.com

OREGONIAN
BYMIL + BIMWICH + DEAVITTE

CH OREGONIAN RAISE AN EYEBROW

by CC winner Barwal Brave Beau, grandson of our Ch Woodbine Aladar,
ex dual CC winner Oregonian Fay Wray, granddaughter of our Woodbine Alyssum

Fewer shows than usual have been attended this year but Rufus won his fourth **CC and BOB** at Bournemouth and has represented the breed on a number of television programmes.

SARAH TAYLOR	DIANA KING	SIMON PARSONS
bymil@btopenworld.com	bimwich@btinternet.com	wortencottage@hotmail.co.uk

BYMIL

CH BYMIL SMILE PLEASE

by Ch Belroyd Pemcader Cymro
ex Ch Bymil Picture This

Daisy gained her title in three consecutive opportunities, at Bournemouth, City of Birmingham and South Wales, thus going one better than her history-making dam whose title came in four shows! Her dam's dam **Ch Blondie's Read My Lips for Bymil** completes three generations of champion bitches at home.

SARAH TAYLOR
bymil@btopenworld.com

Clynymona

The most successful Bolognese and top winning kennel in the breed in UK

Based on the Isle of Man & Gibraltar
Breeding, showing 22 years
in association with
Clarchien, Kathryn Begg &
Havanese Stars, Marguerite Seeberger

BOB & Best Puppy at Crufts
multi BIS at Club and Open Shows

Top Dog 2008, 09, 10, 11, 12 & 2013

Top Dog 2013 INT SP GIB MOR CH
Bolognese Star Donald At Havanese Stars

Top Puppy 2013
Clynymona Chelsea Parker at Clarchien
and Top Puppy Toy Breeds*

Top Breeder 2013 Havanese Stars

Top Brood Bitch 2013
Clarchien Ballerina at Starexpress

Top Stud 2013
Multi Ch Lenny Valasske Hory
owners Marguerite Seeberger & Virginia Dowty

Morse

Virginia Dowty
Isle of Man & Gibraltar

+ 44 (0) 1624823539
(answerphone)

vdowty@yahoo.com

Audrey

Donald

Chelsea Parker

Audrey & Donald

©advertising & Photography Croft-Elliott

Clynymona Bolognese

INT SP GIB MOR Ch Bolognese Star Donald At Havanese Stars
Top Bolognese 2013
Top Puppy 2012
BIS Club show at 6 months old
2013 Multi BOB Ch shows,
Championnat de France,
RSCE (Madrid)

Clynymona Hercules Morse At Ingerdorm ShCM
Bred on IOM Top-winning Bolognese of all time, multiple BOB Ch shows,
18 Toy Groups at OS
1st group place for Bolognese 2013
youngest and first British-bred ShCM

INT CH IR SP CH Bolognese Star Audrey At Havanese Stars
Top Bolognese 2010, Top bitch 2011
and Top bitch 2013* Multi BOB

Clynymona Chelsea Parker At Clarchien
Top Puppy 2013 and
Top Puppy Toy Breeds*
BOB at Ch shows

Keeping the Bolognese community talking Globally

www.kennel **Prefix** .com

Gunilla & Rebecca Agronius • Sweden
www.kennelprefix.com
Top Crested breeder in Sweden for 15 years.

20 Year Club

Shakespeare

Shakespeare

Prefix Shakespeare

**3 CACs
Best Dog wins
Crufts Qualified**

Ex: Ch/Int/Nordic/Swe/Dan/Norw/Lux/Dutch Ch
World Winner '09
Nordic Winner '06, Brussels Winner '06
Prefix Swede Smell Of Success

Grand sire: Ch/Int/Nordic/Swe/Dan/Norw/Lux/Be Ch
World Winner '08, Veteran World Winner '13
Nordic Winner '07, Belgian Winner '09
Crested of the Year '07 and '09
Prefix Singapore Sling

photos Agronius & Nilsson

Sh Ch Shannas Wavedancer at Tarcoulter

BOB Crufts 2013

"Travis" is owned by Kate McKnight, handled and presented by Susan

Bonnie and Ronnie Scougall
Shannas Kennels
Tel 01771 624327 email Bonnie@shannas.co.uk shannas.co.uk

Ingledene
Est 1967

Featuring our star of the year

Ingledene Spirit Of Legend
(dob: 11/10/12)

Sire : Ch/Ir Ch EuW'09 Ingledene Late Nite Legend JW ex Barksdale Ingledene Burning Blushes (Imp USA)
In his first six months of showing Cooper has attained - 16 Ch. class wins - 10 BPIB - 4 BPIS - 2 RBD - 1 RCC - 1 CC - 2 BOB - Puppy Group 4
We are delighted with how this young dog is developing and take this opportunity to thank all the judges, breed and all rounder alike, who have appreciated his many outstanding qualities.

All enquiries contact:

VALERIE and JOHN GEDDES
Email ingledenecollies@btinternet.com
Tel 01938 811846 Val: 07429 437481 John: 07429 429469
http://www.gamma.nic.fi/~geddes

BYQUY and VALINDALE

are privileged to introduce our new kid from
Klompen's Keeshonden Canada

Klompen's Who's Your Daddy

'Richie' PHPT neg. by descent
Sire: Am Ch Skyline's Unit of Measure
Dam: Can Ch Klompen's Gabriel

Our thanks to Richie's breeders Kathy and Bruce Stewart (Klompen's) for entrusting this young boy to us

Owners: **David Peck and Malcolm and Linda Matthews**

Tel: 01223 812105
Email: byquy@tiscali.co.uk

Co-owner Kathy Stewart (Canada)

Prior to leaving Canada

ROMAINVILLE GLEN OF IMAAL TERRIERS

Romainville Billy Whizz
1 CC and 4 RCCs

Sire: Bailielands BB Ben
Dam: Romainville Rhian
Crd3/GPRA Clear

Our dogs have had a good year, Billy's sister Jean Genie gained her first Res CC, as did Ellie Ruby had many Best Puppy wins, her sister Cinders 'n Ashes in Ireland is a Green Star winner. Ch Johnny Be Good Top Glen 2013. Bodrhan and Moira all owned by others. Our two other stud dogs R Rock On and Feohanagh Bryan are both Crd3 Clear.
Our Glens proudly owned by
Kathy and Natalie 01432 880819
www.glenofimaalterriers.co.uk
Kathy@romainvillegsd.freeserve.co.uk

Champion Romainville Aoife at Pajanticks
3 CCs, RCC

Sire: Feohanagh Bryan at Romainville
Dam: Romainville Ali Oop (RCCs)
Crd3/GPRA Clear
Puppies expected from Aoife in the new year

Presenting Pajanticks Star Trooper
Sire: Feohanagh Bryan at Romainville
Dam: Pajanticks Patsy Jane
Crd3/GRPA Clear, BOB Paignton,
BOS Bournemouth, RCC SWKA
Handled by Lydia Hogburn.
Jane Withers jwgranarykennels@aol.com

THE GLEN OF IMAAL TERRIER ASSOCIATION

The original Glen of Imaal Terrier Club has been registered for over thirty years with the Kennel Club and has CC status.

With over thirty years of serving the Glen we take every opportunity to showcase our wonderful breed.

Come and meet us at Discover Dogs, game fairs and shows.

We organise an open show and a championship show every year, print a magazine for our members and also organise fun days, especially for all Glen owners.

For more information on the breed and what you need to know about buying a puppy visit our website at www.goita.co.uk. Secretary Anne Hardy, email anne@goita.co.uk, phone 01777 703417

Romainville Typhoon
1 CCs, 3 RCCs

Sire: Amhard Damson Sauce
Dam: Romainville Briar Rose

Typhoon has now matured into one of the top males in the country. **Romainville Moira**, BOB winner, is also maturing into a very good bitch. Proudly owned and shown by Steph and Ruth Ashcroft.

WINUWUK

20 Year Club

We won CCs with six different Boxers in 2013 and two of these are pictured with Julie

We made up our 23rd UK champion Ch Maromad Kiss the Girls at Winuwuk, bred by Malcolm James and sired by our breed record holder Ch/Ir Ch Winuwuk Lust at First Sight who is the year's Top Stud Dog

We bred and own the 2013 British Boxer Club Champion of Champions, Sire of Merit and Dam of Merit

The girls

Winuwuk Maid Marion
1 CC, 2 RCCs

Winuwuk Rumour Has It
2 CCs, 2 BOB, 3 RCCs

Julie Brown and Tim Hutchings
Winuwuk Cottage, Heathfield, Berkeley, Gloucestershire GL13 9PN
t: 01453 511303   e: winuwuk@btinternet.com   w: winuwukboxers.com

our Havanese...

Myhav Iz Mybeards

(Newtonwood Amazing Grace
ex Mybeards Dandelion)

BOB Leeds 2013
BOB City of Birmingham 2013
BOB SWKA 2013

And still only 20 months old

Bred, owned and handed by Lucy

Special thanks to all the Breed Specialists, All-Rounders and Group Judges for our super awards.

Diane and Lucy Mottram
www.mybeards.co.uk

Charney Japanese Spitz
Top Kennel 2006-2012

Our Latest Champion

Ch Charney Azami

Dulcie is a daughter of our Swedish Import (Quinton) Enfloy'z Quinton the Snow Prince with Charney

Charney Shiro Sora

1 CC and 2 RCCs

Tonto is a son of Quinton who is consistently siring winning stock

Enfloy'z Quinton the Snow Prince with Charney

Patella tested 0/0 graded
At limited stud in 2014

My thanks to to Ewa and Helene who kindly allowed me to have Quinton in 2011

Enquiries welcome for our lovely breed,
www.charney-kennels.co.uk
email charneykennel@btconnect.com

Steph Bliss
Charney Kennels, Stanford Road
Faringdon, Oxfordshire SN7 8ET

Gaesten Italian Gundogs

Pioneer breeder of

Italian Spinone 1982   **1996 Lagotto Romagnolo**

Top Lagotto/Top Import Breeder and runner-up to overall Top Breeder 2012 and at time of writing (November) Top Lagotto/Import Breeder 2013.

2012 was a memorable year for the Gaesten kennel with eight different Lagotto taking Ch Best/BOS Import. Featured below four of the Lagotto who started 2013 in style winning at Crufts 2013 (the first time Lagotto were eligible to enter)

Gaesten Ziggy Pop del Aquitrino
(Int/It Ch Rocco del Gaesten (Imp Ital) ex Int/Ir Ch Gaestendown Dilly) owned by Trish and the late Phil Owens. RBD to the famous Alfredo at Crufts. Best In LRCGB Speciality 2011 and 2013.

Gaesten Just Jago at Joyden
(Int/Ir Ch Gaesten Razz N Roll ex Gaestengaily Gertie) owned by David Lightfoot. 1st Limit Dog at Crufts. Top Lagotto and Import Gundog 2012 and currently in the lead 2013. Best in LRCGB Speciality 2012.

Gaesten Jentle Jamena
(Il Granaio del Malatesta Nereo del Gaesten (Imp Ital) ex Gaesten Razzle Dazzle) owned by Mandy Barker.

1st Puppy Bitch and BP Crufts and currently Top Lagotto Puppy.

Gaesten Desirable Danny CJW 13
(Il Granaio dei Malatesta Mario Martino del Gaesten (Imp Ital) ex Gaestengaily Gertie) 1st Puppy Dog Crufts, Celtic Junior Ch, Best Junior LRCGB Speciality.

I first came across the Lagot (then unrecognised even in Italy) at the Florence Int show in 1990 whilst showing a grandson of my first Spinone. Twenty three years later I no longer share my home with Spinoni - the Lagotto have taken over but I am always happy to give help and advice on both breeds.

Contact **GAEL STENTON**
01403 790140   gaelsc@msn.com
Eagle Cottage, Stane Street, Slinfold, Horsham, West Sussex RH13 0QX

Africandawns

20 Year Club

AFRICANDAWNS RUMOUR RUMBLE
1 CC

AFRICANDAWNS NIGHT HAWK
1 CC 2 RCCs
owned in partnership with
Miss K A Mitchell

AFRICANDAWNS LILLY'S LEGACY AT BRONIA
Owned by Fran Mitchell

AFRICANDAWNS NIGHT KISSES AT DARSOMS
owned by Cindy Dare

AFRICANDAWNS NIGHT GARDIAN AT BRSYDAX Owned by Mr and Mrs L A Fossit
AFRICANDAWNS LARRY'S LEGACY Owned by Miss Lorraine Bedford
Puppies or a nice adult sometimes available

T L Johnson, Old Whistling Pig, Heath Road, Warboys, Huntingdon, PE28 2UJ 01487 822630

LONG HAIRED DACHSHUNDS, TIBETAN TERRIERS, BEAGLES AND DOG TRAINING CENTRE

AFRICANDAWNS LORD GADROON

DOG TRAINING

- GROUP CLASSES
- ONE-TO-ONE LESSONS
- RESIDENTIAL TRAINING
- PET OBEDIENCE
- GUNDOG
- PUPPY TRAINING
- HOUSE TRAINING
- SOCIALISING

- GREAT FACILITIES:
- LARGE, ENCLOSED TRAINING PADDOCKS
- LIVESTOCK ENCLOSURE (LARGE RABBIT PEN)
- INDOOR CLASSES AT RAMSEY DRILL HALL, TUESDAY EVENINGS FROM 7PM

CONTACT INFO:
AFRICANDAWNS TRAINING CENTRE
OLD WHISTLING PIG, HEATH ROAD
WARBOYS, PE28 2UJ
TEL: 01487 822630
MOB: 07736 500893
Email: tl.johnson@btconnect.com

PLEASE CONTACT US OR VISIT OUR WEBSITE at
www.africandawnsdogtraining.co.uk
FOR MORE DETAILS

MEADOWPARK

CH Meadowpark Whispers Breeze
TOP BMD 2012 and 2013
Crufts 2013 BOB and Working Group 1
Crufts 2012 BOB, 3 x Group 2 placements
16 CCs, 13 Res CCs

CH Meadowpark Sugar Daddy
3 CCs 7 Res CCs

CH Meadowpark Living The Dream JW
2 x Group 3 placements
9 CCs, 4 Res CCs

Meadowpark Perfect Blend
Top BMD Puppy 2013
12 BPIB, 1 x PG1

Thank you to all judges who have appreciated our dogs and fellow exhibitors for their support this year.

Homebred by Bernice Mair and Carole Hartley-Mair, co-handled by Gary Dybdall

Lawn Cottage Boarding Kennels and Cattery
Telephone 01706 649900 Email carolehartley@hotmail.co.uk

MEADOWPARK

Top Bernese Mountain Dog Breeder 2012 and 2013 and winners of Kennel Club Breeders Competition at Crufts 2013

Introducing...

Meadowpark One Lover
at 6 months old

Meadowpark The Temptress
at 6 months old

MILLBONE GINGERBREAD

20 Year Club

CC and BIS
Northern Griffon Club

BOB and Group 3
Windsor

BIS
GBBA Open Show

BIS
GBA Open Show

5 RES CCs

Loved and owned by:

Jill Lee
01945 410332

Lynda Cooper
01945 466691

Steven Seymour
01223 845542

NERADMIK, SKYLINE, LEKKERBEK

BIS, BISS, AMERICAN, CANADIAN AND ENGLISH CH KEMONTS SKYLINE'S GAME BOY HOF, ROMX (Imp USA)

'Ferris'

Breeder: Mrs Jan Corrington
Sire: Am and Can Ch Keeshee's Lock Stock 'N Barrel RoM
Dam: Am Ch Skyline's Material Girl
Owners: Dr Kristen Cullen DVM and Mrs Susan Cullen in the USA and Mrs Joan Miles in the UK, 75 Chalvington Road, Chandler's Ford SO53 3EF
023 8026 1621   jad@barton.ac.uk
In the UK for less than two years, Ferris won
17 CCs, 1 Reserve CC
Utility Group 2 Crufts 2012
Best in Show Keeshond Club Championship Show 2012
Top Keeshond 2011 and 2012
Top Keeshond Stud Dog 2012

CH LADY GODIVA'S GUILTY PLEASURES WITH NERADMIK (IMP FIN)

'Tallulah'
16 CCs
including Best of Breed Crufts 2009, Bitch CC Crufts 2010 and frequently placed in the Utility Group
Top Keeshond Bitch 2009 and 2010
Top Keeshond Brood Bitch 2012
Bred by Mrs Annamaija Tuisku

CH SLO JNR CH MLT CH NERADMIK LATE NIGHT LOVE

'Sheva'

4 CCs and 4 Bests of Breed, unbeaten in the breed
Best of Breed Crufts 2013
Group 4 City of Birmingham 2013

making her the 33rd English Neradmik Champion bred at the Neradmik kennel resulting in the record for English Keeshond Champions previously held by the Wistonia kennel for almost 60 years
Owned by Mr Victor Gatt, Malta

Tallulah and Ferris produced ten puppies (seven girls and three boys) in October 2011, resulting so far in three English champions: Neradmik Handsome Hero (7 CCs, 4 BOBs, 1 Group 3), Neradmik Steppin' up the Game at Norkees (7 CCs, 2 Res CCs), Neradmik Late Night Love, see above. Neradmik Kissing Game has 1 CC and 1 Res CC. Neradmik Help The Hero has 1 Res CC.

Good luck to the other puppies from this litter who have done so well in the show ring during 2013. Neradmik Sunday Lovin' will be campaigned in 2014.

A repeat mating resulted in eight puppies (four girls and four boys) being born on 22 February 2013 and seven are being shown.

Neradmik High Society at Skathki – Res CC City of Birmingham 2013 at 6 months
Neradmik Uptown Girl Deminiac – Res CC Midland Counties 2013, 1 Green Star and Puppy Stakes in Ireland at 6 months
Neradmik Family Affair with Lekkerbek – Best Puppy in Show, Keeshond Club Open Show October 2013
Neradmik All About The Boy for Watchkees – Minor Puppy Stakes South Wales
Neradmik Boy Next Door
Neradmik Academy Award – 2 Best of Winners awards in Canada
Neradmik Gossip Girl – good luck to Annamaija's Lulu on her debut in Finland at the end of the year

Not forgetting Ferris' second litter in the UK to Ch Neradmik Chanel
Ch Neradmik Hollyberry – 7 CCs, Group 4 Leeds
Neradmik Miss Mistletoe – in Finland, waiting in the wings to receive her championship titles when she reaches the age of two
Ir Ch Neradmik Beach Boy avec Deminiac – 1 Res CC
Neradmik Game Plan for Lekkerbek – 3 Res CCs, Best in Show North of England Keeshond Club Open Show

All bred by JEAN SHARP-BALE
Wiggs Cottage, Plumley, near Ringwood BH24 3QB   Tel 01202 824368   jsbneradmik@hotmail.co.uk

Ferris is currently Top Keeshond Stud Dog for 2013, Top Utility and 4th overall all breeds
Tallulah is currently Top Keeshond Brood Bitch for 2013, Top Utility and 4th overall all breeds
Sheva is currently Top Keeshond

ORAKEI

Photo By Dave Morris

THE BOUVIER IS MORE THAN GREEN & **WHITE** BITS OF CARD!

Character & temperament are always No 1 at ORAKEI.

The late Orakei Dragonbank Sky Viking & Nikolaev Tanzanite of Orakei (1CC & 1RCC)

Frances Jonas - 7 Chapel Street, Cromer, Norfolk, NR27 9HJ - 01263 514121

NIKOLAEV

Celebrating Thirty Years in Bouvier des Flandres.

Top breeder, top stud dog, and top brood bitch, for 2011. 2012. I would like to thank all the judges who have thought so highly of the dogs that I have bred over the years awarding them many CC's, B.O.B's and B.I.S's. To all the owners who have owned, campaigned, and enjoyed the dogs that I have bred, a very big thank you to you all.

Nikolaev Evangeline, unbeaten in all her puppy & junior classes. Nikolaev Cersei waiting in the wings.

A Typical Nikolaev Puppy.

New Ch for 2013 Ch N AMARANDE AT ABBIVILLE (Jones), her litter brother N TARIQ (Pilsbury) shown only twice this year won DCC, BOB, GRP3, East of Eng & DCC & RBIS Club Ch Show.

Lee Nichols - The Hollies, Aldham Nr Hadleigh, Suffolk, IP7 6NS - 01473 827620
nikolaev.bouvier@btinternet.com

ARANY
DEUTSCH LANGHAAR
(German Longhaired Pointers)

"Hard mouthed, uncontrollable, aggressive and German"
We must have got it wrong over the last 15 years!

Consistently placed at Championship Show Group level and in Field Trials.
Finnish Champion, Irish and Slovac Show Champions
Bests of Breed, BIS CG Open Show x 2
Top Breeder, Top Stud Dog and Top Brood Bitch 2000-2013 UK and Ireland

Larry Wilks and Brenda Moss
01869 340044 aranygundogs@btinternet.com www.aranygundogs.co.uk

MERRYBEAR NEWFOUNDLANDS

Ch Kenamu Break The Mould Merrybear

Sire: **Ch Joy To The World For Shadows Eternity**
Dam: **Ch & Ir Ch Merrybear Pattie Labelle Kenamu**

Our 44th Champion owned or bred
Gordon Cutts and Patrick Galvin
Merrybear, 129 Thornhill Park Road, Thornhill Park, Southampton SO18 5TE
02380 570070   07770 624738
Email merrybear2000@hotmail.com

STARVON SWEDISH VALLHUNDS

Photo Janet van Iperen-Hoevens

At time of press
TOP BROOD Diarah Summer Rain at Starvon (Australian import)
TOP STUD ARBA Ch & Ch Sunfires All Riled Up at Starvon (STDC) (American import)
AND TOP VALLHUND AND THE NEW BREED RECORD HOLDER
Kassi
CH STARVON RUMOUR HAS IT

A HUGE thank you to ALL the judges who have enabled us to be privileged enough to have achieved these awards. Without the wonderful owners of TEAM STARVON we would not be flying so high.

Stud and puppy enquires welcomed
ADA and TIM WEST
01672 540900   starvonsv@aol.com   www.freewebs.com/starvon

Kassi's wins and breed record we dedicate to those who we have loved and lost, our beloved Reg, husband, father and the driving force from behind the scenes, and Leonie Darling, breeder of Kassi's mum Gilli.
Good luck to all our friends across the breeds, YOU are what has kept us going.

MOLOSSER BULLMASTIFFS

The generation gap!

'Wise One'

OPTIMUS GALILEO OF MOLOSSER

Born 16.01.09

COPPERFIELD HENRIETTA OF MOLOSSER

Born 04.06.12

'Wild One'

Owned and much loved by
Pamela and Robert Jeans-Brown
Tel 0044 (0) 121 779 2692
pamela@bourgueil.co.uk

Nadavin Field Spaniels
Top Breeders, Top Stud Dog, Top Brood Bitch and Top Puppy*
Our Stars of 2013

Top Brood Bitch
Sh Ch Nadavin Nobility JW

New Show Champion
Sh Ch Nadavin Quinevere JW

Three new Nadavin Show Champions in 2013

Congratulations to

Sh Ch Nadavin Quintessa at Tayowen
owned by
Sheila and Howard Taylor

and

Sh Ch Nadavin Quany at Vrackie
owned by Anne Menzies and Mo Henderson

and our own
Sh Ch Nadavin Quinevere JW

Sh Ch Nadavin Julianna JW ShCM
The breed record holder

A special thank you to the judges who have thought so highly of our dogs.

To the special friends who have supported us and to the amazing owners of the Nadavin dogs.

Proudly bred, owned and most definitely loved by Jill and Charles

Jill and Charles Holgate
01282 865705
www.nadavin.co.uk

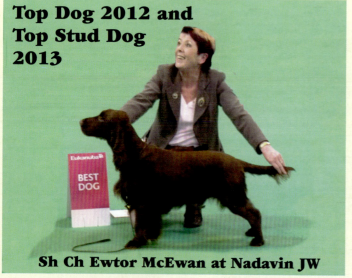

Top Dog 2012 and Top Stud Dog 2013
Sh Ch Ewtor McEwan at Nadavin JW

Top Puppy
Nadavin Thistledown

*at time of going to press

GLENIREN - SUNSHOO

Top Bitch - Top Stud* - Top Brood* - Top Toy Puppy* - Top Breeder*

**HOME AND BREEDERS OF THE ALL TIME
PAPILLON BREED RECORD HOLDER 43 CCs and
ALL TIME PHALENE RECORD HOLDER 22 CCs**

**GLENIREN SHOOTIN '
STARMAKER SUNSHOO**
TOP TOY PUPPY 2013*
'Travis'

TOP PUPPY 2013 - 10 BPIB - DCC/BOB (10 mths) and RDCC - BPIS BREED CH SHOW
RBPIS BLACKPOOL CH SHOW '13 - 2 x CH TPG1 and TPG3 - JUNIOR STAKES DAY WINNER
(10 mths) - BPIS CLUB CH SHOW

NEW CHAMPION 2013

TOP BITCH 2013*
**CH GLENIREN KISS ME
KATE SUNSHOO** 'Kate'
RBIS CLUB CH SHOW -
5 CCs BOB

TOP BROOD 2013
CH GLENIREN JUNIPER STARMAKER SUNSHOO

NEW CHAMPION 2013
TOP STUD*

**CH GLENIREN NIKOLIA
MANIA SUNSHOO**
MULTIPLE CCs -
RBIS PAPILLON
CLUB CH SHOW

IRENE AND GLENN ROBB
AND CAROLYN ROE
+44 (0) 1829 770909

20 Year Club

Pendley

Ch PENDLEY PLAYAWAY JW
4 CCs 5 RCCs

PENDLEY HESTER
1 CC 1 RCC

(Ch/Sw Ch Raskens Romping Playboy ex Birselaw Only Make Believe to Pendley)

(Ch Larchlea Licence To Thrill at Stanedykes ex Birselaw Only Make Believe to Pendley)

These two homebred girls have given us a wonderful year in the ring and we thank all the judges who have appreciated them. After owning and breeding thirteen Rottweiler Champions we were delighted to make up our first homebred Cairn Champion. We aim to stick to our principles of quality not quantity with health and soundness a major factor in our breeding plans.

Mrs June Yates and Mrs Joanne Johnson
Newstead, Robins Folly, Thurleigh, Beds MK44 2EQ
www.pendleyrottweilers.co.uk 01234 772542 07970 758291

Robroyd Russian Black Terriers
ROBROYD I LYKALOVE

'King'
8/1/2010
25 BOBs
Windsor Group 3,
South Wales Kennel
Ass Group 4,
European wins:
Bergamo (Italy)
Group 2-2nd, Avignon
(France) Group 2-2nd,
4 CACs 2 CACIBs

Andrea Gaviraghi

Thank you to all the judges who thought so highly of our dogs
Owner/breeders TOM and JANET HUXLEY (ROBROYD), Robroyd Kennels, Robroyd Cottage, Barnsley, S Yorks. S70 6TY
Tel 01226 285822 email janet@robroyd.co.uk web www.robroyd.co.uk

Liric GORDON SETTERS
(established 1976)

Consistently winning stock producing consistent winners
Fit for function, fit for life

Liric Gordons have again had another good year -

Sh Ch Liric Blac Onyx JW taking 7 CCs and 2 RCCs bringing her total to 15.

Liric Rhapsody in Blue has won 10 Junior Bitch classes from her 11 champion shows, and

Drumdaroch The XPat to Liric (Imp Aus) is Dog World/Royal Canin Top Stud[*].

Liric Xtra Special JW is the Dog World/Yumega Top Brood Bitch and

Our Dogs Top Breeder for 2013 is myself **LIRIC Gordons**

Good breeding speaks for itself
All stock is health tested

MAUREEN JUSTICE
Hilltop, Pudding Lane, Barley, Hertfodshire SG8 8JX
Tel 01763 849749   email liricwithjustice@talktalk.net

www.liricgordonsetters.com

[*]at time of going to press

Soft-Coated Wheaten Terrier Club of Great Britain

Forthcoming events 2014

Open Show South:
March 30, Haddenham

Open Show North:
September 13, Carlisle

Championship Show:
October 19
KC Building, Stoneleigh
+ 4 fun days, grooming workshops etc

For information pack and enquiries for puppies from health-tested parents:
Hon Sec: Mrs Linda Salisbury
Big House, Hardwick Wood
Chesterfield S42 6RH
sec.scwt@hotmail.co.uk

Breed Handbook, Expanded Standard and DVD 'Guide to the Care of the SCWT' available

www.wheaten.org.uk

MARKSBURY BLOODHOUNDS
present this kennels' 28th champion

Current top Bloodhound 2013
CH MAPLEMEAD MELODEON FROM MARKSBURY
(DOB 21.09. 2011)
9 Challenge Certificates, 7 with BOB Top puppy 2012
(Short listed in the Hound Group Crufts 2013)
(Marksbury Forgery at Maplemead ex Ch Marksbury Serious at Maplemead)
Also made up this year Ch Marksbury Ruin and
current top stud in the breed Ch Marksbury Scribble

All enquiries welcome: **Suzanne Emrys-Jones**
sue@penwesta.demon.co.uk   Tel 01637 880443   www.marksburybloodhounds.com

Miccosukees Schnauzers

Standard and Miniature Kennel Club Assured Breeder with Accolade of Excellence

Record Alarm Beskyd at Miccosukees (imp CZ)
2 CCs and 1 RCC
CC and BOB Midland Counties, judge Mary Deats
He has produced some lovely puppies, 3 of which out of **Miccosukees Honey Honey** are in the ring, their results listed alongside:

Mrs Hilary Lockyer
01992 892256   hilarylockyer@hotmail.co.uk
Dogs at stud. Quality puppies for show or pet homes.
We pride ourselves on good termperament.

Miccosukees Rumour Has It
RCC at Welsh Kennel Club, judge Jan Rual

Miccosukees For The Record (Jay)
has 2 RCCs, at Welsh Kennel Club and South Wales KA, judge Mary Deats

Miccosukees Hit Single (Meg) won RCC at Midland Counties, judge Jeff Luscott

Visit our website www.miccosukees.co.uk

Louieville LAKELAND TERRIERS

20 Year Club

In 2014 we celebrate our 40th anniversary in the breed. It all began in 1974 with the purchase of two 4-month-old pups from the Kelda kennel. The dog Ch Kelda Master Mind went on to be top Lakeland Terrier 1978, trimmed and handled by myself when I was only 18 years old. We have had some lovely dogs over the years, Ch Louieville Imperial was a special favourite of mine in the '80s. Special mention to Ch Louieville Red Prince, the Lakeland CC record holder, and his sire Louieville Ploughman, Top Lakeland Stud Dog 2005 who has proved to be such an influential dog in the breed. Our latest puppy Louieville Making Waves has attended two shows and already has 1 CC and 1 RCC at only 7 months old. We look forward to campaigning him in 2014.

Wendy Johnston

Ch Louieville Red Prince

CC RECORD HOLDER
BIS MANCHESTER 2007
BIS CITY OF BIRMINGHAM 2007
RBIS NATIONAL TERRIER 2008
25 CCs
TOP LAKELAND TERRIER
2006, 2007, 2008

Louieville Making Waves

CC AND BEST PUPPY IN SHOW MLTC CH SHOW 2013
RES CC AND BEST PUPPY IN SHOW LTS CH SHOW 2013
FANTASTIC RESULTS FROM HIS FIRST TWO SHOWS AT ONLY 7 MONTHS OLD

We strive to produce Lakelands of the correct type and temperament, with sound movement.
Many thanks to the judges who have appreciated our dogs over the last 40 years.

JOE THORBURN 01461 338287
WENDY JOHNSTON 01931 715352   whitefoldwendy@hotmail.co.uk

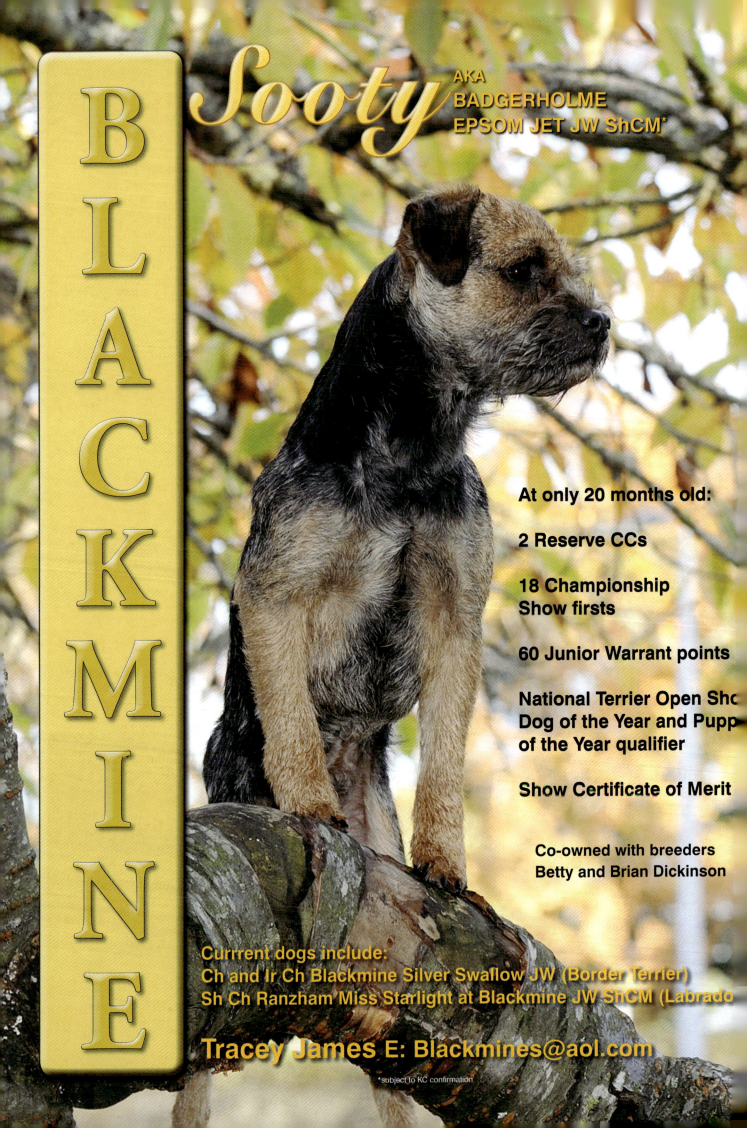

GILCORU

We have bred or owned more Champions than anyone else in the history of the breed in the UK

THE GILCORU GIRLS – NIKKI and LISA with FORTE and EVIE

French & UK Champion Forte Negro at Gilcoru Duovarious (Imp Poland)

Multiple CC and BOB winner, many Group placings
Best in Show UEBB Club Show - Holland
200 Briards from 12 different countries
CAC Black Male National D'Elevage,
France, 20 Black Males, 12 different countries
Best in Show British Briard Club
and Briard Association

**GILCORU ARE THE RUAL FAMILY –
JAN, GORDON, NIKKI and LISA
WWW.GILCORU.CO.UK**

**FORTE'S DAUGHTER
Ch Gilcoru Trueste D'brie at Arrowflec**

1st CC Brenda Banbury, 2nd CC & BOB Frank Kane,
3rd CC Darren Clarke, 4th CC Mr T Jones, 5th CC & RBIS
Briard Association Ch Sh Elia Alia Benitez (Spain)
and 6th CC & BOB Leanne Lewis.
Belgian Briard Club Ch Sh Black Bitch CAC
Corrine de Brouwer (France)
Currently Top Briard Bitch in the UK for 2013
Best in Show Briard Association Open Show Mr G Lawler

Trueste (Evie) is owned and loved
by Dave and Karen Fletcher

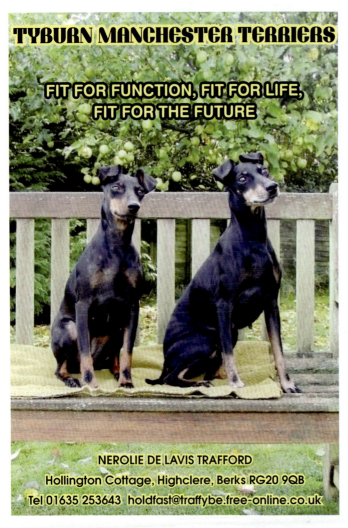

TYBURN MANCHESTER TERRIERS

FIT FOR FUNCTION, FIT FOR LIFE, FIT FOR THE FUTURE

NEROLIE DE LAVIS TRAFFORD
Hollington Cottage, Highclere, Berks RG20 9QB
Tel 01635 253643   holdfast@traffybe.free-online.co.uk

Penrose Chesapeakes
Top UK Kennel, Top Breeder, Top Dogs

Over 50 CCs and 9 Penrose Champions in 5 years, FT awards, WT awards, BIS, RBIS, BPIS, BVIS, 6 Ch Show Group placings, Top Stud, Brood etc

Almost 40 champions, working and wildfowling dogs worldwide

JANET MORRIS
ABS Accolade of Excellence
www.penrose-chesapeakes.co.uk

BLOMENDAL SEALYHAM TERRIERS

Ch/Am Ch Blomendal's Born In USA at Thunder Road

Ch/Am Ch/Can Ch Thunder Road This Kiss

TOP SEALYHAM TERRIER 2012

CC and BOB Scottish Kennel Club 2011 and 2012
CC and BOB Crufts 2012 and 2013
CC and BOB Welsh Kennel Club 2011, 2012, 2013
CC and BIS Midland Sealyham Terrier Club 2011
CC and BIS Sealyham Terrier Club 2012
CC and BIS National Dog Show 2013
CC Sealyham Terrier Breeders Club 2012
CC Ladies Kennel Association 2012

Bliss arrived in the UK in time for Crufts 2013 and in only three months gained her UK title
CC Crufts 2013, CC Scottish Kennel Club 2013
CC and BOB Three Counties 2013

Our sincere thanks to all the judges who thought so highly of our dogs

In 2013 we attended only seven championship shows but gained 6 CCs from them

Owned by **Ms S Hawks and Mrs J A Bledge**
Blomendal, 20 Vicars Road, Stonehouse, Lanarkshire   01698 791443

Sevray and Harrisclub have joined forces....

Viv Rainsbury and Joan Hamilton have had a great year, with:

Jetsway Chaser (jointly owned by Viv and Joan)
(Ch Rathsrigg Millrace – Jetsway Absolut Bling)
Among his many successes in his first months in the ring, **Flint** has won BPIB National Terrier, Darlington and Driffield, BPIS Bedlington Terrier Association, BAVNSC Terrier/Terrier Puppy East of England Ch., RBIS Lowestoft Open and many breed and group wins at Open shows.
He will be at limited stud to approved bitches in due course

Ch Benjique Whistle in the Wind
(owned by Joan)

Although only lightly shown, **Rowan** has 4 CCs, with 3 BOB (including Crufts 2011) and 3 RCCs

Photo by Terry Pover

and it has been a successful time for Viv exhibiting in the art world

Viv is now able to accept commissions for paintings in pastel or acrylics of your dogs, cats, horses, other animals and wildlife. Take a look at
www.blueartsfly.com

Acrylics portrait of my beloved Krystal, my constant companion, muse and artist's model

Viv Rainsbury and Joan Hamilton
(01493 440972 / 01493 669138)
(Norfolk)

CHANDHALLY DALMATIANS AND ITALIAN SPINONE

A small but caring kennel established in 1989. We aim for conformation, movement, temperament and healthy – fit for function dogs. We have great fun showing our dogs and do extremely well both here at home and across Scandinavia & Europe. We are proud to present our newly crowned Multi Champion - Our Italian Spinone Norw/Danish/Med & Int Ch Redrue Cherriecola to Chandhally. Winner of and placed in Gundog Groups (Group7) at Major National and International Shows and a FAB 3rd BIS in Norway. Also at home our Dalmatians Norw Ch Chandhally Snow Queen and her son Chandhally Cuvee du President- a successful and proven sire. Stud and Puppy enquiries welcome. Spinone litter planned 2014

Breeder, Exhibitor, Owner and Judge – Mrs Nina R Fleming,
Cae Bach House, Cae Bach Machen,
Caerphilly CF83 8NG, UK
Tel: (0044) 01633 440371
Email: n.fleming27@btinternet.com
www.chandhally.co.uk

Sh Ch Luneville Honey Moon at Brent ShCM

Crookrise Floyd ex Crookrise Moondance at Luneville
CC & BOB at Midland Counties 2013 - Flo Barker
CC at East of England 2013 - Helga Edmondson
CC & BOB at Border Union 2012 - Gail Simmons
'*Dilys*' has also gained **2 RCCs**

All her awards have been won under breed specialists. Thank you to all judges who have thought so highly of our girl and a very special thank you to her breeders, Michelle and Nigel MacManus, without whom none of this would have been possible.

Puppies are hopefully planned for 2014

Owned and loved by **Roger and Colette Perkins**
Colette.p@hotmail.co.uk

Kanix Fate of Brent JW ShCM 'Olly'

1 RCC
UK Sh Ch/NZ & Aus Gr Ch Robwyn Dreams are Free at Ridanflight ex Sh Ch Kanix Beatrice

Our lovely young boy is only 22 months old and has had a super career in the ring so far.

He has sired some very promising puppies and is available at stud to approved bitches.

Introducing 'Huw' Kanix Joker of Brent

Kanix Fate of Brent JW ShCM ex Sh Ch Chesterhope North 'n' Breeze at Kanix

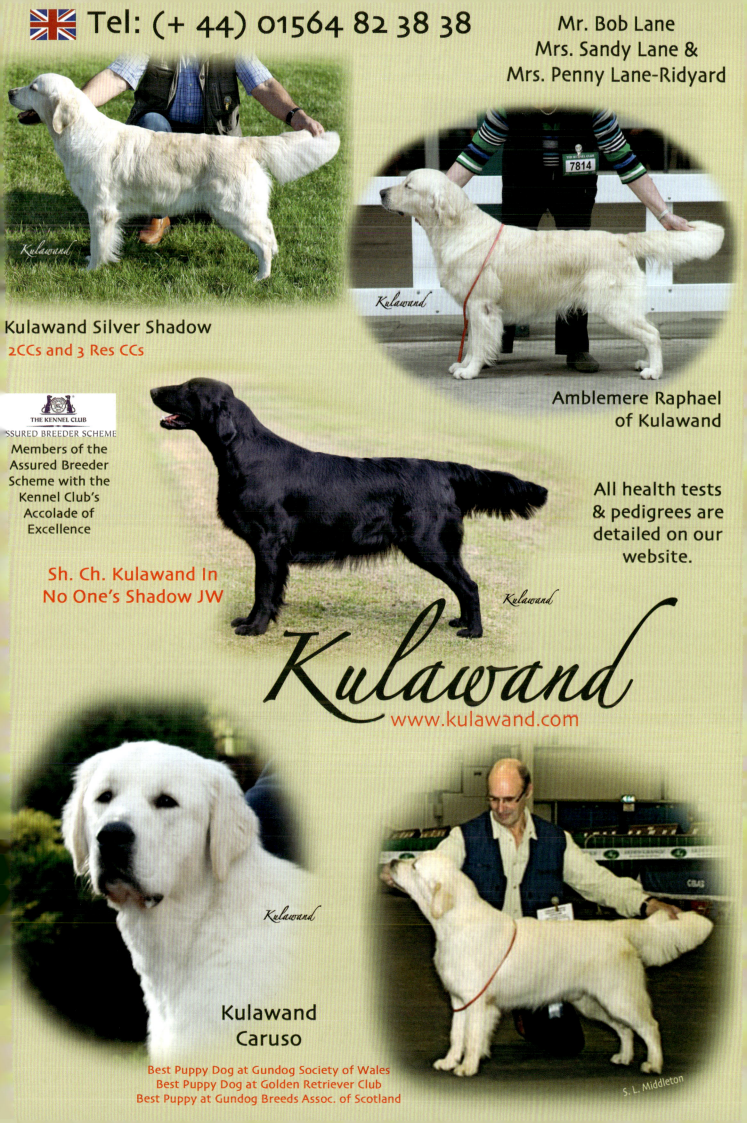

GORTHLECK

20 Year Club

Ryan
Whitepoint Wishful Thinking for Gorthleck
(Hillberry Fox In Socks ex Whitepoint Breeze With Ease)
Breeder of both Ms L Campion

Daniel
Whitepoint Don't Look Back for Gorthleck
(Hillberry Fox In Socks ex Whitepoint Breeze With Ease)

Cush MacNally and Pat Piper
Perrywood, Peeks Brook Lane, Smallfield, Surrey RH6 9PP
Tel: 01342 842639 email: gorthleck@btinternet.com

TOP KENNEL*
TOP BROOD BITCH*
TOP BREEDER*
TOP STUD DOG*

ASTEREL Est 1977
Estrela Mountain Dogs
TOP WINNING KENNEL IN THE UK

Although I wasn't able to attend as many Ch shows as usual in 2013, due to my knee surgery, 'Asterel' still made their presence felt in the showring. Once again 'Asterel' is responsible for the #1 Estrela dog, Asterel Sabugeiro at Bamcwt and runner up with Asterel Fernando, #2 bitch with Asterel Bohemian Rhapsody. Of the 12 shows attended we have won 8 BOBs, 4 BOS and did the double no fewer than 6 times. We also won BIS at both the EMDA club shows in 2013. 'Asterel' will once again be representing the breed in the KC breeders finals to be held at Crufts. I'm thrilled that Asterel Sir Launcealot is once again Top Rare Breed Stud Dog, he is a very special boy!
There are some new pups waiting to make their debut in 2014, so watch this space! The first 'Asterel' will also be going to Australia, he will be upholding the kennel name the other side of the world.

Fernando BOB Crufts 2013

EMDA April 2013
XUVA BIS   RHAPSODY ResBIS   CALI BVIS

Advice and information is always freely available from the most experienced and successful breeder ever in the UK
TRISHA DEAN
email trisha@asterel.co.uk
tel 01994 231052

*at time of going to press

Coalacre Portuguese Podengo
Garrote de Viamonte x Coalacre Geleira
TOP STUD (at time of going to press)

Left to Right: **Norw. Ch Coalacre Tommy Tucker** # 1 Wire Podengo in Norway – 2012 & 2013. BIS Podengo Specialty under Gabriela Veiga. Loved by Gunn Halle ~ www.gerseme.no ~ 0047 92608084
Ir & Int Ch Coalacre Georgie Porgie # 1 Podengo in Ireland. Placed in Group 5. This versatile boy has also won in Agility. Loved by Amanda Lattimer ~ 02890 878260
Ir Ch Coalacre Tom Thumb #2 Podengo in Ireland. Although shown lightly he has been placed in Group 5. Loved by Paul & Amanda Anderson ~ 02890 410274

Pomar Do Vale Do Cutileiro Da Caldermist x C Geleira

Left to Right: **Coalacre Bithisarea at Bryndingo** several BPs & BPIS at the NPPA Open Show. BOB South Wales Loved by Tom & Iona Bailey ~ 01974 831580

Coalacre Gabriela at Bleyos 3 BOBs, 5 x Best Bitch, 2 x Res. Best Bitch & 8 BP awards, including Group 4 & Puppy Group 2 – Belfast.
TOP PUPPY IN BREED (at time of going to press)
Loved by Graham & Tracy Boyles ~ 01838 200301

Left: **Readwald Muddy Waters** (Garrote son) BD Darlington, RBD Driffield. Puppies hopefully expected end 2013 by Muddy & Geleira's sister Nevada.

Lesley Tomlinson
01332 880793 ~ 07832 37403
www.coalacre.com ~ coalacre@btconnect.com

CHAMPION COPPERGOLD SIMPLY SURREAL AT TIGRATO

Many thanks to the knowledgeable judges who have appreciated her many qualities
Driffield 2011 – William McKay – BCC, BP
Crufts 2012 Doreen Cram – RBCC
Birmingham 2012 – Andrew Brace – BCC
BTC 2012 – Frank Kane – RBCC
BTC of Scotland 2013 – Chuck Winslow (USA) – BCC and RBIS
East of England 2013 – Andy Hamilton – RBCC

Dr A and Mrs V Jackson
Haddington, East Lothian

photo Photocall

---

20 Year Club

take a Dog World premier subscription and get a free Pooch and Mutt product* worth up to £15

premier subscription: £29 per quarter

full access: Dog World newspaper and Dog World Annual delivered to your door, the Dog World digital edition plus full access to the Dog World website including breed notes and show reports (now updated daily).
Pay by direct debit only

All these extras for 3p per week

To get your free Pooch and Mutt products call 01795 592854 to take out your premier subscription.

Choose from these three health supplements for dogs: • **Bionic Biotic**: Helps skin health, coat quality, digestion and overall health and condition. Also stops problems like runny stools, itching and scratching • **Mobile Bones**: A joint and bone supplement for dogs. To help all mobility problems and help stop dogs getting stiff joints • **Slimmin' tonic**: A weight loss supplement for dogs. *Please allow 28 days for delivery

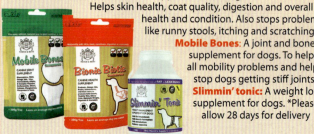

subscription hotline: 01795 592854 or
subscribe online at: **www.dogworld.co.uk**
and click **'Subscribe'**

COPPERGOLD
BOSTON TERRIERS

Joss
COPPERGOLD SIMPLY A SWAGMAN
Crufts 2013 Res Dog CC and 1st PG Dog

Diddy
COPPERGOLD SIMPLY STUNNIN
BPIS - 2013 NBTC

Phinn
TOPTUXEUDO ROCKET SUPREMO AT COPPERGOLD
Crufts 2013 – 2nd Junior Dog

Congratulations to **Ch Coppergold Simply Surreal at Tigrato** (sister of Swagman) on gaining her well deserved title.

Mrs K M GLYNN, Ms J GLYNN and Miss J K WILLIAMS
Coppergoldbostons@ntlworld.com

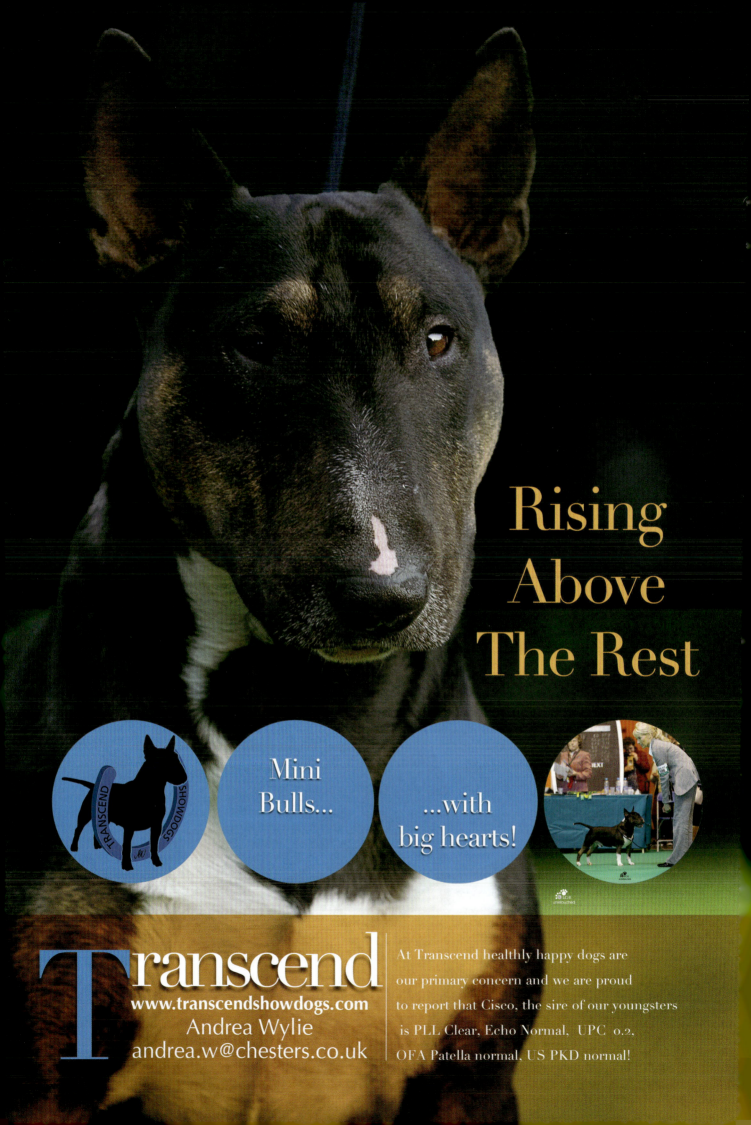

Benatone

Top Breeders 2013
3 New Champions in 2013

CH AM CAN CH Hi-Lite Come Dance With Me   CH Benatone Bossy Boots   CH Benatone Bands Of Gold

CH AM CAN CH Hi-Lite Come Dance With Me

- Co-Owner Andrea Wylie
- Breeder Pamela Armstrong

- Number one Maltese 2013
- RBIS Boston CH show
- CC and BOB at Crufts 2013
- 7cc 5 bob
- Group 2 at Manchester

Sarah & Rosemarie Jackson
www.benatonemaltese.com
maltesesarah@aol.com
tel: 01604409995
mob: 07919160770

Boss

Ch Benatone Bossy Boots

Owned by Andrea Wylie, Tarmara Dawson, and Sarah Jackson

- Number 2 Maltese 2013
- BIS Club CH Show
- Group 1 Welsh Kennel
- Group 1 South Wales
- 6 cc 6 bob

©advertising & photography Croft-Elliott

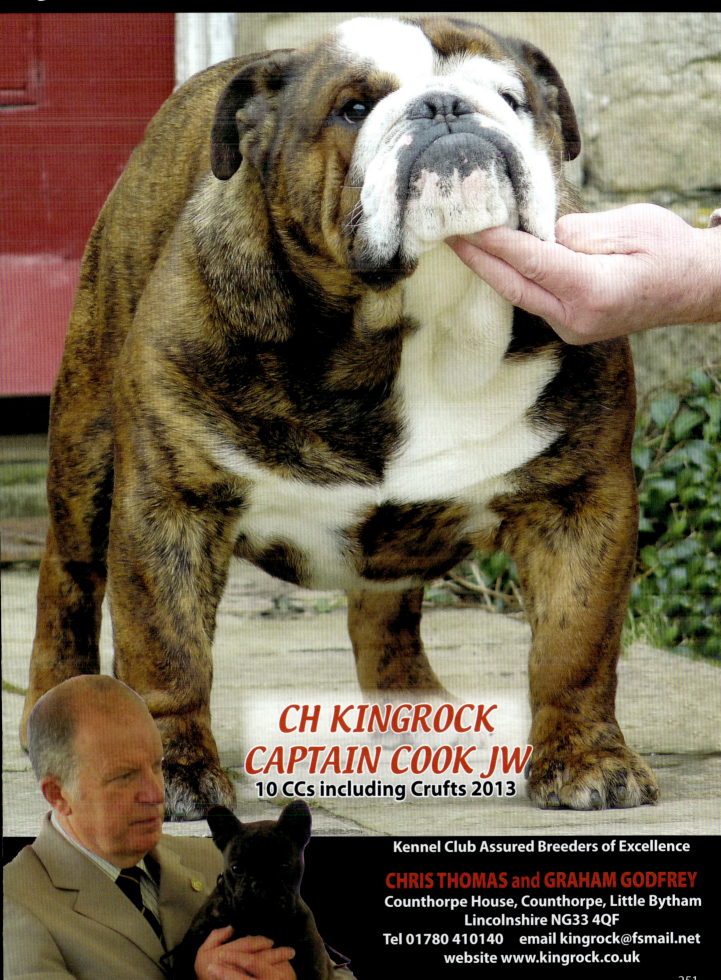

Bart
CH Chayo My Prerogative

2013
#1 Alaskan Malamute
#1 Alaskan Malamute Puppy
#1 Alaskan Malamute Female
#1 Alaskan Malamute Brood Bitch
#1 Alaskan Malamute Breeder
#1 Working Group Breeder

Top Malamute 2010 -> 2013
Breed Record Holder
BIS/RBIS Winner
4 Group 1
26 Group Placings
19 CCs

Enzo
CH Chayo All Eyes On Me

Youngest Champion In The Breed
RBISS and BJISS Winner
Group Winner
Multiple Group Placements
#2 Malamute Overall
7 CCs

Reserve Winners Dog
Alaskan Malamute Club of America
Regional Specialty

Dedicated to producing quality Malamutes that are sound in both body & mind

The Top-Winning Record-Holding Malamute Kennel In Great Britain

Gypsy Crystal

Chayo Blue Velvet

RBIS Windsor 2013
Group Winner
2 CCs 4 rCCS

AM HR CH Chayo Pure Crystal

Multiple BOB Winner
Group placement
2 CCs 3 rCCs
4 CACIB

Where Malamute history continues to be made in the UK

Breeder/Owner/Handler: Sue Ellis
Telephone: (+44) 0161 973 3207
Mobile Phone: 07887607445
Email: sue.chayo@gmail.com
www.alaskanmalamute.uk.com

©advertising Croft-Elliott

The indomitable
CH/IR/FR CH AVIGDOR JARKO
(7th Generation home bred Champion)
Top Tibetan Spaniel UK 2010
BISS TSA'13, SWTSA'12, SE&EA'10
14 BOBs, 16 CC's, 9 RCCs (including Crufts '11 and '12)
Group 3 Three Counties '10, Group 4 WELKS '13, Group 4 Birmingham National '13

Top Tibetan Spaniel Ireland 2010
Group 1 Tralee '12, Group 2 Portadown '10, Group 3 Limerick '12, Group 4 Swords '10, Group 4 ILKA '13
Multi BOB, Green Star and CACIB winner

www.avigdor.eu

'Matka'
Multi Ch
Elbereth Matkamies ShCM

Breed record holder with 9 CCs
Top Dog 2013

'Hessu'
Multi Ch
Lapinpeikon Hanta Heikki
Owned with Kirsi Vallittu
Winner of 2 CCs and 5 BOB

'Mimmi'
Bridus Pikkumimmi
Winner of 2 CCs whilst a puppy, Top Puppy 2013
Owned by Alex Lock

Elbereth & Bridus

'Kia'
Multi Ch Elbereth Kia Joins Bridus ShCM

'Miska', 'Tuuli' & 'Kaikki'
Elbereth Miskakarhu, Elbereth Suvituuli and Elbereth Kaikki Meille Allforus

Special congratulations to David & Judi Cross' Ch Elbereth Marja on becoming the third Elbereth UK Champion

SH. CH. TREVARGH THE ENTERTAINER AT BRIZEWOOD

1st UK TOLLER SHOW CHAMPION - MAKING BREED HISTORY

5 CCs ALL with BOB

74 CH.SH.BOB, 2 X GRP 4, 7 BIS, 2 RBIS

FULLY HEALTH TESTED

HIPS 3/3 = 6, ELBOWS 0/0, OPTIGEN TESTED CLEAR PRA/CEA

HEART TESTED NORMAL, DM TESTED NORMAL,

CURRENT CLEAR EYE CERTIFICATE

PHOTO TIM ROSE/DOGS TODAY   **"WOODY"**

DOG CC & BOB CRUFTS 2013 FROM A RECORD ENTRY

OUR SINCERE THANKS TO ALL JUDGES WHO APPRECIATE HIS QUALITY & STYLE

PROUDLY OWNED BY BABS HARDING & ELAINE WHITEHILL

uk.toller@btinternet.com   www.brizewood.org.uk

Eardley
2 New Champions Home & Away

Am Ch Eardley Barb Dwyer

Ch Eardley Duncan Disorderly ex Ch Eardley Early Opening
(Duncan is MLS-NCCD-FactorV11 Clear)

We have had great fun showing Barbi to her American title this year

Between travelling to the States, back home we have made up our GBGV

Ch Gairside Farfelu for Eardley
4 CCs, 2 BOB and 3 RCCs

Claela Avrille at Eardley
1 RCC, multiple BPIB

Duncan's progeny are doing well in the Beagle ring

Debucher Bubbles at Eardley
1 CC

Seiont Ieuan ap Duncan from Eardley
2 CCs, 1 BOB and 1 RCC

We wish all our fellow exhibitors a happy and successful 2014

Tim Jones and Steve Jepson
ST7 8ND

www.eardleybeagles.com Eardleyhall@aol.com

Breeding quality dogs since 1982

Alncroft

Ch Alncroft I Spy

Top Parson Russell Terrier 2013

10 CCs
8 BOB

"Excellent in such moderation, there is no extreme at all, everything breathes Parson Russell and she moves with free reach and drive."
CC and BOB
Harold Gay

DW/Arden Grange Top PRT 2013

DW/Royal Canin Top PRT Stud Dog
Ch Alncroft Blackthorn
(7 CC and RCC winning progeny)

DW/Yumega Top PRT Brood Bitch

OD Top Breeders

photo George Blair

www.alncroftkennel.co.uk
AlncroftParsonRussellTerriers
Kate Smith and Michaela Moon

Thendara
CHAMPION

G
GUILLAUME
DU MENUELGALOPIN JW
Imp FRA,bred by MARTIAL ROBIN

Achieving
The Spectacular

SH. CHAMPION
THENDARA POT
NOODLE

www.thendara.co.uk 0116 2403497 deemilligan@btinternet.com
Dee Milligan-Bott & Jeremy Bott. 'G' co-owner Julie Noble.

WAVENEY KOZMONAUT

BIS AUS. CH. UK SH. CH.

8 CCs
5 BOB

GROUP 1
WINDSOR
(Rodney Oldham)

GROUP 1
MIDLAND COUNTIES
(Ferelith Somerfield)

TOP UK BORDER COLLIE 2013

Owners: Gary & Marina Clarke & Jacquie Johns

Breeder: Jacquie Johns

claygar@btinternet.com

Arnscroft Norwegian Buhunds

Top Breeder 02-03-04-05-06-08-09-10-11-12-13
Top Kennel 02-03-04-05-06-07-08-09-10-11-12-13
Top Buhund Dog/Bitch 03-04-05-06-07-08-09-10-11-13
Top Brood Bitch 02-03-04-05-06-07-08-09-13

CH AND IRISH CH ARNSCROFT DI DI DI DELILAH
(Fag Ash Lil)
Group winner and multiple group placings
18 CCs 12 green stars

CH AND IRISH CH ARNSCROFT KIMURA
(Kato)
Sire of Arnscroft Champions in Norway, UK and America

CH AND BELGIAN CH ARNSCROFT DI HARD (Rossi)
Multiple group winner and placings here and abroad
23 CCs

CH AND IRISH CH ARNSCROFT DI-NAHS-MITE
(Mia)
Breed record holder 35 CCs
Multiple group placings
Dam of Champions UK, Norway and America

Our Darling Dinah
now almost 17 years young
Top Pastoral Brood Bitch 2008, she is the heartbeat of the kennel

CH ARNSCROFT DI CLAUDIUS
(Claude)
Group winner and multiple group placings

ARNSCROFT ACES HIGH DI
(Baxta)
Junior Luxemburg Champion
Owned by Di (Butler)

NUCH DKCH ARNSCROFT DI VERT TIMON TO KIMURA (Timon)
Owned by my darling little sister Kathrine

LUX CH ARNSCROFT GLA DI OLA (Freya)
Luxemburg Ch and Junior Ch
Owned by Brenda and Tony

NUCH ARNSCROFT DI TO BE A LADY (Daisy)
Group placed
Owned by Kathrine and Janne

See the kids at
WWW.ARNSCROFT.CO.UK

Over 120 Challenge Certificates won in since 2001

In 2012 the kennel had a rest and the kids were not campaigned but our wonderful Arnscroft owners still brought home Top Kennel and Top Breeder for the A team. In 2013 we were back and the kids have made history for the breed once again. So take a bow my Amazing Arnscrofts and their owners who have won the following in 2013

Top Buhund UK 2013
CH ARNSCROFT KISS AND TELL DI
(Ice)
Owned by Sue, Milly, Ian and Toni

Top Buhund Dog 2013
CH ARNSCROFT DI NA MO FARRAH OF KOROMANDEL (Mo)
Pastoral group and Puppy Group 1 Southern Counties
Ch Show. BIS NBC Ch Show Oct 2013
Owned by Jenny

Top Puppy 2013
IRISH CH ARNSCROFT DI TO BE A SAILOR IJCH (Sirius)
Top Puppy UK 2013. 1 CC. BPIS Bath Ch Show. Pastoral puppy group winner. Dublin International Adult group four.
Owned by Alf, Shirley, Nancy, Sue

Top Brood Bitch 2013
ARNSCROFT DI SING ON ICE
(Tusk)
Top Brood Bitch UK 2013. 1 CC.
Owned by Di, Margaret and Treena

ARNSCROFT DI OR COMPLY
(Fli)
2 CCs shown only twice in a year winning both CCs. owned by Mel, Nancy, Clive, Pauline and Martin

CH ARNSCROFT DI NAH SAWR US REX
ShCM (Dino)
Made up 2013. Owned by Neil

I strive to breed quality not quantity a repeat mating of the history – making litter from Tusk and Casper (UK Ch/Am Ch Visions Dino of Trollheimen) is planned however interviews and checks are imperative prior to booking

Please note, win or lose, Arnscrofts are loved and cherished from cradle to grave – if this is not the way you see owning, showing or working please do not contact us.

To all Arnscroft owners and helpers, thank you for your friendship and for loving my babes. I could not do it without you and our success is down to you and my kids and the judges who have been kind enough to reward the quality of the kennel

DI STIRLING   Arnscroft@aol.com   01724 732398   www.arnscroft.co.uk

Dog World Annual 2014   The Basset Griffon Vendéen Club

Eardley GBGVs

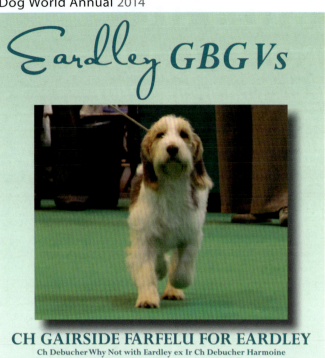

CH GAIRSIDE FARFELU FOR EARDLEY
Ch Debucher Why Not with Eardley ex Ir Ch Debucher Harmoine

Franny has had a wonderful year pictured at Crufts picking up a RCC,
2nd CC at Birmingham National,
Gaining her crown at Paignton,
4th CC at Scottish Kennel Club

Thanking all judges for their kind words

TIM JONES and STEVE JEPSON
For details on our GBGVs and Beagles
www.eardleybeagles.com
eardleyhall@aol.com

BRAEGO PBGV's

MARCUS   **HOLLY**

RUPERT

ERNIE   **GLADYS**

11 CCs and 20 RCCs in our first three years in this "Happy" Breed.
Thanks to all of the judges, who have thought highly of our dogs.

PAUL and MAUREEN OSBOURNE
01366 378497   **07585 979022**

Soletrader Poker Face from Wyvisview

Ruby

Proudly
owned, shown and presented
by Jackie and Lewis Fraser

RCCs at BGV World Congress 2012
The National 2013
Houndshow 2013
City of Birmingham 2013
Plus many class wins

www.wyvisview.com
Beagles and PBGV in the Highlands of Scotland

photo S & S Productions

Maudaxi

PBGVs and Griffon Fauve de Bretagne

2013 sees 3 new champions in PBGVs:
Ch Soletrader Rant Or Rave (owned in partnership with Mrs S Robertson)
Ir Ch Maudaxi Bridget Bordeaux Ir Jun Ch
Ir Ch Trezeguet Treacle Sponge at Maudaxi

2014 sees some exciting youngsters entering the show ring:
Trezeguet Plum Crumble at Maudaxi
Maudaxi Tommy Holedigger

Maudaxi Chewy Vuitton (Elvis)

CC and BPIB East of England,
Mrs Jenna Betts

BPIB SKC May,
Mrs Linda MacKenzie

BPIB Darlington,
Mr Nigel Luxmoore Ball

Phil and Dianne Reid
maudaxibgv@gmail.com   www.maudaxibgv.co.uk
07801 950895

Dog World Annual 2014 — The Basset Griffon Vendéen Club

OVERBECKS

CH OVERBECKS CHEDDAR GEORGE

CCs from Mrs J Pain, Mr R Price and Ms M Persson
RCCs from Mrs E Bothwell, Mr A Rees, Mr J Pepper and Ms S Parker

Bred, owned and loved by
LYNNE SCOTT
Tel 01258 452620
Email lynne.scott@overbeckspetits.co.uk

OVERBECKS ARTIE FISHEL

During 2012 whilst a puppy Archie attended only 3 Championship Shows gaining one 1st and two 2nd places. He has had numerous wins at Open Shows including 4 Puppy Groups and 1 RBPIS.

In 2013 Archie carried on his winning ways with five 1st and seven 2nd places at Championship Shows.

We were thrilled to win the RCC at Paignton and of course all his fans know about his 'literary' talents which continue to make everyone laugh.

Bred by Lynne Scott
Owned and loved and sometimes 'cursed' by
JOAN and **STUART PUCKETT**
Tel 01305 782648 Email joanpuckett@hotmail.co.uk

MARUNNEL

Mrs Ceri McEwan

cerimcewan@googlemail.com

Ch Maudaxi Tycoon Ginger from Marunnel ShCM
(Ch/Am Ch Gebeba Texas True Grit ex Ir Ch Soletrader Sherry Trifle at Maudaxi ShCM)
6 CCs including Crufts '13 and BGV Club '13
G3 Boston '13
G2 Limerick '13 and
2 Green Stars on the Circuit
3 RCCs

Culdaws Diesle from Marunnel
(Ch Gemshorn Rocky ex Monkhams Hippy Chick)
RBIS Hound Club of Ireland '13
1 RCC and 1 Green Star
Numerous Championship Show Stakes Class wins
Best Scent Hound – Hound Club of East Anglia '12 and '13

Maudaxi Coco Chewnel from Marunnel Ir J Ch
(Gaelmarque Bon Ventura with Soletrader ex Maudaxi Cosmopolitan)
4 Green Stars and Ir J Ch title gained at 8 months old
RBB Midland Counties '13
BP WKC '13 and Driffield '13

The Basset Griffon Vendéen Club — Dog World Annual 2014

CH SOLETRADER NAPLES
5 CCs
Owned and shown by Paul Sparks

PAUL SPARKS
paulsparks335@gmail.com
07966 324401

www.soletraderpbgvs.com

CH SOLETRADER SUCH A TUPENCE
3 CCs, 3 BOBs
Owned by Paul Sparks and Sara Robertson

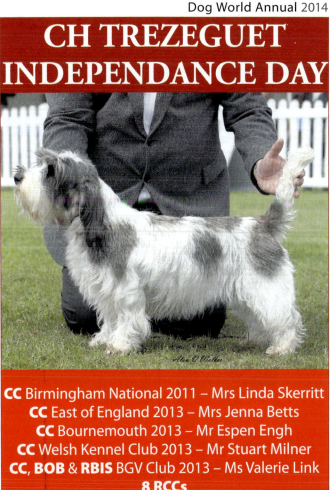

CH TREZEGUET INDEPENDANCE DAY

CC Birmingham National 2011 – Mrs Linda Skerritt
CC East of England 2013 – Mrs Jenna Betts
CC Bournemouth 2013 – Mr Espen Engh
CC Welsh Kennel Club 2013 – Mr Stuart Milner
CC, BOB & RBIS BGV Club 2013 – Ms Valerie Link
8 RCCs

Owned by **CHRIS BLAKE**   01454 884492

Maudaxi

PBGVs & Griffon Fauve de Bretagne

'Arnie'
IR CH ALGERNON PRINCE

From the first litter born in the UK
(Ir Ch Hovriket's Baladin ex E'Mia De L'Equipage Las Fargues)
7 Green Stars, 1 Group 4

We are indebted to Jean McDonald-Ulliott for introducing us to this lovely breed and for entrusting us with one of the foundation males for the UK

Phil and Dianne Reid
maudaxibgv@gmail.com   www.maudaxibgv.co.uk
07801 950895

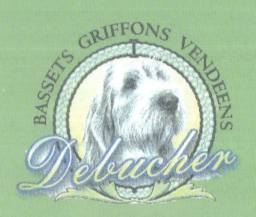

CH DEBUCHER RIGOLE

Co-owned with Claire Cooper
Top GBGV 2012-13, 11 CCs, 11 RCCs
Sire of Debucher X Factor,
Denny's Debucher D'Artaganan at Janimist
and Debucher Delicieuse,
Top GBGV bitch in the USA

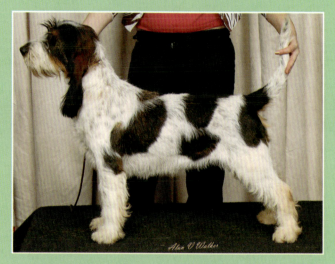

DEBUCHER BIEN CONNUE

Another of our bitches who
will be campaigned in 2014

DEBUCHER X FACTOR

2 CCs, 2 BOB, 1 RCC, BIS BGV Ch Show 2013

DEBUCHER MATISSE

2 RCCs, 2 BD, 1 BOB, 5 BP,
BPIS BGV Ch Show 2013

Both owned, shown and loved by CLAIRE COOPER 07855 255287
Bred and cared for by VIVIEN PHILLIPS

All bred by VIVIEN PHILLIPS 01442 851225
www.bassetsgriffonsvendeens.me.uk
vphillips@btinternet.com

Sh Ch Ferndel Butterkist Cwsscwn JW

the beautiful Fern

Chrisses
Morgan & Schofield

Photos courtesy
Red Ember Photography
and Linda Tyler

PENLI

PHOTOS CAROL ANN JOHNSON · DESIGN EPDCREATIVE.CO.UK

PENLATH VANILLA ICE

Chris and Nicki Blance · 01268 745164 · www.pembrokecorgis.co.uk

Laurelhach
Gordon Setters With Personality Plus
www.laurelhach.co.uk

Laurelhach Legacy JW
1CC~8RCC

Triseter Celtic Link
With Laurelhach
2CC~1BOB

Sh Ch Aust Ch Triseter Ebonie
Zena With Laurelhach
3CC~1BOB

copyright lps2013

WWW.SERENAKER.CO.UK
SERENAKER@GOOGLEMAIL.COM
07792570307

©advertising
& photography
Croft-Elliott

SERENAKER MEMPHIS BELLE

Owners: Parker & Stevens

2 CCs 2 Rccs
1 BOB
1 GROUP 2

S&S Productions 2013

SERENAKER STROCCO

SELECTIVELY SHOWN
MULTIPLE BPIB

Owners: Parker, Stevens, Norridge, Carota & Sipperly

SERENAKER FIGARO

2 CCS
1 BOB

Owners: Parker, Stevens & Norridge

SERENAKER

Serena Parker & Graham Stevens

CH JANEYJIMJAMS JENSON JW ShCM

TOP SOFT-COATED WHEATEN 2013

Owners Michael and Alison Fallon
Handled by Alison Fallon
01252 875852
website www.janeyjimjams.com

CASSOM
COCKER SPANIELS

Cassom Bea Dazzled
Sire: Sh Ch Lindridge Star Quest
Dam: Cassom Busy Bea

Cassom Skyfall
Sire: Sh Ch Cassom Hey Jude JW
Dam: Cassom Cristal

Cassom Olive Oyl
Sire: Sh Ch Joaldy Mandolin Wind
Dam: Cassom Penny Lane

Cassom Amaze N Grace
Sire: Sh Ch Charbonnel Life N Times
Dam: Cassom Calamity Jane

This year the show team has consisted of our four girls. All have been consistent winners at Championship shows and breed club shows, but our star this year has been Cassom Skyfall 'Adele' who (at time of going to press) is current leader in the Our Dogs Top Puppy competition and joint current leader in the Cocker Spaniel Club Puppy of the Year competition.
All this despite losing her coat half way through her puppy career. We hope to have her back out in 2014!
Sh Ch Cassom Hey Jude and **Cassom Rock Star (RCC)** remain available at stud.

Thank you to the judges for a fantastic year.

Bred and handled by **SARAH AMOS-JONES**
Tel: 07950 117361 Email: sarah.cassom@gmail.com
web: www.cassomcockers-vizslas.co.uk

FLO

TOP POINTER 2013 & 2012

RUNNER UP TOP GUNDOG 2013*

SH CH WILCHRIMANE ICE MAIDEN JW WW '13

RBIS BLACKPOOL 2013

7 X GROUP 1

CONTEST OF CHAMPIONS WINNER 2013

KENNEL GAZETTE JW FINAL WINNER '13

WORLD WINNER & GROUP 2 WORLD SHOW '13

17 X CC

* AT TIME OF GOING TO PRESS

ANNETTE & AMELIA SIDDLE   WILCHRIMANE POINTERS   01404 812624   SID.EASTHILL@BTCONNECT.COM

Ice
'Alouann Steal N'The Show'

Marcus
'Alouann Mr High N Mighty at Grenowood'

Gracie
'Alouann Glitz N'Glamour'

Cinnamon
'Alouann Cinnamon N'Nutmeg of Lelaps'

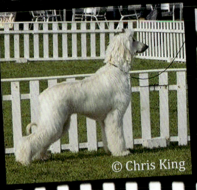
© Chris King

© Leanne Trethowen

© Pauline Oliver

© Dom Santoriell

Claire and Liz Millward - Sheffield UK
ALOUANN
Starring...

Presents Our Top Winning Litter of 2013

Natalie -
1 x RCC SWKA, 3 x Ch Show BPIB, BOB & BPIB Darlington Ch show
Owned by Alouann and Pamela Mottershaw.

Ice -
1 x Ch Show BPIB, 3 x Ch Show BPD, 1 x BPIS & RBPIS Club Ch Show
1 x BPIS Club open show, 1 x Open Show PG1 & PG4.
Owned by Chris and Debbie King and Alouann.

Sassy -
1 x BPIS Club Ch Show, 1 x Ch Show BPIB, 1 x Club Open Show
BPIS & RBPIS. Owned by Lesley, Alister and Dawn Currie (Australia)

Gracie -
2 x Ch Show BPIB. Qualified for Welsh Top Puppy.
Owned by Annalise Gray.

Marcus -
3 x Ch Show BPD, 1 x RBPIS Club Open Show.
Owned by Susan Brookes and Kristina De Havilland.

Cinnamon -
1 x Ch Show BPB, 1 x Open Show BPIS & RBPIS, numerous Open Sh
PG1 & PG4, qualified for East Anglia Supermatch competition.
Owned by John Stokes & David Knights.

Persia -
1 x Open Show BPIB, 1 x BPIS Club Open Show & Crufts qualified
Owned by Kristina De Havilland and Susan Brookes.

www.alouann.com

Persia
'Alouann Diamonds N'Pearls with Purplequeen'

Natalie
'Alouann Wishes N'Dreams'

Sassy
'Alouann Red Hot N'Sassy to Tico'

© Leanne Trethowen

© Will Harris

© Angela Brown

The full litter of 8 is Crufts qualified. The litter has also competed occassionally in the KC Breeders Competition and won the Hound Group at 3 Ch Shows. All achievements were won before they were 10 months old. We are so proud and would like to thank all judges concerned for thinking so highly of the litter.

WHITTIMERE
Norwegian Elkhounds & Finnish Spitz

Whittimere celebrated their 100th CC and 14th UK Champion during 2013
Top Finnish Spitz 2013* ~ Top Norwegian Elkhound 2013*
(*at time of going to press)

Ch/Ir Ch Ennafort The One And Only ShCM

(Sired by Ir Ch Whittimere Pandemonium)

Ir Ch Whittimere Pandemonium

Well done to Will on being JHA Handler of the Year 2013 at Discover Dogs in November.
We are so very proud of you Will – 'Mum' and Robert.

Ch/Ir Ch Kunniakas Look No Further For Whittimere

Robert Greaves,
Nicola and Will Croxford
www.whittimere.co.uk

THE JACK RUSSELL TERRIER

Originated in England, developed in Australia and now a show dog everywhere but the UK

by Kao Miichi and Christina Areskough

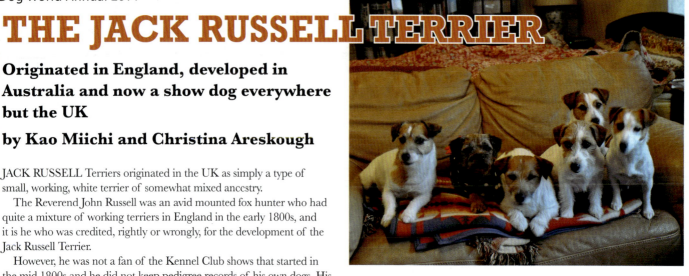

JACK RUSSELL Terriers originated in the UK as simply a type of small, working, white terrier of somewhat mixed ancestry.

The Reverend John Russell was an avid mounted fox hunter who had quite a mixture of working terriers in England in the early 1800s, and it is he who was credited, rightly or wrongly, for the development of the Jack Russell Terrier.

However, he was not a fan of the Kennel Club shows that started in the mid 1800s and he did not keep pedigree records of his own dogs. His terriers did not follow a written Standard; the only requirement was that they be good workers.

Thus, the Jack Russell Terrier was never incorporated into the KC in the UK. It was not until 1990 in the UK that a Standard was written for a taller version of the Jack Russell Terrier (12-15 inches) and given the name Parson Jack Russell Terrier and updated ten years later to Parson Russell Terrier. The US followed suit and adopted the Parson Russell Terrier into the American KC around the same time.

Independent of what was happening in the UK or USA, Australia was working on the breed. Migrants from the UK had brought terriers Down Under, most of these having Parson ancestry with heights up to 15 inches.

Dedicated breeders in Australia fought, through line-breeding, to bring this height down to 12 inches and under.

A Standard was adopted to denote this 'new' kennel club breed in Australia as a Jack Russell Terrier, and the breed was allowed to be shown at Australian National Kennel Council (ANKC) shows.

In July 1991 New Zealand adopted the Australian Standard and 'Jacks' were shown in that country from then on. Jacks hit the terrier ring with a flourish and it was not long before they were featuring in group and in-show awards.

The Fédération Cynlogique Internationale recognised the Jack Russell Terrier as a breed in 2001 with the Australian Standard.

Since FCI recognition, this has become one of the most popular breeds in the terrier group all over Europe, except in the UK, where it remains outside the KC (in the vein of Reverend Russell).

Although everyone acknowledges that the country of origin of the Jack Russell Terrier is the UK, Australia must be given credit for developing this terrier into a kennel club breed, with a written Standard. The AKC finally followed suit and recognised it as a 'Russell Terrier' in 2012. The US chose to alter the name as a nod to those who remained staunch in their beliefs that the Reverend John 'Jack' Russell was the forefather of a 'type' of working terrier and not a kennel club 'breed'.

The UK remains the holdout, sticking with the tradition of the Jack Russell Terrier as a 'type' of small working terrier and not a purebred dog for the show ring.

On the other hand, kennel clubs in most modern countries in the world have recognised this dog and it is a shame that it cannot be shown in its country of origin at all-breed shows.

This is a breed that cannot be ignored. It is impossible not to adore these little terriers, and somehow they are going to find their way into the show rings in their country of origin!

The progress of the FCI Jack Russell Terrier in Scandinavia

Christina Areskough and Lena Lövdahl

AFTER the Jack Russell Terrier were recognised by the FCI in 2001, an assessment of the breed started in Scandinavia. Breed clubs were started with devoted people, all for the benefit of the breed.

A handful of breeders in each country, Sweden, Norway, Denmark and Finland, imported dogs mainly from Australia but also from New Zealand and a few from Europe. The imported puppies and young dogs, adult males and pregnant females, were of very high quality and became the foundation of what we have today.

The imports were cleverly bred and sometimes mixed with the local assessed dogs and the breed type was established fast. The demand for the FCI registered quality puppies was and still is very high and Scandinavian puppies are exported all over the world.

The FCI JRT has become a popular show dog and is often seen among the terrier group placings. They are also popular companion dogs and many are seen in other dog sports, such as agility and freestyle.

Many Scandinavian breeders also find it important to test their JRTs' hunting and tracking abilities, to maintain the purpose of the breed as a small working terrier.

The health situation of the breed looks good; many breeders test their dogs for luxating patella and hereditary eye disease before breeding.

The future looks bright for the lively, alert and active little terrier with the keen, intelligent expression, so bold and fearless, friendly but quietly confident.

MONAMOUR Jack Russells

What we show, what we Believe...

The FCI/Australian Jack Russell Terrier
- Strong, active, lithe, medium-sized (25-30cm), working terrier
- Body marginally longer than tall, with short strong loin and visible forechest
- Girth spannable by a medium-sized man's hands; The depth of the body from the withers to the brisket should 50:50 the length of foreleg from elbows to the ground.
- The girth behind the elbows should be about 40 to 43 cms.
- Forelimbs straight from elbow to toes; shoulders layed back; hindlimbs well angulated
- A balanced terrier with true reach and drive in their movement

We have bred this wonderful terrier since 2000, when it was first recognized by the FCI.

KAO MIICHI & HIROSHI TSUYUKI clumberup@gmail.com +81-53-545-0537

MONAMOUR, home of the Jack russell terrier since 2000.

Dog World Annual 2014

Dog World Annual 2014

Chelsea

Owned by Elaine Reiseman   Presented by Andrew Green & Amy Kiell-Green

Bred by Kao Miichi, Monamour Jack Russell Terriers

Am.JKC.CH,Monamour Energy of Kiss
Sired by WW12,Multi.CH.Lemosa Mr.Energizer From Monamour JP Monamour Forever

American Grand Champion
DBF Trophy Wife CM
Bred/Owned/Shown by DBF Russell Terriers and Lynn Norley

American Champion
DBF Woodsong Hot in Cleveland
Bred/Owned/Shown by DBF Russell Terriers and Melissa Dodge

American Champion
DBF Woodsong of KCR
Owned by Pam Bailey
Bred/Shown by DBF Russell Terriers

American Champion
DBF Shez a Golddigger at Woodsong
Bred/Owned/Shown by DBF Russell Terriers and Melissa Dodge

American Champion
DBF Hez a Jetsetter
Bred/Owned/Shown by DBF Russell Terriers

American Champion INTERRA Junior Champion
Mon Amour Afterglow
Bred by Kao Miichi, Owned/Shown by DBF Russell Terriers

DBF Russell Terriers
Virginia, USA

Producing and Exhibiting Quality Jack Russell Terriers

Dr Candace Lundin and Frank Zureirck

DBF RUSSELL TERRIERS

Phone: 1-540-554-4525
Email: FZureick@earthlink.net

TAYLORTAY TERRIERS

Bred with integrity, for temperament, health, longevity, character, working ability, agility and show quality

Anne Taylor
00353 86 3559173
taylortay2@gmail.com
www.taylortayterriers.weebly.com

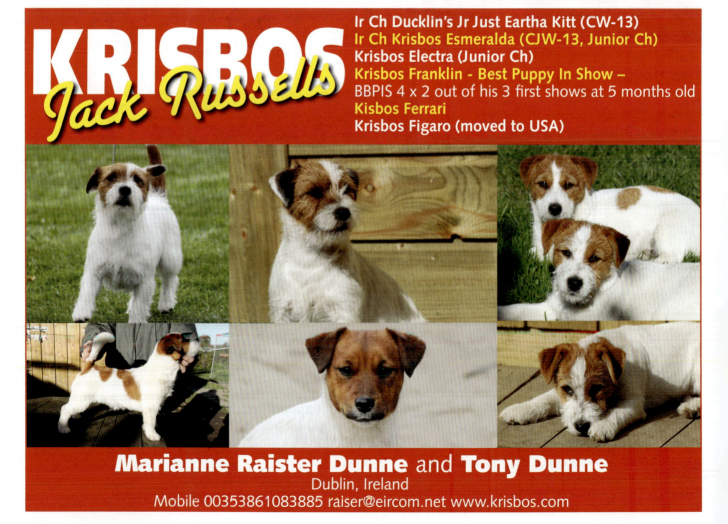

KRISBOS Jack Russells

Ir Ch Ducklin's Jr Just Eartha Kitt (CW-13)
Ir Ch Krisbos Esmeralda (CJW-13, Junior Ch)
Krisbos Electra (Junior Ch)
Krisbos Franklin - Best Puppy In Show –
BBPIS 4 x 2 out of his 3 first shows at 5 months old
Kisbos Ferrari
Krisbos Figaro (moved to USA)

Marianne Raister Dunne and **Tony Dunne**
Dublin, Ireland
Mobile 00353861083885 raiser@eircom.net www.krisbos.com

JOJAVIK

Dobermanns
WWW.JOJAVIK.COM
Jackie & Victoria Ingram

2 CC's
South Wales 2013
Mr Bob Gregory

The Midland Dobermann Club 2013
BEST IN SHOW
Mr Richard Thorpe / Mr Dave Anderson/ Mrs Maggie Spindley

4 RCC's
The Dobermann Club 2012
Mrs June Higgins / Mr Joel Vanlerberghe

North Eastern Counties Dobermann Club 2013
Mrs Lita Lainchbury

Midland Counties 2013
Mr Micheal Quinney

Working & Pastoral Breeds Of Scotland 2013
Mrs Roberta Wright

TOP DOBERMANN PUPPY 2012
Junior Luxembourg Champion

BEST BITCH & RESERVE BEST IN SHOW
South West Dobermann Club 2013
Mr Geoff Duffield

BEST OF BREED WG1 & BEST IN SHOW
SWECA 2013
Mr Steven Walker / Mrs Suzanne Archer / Mrs Eileen Gecson

RESERVE BEST BITCH
Boston 2013
Mrs Sue Coster

RESERVE BEST BITCH
The Dobermann Club 2013
Mr Mike Vines

Molly

JOJAVIK MOLLY MOBSTER JW SHCM
CH Krieger's The Wizard Of Oz JW x CH/LUX CH Jojavik Gangsters Moll JW

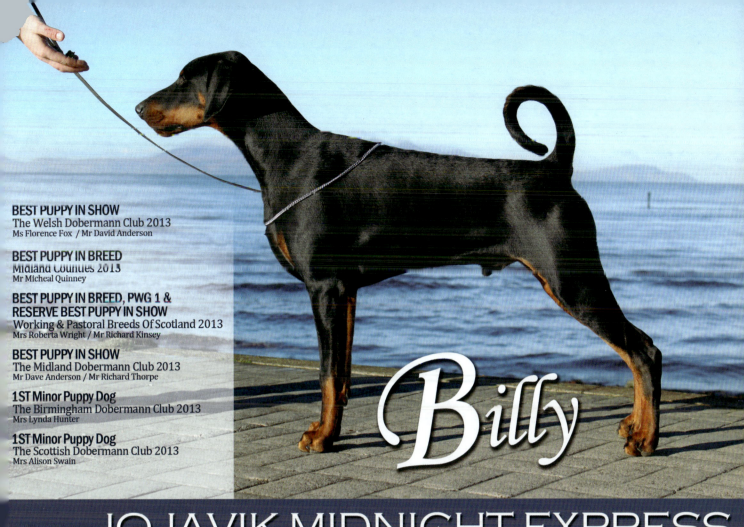

BEST PUPPY IN SHOW
The Welsh Dobermann Club 2013
Ms Florence Fox / Mr David Anderson

BEST PUPPY IN BREED
Midland Counties 2013
Mr Micheal Quinney

BEST PUPPY IN BREED, PWG 1 & RESERVE BEST PUPPY IN SHOW
Working & Pastoral Breeds Of Scotland 2013
Mrs Roberta Wright / Mr Richard Kinsey

BEST PUPPY IN SHOW
The Midland Dobermann Club 2013
Mr Dave Anderson / Mr Richard Thorpe

1ST Minor Puppy Dog
The Birmingham Dobermann Club 2013
Mrs Lynda Hunter

1ST Minor Puppy Dog
The Scottish Dobermann Club 2013
Mrs Alison Swain

JOJAVIK MIDNIGHT EXPRESS
CH Chancepixies Locomotive X CH Tronjheim Belladonna From Jojavik JW ShCM
JOJAVIK POISON IVY

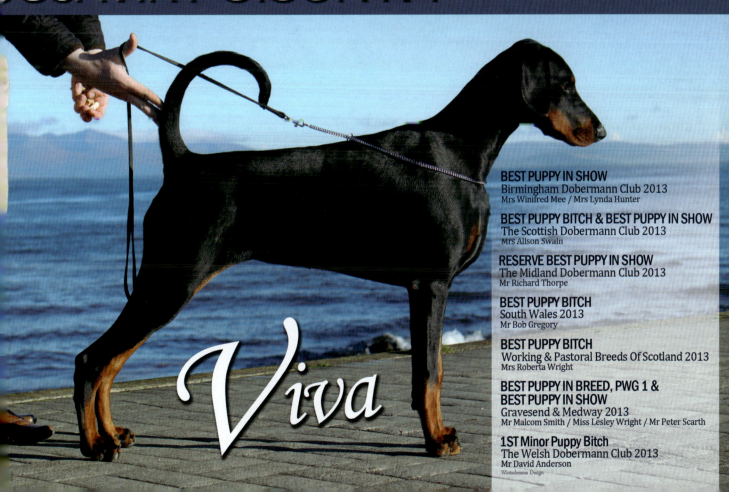

BEST PUPPY IN SHOW
Birmingham Dobermann Club 2013
Mrs Winifred Mee / Mrs Lynda Hunter

BEST PUPPY BITCH & BEST PUPPY IN SHOW
The Scottish Dobermann Club 2013
Mrs Alison Swain

RESERVE BEST PUPPY IN SHOW
The Midland Dobermann Club 2013
Mr Richard Thorpe

BEST PUPPY BITCH
South Wales 2013
Mr Bob Gregory

BEST PUPPY BITCH
Working & Pastoral Breeds Of Scotland 2013
Mrs Roberta Wright

BEST PUPPY IN BREED, PWG 1 & BEST PUPPY IN SHOW
Gravesend & Medway 2013
Mr Malcom Smith / Miss Lesley Wright / Mr Peter Scarth

1ST Minor Puppy Bitch
The Welsh Dobermann Club 2013
Mr David Anderson

Wustadonna Design

Blake
Owned by Mervyn & Michelle Campbell

JOJAVIK PINBALL WIZARD AT RAITHCOR JW
CH KRIEGER'S THE WIZARD OF OZ JW X CH/LUX CH JOJAVIK GANGSTERS MOLL JW

In 2013 Blake's highlights were....

1ST Yearling Dog
CRUFTS 2013
Mr Stuart Mallard

1ST Yearling Dog
The Scottish Dobermann Club 2013
Miss Bridgette Bodle

1ST Yearling Dog
Working & Pastoral Breeds Of Wales 2013
Mr Kevin Young

1ST Post Graduate Dog
The Scottish Kennel Club 2013
Mr Sigurd Wilberg

1ST Post Graduate Dog
Three Counties 2013
Mr Mike Mullan

1ST Post Graduate Dog
Blackpool 2013
Mrs Irene Rushfirth

1ST Post Graduate Dog
The Welsh Kennel Club 2013
Mr Albert Wright

1ST Post Graduate Dog
Driffield 2013
Mrs Wendy Meikle

1ST Post Graduate Dog
South Wales 2013
Mr Bob Gregory

JOJAVIK
BRED with CARE
RAISED with LOVE
SHOWN with PRIDE

CRAIGYCOR CORGIS

Erin

UK's #1 Corgi in 2013*

BIS/BISS Eng/Ir/Int Ch Craigycor Viva La Diva

(BIS/BISS Eng/Ir/Am Ch Shavals Fire Classic at Craigycor
ex BIS Am/Ir Ch Elfwish Sally Ride)

**Multiple Best of Breed, Group and
All Breed Best in Show Winner**

The highlight of our memorable year was winning the
Bitch CC and Best in Show at the Welsh Corgi League Diamond Jubilee
out of a cosmopolitan entry of 280 Pembrokes

Alan, Sarah, Emily and Jessica Matthews
Tel: +44 2892 611317 / Email: craigycor@lineone.net

*at time of going to press

KEBULAK
Home of World Winning Terriers

- 46 champions to date
- Top UK breeder Kerry Blue Terriers '11, '12, '13
- Top UK breeder Lakeland Terriers '13
- Top Lakeland Terrier '13
- World Winner '13

Ch Kebulak Man After Midnight
'Vegas'

UK's Top Lakeland '13, World Winner and BOB '13
17 CCs
Multiple Group Placements
RBIS National Terrier '13
Group 1 Boston '13

Cara Davani and Andy Potts
www.kebulak.com

cdavani@live.co.uk   01473 785411   07717 692854

KEBULAK
Home of World Winning Terriers

Ch Kebulak Kiss This 'Romeo'

Co-owned with Cathy Neil
4 CCs, 3 BOBs
Multiple group placements in UK and Ireland

Ch Kebulak Striptease 'Shakira'

Other CC winners in team Kebulak:
Kerries –
Kebulak Bare All, 1 CC Kebulak Rockin Robin 2 CCs Kebulak Filthy Love 1 CC
Irish - Photo Finish at Kebulak 1 CC

Irish Champions '13:
Welsh:
Ir Ch Kebulak Trigger Happy
Lakies:
Ir Ch Kebulak Lady Madonna and
Ir Ch Kebulak Sixty Minute Man

Cara Davani and Andy Potts
www.kebulak.com

cdavani@live.co.uk   01473 785411   07717 692854

Winterkloud Portuguese Water Dogs

Proud owner of the first CC winner in the UK and currently the only dog to win a group placing at Crufts, the Top Stud for 2011, '12 and '13 Ch Bregantia The X-Factor at Winterkloud

Ch Rarjo Revolution at Winterkloud
'Rico'
(Ch Bregantia The X-Factor at Winterkloud ex Bregantia Funky Diva)
3 CCs, 5 RCCs, 1 CACIB and CAC, 1 RCACIB and RCAC, 2 Group 4s

Ch Digadogs O'Cornelia (imp Swe)
'Connie'
(DK,UCH Camlin Seadancer Salute 2 Rodtop ex Digadogs You're Made For Me)
3CCs, 5RCCs, 1 RCACIB & RCAC, 1 group 3, BPiB & RCC Crufts 2011.

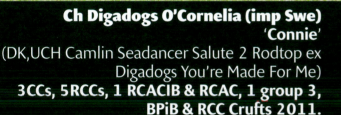

Winterkloud Mad Moments
'Edna'
(Ch Bregantia The X-Factor at Winterkloud ex Bregantia Don't Stop Me Now at Winterkloud)
1CC, 2RCCs

Winterkloud Hugo Boss
'Hugo'
(Ch Rarjo Revolution at Winterkloud ex Ch Digadogs O'Cornelia)
The new generation of 'Winterkloud Winners'

Sarah McGill
Tel: 07773 335641
Email: winterkloud2000@yahoo.co.uk

ALKINRA WIRES

Bart

Alkinra Making Mischief

CC & RCC Winner

Reserve CC at the WFTA Centenary Show under breed specialist Peter Green with an entry of 83

Co-Owned with Beverly Deacon

BREEDING WITH THE BREED AT HEART

RACHEL PEARCE

+44 (0) 1584 711441

+44 (0) 7788 721082

alkinra@yahoo.co.uk

©advertising & photography Croft-Elliott

Ankors
Winners, champions and history makers

ANKORS VASSUD and ANKORS FREYA

Featured at the First World Meeting of the PWD in Portugal where Freya went BPIS under breed specialists Luis Catalan and Carla Molinari, Vassud went RBPIS among international competition. Vassud is top puppy '13* and puppy group winner at Bournemouth, his sister is one point behind with PG4 at Brmingham City and PG2 at Darlington. We look forward to an exciting 2014 with them.

LIDDYLEAZE LADY GODIVA FOR ANKORS
Evie
*2 CCs, 7 RCCs

Our thanks to all those who have thought so highly of the girls and special thanks to Ruth Bussell, Rachael Reddin, Rose Turley, Louise Turley and Sarah McGill.

ANTONY BONGIOVANNI and JOHN HEARD
Portuguese Water Dog
ankorsph@aol.com

LINDA BISS and JIM SAWYER
Chinese Crested and Mexican Hairless
ankorsch@aol.com

*at time of going to press

BELLE VILLE
2013 Another Fabulous Year!

CH BELLEVILLE HONEY NUT CRUNCH
BOB Crufts
Photo Ira Karvo

BELLEVILLE ANJO DE NOITE
CC & BOB
Goup 3
Birmingham City

BELLEVILLE LUA DA NOITE
RBCC Border Union and WKC

BELLEVILLE JUST MAGIC
5 x RBCC from Puppy
Puppy Group 1
Bournemouth

CH BELLEVILLE SILK SLIPPERS
BCC WKC

BELLEVILLE SEDUCTION
BP and Puppy Group 3
South Wales

Lua and Claudia congratulate their PWD Litter broithers: Heather Gibson's Belleville Noite Preta At Majesixs DCC Leeds + 2 RCC's and Kate Holness' Belleville Guarda De Noite at Ricci RDCC PWD Club

Cathy Thompson-Morgan & Ed Morgan
www.bellevillenorfolkterriers.co.uk

Dog World Annual 2014 — The Irish Terrier Association

MONTELLE IRISH TERRIERS and Toy Poodles

MONTELLE VISION IN RED JW ShCM
Owned by Lucy Jackson

MONTELLE GOING FOR GOLD JW
Age 14 months
Owned by Joanne Bradbury

MONTELLE VISION IN RED JW ShCM winner 9 RCCs and 1 CC. Lightly shown during 2013 gained the **RCC** Three Counties, judge Bill Browne-Cole, **RCC** SITS, judge Liz Cartledge and CC and RBIS NEITC, judge Phillip O'Brien.

MONTELLE GOING FOR GOLD JW has had a successful Puppy career gaining **4 BPIS and 3 RBPIS** including **BPIS & RCC** ITA Ch Show Judge Les Aspin.

CH MONTELLE MI'LADY JW ShCM (owned by M Williamson & B Stirling) has continued to be a strong contender in Veteran Classes gaining a number of **Best Veteran in Show, including Best Terrier Veteran** at Darlington Ch Show under Judge Tom Mather. 2013 has seen the debut of the homebred **Black Toy Poodle Montelle Look At Me** who has gained **3 RBPIS, 2 BPIS and a RCC**, a descendant of the influential sire **Ch Montelle Just As Smart for Fabuleux**

Enquires to: **Ann Bradley** 170 Glassmoor Bank, Whittlesey, Peterborough PE7 2LT Tel: 01733 205386

LAKERIDGE
Irish & Lakeland Terriers

WYNDAM RIONACH AT LAKERIDGE 'Lucy'

A consistent winner at all the championship shows Lucy attended in 2013 before retiring for maternity duties in July.

Thank you to the judges for their awards.

Lucy will be returning to the ring in 2014 where she will be joined by her daughter **LAKERIDGE NIAMH**.

Keith & Wendy Bower
11 Pennys Lane, Lach Dennis
Cheshire CW9 7SJ
Email: wendy.bower2@btinternet.com
Tel: 01606 333672

SUJONCLA IRISH TERRIERS
KENNEL CLUB ASSURED BREEDER

SUSAN SEABRIDGE

Four Winds, Hurnbridge Road, Hawthorn Hill, Coningsby, Lincoln LN4 4UP
Tel: 01526 345374   web page www.sujoncla-terriers.co.uk   email jonsue@globalnet.co.uk

CHAMPION SUJONCLA POWDER RIVER (Spence)
Sire UK/Am Gch Fleet St Fenway Fan   Dam Champion Sujoncla Tecumseh

From this (National Terrier) April 2012
Six months old

To this (North of England Irish Terrier) November 2012
Twelve and a half month old gaining his Champion status

STUDS AVAILABLE TO APPROVED BITCHES ONLY

Champion Balengro Tben Tainte at Sujoncla – 10 CCs, 9 BOB, 11 RCCs, 3 BIS and Top Irish 2008
Champion Sujoncla Powder River – 3 CCs 1 RCC, 1 BIS and Top Puppy 2012
Sujoncla Kowtolik – 5 RCCs and 1 BIS

Champion Balengro Tben Tainte at Sujoncla
(Jimmy)
Sire Sujoncla Blackfoot   Dam Yewood Amber

Sujoncla Kowtolik
(Boulton)
Sire Ch Balengro Tben Tainte at Sujoncla Dam Ch Sujoncla Tecumseh

BREEDING AT ALL TIMES FOR TYPE AND TEMPERAMENT
All dogs owned, handled and prepared by Susan
We also wish all Sujoncla progeny, both home and overseas, a happy and successful 2014

Holbam Irish Terriers

HOLBAM PEARLY STAR made her debut at the Irish Terrier Association Open Show winning **Best Puppy in Show**. Other wins include Belfast **Best Puppy in Breed**, South Wales **Best Puppy Bitch & Reserve Best Bitch**, Midland Counties **Best Puppy Bitch**, Southern Irish Terrier Society Ch Show **Best Puppy in Show**, Northern Irish Terrier Society Ch Show **Best Puppy in Show**, Worthing Open Show **Best Puppy** and **Reserve Best of Breed**.

The Holbam Breeders Team featuring **HOLBAM CELTIC KATE** (handled by Mary Bradshaw) whose wins include Richmond **Best Puppy** and **Best Bitch**, Windsor **Best Puppy Bitch**, Blackpool **Best Puppy Bitch**, South Wales **Best Bitch**, Witney Open Show **Best Puppy** and **Reserve Best Puppy in Show**, Worthing Open Show **Best of Breed**.

Her dam **HOLBAM TIERNEYS GIRL** (handled by Mary Ruffles) was lightly shown in 2013 and **HOLBAM PEARLY JACK** (handled by Claire Nolcini) many open show Best of Breeds and group placings including Richmond **Best of Breed**.

The Holbam Irish Terriers are handled by Mary Bradshaw.

All enquiries to **Mrs Carol Bamsey**
Tel 01296 713045
Mob 07703 692887
Email holbam1@gmail.com

KERRYKEEL

KERRYKEEL AOIFE
BP National Terrier 2013
2 RCCs from puppy

CH KERRYKEEL EOGHAN
BP National Terrier 2012
BOB National Terrier 2013
5 CCs

Owned and loved by Wendy and Kevin Anderson
Bred, trimmed and handled by Kevin
01453 825737

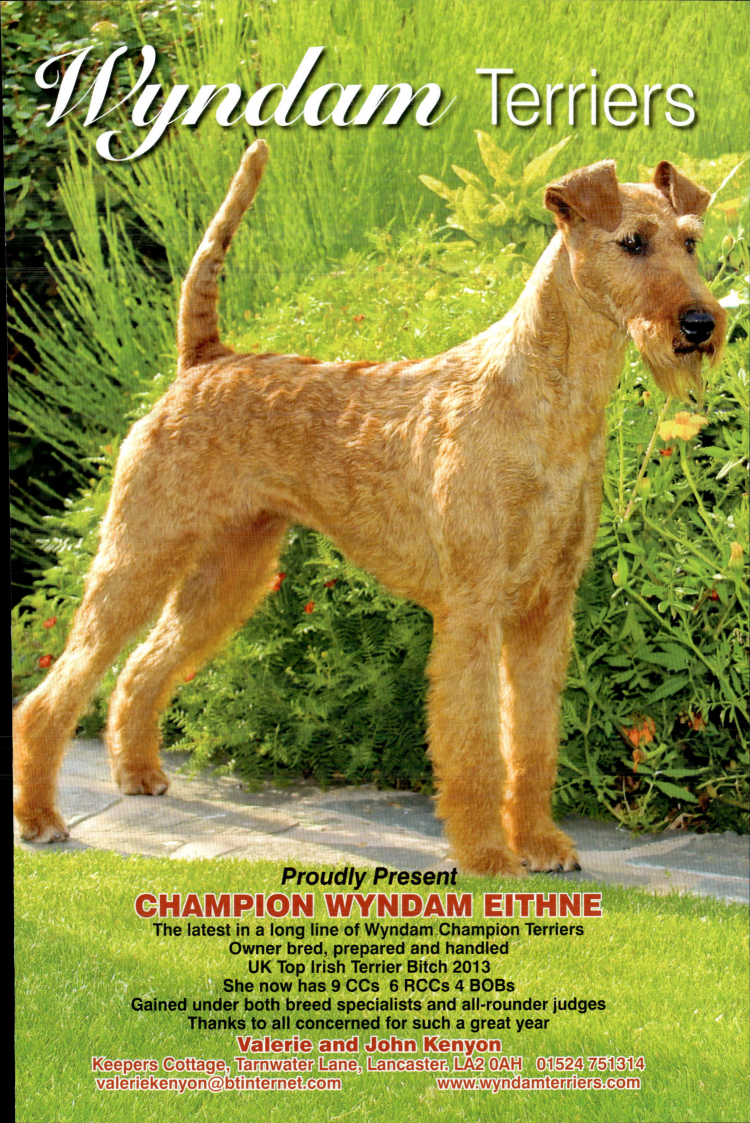

Dog World Annual 2014 — The Irish Terrier Association

The Irish Terrier Association
www.irishterrierassociation.co.uk

Patron Ferelith Somerfield   **President Lucy Jackson**

Aiming to promote and encourage the wellbeing of dogs in general and Irish Terriers in particular

Main events include:
Championsip Show June 22, 2014
at Markfield Canine Centre, Leicestershire
Our judge is breed specialist
John Stewart (Drumshaw) Scotland.

Open Show and Fun Day September 14, 2014
at Roade Village Hall, Northants.
A great day not to be missed!

New members always welcome. Membership includes our annual year book. This publication is a valuable source of information and also offers a wide variety of reading relating to the breed.

Puppy Line enquiry co-ordinator Angela Cook, 01519 311290. Along with the breed clubs we aim to ensure enquiries are dealt with efficiently to achieve a well bred and reared puppy at a sensible price. Rescue officers Ann Bradley (ITA), 01733 205386 and Jill Looker (SITS) 01264 850255
Working together with the breed clubs providing care and advice.
We run a home from home rehoming service

For membership details see our website
www.irishterrierassociation.co.uk or contact
secretary Ann Bradley 01733 205386

Labanjo French Bulldogs

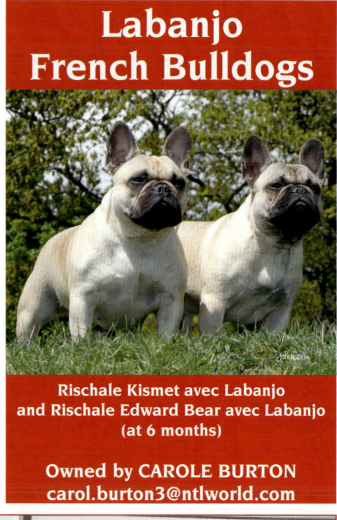

Rischale Kismet avec Labanjo
and Rischale Edward Bear avec Labanjo
(at 6 months)

Owned by CAROLE BURTON
carol.burton3@ntlworld.com

Sandbears Newfoundlands

Top Breeder 2013

Top Newfoundland 2012 and 2013

Ch Sandbears Stride N Style (aka Stride)

15 CCs, 17 RCCs
12 BOBs
2 x BIS
3 x Group 1
Multiple group placings

Sandbears Better Than Ever (aka Tyler)

Top Puppy 2013

Thanks to all the judges
Breeding for health, type and temperament
Puppies occasionally available

Bred, owned and very much loved by **SUZANNE BLAKE**
www.sandbears.com

STANEGATE

Says A Huge THANK YOU to…

…the One and Only Merlin

Sh Ch Am Ch Whistlestop's Elements of Magic CD RN
(co-owned by Colleen McDaniel)

Top IWS 2011, '12,'13
Multi All Breed BIS winner
Multi Group Winner including Crufts 2012
Sire of Champions including UK Top Bitch
Attwood's Sh Ch Doonbeg Magic Dust (BIS IWSA Ch Show 2013)

…and the Beautiful Tallulah

Sh Ch Foulby Fired Up

Top IWS 2007
BIS IWSA Open Show 2013 from Veteran
Dam of :
Sh Ch Stanegate Sparks Will Fly – Top IWS 2010, BIS Midland Counties 2010, Group 2 Crufts 2011, and dam of Ir Sh Ch Stanegate Firefly and Am Ch Stanegate Second Thoughts (CD JII)
Sh Ch Stanegate Sorceress at Foulby (4 CCs 2013)
BIS Am/Can Ch BISS Stanegate Supertramp WC
Am GCh Stanegate Slippery When Wet
Ir Sh Ch Stanegate Storm Warning at Sosteli
Am Ch Stanegate Just An Illusion (WD IWSCA 2013)
Stanegate Burnt Biscuit at Foulby (BCC Blackpool 2013)

We are so proud of all Stanegate Irish Water Spaniels all over the world and thank their owners for cherishing them like we do.
All dogs are hip and elbow scored and eye tested.
JUDITH CARRUTHERS   0044 1697 343480   knxhll@aol.com

Ch Friend De La Parure

Top UK stud for 5 years and top producing French Bulldog in the history of the breed

Producer of Champions Worldwide

www.KingFriend.co.uk

Darren & Natalie Friend   kingfriend1@msn.com   +44 1582 738976

Westaway
of Norway

Made up this year

Norw Sh Ch Westaway In For A Penny
by Swed Sh Ch Alanea Landcruiser
ex Westaway Billie Holiday

In the lead for Top English Springer in Norway 2013 at time of going to press

Norw Sh Ch Westaway Beggars Belief
by GB Sh Ch Ferndel Aeron Magregor
ex Norw Dan Sh Ch Westaway Reds Have More Fun

Litter sister to Beggars Belief
Fin Sh Ch Westaway Beyond Belief With Benton
was made up in Finland

Co-owned with Marjo Jaakkola and Marianne Forsell

Norw Sh Ch Troon The Blue Magic at Westaway
by GB Ch Gentom Peacemaker
ex Int Nordic Sh Ch Troon Shadow of A Doubt

Bred by Liv Vogt Johansen

Waiting in the wings — with two CCs each

Westaway Don't You Forget About Me

Westaway Better Believe It

Stig A Kjellevold & Frank W Bjerklund • Kleven Cottage • NO-3178 Våle • Norway
www.westaway.no • westaway@online.no • Telephone 00 47 33 06 20 90

Make a Good Dog Great

AMSCOT GORDON SETTERS
'TRULY DUAL PURPOSE'

AMSCOT REBEL WITH A CAUSE (AI) JW
AM Dual Ch Sun-Yak Spellbound Heaven Scent (ET) ex Amscot Unbeliva Belle
Hip Score 6/4 - DNA CLEAR for PRA and Cerebellar Degeneration
1 Reserve CC 4 Field Trial Awards

Dallas has become the first male Gordon Setter with show awards to win an OPEN FT Stake in almost 60 years!

Dallas' First Kids

Black Mystery Peggy Sue

Black Mystery Phantom of the Opera by Amscot (AI)
Pictured at 12 months. Has already won a Res CC from Junior.
Hip Score 4/4 PRA Clear

Dallas' Sister

American Ch Amscot Shadowmere Fame JH

Ch Amscot Dramatist
Hip Score 5/3 DNA Clear for PRA and Cerebellar Degeneration
3 FT Awards

Dual Champion Amscot Irresista Belle
1995-2010
Still the ONLY DUAL CH Setter in UK history

All three boys are available at stud to approved bitches
(AI available)

JEAN COLLINS-PITMAN

amscotgordons@aol.com
+44 (0) 7877 286702

Mariglen
Jane Dennis
janemariglen@yahoo.com   www.mariglen.com

top breeder, top puppy, top stud dog, top brood bitch 2013
all the dogs featured excluding Audi were CC winners in 2013

Mariglen Xanthe

BPIS at National Gundog
Gundog Puppy group winner Blackpool and City of Birmingham, top puppy in breed, RCC from puppy and CC at thirteen months Midland Counties.

Mariglen Crystal Gayle

Sh Ch Mariglen Pengtsson's Legacy ex
Sh Ch Mariglen Princess Royal at Gemsett
1 CC, 1 RCC

Crystal Gayle, is my first show English Setter and is a consistent winner at Championship Shows

I would like to thank all judges who have thought so highly of her and a big thank you to Jane for entrusting her to me.

Mel Sharples Tel 01242 87020

Mariglen Audi

"Vorsprung Durch Technik"
Featured winning Pro Plan/Dog World Puppy Dog Stakes, Gundog and Toy day, Darlington at seven and a half months old

Sh Ch Mariglen Ice Crystal JW ShCM

TOP ENGLISH SETTER PUPPY 2009
5 CCs, 5 RCCs
CC + RBIS English Setter Association 60th Anniversary Championship Show, CCs SKC + East of England
RCC's Manchester + Birmingham National
1st Limit Bitch CRUFTS 2013
Muliple Ch Show Stakes + Open Best In Show Winner.

Linda A Lawson   l.lawson@beverleyhigh.net

Sh Ch Mariglen Blue Flame for Christter

(Sh Ch Mariglen Pengtsson's Legacy ex Sh Ch Mariglen Flaming Colours)

Owned in partnership with and bred by Jane Dennis

26 CCs, 14 BOBs, 8 RCCs, G1, G3, 2 G4s
BIS - ESSS 2011, ESA 2012, MESS 2013

Dog World/Arden Grange
Top Winning English Setter for 2012

CHRIS SAYERS
01892 740170 chris.sayers@caravan-club.co.uk

Sh Ch Mariglen Snowdrift at Hayworth

5 CCs, 9 RCCs, RBIS Gundog Society of Wales Ch Sh 2011
Josh is a proven stud with championship show winning progeny

Tereza Watkins Tel 01452 859232

SMILE ANJO CORGIS

Norimoto&Yumi Murase

+0566-98-1912

clumberup@gmail.com

Handled by Hiroshi Tsuyuki

SUP.CH.Jacky of Yumi Anjo Jp

AM.G.CH.JP.CH.Ever Green of Yumi Anjo JP

INT.JP.CH.Towernaglen Luck Irish

GREEN

AM.Gr.CH.JP.CH.Ever Green of Yumi Anjo JP
Sired by AM.G.CH.Tallyrand Halo Chaser/ From SUP.CH.Sieva of YumiAnjo JP

OWNED, BRED and Loved by Norimoto&Yumi Murase
Shown by Sherri Hurst(USA) and Hiroshi Tsuyuki (Japan)
SMILE ANJO WELSH CORGI PEMBROKES

Davricard

proudly present the TOP WINNING BEAGLE 2013

CH DAVRICARD BUTTERCUP

Made up in 2012 at 14 months of age, 'Lucy' won 9 CCs, 9 BOBs, 4 Hound Group 2 placings and 1 Hound Group 4 placing during 2013.

Her younger kennelmate, Ch Davricard Martina gained a further 2 CCs and 2 BOBs whilst our new youngster, Davricard Moonlight has been BPIS at several breed club championship shows.

DAVID CRAIG
Tel (01325) 285485   Email: davbeagle@hotmail.com

LEXI
Tuwos Jackie 'O' at Dronski JW ShCM

1 C.C, RBIS, 1 RCC, 1 Green Star, 1 B.O.B,
6 Res Green Stars, Multi Group Winner
Irish P.O.T.Y Qualifier

ADELE
Dronski's Adele at Lintoya

Best Bitch & B.I.S N.E.C.D.C Open Show.
Multi Class Winner

Owned by Tony & Linda Fisher

ERIN
Dronski's Bang Tidy

Only 7 Months old
B.P.I.S All Breed Open Show
R.B.P.I.S IKC Int Ch Show

www.dronskidobermanns.co.uk

TRIMERE
The first ladies of Springers
Where the ladies come first

Trimere Teresa Green
Sh Ch Peasblossom Escape to Beresford
x Sh Ch Trimere Tantrums and Tiaras

CH Trimere Tigra
Sh Ch Mompesson Royal Destiny
x Sh Ch Trimere Tuscany

Trimere Tough Cookie
Bercanbar Angelo
x Trimere Twist of Fate

Ann & Sarah Corbett
esstrimere@me.com
www.trimere.co.uk

BRED BY EXPERTS. FED BY EXPERTS.

www.Breeders.Eukanuba.co.uk

Elegance with strength

Grafmax Louis Armstrong Sh CM BW'13

(Int/Lux Ch Arttuur Histabraq ex Cosajoro Nina Simone at Grafmax)

BOB Crufts 2013 and shortlisted in the group

1 CC
2 RCC
2 CACIB
BIS Dobe Club September 2013

'All male, he is muscular, classy and totally harmonious from all angles...
Punishing hindquarers complement front construction to produce super sound, easy action and impressive deportment that was a joy to watch'

Thanks to Stuart Mallard for this lovely critique.

vWD clear, PHPV clear, Troponin normal 2013, hips 5:4

Grafmax Ninette de Valois

GRAFMAX
Dobermanns

SATCHMO

GRAFMAX LOUIS ARMSTRONG SH CM BW'13

CRUFTS BOB

Photos by Will Harris | Design by Zara Boyle

CH MORALACH THE GAMBLING MAN JW

(aka Cookson)
DOB: 16/4/11

Dam - Ainsea First Lady at Moralach

Sire - Ch Mascotts Another Stripe

We are very proud of Cookson's achievements so far at only 2½ years old, and as of Nov 2013 Cookson is Top Irish Wolfhound.

9 CCs
8 RCCs
6 Best of Breeds
Group 2 and group 4 placings.
Pet Plan Junior Stakes Winner
East Anglia Super match Winner 2013
Junior Warrant Finalist 2013 (first Irish Wolfhound to reach the final)
Eukanuba Champion Stakes Finalist 2013
Numerous class and stake wins
Chosen to represent the breed in the Dog Encyclopaedia

We would like to thank all the judges who have thought so highly of Cookson so far, in his short show career.
Special thanks to Maggie Holder/Dave Howe (Mascotts) and Jean Malley (Ainsea). Maggie and Dave for letting us use their magnificent dog, Ch Mascotts Another Stripe, and Jean for allowing us to have Annie (from what transpired to be her last litter of Ainsea bred Irish Wolfhounds) and from which, apart from his wonderful "type", Cookson also inherited his superb temperament and tolerant nature.

Bred, owned and loved by
Carole Goodson
Tel: 01205 870730
Email: Moralach@aol.com

Larhjelm

In the lead for Top Breeder all breeds in Norway 2013 at time of going to press

BIS breeders Oslo 2013

Norw Swed Sh Ch Norw Tracking Ch Visvas av Larhjelm here winning the group in Rogaland

NJW-12 XI av Larhjelm - 7 CCs at eighteen months

Lars Hjelmtvedt • Odderudveien 20
NO-3089 Holmestrand • Norway
Tel: 00 47 416 60 485
www.larhjelm.net • larhjelm@online.no

Design: westaway.no

Eukanuba

Dog World Annual 2014 — Kent, Surrey & Sussex Labrador Retriever Club

Kent, Surrey & Sussex Labrador Retriever Club

Celebrating the successes of all its members during 2013

In 2014 we will be celebrating 40 years of the club's dedication to maintaining the uniqueness of the Labrador Retriever.

We support and run Field Trials, Working Tests, Shows, Obedience, GCDS, Canine Health/Breed Seminars & Discover Dogs throughout the year

www.ksslrc.co.uk

Secretary: Alison Scutcher 01255 871489
secretary@ksslrc.co.uk

Lyndham

Some of our dogs past, present and hopefully, *one for the future!*

Keith and Dale Elliott
email: keith-elliott@hotmail.com   www.lyndhamlabradors.co.uk

LEOSPRING LABRADORS — Assured Breeders
LEOSPRING GOLD GILI
(Ch Warringahs Gundaroo ex Leospring Rapid Reaction)

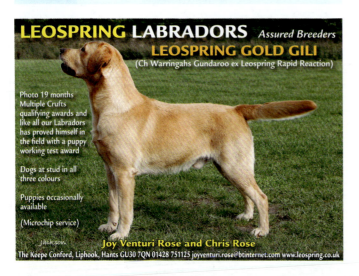

Photo 19 months
Multiple Crufts qualifying awards and like all our Labradors has proved himself in the field with a puppy working test award

Dogs at stud in all three colours

Puppies occasionally available

(Microchip service)

Joy Venturi Rose and Chris Rose
The Keepe Conford, Liphook, Hants GU30 7QN 01428 751125 joyventuri.rose@btinternet.com www.leospring.co.uk

Millerdan Labradors

Aspiring to the dual purpose ideal with our first homebred girl Lola, aka

Ch Millerdan Vision of Love JW ShCM

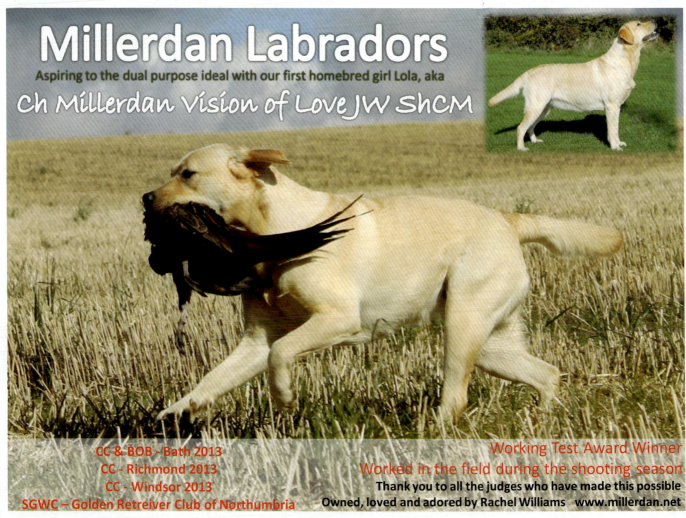

CC & BOB - Bath 2013
CC - Richmond 2013
CC - Windsor 2013
SGWC – Golden Retreiver Club of Northumbria

Working Test Award Winner
Worked in the field during the shooting season
Thank you to all the judges who have made this possible
Owned, loved and adored by Rachel Williams   www.millerdan.net

Loch Mōr

MAKING HISTORY! YEAR OF EXTRAORDINARY SUCCESS FOR "ROMEO & GIULIETTA"

BOB, BIG & Res. BIS at Crufts

Both winners of World and European Titles

Both new UK Champions

Top Labrador UK (1st and 2nd) 2013

won in the UK this year:

12 CCs

3 x Gundog Group

2 x Gundog Group 2

3 x Breed Club Best in Show

1 x Gundog Best in Show

1 x Reserve Best in Show

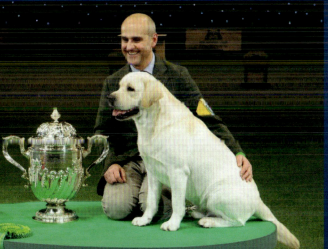

RESERVE BEST IN SHOW - CRUFTS

World Winner & Group Winner
WDS Budapest

European Winner & Group 2
EDS Geneva

Best in Show
National Gundog Ch Show

Best in Show
The Yellow LRC Ch Show

World Winners BOB & BOS
WDS Budapest

Gundog Winner
East of England Ch Show

Many thanks to all judges who appreciated them and all the people who with their support have made all this possible…Thank you!

Breeder & Owner by Franco Barberi

Mobile +39 335 8333146 - www.lochmor.it - lochmor@alice.it or see Facebook

TALLOWAH *Beaucerons*

Haureole des Feux de l'Ange (imp Fra)
DOB 05/01/2012 Hips 4/6
CSAU, 5 CACs

Introducing...
Miss Scarlet du Regard Mordant (imp Bel)
DOB 27/03/2013. Photo at 6 months

Jupiler du Regard Mordant (imp Bel)
DOB 24/09/2010
Hips 7/7, Elbows 0/0,
Eyes clear (9/2012)
Cot 4, CSAU, CANT, CACIB,
6 CACS, 2 RCACS,
Belgian Selection

Stop Press
Kortrijk 16/17 Nov '13.
Jupiler - RCAC (Sat) and
Scarlet Best puppy in breed
(Sat and Sun)

STEVE and JACKIE BARNES
+44 (0) 1452 831546
Tallowah@btinternet.com
www.freewebs.com/tallowah

Sw/Sp Ch Curioso De La Ribera Del Genil Del Valentisimo

PACO IS TOP SWD 2012 AND 2013!
CRUFTS BOB 2011, '12 AND '13!

- Crufts 2013 **group shortlist**
- **Group 3** at Windsor Ch Sh 2013
- **Group 4** at Windsor Ch Sh 2011
- **Group 4** at Richmond Ch Sh 2012
- **BVIS** at SWDC Open Show 2013
- **BVIB** at Darlington Ch Sh 2013
- **Contest of Champions** participant
- **Ch of Andalucia** '08, '09 and '10
- **BIS** Spanish Monografica '09
- **BIS** Swedish Monografica '11
- **BIS 3** Tvaaker National and Internationa Show '11 (both days)

IN PACO'S THREE YEARS IN THE UK HE HAS GAINED 22 BOB'S!

Valentisimo's Gordviday

'Shanti'

Lizar Del Valentisimo

'Lizar'

- BIS at the SWDC Show 201?

Valentisimo

We have had another truly unforgettable year and our thanks go to all the judges who have thought so highly of all the dogs we have exhibited and those we have bred. A huge thanks must also go to all our friends across the world who carry on supporting us in our mission to promote and preserve the rustic and untainted qualities of the true

Spanish Water Dog

We are also proud and lucky to have the help of our young handlers; James Newton, Lizzie Greenslade and Hanna Wiseman who all do a superb job and we are sure all have great futures ahead of them.

Valentisimo
Spanish Water Dogs

'Balou'

Valentisimo's Guerrero
- BPIB at Midland Counties '13
- 1 PG2

'Norte'

Valentisimo's Tuvida
- BIS at the SWDC Show 2013
- 1 BOB and group shortlist
- 2 BD's

'Tica'

Valentisimo's Pacopilik
- BOB at SKC

TOP GUNDOG & SWD PUPPY 2013! (at time of press)
Valentisimo's Castro

Castro has taken the show ring by storm, both in the UK and Europe! He has continued his winning ways throughout the year by racking up an astonishing:

- 2nd Male Puppy at the Spanish Monografica '13
- 12 UK BPIB's
- BPIB and puppy group shortlist at the WDS'13
- World Winner at the World Dog Show '13
- 1 PG3
- 2 PG4
- BPIS at the SWDC Open Show '13
- 1 BD (BOS)
- 4 RBD's

email: nigel@spanishwaterdog.net
Telephone: 01246 888081
www.spanishwaterdog.net

Nigel, Jenny and Ben Egginton
or follow us on Facebook:
www.facebook.com/spanishwaterdogs

Maibee

Ch Maibee Theo

Celebrated 2013 with a new
Breed Record Holder
49 CCs, 48 BOB

Best in Show
East of England Ch Show

Toy Group Winner
CRUFTS 2013

Group wins at Bath
and Paignton 2013
Blackpool and Driffield 2012
City of Birmingham 2011

Several other group places duing
2011 and 2012

Ch Maibee Make Believe

During 2013 'Hairy' won
CCs from breed specialists:
Bath - Virginia Barwell
SKC - Elaine Waddington
Darlington - Philip Lovel

Many thanks to my friends
who have continued to support
the Maibee kennel

Looking forward to meeting up
with you all at Crufts.

Both these boys are a tribute to my wonderful late wife Shealagh.
Maibee CKCS and KCS are loved, cared for and handled by
BILL MOFFAT, JOYCE ROBINS and TANYA IRELAND
01207 561249

BITCON & FERNDEL
The brother & sister

Sh Ch Bitcon Wizard of Oz ex Sh Ch Bitcon Merely Magic
Their wins at 15 months old:

Bitcon Potions and Spells
1 CC and 2 Res CCs
Owned by Karen Anderson

Ir Ch Bitcon Card Tricks for Cooley
Many group places
Owned by Sinead Taggart

Congratulations to Andrew and Christine MacDonald and Dual Ch Bitcon Gold Coast at Northey the first ever Dual Champion Vizsla, made up in both show ring and field.

Sh Ch Ferndel Aeron Magregor (centre) - 37 CCs 3 Group 1s, many group places, Top Welsh Springer 2012 and 13 Sh Ch Ferndel Voyage to Vynesbrook JW ShCM (left) owned by Mike Lewin
Sh Ch Ferndel Butterkist Cwsscwn JW (right) owned by Christine Morgan and Chris Schofield

Congratulations to the two New Champions made up during 2013

Moray Armstrong
01228 674318

ferndel@jthirlwell.fsnet.co.uk

John Thirlwell
0191 4887168

345

SILVANUS

Home of the Ginger Nuts where temperament is paramount!
Silvanus Quality Speaks Volumes

CRUFTS ROLL OF HONOUR

2002 BB & Best of Breed
Silvanus Queen Victoria Ruling Bardantop
Borostyanko Marci x Silvanus Absolutely Fab

2003 BB & Best of Breed
Silvanus Nell Gwynne to Tragus
Borostyanko Marci x Silvanus Absolutely Fab

2007 BP, BD & Best of Breed
Farnfield Cock Robin
Sh CH Silvanus Oh Oh Seven x Silvanus Fanny By Gaslight

BB & Best Opposite Sex
Tragus Ginger Rogers
Sh CH Silvanus Oh Oh Seven x Silvanus Nell Gwynne to Tragus

2008 BB & Best Of Breed
Cwsscwn Chintz
Silvanus Prince Albert x Silvanus Ezmi

2009 BB & Best of Breed
Cwsscwn Chintz
Silvanus Prince Albert x Silvanus Ezmi

BD & Best Opposite Sex
Sh CH Silvanus Oh Oh Seven
Blamtrinever Bombadier x Lilymere Delilah of Silvanus

2010 BD & Best Opposite Sex
Tragus Fred Astaire
Sh CH Silvanus Oh Oh Seven x Silvanus Nell Gwynne to Tragus

Silvanus Absolutely Fab (Patsy)
1996 Puppy Bitch States Winner at Three Counties CH Show
Top Brood Bitch 2004 & 2005, Runner Up 2007
Test of Work 2nd ... WC of GB and many more
Very many BOBs over the years

Silvanus Lady Hamilton
First HWV in New Zealand

Silvanus Moll Flanders
Dam of Cwsscwn Chintz

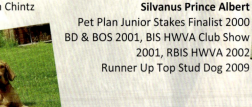

Throstlenest Siren by Silvanus
Crufts BPB 2008

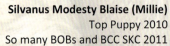

My Solitaire for Silvanus (Doris)
1 CC & BOB WKC and 1 RCC National Gundog 2013
Reserve Puppy Stakes Darlington 2013
8 BP in Breed, 2 BOB & RBPIS HWVA CH Show
Puppy Group Winner Open All-Breed
All whilst a puppy and now just 13 months old now

(James) First Male Champion
Top Sire 2007, 2008, 2009 and 2010
Sire of so many winners at shows including - **Australian CH**
Miz Monipenny of Silvanus

Lilymere Delilah of Silvanus
Born April 1995
Top Brood Bitch 1999, 2001, 2002 & 2003

Australian CH Silvanus Lord Nelson
First HWV Champion in Australia

Ir CH Silvanus Fanny By Gaslight
First Irish Champion
Top Brood Bitch 2009

Silvanus Prince Albert
Pet Plan Junior Stakes Finalist 2000
BD & BOS 2001, BIS HWVA Club Show 2001, RBIS HWVA 2002
Runner Up Top Stud Dog 2009

Silvanus Modesty Blaise (Millie)
Top Puppy 2010
So many BOBs and BCC SKC 2011

Alastair's
Silvanus Simply Does It (Sarah)
Just 8 months
Qualified for Crufts

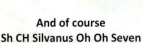

And of course
Sh CH Silvanus Oh Oh Seven

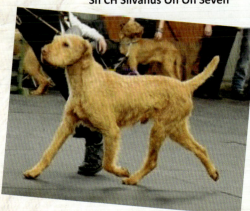

Donna, Millie (Modesty Blaise 1CC) & Alastair Moss

Designed by www.HaveADogDay.co.uk

Donna Holman T: 01257 453111 www.wirevizslas.com wirevizslas@aol.com

BLAMTRINEVER

Brig

Hungarian Wirehaired Vizslas

Oddley

Also: Basset Fauve de Bretagne

Tricia Turton
A Kennel Club Assured Breeder of Excellence

ricia@blamtrinever.com   www.blamtrinever.com

ANT & BRAD

Spellcast Shout About It (Black)
CH.Spellcast Secret and Lies JW (Cream)

Ant (Black)
CC & BOB – City of Birmingham 2012
4 RCC's & Joint Top Puppy 2012

Brad (Cream)
7 CC's 5 BOB 6 RCC's 3 BPIB
Owned by Lynda Hewett

DAISY

Spellcast Talking Secrets with Azkaban
BB & BOS – German Spitz Club of GB
BB & BOS – Darlington 2012
Multiple Class Winner
Owned by Gwynne Pooley

REGAN

CH.Spellcast Jivetalking*
(*Subject To KC Conformation)
CC & BOB – Blackpool 2013
CC & BOB – East of England 2013
CC & BOB – GSC of GB 2013
4 RCC's 3 BPIB
Owned by Jenny & Mark Smith

KEVIN

Spellcast Talk To Da Paw at Trebettyn
CC, BOB & BPIB – Manchester 2012
RBD & RBOB – GSC of GB
BD – SKC RBD – Leeds RBD – Paignton
RBIS – Swansea & DCS
Owned by Bethan Williams

spellcast
german spitz
bred by lynda hewett
top breeder '07 '09 '10 '12

dogs available at stud to approved bitches

Dachida's Chihuahuas

Breeders of 28 UK Champions and Multiple Champions Worldwide, including Ch Dachida's Master Angel, the Top Winning all-breed BIS and Group Winning Chihuahua to date

Ch Sundowner Play Misty For Me at Dachida's (Misty)

Ch Veejim Delta Force at Taradona
ex Sundowner Spice Girl

Breeder: Mrs J Day
Owned by Miss A Davies and Mrs J Day

By the tender age of 18 months
Misty has achieved:
Top Chihuahua 2013 and
currently #4 Top Toy 2013
Top Chihuahua Puppy 2013
Toy Group 1 and RBIS – SKC
Toy Group 1 and RBIS – Richmond
4 x Toy Group 2s and 1 x Toy Group 3
1 x Puppy Toy Group 1
9 CCs and 15 BOBs
BIS at the Ulster and British Chihuahua Club
Championship Shows 2013

Thanks to Tuija and Mattl Varpula (Owelan) who have been campaigning **Ch Dachida's Colour Me Blue (Mav)** (Master Angel daughter) in Finland for the last 6 months and have achieved the following fantastic wins: Champion titles in Finland and Denmark, DKV-13 and Super BIS at the Finnish Chihuahua Speciality 2013.

With thanks to all the judges concerned for the fantastic wins

**Dachida's
Carol, Bob and Aimee Davies
Tel: 0161 430 6030**

Amanda Carter (Afilador) and Roberta Hozempa (Amahte) present our boy

Amahte Runnin On Jamaican Time (imp Can) JW ShCM

Bolt

Bolt has continued his winning ways, winning Best in Show at Exonian Open Show, qualifying for the Top Dog of Devon 2013

Bolt won his first CC at Paignton Championship Show (under the single CC system).

Bolt is proud to present his son, out of Diecisiete Mandarina at Afilador ShCM

Afilador Thunderbolt

Torran

Pictured here at 4 months old, will be debuting soon.

Thank you to all the judges who have made this all possible, and to all who have sent messages of support

Thank you to Bolt's co-owner and breeder Roberta Hozempa for allowing Bolt to come and be part of my family

Please visit us at www.afilador.co.uk and follow us on Facebook

Afilador show team

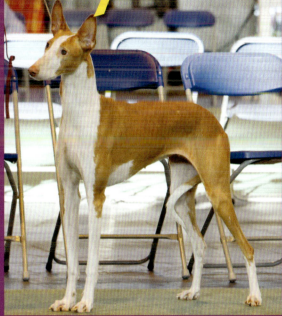

Diecisiete Mandarina at Afilador ShCM
Kalusha
Kalusha took some time out of the ring to have her boy Torran. She has returned to the ring with a bang, winning many Best Veteran awards, both at Open and Championship Shows.

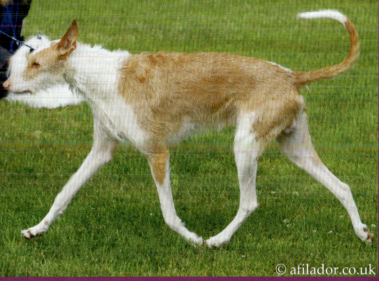

Afilador Moonlight Shadow ShCM
Bandit
Bandit has had another great year in the ring, and was handled by Caitlin Channon who won 2nd in Hound Junior Handling class at Richmond Semi-Finals with him.

Afilador A Hint Of Jasmine
Jazmin
Jasmine has also continued to have a great year in the ring, winning Best of Breed and Hound Group 1 at Exeter and County Show, handled by her Dad. Her mother, Afilador Spark to a Flame, aka Juno, has now retired from the ring.

Amahte's Bewitched
Tabitha
Tabitha made her début at Liskeard show, winning BPIB and Hound Puppy Group 4. I would like to thank Roberta Hozempa for allowing Tabitha to come and be part of our family.

Please visit us at www.afilador.co.uk and you can follow us on Facebook too.

Briarmoor Australian Cattle Dogs
A Mooving Experience Since 1989

American Grand Champion Briarmoor's Uncrowned King 'Chunk'
2011 National Specialty Winners Dog

30+ Conformation Champions, multiple obedience, agility and herding titleholders

Breeder of the First ACD import to finish a UK Championship plus win the ACD Society Great Britain Club Show!

Breeder of Most Champions (US) for 2012

PAM GIPSON
Chattanooga, Tennessee USA
www.facebook.com/Briarmoor 423-240-4840

Tidemill Pugs
Established 1978

CHAMPION TIDEMILL CHERRY COLA
Homebred
Top Pug 2011

CHAMPION YORLANDER RONALDO AT TIDEMILL JW
Bred by Mrs Kath Hindley
22 CCs
Top Pug 2009. Top Stud Dog 2011, 2012 and 2013

CLARIPUGS CELTIC STAR OVER TIDEMILL
Bred by Lundi Blamey
CC & Best of Breed at Paignton 2013, RCC at Leeds 2013

CHAMPION YORLANDERS MAX AT TIDEMILL JW
Bred by Mrs Kath Hindley
Top CC winner in Pugs 2012

DYLVILLE LILYBETH AT TIDEMILL JW - IMP BELGIUM
Bred by Ingrid & Jan Mylemans
CC at City of Birmingham, CC at Driffield, RCC at Blackpool 2013

CLARIPUGS SECRET AGENT AT TIDEMILL JW
Bred by Lundi Blamey
Reserve Best Puppy In Show UK Toydog Championship Show 2013
RCC at Driffield 2013. Top Puppy in the breed 2013

TERRY PURSE and **NIGEL MARSH**
Tel 023 8086 4963   Email nigel@tidemillpugs.co.uk   www.tidemillpugs.co.uk

Fralex

Champion Fralex Dark Mystique

7 CCs, 3 BOBs, Champion Stakes Day Winner

Alan V Walker

Toy Poodles and Bedlington Teriers

Champion Fralex Culibre Pharos

5 CCs, BOBs, Group 2, Junior Stakes ~ Bath Championship Show

Mr A and Mrs J Hurley B Phil MA
Fralex, Middleton Road, Winterslow Wilts SP5 1QL
Tel: 0044 (0)1980 862600
Email: jacqui@fralex.co.uk

Alan V Walker

Ch Shanitau's Mane Attraction JW
'Baxter'

Many thanks to judges - Peter Jolley, Kenneth Roberts and Albert Easdon

Dearly loved, bred and owned by - Dorothy McIntyre, 90 Babbacombe Road, Styvechale, Coventry CV3 5PA

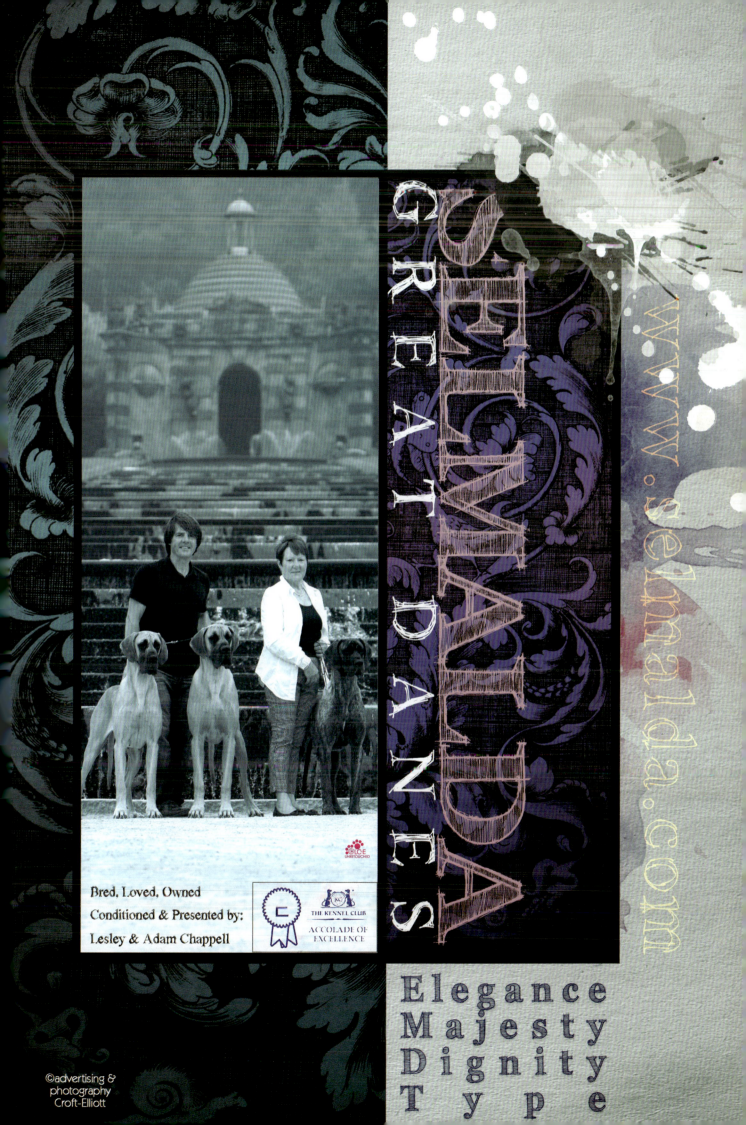

ANDLARE

Triarder Dreamseen at Andlare

Andlares Late Fall

Andlare Shooting Star

Introducing our new show girl

Andlare Ruby Rainbow

Andrew and Clare Bannister.
Tel 01246 860393
07970 545025
www.andlare.co.uk

TRIARDER

Always 'trying harder' to produce the best

Triarder Likeadream

Multi Ch Jabberwocky's Cloudless ex Triarder Abitdreamy

Florence is Triarder's 5th generation of happy healthy show winning Bulldogs

Also Introducing our new star

Wildax Secret Wish of Triarder

We are looking forward to campaigning 'Mrtyle' in 2014

We are proud to say all our exported dogs that have been shown have gained their champion titles – we only export dogs we would be happy to show ourselves!

Bred, handled and cherished by Amanda Bentley
Tel 07462951532
www.triarderbulldogs.com
triarder@gmail.com

Honeymist Bedlingtons

Where style meets the Standard
Breeding for type, soundness and quality

Honeymist Posh Dreamz
Top Puppy in Breed* with 5 Best Puppy and a RCC at shows with CCs.
Pictured (with Lorraine) winning BPIS at NBTC Championship Show.

Ch Honeymist Crazy Rhythm
BCC and BOB Midland Counties

Honeymist Sunny Delight (Sunny)
DCC and BOB Darlington

In 2013 we said a very sad goodbye to a lovely old friend, Ch Honeymist Little Sunflower

For information and advice on grooming, the breed Standard, copper toxicosis, health and care of Bedlingtons, breed history, and much more, visit my website **www.honeymist.com**

Mrs SHIRLEY DAVIES, MPhil, BSc, Dip Ed, MIBiol, CBiol, Struthers Kennels, London Road, Kilmarnock KA3 6ND
Tel 01563 533671   email sd@honeymist.com

*at time of going to press

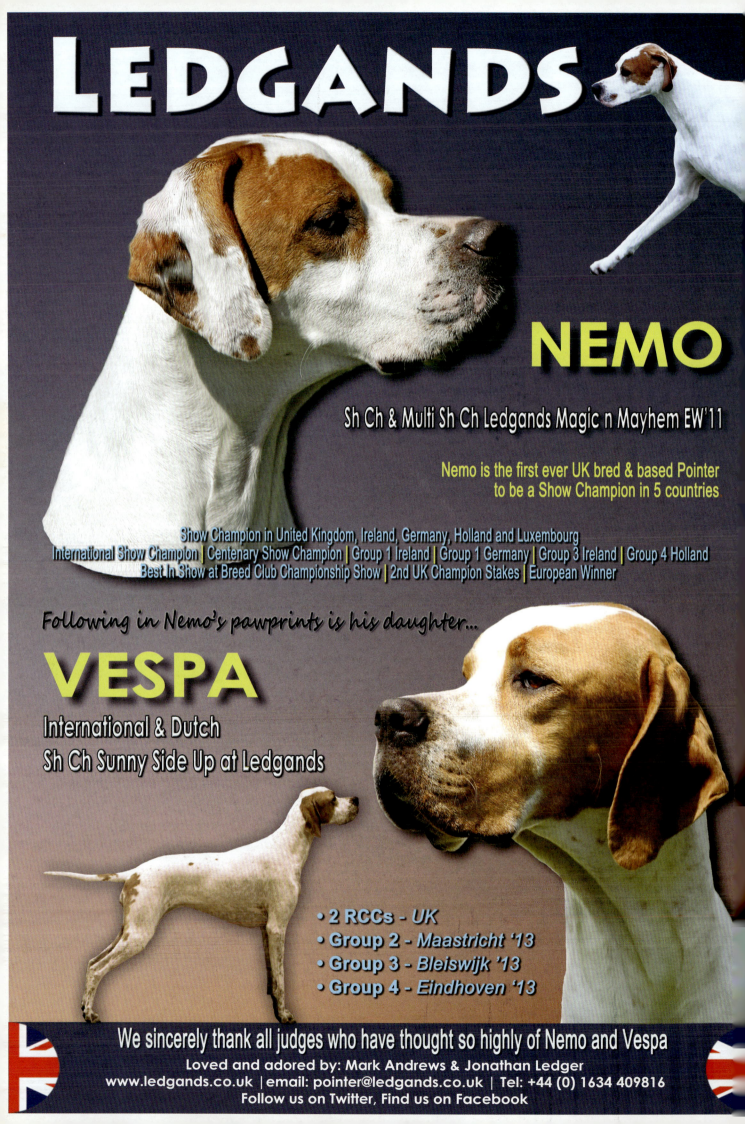

Kazval and Feldkirk

Another 'Fabulous Year' 2013 and very much appreciated.
We would like to say a big thank you to all those judges who have
thought so highly of 'Fashion', 'Blake', 'Asia' and 'Kanga'

SH CH FELDKIRK FASHION
Top CC winning Flatcoat
2011, 2012 and 2013
BIS United Retriever 2013
28 CCs, 20 BOB, 6 RCCs, 4 x Group 2
and 2 x Group 4
RBIS Gundog Society of Wales

SH CH BALLYRIVER BLAKE
BIS United Retriever 2012
13 CCs, 5 BOB, 5 RCCs
Group 2
Group 3

BITCON POTIONS AND SPELLS (Hungarian Vizsla)
At 15 months, several Best Puppies, Puppy Group 3 Windsor, consistent wins in Junior and
1 CC, 2 RCCs to date and winner of Junior Stakes at Midland Counties

'Kanga' (Rhodesian Ridgeback) shown lightly but also
has BP wins and BPIS at a Club Open Show

Dogs are health checked, studs to approved bitches, puppies occasionally available, friends welcome
and hopefully new youngsters will be entering the ring in 2014

FRANK H WHYTE
Mob 07775 701057
Frank.Whyte@pinneys-scotland.co.uk

TOM H JOHNSTON
Tel (0044) 01461 800372
tomstjohn17@yahoo.com

Haley and Sarah
Dog Handlers

We are both ex-Junior handlers who have a passion for dog showing which we have continued on long past our junior years. We attend almost all championship shows, usually on a number of days, to show not only our own dogs but other people's too.

We compete not only in the breed ring but also in the handling ring. Over the last twelve months we have both won a handling class with a different breed from each of the seven groups and in total have won 24 classes. Along with competing in handling ourselves we also have the pleasure of training junior handlers. We regularly train three girls and we couldn't be more proud of them. Although none of them have been handling for much longer than 12 months they have won a total of 32 handling classes, have all qualified for Crufts and Richmond JHA semi-finals where in September 2013, Tamsin Blyton took 2nd in Working 6-11 years with her Boxer and Paige Spencer took 4th in Pastoral 6-11 years with a Shetland Sheepdog. Megan Rayner qualified for Crufts 2013 with her Akita, as well as for 2014, meaning she qualified within six months of beginning showing.

Pictured above: *Casper*
Ch Allmark Spirit Of St Louis ShCM
(Australian Shepherd)
2 x Group 4, BIS NASA Ch Show 2013,
3 BOB, 6 CCs, 5 RCCs and YKC stakes
2014 qualified
Sarah handled Casper to
BIS NASA Ch Show, 2 BOBs,
2 CCs all within a month.
Owned by Mr P and Mrs J Longhurst,
Mr P Routledge and Miss S Gibbons
New Champion

Allmark Electric Avenue
Sarah also began handling another
Australian Shepherd, Marley who was
born April 2013. At 6 months old he
won BPIS at NASA Ch Show.
Owned by Miss T and Mr G Weaver

Pictured below: *Bess*
Ch Nikolaev Amarande at Abbiville
(Bouvier des Flandres)
3 CCs, 2 RCCs, 2 BOB,
working group shortlist
Owned by Mrs A and Miss H Jones
Jasper
Abbiville Avitus (Bouvier des Flandres)
3 RCCs, YKC Working Stakes Final
Winner 2012, RBIS, BVIS, Best Working
Veteran
Owned by Miss H Jones

Pictured above: Tunya and Tannu (Hungarian Vizslas) two of the dogs we have qualified for Crufts.
Crufts Qualified: ASDs Bud (**Bordertime Special Choice**), SCWT Maggie (**Emalot Little Miss Magic**), Lillee (**Orliscwt Lillee The Pink**), Ennis (**Killeshin Reagan**), Dogue de Bordeaux Chilli (**Sweet Chilli Pepper**), Hungarian Vizslas Tannu (**Sirius Bell Resze**) and Tunya (**Siriusbell Hengill**)

Rosie
Nikolaev Osha (Bouvier des Flandres)
Haley has handled her young pup to BPIB and WPG2 at
Pollard Open Show and RBPIS, BMPIS at BDF Ch Show
at her first two shows.

Haley handled *Donny*, **Alpencrest Donatus**
(Great Swiss Mountain Dog) once and they took
Best Import Reg at Blackpool 2013.

Sarah handled *Millie*
Ch Silkcroft Colour Of Magic ShCM (SCWT), for the
first time and they took BCC at the National 2013.

Sarah has also handled *Keyser*
Ch Elkis Aquila of Silkcroft JW ShCM (SCWT) to RBD at
Boston along with BIS at Retford Open Show 2013.

Pictured above: *Derfel*
UK/Ir/Int Ch Hobel Joe O' Brien
(Soft-coated Wheaten Terrier)
3 CCs, BOB, 4 RCCs, BVIB,
Haley handled him to
Terrier Veteran Group 2 at Darlington
Owned by Mrs D Evans-Barry
New Champion

Pictured Below: *Zube*
Rohantia Nikolai at Fernwood
(Russian Black Terrier)
8 BOB, 8 BDs, 8 RBDs, BNSC
working, working group shortlist,
multiple open show group wins.
Current Top Russian Black Terrier 2013
(at time of press), joint top working
import register/rare breed pup 2012
Owned by Mr L M Smith
Riley
Silkcroft No More Games
(Soft-coated Wheaten Terrier)
4 BPIBs, Current Top SCWT Puppy
2013 (at time of going to press),
YKC stakes 2014 qualified,
RBPIS, 2 Terrier Group 1, 2 Puppy
Group 1s all under 12 months old
Owned by Mr and Mrs C Satherley and
Miss S Gibbons

Haley
07930485587
haleymariejones@hotmail.co.uk

Contact us
www.haleysarahdoghandlers.webeden.co.uk

Sarah
07517 656006
sarahgibbons@hotmail.co.uk

JANMARK Bedlington Terriers
& Manchester Terrier

Many thanks to all the judges who have thought so highly of our current dogs at championship and open show level through 2013, continually rewarding all our dogs with top honours & making it a memorable year.

Ch Janmark Blue Encounter JW ShCM. 14 CCs, 16 RCCs, 8 BOB and Group 4
(right)
CH Janmark Misty Horizons JW ShCM. 7 CCs, 6 RCCs, 1 BOB
CH Janmark Jeremiah JW Shcm (co-owned with Paul Richardson),
3 CCs, 1 RCC, 1 BOB
Janmark Justintime JW ShCM 6 RCCs

We look forward to introducing the next generation and having some fun with them in 2014…
We have already introduced 'Wilma' to the team & she was off to a wonderful start in late 2013. In the space of a couple of weeks she was awarded Reserve Best Puppy in Show (Hillsborough Open Show), Best Puppy in Breed and Reserve CC (Midland Counties), Best Puppy in Show (Chester le Street Open Show) and Reserve Best Puppy in Show at The Yorkshire Sporting Terrier Show, all at just 6 months.

Digelsa Diva avec Janmark
(bred by Mick, Gill and Stacey Oxley)

Mark and Jan Walshaw
Tel: 01287 652860
www.janmark.co.uk

Carrustead My Cup Of Tea JW
(Imp Nor)

Bred by Nina Skjelbred
Owned and loved by **Netty and James Morrissey**

Bregantia and Rarjo Portuguese Water Dogs

Breeders and/or owners of:
Top Dog 2008, 09,11,13   Top Brood 2011,12,13   Top Working Brood 2012
Top Stud 2011,12,13   Top Breeders 2009,11,12,13
Owners and Breeders of the CC record holder Ch Rarjo She's The One

Ch Rarjo For Your Eyes Only (Jimmy)

Ch Bregantia The X-Factor at Winterkloud ex Bregantia Funky Diva

9 CCs, 8 RCCs, 1 Group 3, 3 x shortlisted, Dog CC record holder, Top Dog 2013

Aviators Epitome Of A Bygone Era at Rarjo (Imp USA) (Webster)

(Keel Tonel ROM (Toby*) all-time top producing PWD (2,776 down line champions) ex MBIS, MBISS, Gr Ch Aviators Luck Be A Lady (Ladybug) the all-time top winning PWD bitch in the US). Webster's father Toby is a direct link back to the original PWD lines of Do Al Gharb and Algaborium. Thank you to Websters breeders Mike and Cathy Dugan and Maryanne Murray for sending this very special boy to the UK

Winterkloud Coco Chanel at Bregantia (Coco)

Ch Rarjo Revolution at Winterkloud ex Ch Digadogs O'Cornelia (Imp Swe)

Thank you to Sarah McGill for allowing us to have Coco. She is under the skillful direction of my son Byron Williams who has successfully trained her and is currently campaigning her here and abroad.

RACHAEL REDDIN, BYRON WILLIAMS and the late RUTH BUSSELL
Tel 01945 440431   Email rachael-reddin@supanet.com

Teckelgarth Otterhounds

Ch Teckelgarth Horus

Top Otterhound 2012 and 2013, 11 CCs all with BOB, 11 RCCs and Group 3. Jointly owned with Mrs Jan Court

Teckelgarth Faith

1 CC
Owned by
Mr and Mrs T Scott

Teckelgarth Jollity

1 CC and 2 RCCs.
Jointly owned with Mrs C Scott

Ch Teckelgarth Calista

6 CCs
2 CCs this year
2 RCCs

Ch Teckelgarth Cerys

3 CCs with 2 BOB, 1 CC and BOB this year. Jointly owned with Mrs I Knight and Mr W March

T Fabius, T Iolanthe, T Julius, T Hyacinth and Ch T Quintus have also won RCCs for us this year.

I am so grateful to all the Teckelgarth owners for all their hard work and effort over the last 12 months, especially those who have given up their holidays to help in the rearing of two very promising litters.

Thank you Lynn for the use of T Eros, his children will do you both proud

For more information about this wonderful, but vulnerable breed please contact MARIA LEREGO via www.teckelgarth.org

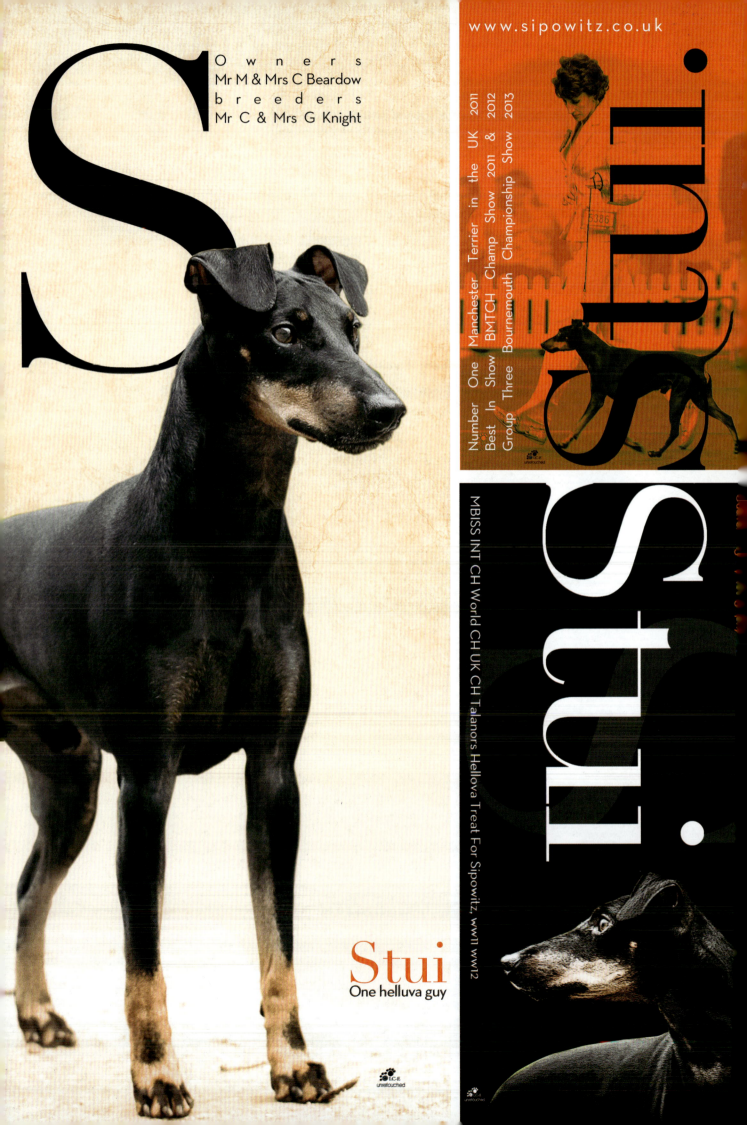

Snugglepug
BLACK AND FAWN PUGS

INTRODUCING OUR TWO IMPORTS

CH LOVEKLIPPENS DINGAAN BIMO SON AT SNUGGLEPUG JW ShCM (IMP NORWAY)
Milton
Tangetoppen Spitfire ex Tangetoppen Khula
Top Puppy 2012, Youngest Pug to gain JW
3 CCs, 2 RCCs, Group 2 Leeds
Thank you to Sonja and Trond Torres and Elisabeth Olsen for my very special boy

NEMO BLACK MY LITTLE GIANT AT SNUGGLEPUG (IMP HUNGARY)
Nemo
Yankee von Baden-Wurttemberg ex Elisa Sun-Lee My Little Giant
Hungarian Junior Champion
Nemo has just arrived in the UK
Thank you to Aniko Nagy for entrusting us with this lovely boy

SNUGGLEPUG JUST LOOK AT ME
Malani 1 CC

SNUGGLEPUG LOOKING FINE
Cricket

BOTH BY SNUGGLEPUG HOW'S THAT

Thank you to all the judges who have thought so highly of all our Snugglepugs and to all our owners who do use proud in the ring

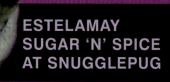

ESTELAMAY SUGAR 'N' SPICE AT SNUGGLEPUG

Proudly bred and owned by Elaine Arnold
01428 708014   07710 169937
www.snugglepug.co.uk   snugglepug@hotmail.com

Stormchaser
Generation after generation of Top Winning Leonbergers

Top Breeders   Top Dog   Top Brood Bitch   Top Import

All present day Leos come down from Khan and Storm, bred from International Champions and Top Winning European lines, proving that quality breeds quality! Every generation has produced CC winners. With their strong working instinct, many of our Leos are involved with draught work, water rescue and PAT.

CH STORMCHASER ANDALUCIA JW
The first and only female to win Working G1 at a Championship Show

'Tomba' CH STORMCHASER TA PINU JW ShCM
Supreme BIS, 6 BPIS, 3 BDIS at LCGB shows

CH STORMCHASER ANOUSHKA JW
Female CC record holder

and with her daughter **CH STORMCHASER FALLON JW**
BIS and RBIS at the LCGB Ch Show

The first breeders to 'do the double' at Crufts (twice). This mother and daughter are the two youngest UK champions. Our Leos have won 12 x BIS and Supreme BIS awards : 12 x BPIS awards and many Res BIS.

CH STORMCHASER SORAYA OF TANYVSKA

Sue and Lyn with puppies

Stormchaser have bred more winners of CC and RCC, than any other UK breeder (over 90). Between us we have 40 years of experience in breeding for health, temperament, longevity, quality and type. KC Assured Breeders, proud to have been awarded the prestigious KC Accolade of Excellence in 2013.

Lynette Hodge : 07966 299112 : stormchaserleos@yahoo.co.uk   Sue Brailsford : 0115 926 6124 : samfio@hotmail.com

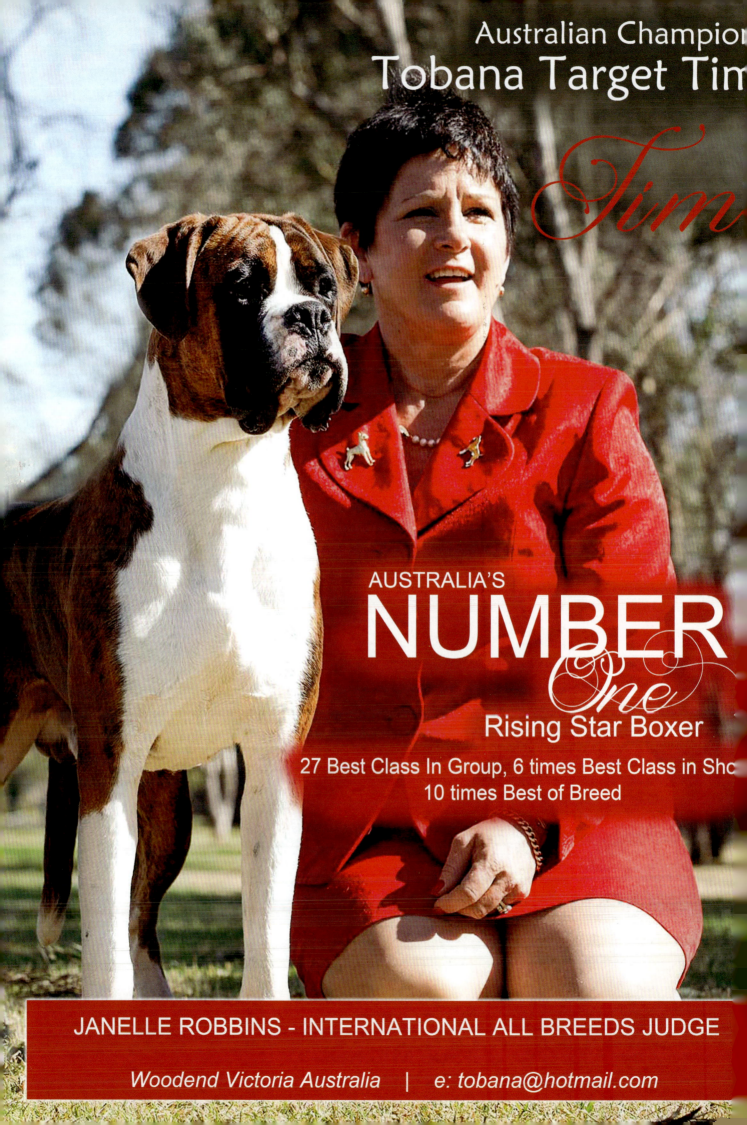

WYNELE BOSTON TERRIERS
Halfway Top Breeder 2013

CHAMPION ANDRIDZ WICKED WYNELE

6 CCs and BOBs
4 RCCs

and his daughter

CHAMPION WYNELE CLASSIC TOUCH

At just 14 months this young lady has won 3 CCs, all with BOB, and a Group 3 BUBA – AV Puppy Stakes, Best Bitch Puppy Blackpool – 4th in Junior stakes

Bob Naulls
01775 750089   wynele_boston@hotmail.co.uk

RUDDYDUCK
Nova Scotia Duck Tolling Retrievers and Finnish Lapphunds

Celebrate their success in the first year of KC Rally.

Blairswolf Tulikki of Ruddyduck WW'12 RL1-A.Ex
3rd in Level1A - Blackpool Jul '13
3rd in Level 1A - Doncaster Aug '13
3rd in Level 1A - Runcorn Aug '13
Eeva also has 2 x Level 1B Qualifiers

Camusmor Knockando at Ruddyduck Beg Ex RL1
Rupert gained his RL1 at his first 3 Trials
Winner Special Level 3 - Blackpool Jul '13
Winner Level 1B - Doncaster Aug '13
2 further Level 1B & 1 Level 2A Qualifier

Eeva and Rupert are loved, trained and handled by Rachel Bradley
Tel: 01527 591519   Email: ruddyduck@duck-toller.co.uk

Camusmor
After a successful year, we are looking forward to the future

Camusmor@btinternet.com
Proudly loved and owned by: Margaret Hussey, Carol and Ailsa Macleod

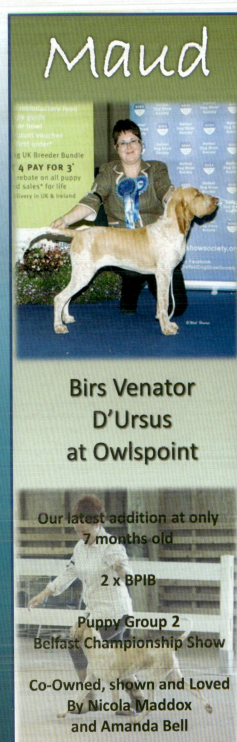

MISWAKI Show Dogs from Spain

EWC SIEGER'S MATCH POINT

Junior World Winner '12

Junior European Winner '12

European Winner '13

Multi Champion

International Champion

Multi BIS Winner

#1 Top Dog all-breeds in Spain

American Champion

Junior European Winner '13

SEASYDE HEAVEN SCENT

The MISWAKI show dogs are owned and handled by
ALBERTO ABAJO
email: alberto@miswaki.es

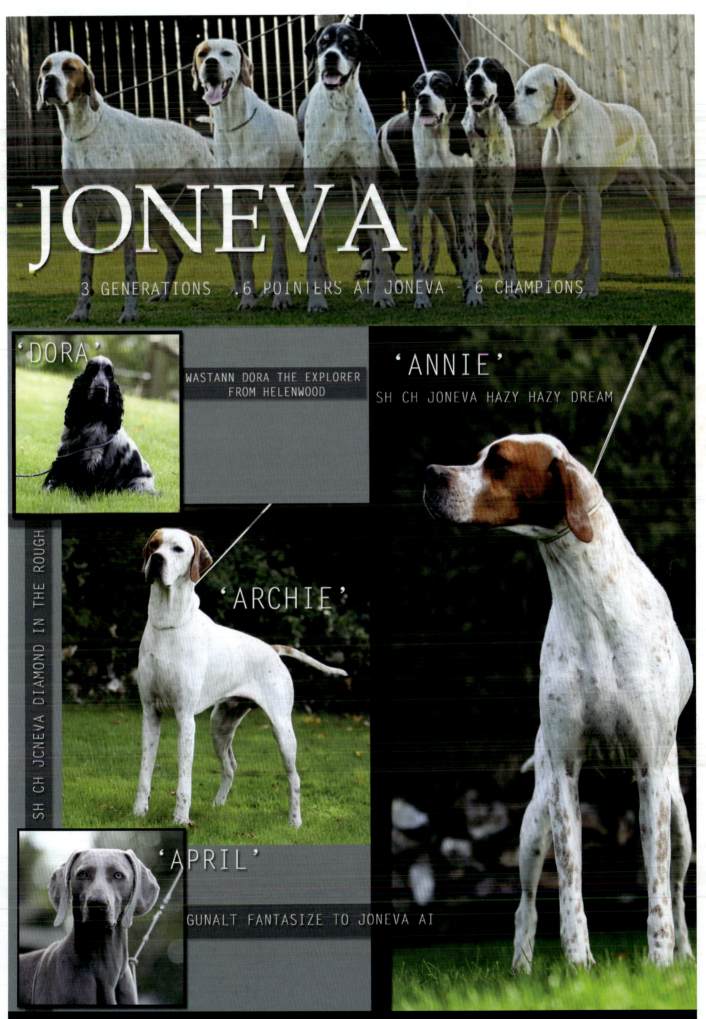

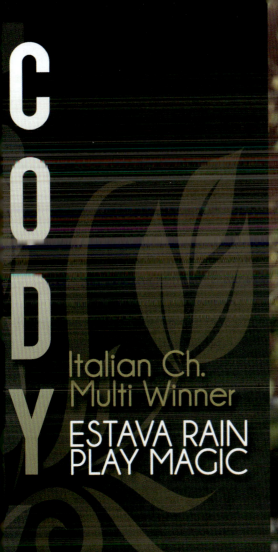

TRAGUS H.W.V
TOP BREEDERS 2012 and 2013

SH CH TRAGUS JAKOBI
3 CCs 4 RCCs

TRAGUS HONEY BUZZARD JW
1 CC Top Puppy 2012
First JW Winner for the Breed

RAGNOLDS FANTASTIC MR FOX (Foxy)
2 Reserve CCs

12 Shows, 12 wins:
1 BOB, 4 Best Dogs, 8 Best Puppys
HWV Open Show RBIS Best Puppy in Show
National Gundog Championship Show First Wire to win an overall heat in the ProPlan/ Dog World Puppy Stakes

Breeders of Top Wire for 2013 Sh Ch Tragus Zuri – sister to Jakobi
Tragus Ginger Rogers – Top Brood Bitch 2013

PETER and LINDA and GARY UPTON
Tel Luton 01582 581806

Awards at time of going to press

STARWELL CATALAN SHEEPDOGS AND BRIARDS

We have had an amazing year up to now since Catalan Sheepdogs were taken off the AV Imported Register on April 1, 2013 and our fabulous team has taken the show ring by storm. We would like to thank all the judges who have thought so highly of all the dogs we've exhibited this year.

Top Overall Catalan 2013
Ir Ch Mei D'Espinavesa at Starwell (Imp Esp)

has collected an astonishing:

Best Import Register Pastoral Crufts 2013, BIS/BVIS at the first CSCoGB Open Show 2013, 7 BOB, 2 AVNSC BB (1 Best AVNSC) and 1 Best AVNSC Veteran. Not only is Mei a show winner but so are her daughters. Handled by Toni Westcott-Smith

Kerry Rushby 2013

Irish Ch Starwell Mistletoe at Tisalmyn
Owned by Debbie Theaker

Irish and International Ch Starwell Prinesi at Bernemcourt
Ir Junior Champion, An Ch 11, 12. CJW 12. CW 12, 13
Owned by Mr and Mrs Embleton

Starwell Ilex at Kiandra
BOB Winner – Andy Bland

Also **Starwell Aphrodite** Crufts Qualified and **Starwell Dream Girl** Dr F Humphries Crufts Qualified

Top Catalan Puppy 2013
Kawanna Zena at Starwell

has racked up an amazing:
2 Best Baby Puppy in Breed in Ireland, 1 Reserve Best Baby Puppy in Show, 1 PG1 (Open Show), 1 PG2 (Open Show), 10 BPIBs (1 Rare Breeds BP, 6 Breed Class BPs and 3 AVNSC BPs), 4 RBB, two 2nd places in Pup of the Year Stakes and one 3rd place in Pup of the Year Stakes

Top Male Catalan 2013 – **Ir Ch Atengos Made in Heaven at Starwell (Imp Swe)** since his return from being campaigned in Ireland has collected: 4 BDs (1 BOB) and 1 RBD
Charlie is the sire of **Starwell Alfie** Crufts Qualified (J Hampson) Crufts Qualified and **Starwell Scarlet Lady at Sevarna** (S Peters) Crufts Qualified

We also had the pleasure of handling **IR CH LA PETIT RANA'S AIKOS XENIA AT KAWANNA (IMP SWE)** CW12 (Owned by my parent) many **BOBs and Crufts qualified**

Thank you mum who travels to all the shows with me

Owned and loved by **Angie and Trevor Fieldsend**
01673 818624 angie@brandycarr.co.uk

Our homebred Briard **Starwell Athena** has had a great year and has won: 2 BB (2 BOS), 2 RBPIS at Briard Club Shows, multiple puppy/junior class wins and 1 RBB from AVNSC.

MARINIKS

Celebrates 40 years of working, playing with, breeding, showing and grooming Rottweilers, Miniature Schnauzers and Shih Tzus, winning many awards and Stud Book numbers.

MARINIK are now celebrating ten years in Bichons Frisés and Twinkle in her first litter produced my first CC winner and there followed many CC and RCC winners, including two champions.

I breed only one or two litters a year and always plan and hope they are better than the last. Puppies due out in 2014 and the best of luck to all Marinik owners. Don't forget you always take the best dog home.

SUE DAVIDSON, owner, breeder, Advanced Master Groomer, twice Groomer of the Year, international gold medallist.
52 Castle Road, Rowlands Castle, Hants PO9 6AS
Tel: 02392 410066
Email: Marinikbichon@hotmail.co.uk

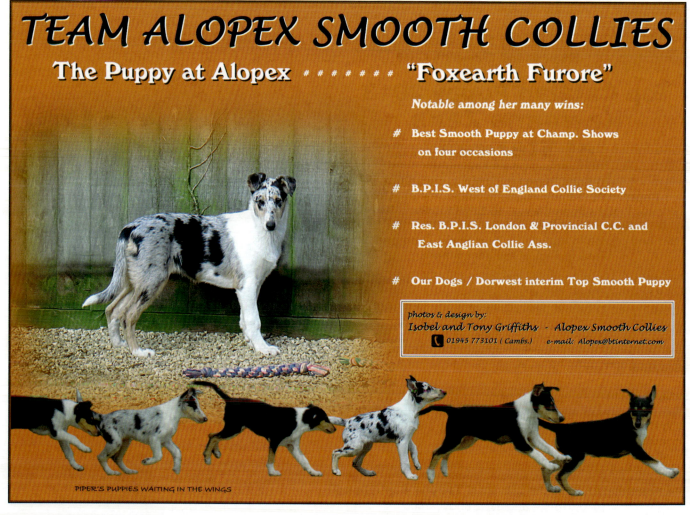

TEAM ALOPEX SMOOTH COLLIES

The Puppy at Alopex ****** "Foxearth Furore"

Notable among her many wins:

Best Smooth Puppy at Champ. Shows on four occasions

B.P.I.S. West of England Collie Society

Res. B.P.I.S. London & Provincial C.C. and East Anglian Collie Ass.

Our Dogs / Dorwest interim Top Smooth Puppy

photos & design by:
Isobel and Tony Griffiths - Alopex Smooth Collies
01945 773101 (Cambs.)   e-mail: Alopex@btinternet.com

PIPER'S PUPPIES WAITING IN THE WINGS

GLEBEHEATH

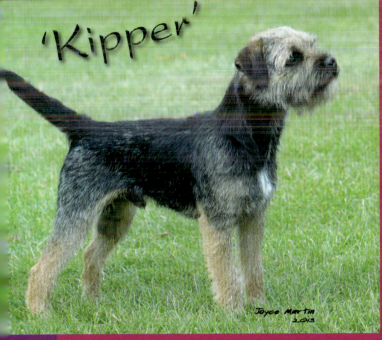

Top Junior '13
Ch Glebeheath Jump The Gun JW
'Kipper'

Ch Achnagairn Code Name Glebeheath JW ShCM
'Codie'
Dam of both Kipper and Rodney, a truly wonderful dam

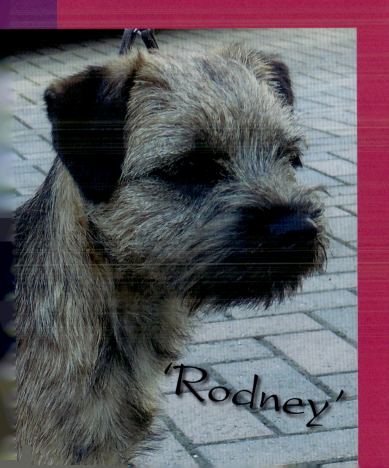

Glebeheath Name That Tune
'Rodney'
Will be campaigned in 2014

Celebrating my 10th UK champion when 'Kipper' gained his title at 18 months old

6 Champion Borders in consecutive years

Mrs Julie Guvercin
Tel: 01793 763987
Mobile: 07825 432378
Email: guvercin@btinternet.com

Glynderys Gwennol

DOB 16.09.11

Drumdaroch The Xpat to Liric (IMP AUS) ex Graylacier Amber Destiny at Glynderys

Another amazing year for 'Iola'

RCC and RBIS Gordon Setter Association Championship show and highly placed throughout 2013

Bred and loved by

Dr Marian Thomas

email glynderys@yahoo.co.uk
Tel 01763 272968

photo Walker

Pinicio's First Generation

Pinicio
MINIATURE PINSCHERS
www.pinicio.co.uk

Beverly
PINICIO JELLY TOT
Owned by Dom Santoriello

Lightly shown during 2013 taking RBB at Driffield 2013, BPIB at Manchester Ch Show 2013 BB, BOS, BP and Toy Puppy Group 1 at Boston Ch Show 2013

Kevin
Owned by Suzanne & Dom Santoriello & Jo Skelton
PINICIO JELLY BEANIE JW

Dog CC, BOB & Group Shortlisted at City of Birmingham Ch Show 2013 at just 17 months old, YKC Stakes winner at East of England Ch Show 2013 & RBIS at Newmarket & DCS 2013

Loved, bred and handled by Dom & Suzanne Santoriello
piniciominpins@hotmail.co.uk
© Pro Paw Design

Cloverwood Dandies...
breeding for type, conformation, temperament... and that little extra something!

Ch Cloverwood Royal George

Expertly handled by Geoff Corish to win
17 CCs –15 with BOB.

George has had numerous Group placings, and was Top Dandie 2012 and 2013.

His sire is Mike Macbeth's beautiful **Am/Can Ch Gateway Sparks at Glahms**.

Thank you to all the judges who have given Cloverwood such a successful year.

Breeder/owner Mrs Joan Glen Tinsley,
Blackboy Farm, Wellington, Somerset TA21 9QD
Email Joantinsley@aol.com

Spinillons Papillons... celebrating 50 Ch titles!

**The ONLY Papillon breeders to win CCs / Top Awards from the Good Citizens Classes!
3 years Top Papillon in the KC Breeders Comp, All Fit For Function!**

CH SPINILLONS REBEL ROWSER JW ShCM
13 x BIS, 4 x RBIS, 5 x GS
Ch Show Group Placer
Champion Of Champion Qualifed (Ireland)
East Anglian Super Match Qualifed

CH & IR CH SPINILLONS SAFFIRE JW ShCM
12 CCs
Multiple BIS and RBIS

IR JUNIOR CH SPINILLONS CLASSIC CARESS JW
JW at 10m, Green Star, Multiple RGS/RCC Winner

SPINILLONS SERANADE JW
Co-owned by Danni Peterson of Remani Papillons, Oregon USA
JW won at 8months
Toy Puppy Group 1 – Belfast Ch Show 2013
4 x BPIS, 1 x RBPIS, BBPIS3, Multiple puppy Group Winner!

SPINILLONS ZUZZI JW
Green Star Winner, Group Winner, co-owned with Karen Farrell, Shown by Karen, Daniel or Jo Davidson-Poston

BISS MULTI CH (7) MAGNOLISE TIAGO FOR SPINILLONS
(Imp Phalene USA)

SPINILLONS SOFISTICATION
BPIS, BBPIS, Adult and Puppy Group winner!

Where Honesty, High Standards, Quality, Soundness and Condition Don't Just Count ... THEY ARE EVERYTHING!
All Spinillons Fit for Function, Health tested Clear, including 0-0 for Patella and OptiGen DNA Tested Clear for PRA1

Owned, bred and loved by
JO DAVIDSON-POSTON BA (Hons)
Email Jo@spinillons.com Website www.spinillons.com

CH HISNHERS DIAMOND GEEZER AT ANFRANJO JW ShCM

4 CCs - 3 RCCs

Yogi

Another successful year in Breed and Stakes classes including winning the Ch Stakes twice on the day
Also qualified again for the Pets as Therapy Stakes Final at Crufts 2014

We are so proud of our super boy, he really is a diamond

Jodie, Ann and Frank Harrison
01375 677026
ann.anfranjo@gmail.com

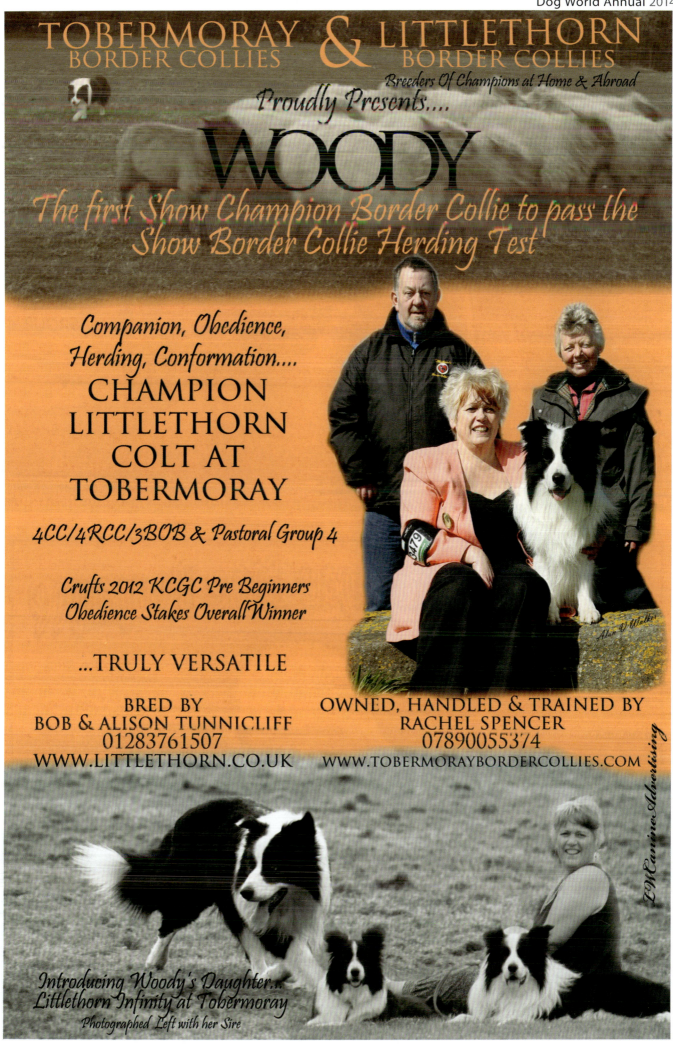

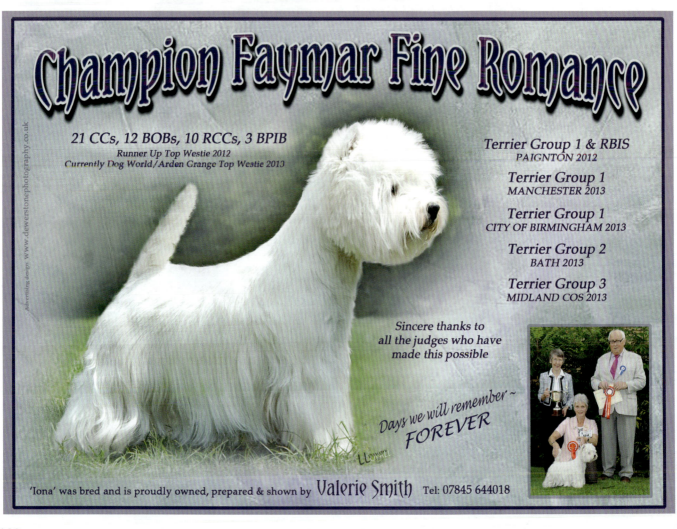

MILLINGFORD

CH MILLINGFORD CLOUDBERRY

TOP UK SCOTTIE for 2013*

Thanks to the following well renowned and respected breed and terrier specialists.

She won **CC and BOB** at these Championship Shows
Manchester - Stuart Plane (Stuane)
National Terrier - Jean Green (Ionascot)
Birmingham National - Susan Gaskell (Mayson)
Windsor - Laurie Herd (Brueik)
SKC (August) - Roger Crooks (Crooksmoor)
Darlington - Sandra Maclachlan (Burnview)
SWKA - Sue Thomson (Ashgate)
NESTC + BIS - Ava Platt (Tamzin)
Blackpool - CC - Jenny Morris (Scotchmore)

At the 16 shows she attended this year, she either won the
BCC or RCC (except at WKC)

Not forgetting the **RCC** at Crufts - David Guy (Donzeata)

Thanks to all who recognised her correct breed type, movement and quality. We are very proud of her.

Alison and Ashley Kenny
amkscotties@yahoo.co.uk or 01204 852934

*at time of going to press

The Canaan Dogs of Anacan keep on setting the standard!

Promoting Canaan Dogs since 1984. Member of the Assured Breeders Scheme.

THE SON

ANACAN ISSACHAR
Top Dog 2012
RBD Crufts 2012

THE FATHER

AM CH HA'ARETZ HAYYIM FOR ANACAN (Imp USA)
& RICHARD BOB CRUFTS 2013
TOP DOG 2013; TOP STUD DOG 2012
Photo by Alan Seymour

THE DAUGHTER

ANACAN HAPPY ANNI
Top Puppy 2011
RBB Crufts 2013
Photo by Yossi Guy

For breed information and details of our upcoming litters contact:
Richard & Ellen Minto
Anacan Boarding Kennels & Cattery
Little Lane, Irby In The Marsh
Lincs PE24 5AX

Tel: 01754 811153; Email: minto@canaandogsofanacan.com

www.canaandogsofanacan.com

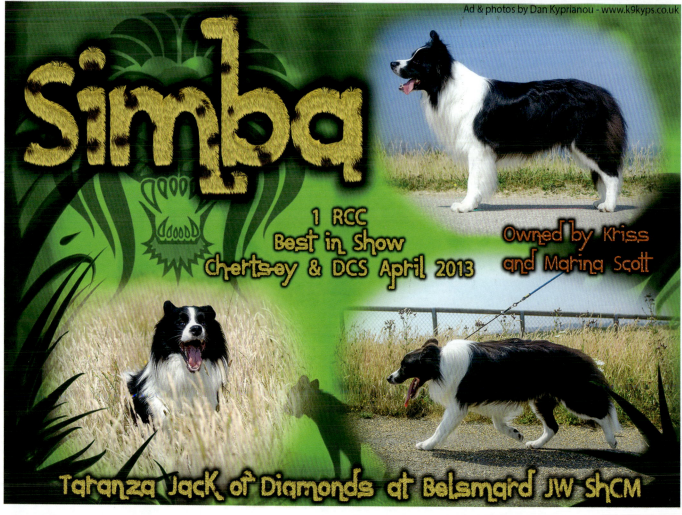

Dog World Annual 2014

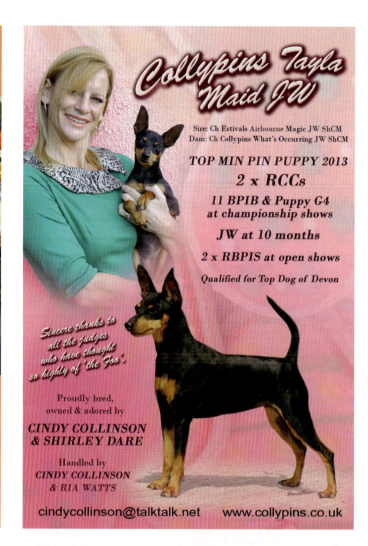

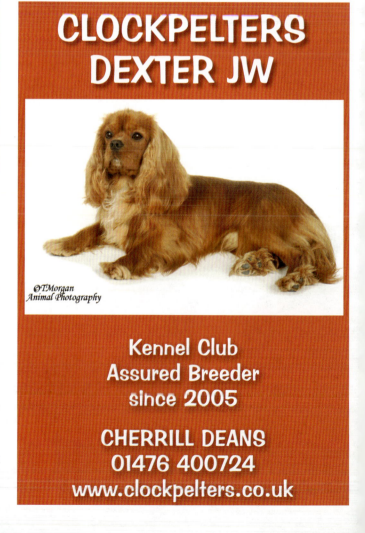

Continuous effort...

...is the key to unlocking our potential
Churchill

Macey
Owned by
Darren Jennings
Nancy &
Rita Walker

Rassi
Owned by
Nancy & Robin Walker

Alibama Talk Talk

Alibama Now you're Talking

ALIBAMA AMERICAN COCKERS
07854421938
DARREN@ALIBAMA.CO.UK
WWW.ALIBAMA.CO.UK

Dog World Annual 2014

Ch Gnejnabay Genegenie Gal at Lowbrook JW ShCM

Top Bedlington 3 years in a row, Genie has 29 CCs, 21 with Best of Breed. Also she has 15 group placings and is the bitch record holder.

Owned and much loved by
Angela and Stuart Yearley
Tel: 01628 630617

SUBSCRIBE to our free weekly newsletter

Receive news of the latest content from our growing portfolio of websites and other interesting information from the world of dogs.

PLEASE VISIT
www.dogworld.co.uk/newsletter
to sign up now!

Memetuka Basenjis

What an exciting year 2013 has been

Freya, our beautiful girl arrived from Finland and exceeded all our expectations by taking the RCC at her very first show at just 6 months of age. Not to be outdone by the new arrival, Rocco, our handsome homebred boy, made us all very proud by gaining his title of Champion.

Hi-Lite Bulldobas Wild Child Of Memetuka (imp Fin) (Freya)
1 RCC, 1 BB with BOB and 3 BPIB

Ch Memetuka Jabali ShCM (Rocco)
3 CCs, 3 BOB, 5 RCCs, 2 BD, 4 RBD, BIS (BOBA 2012), RBIS (BOBA 2013)

Memetuka Juakali (Sunny)
1 BD, 3 RBD, 3 BPIB

Many thanks to all the judges who have thought so highly of our dogs.
For more information visit our web pages at http://www.champdogs.co.uk/breeder/24278
email memetukabasenjis@gmail.com
Bred, owned, loved and handled by **Victoria Gaskell**

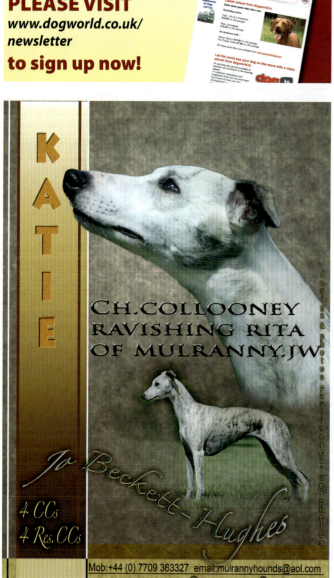

Damai Longhaired Dachshunds
OUR STAR
Damai Master Benedict ShCM
(Sonny)

Multiple Best Veterans in Show including:
Southern Dachs Ch Show
Dachs Club Open
Eastern Counties Dachs Open
Southern Dachs Open
Camberley Open Gravesend and Medway Open
BVIB L/H Dachs Ch BVIB and Veteran Stakes
Bournemouth Ch Show and many more Stakes wins, BOB and Groups

Proudly owned and bred by
June and Ken Sutton
Tel 01424 870683

GRIFFON BRUXELLOIS

VICE WORLD CH. 2012
EUROPEAN WINNER 2011, 2010
ASIA & THE PACIFIC SECTION WINNER 2011
CH. OF KOREA
CH. INTERNATIONAL DE BEAUTE
MEDITERRANEAN CH., CH. DE FRANCE,
CH. DE BEAUTE DE MONACO
FINNISH WINNER 2010
NORDIC CH., DANISH CH.,
FINNISH CH., SWEDISH CH., SWISS CH.,
RUSSIAN CH., CH. OF POLAND
POLAND WINNER, POLAND CLUB WINNER
CH. OF CZECH REPUBLIC,
CH. OF MONTENEGRO
CH. OF REPUBLIC MACEDONIA
CH. OF HUNGARY, HUNGARY CLUB WINNER
CH. OF BULGARIA, CH. OF ITALY
BIG INTERNATIONAL DOG SHOW LATINA (Italy) 22/09/2012
CH. & GRAND CH. OF UKRAINE
LITHUANIAN CH., CH. OF SLOVENIA
AUSTRIAN CH., BIS DE LA NATIONAL D'ELEVAGE PONTOISE – 11/09/2010, BIS FRANCE PONTOISE INTERNATIONAL DOG SHOW – 12/09/2010
RESERVE BIS PARIS DOG SHOW 2011
INTERNATIONAL DOG SHOW – 09/01/2011

*I WOULD LIKE TO SAY THANKS ALL JUDGES WHO EVALUATED MY DOG AT ALL THE SHOWS AND CONTRIBUTED TO ITS TRIUMPH.
SPECIAL THANKS TO LEVINA ELENA AND FIRSOV VICTOR*

HUVIKUMMUN
RED JACKET

DATE OF BIRTH 24/09/2006

s. Barnfall Black Flash d. Huvikummun Red Elegance

OWNER MRS. TATIANA STARIKOVA
REDJACKY@LIST.RU
MOSCOW, RUSSIAN FEDERATION

Dog World Annual 2014

KATHINGTON

MINIATURE SMOOTH DACHSHUNDS

© Photos by Will Harris | Design by Zara Boyle

KATHINGTON CHANCE TO DREAM

(Libby)

Ch Kathington Chance N Counter x Kathington Grace & Favour

Consistently Placed at all Levels

KATHERINE HERRINGTON

01904 761903

www.kathington.co.uk

katherine.herrington@yahoo.co.uk

CH. KATHINGTON COEUR DE LION

(Richard)

Ch Donnadoon Imagination at Barisse x Kathington Chantelle JW

Continues Achieving Top Honours

CATCOMBE CRYSTAL BALL AT PAJULA
'Charlie'

(Sh Ch Charamese Roadrunner to Leighsham (JW) x Catcombe Cha Cha Cha)

Bought as a family pet, he wasn't introduced to showing until he was 15 months old. **He made a good start winning 3 x 1st places at his 1st Championship Show.**

Since then he has been regularly placed at shows and was **shortlisted at his 1st Crufts Show in 2013.**

We are very happy that Charlie won his 1st CC in July 2013.

He has a wonderful temperament and is a delight to own.

PAULA WILKINSON
Appleton, Warrington, Cheshire. Tel: 07810 301802 Email: pjrwilki@aol.com

Dog World Annual 2014

Liric Special Fanfare With Shillay (AI) JW

DOB 20/03/2011
'Cooper'

Sh Ch Shannas Daimler ex
Sh Ch Liric You're So Special JW

Another fantastic year in the ring with Cooper, such a special boy

1 CC, 4 RCCs

Owners
Ian and Connie Ford
www.shillaygordons.co.uk
shillaygordons@aol.com
0168 284142
'Shillay' 5 Darngaber Gardens, Quarter,
By Hamilton,
Lanarkshire
ML3 7XX

Breeder
Maureen Justice
www.liricgordonsetters.com

We're more than just a newspaper!

Design for print or online
Our in-house studio will professionally typeset and design your artwork at a competitive price and delivered on time.
- Stationery, brochures, leaflets and newsletters.
- Adverts, posters, pop-ups and signage.

Prices from £99

eBooks
Reading eBooks is becoming increasingly popular. Do you want to convert a book that is out of print or maybe you have written a book?
We will produce your ebook and help you market it online.
- Includes iPad and Kindle versions.
- Also works on Android.

Prices from £199

Let us help you be part of this exciting new age of digital media.

For further details please contact the sales department on
tel 01233 621877 or email advertising@dogworld.co.uk

JENERELENA

What a wonderful year for ...

DOMBURG LOVE GAMES WITH JENERELENA (pictured)

Leea has had a fantastic start to her show career:
2 x Best Puppy in Show
Best Puppy bitch - Southern Counties
Best of Breed and Best Puppy - Three Counties
Best Puppy and Pastoral Puppy Group 4 - Blackpool
Best Puppy bitch - Leeds

A huge thank you to Linda Collins for entrusting us with such a special girl.

And our homebred Border Collie
JENERELENA AGAIN ITS MAGIC
Alfie
(owned by Debbie and Paul Logan)
Reserve Challenge Certificate - WKC 2013

Handled by Helena Hutchings,
Owned by - **Eric, Jenny and Helena Hutchings and Keith Brooks**

www.jenerelena.com

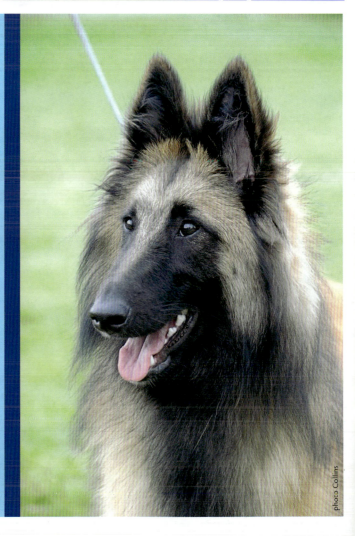

photo Collins

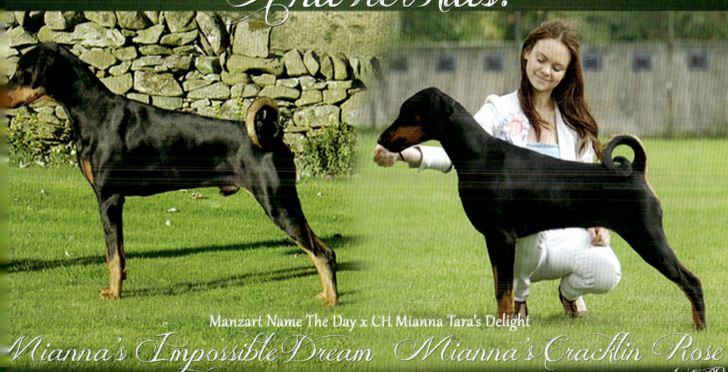

Liwang Basenjis

Krystyna & Janusz Opara, Poland, liwang@wp.pl, www.liwang.pl

International CACIB shows in Denmark 2014

1. Fredericia, 8-9/2 2014
2. Roskilde, 10/5 2014
   Roskilde, 11/5 2014
   (Crufts qualification Sunday)
3. Vejen, 21/6 2014
   Vejen, 22/6 2014
4. Bornholm, 16/8 2014
   Bornholm, 17/8 2014
5. Hillerød, 20-21/9 2014
   (Copenhagen Winner Show)
6. Herning, 1/11 2014
   Herning, 2/11 2014
   (Danish Winner Show Sunday)

Take your dog with you to Denmark

Denmark is a great place to go on holiday with your dog. All year round you are allowed to bring your (nice) dog unleashed in over 175 special "dog friendly woods". In the winter term you can also enjoy the beaches.

You can rent holiday houses through the Danish Kennel Club's partner NOVASOL-dansommer at www.novasol.dk or www.dansommer.dk.

Combine your holiday with one of the Danish Kennel Club's international CACIB shows, which have an international reputation of being very well organised. Read more at www.dkk.dk/en/Shows. It is possible to enter and pay on-line.

MAINTAINING THE STANDARD

www.ridleyceskyterriers.com

RANGALI - Top Fauve 2013*

Heidi Allenby with **Ch/Ir Ch Brequest Bailee Basler and Ch Hirondelle Rangali (imp France)**

Ch Gigolo du Rallye Saint Paul for Rangali (imp France)

*at time of going to press

Ch Hirondelle Rangali Top Fauve 2013*, 5 CCs all with BOB, BIS at the Club Ch Show 2013, youngest ever Fauve champion at just 14 months and another first for the breed, she has become the first Fauve to obtain a JW

Ch Gigolo du Rallye Saint Paul for Rangali 3 CCs, 4 RCCs and BIS at the Club Open Show 2013
Ch/Ir Ch Brequest Bailee Basler (co-owned with Ruth Farrell) 6 CCs and BVIS and RCC at Club Ch Show 2013
Rangali Magic Moment 1 CC and 13 RCCs
Rangali Oh La La BPIS at the Club Ch Show 2013

What a year – doubles at Houndshow, City of Birmingham and Darlington (with CCs), Three Counties and Driffield (without CCs)

Thank you to all the judges who have thought so highly of all our dogs. A huge thank you to Colin and Ann Makey who help show and handle my team and for all the hard work behind the scenes and their constant support. Della and I appreciate you very much!
Thank you to Chris Schofield for handling Magic beautifully at some shows this year.

Della, Gigolo, Magic and Ola are all loved and owned by **Richard and Heidi Allenby** 01327 857886/07886 454587 heidi.allenby@googlemail.com

GILLANDANT PYRENEANS

Breeder of 13 UK Champions,
3 International, 1 American

Top Pyrenean 2011, '12, '13
Top Breeder 2010, '11, '12, '13
Top Brood Bitch 2010, '11, '12, '13

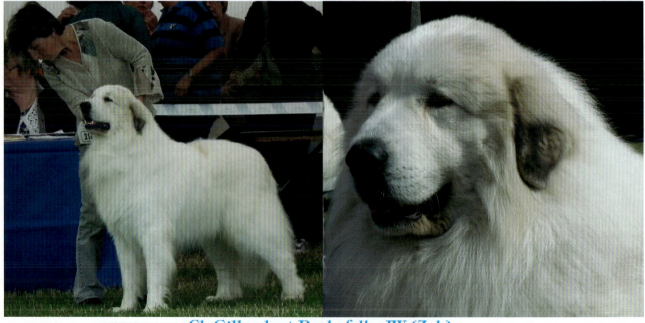

Ch Gillandant Rockafella JW (Zak)
Top Winning PMD 2012, 2013 to date 14 CCs, 3 x Group 3, 2 x Group 4
Ch Gillandant Sugar And Spice JW Top Winning PMD 2011, 25 CCs
Ch Gillandant Annie Oakley Top Brood Bitch 2010, '11, '12, '13
Mother to the above and 4 other Champions

Proud breeder and owner **GILL POLLARD** 01775 640469, tonygillandant@tiscali.co.uk

Holmchappell

Happy, healthy hounds (and their little friends)!

Dr Jessica Holm
KC Assured Breeder
07876 482398
jessica.holm@btinternet.com
www.jessicaholm.co.uk

photo Clifton Photographic

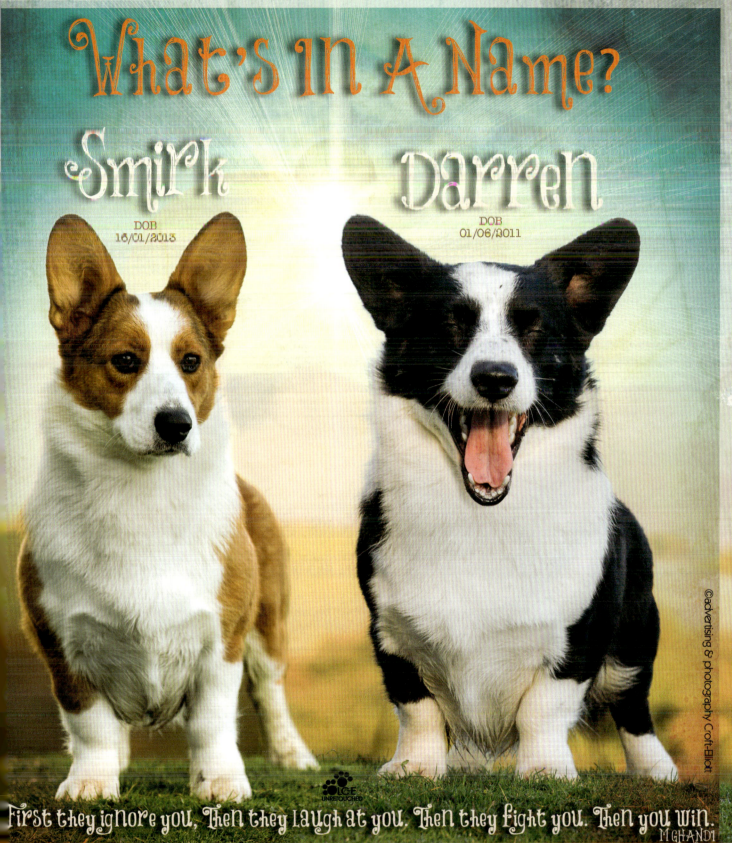

highampress.co.uk

dog.biz

- 🐾 **Show Secretaries Zone for Real Time Show Entries**
- 🐾 **Real Time Dog Show Results**
- 🐾 **Photo Gallery of Winners**
- 🐾 **Downloadable Breed Catalogues**

JOIN THE CC CLUB for:

- 🐾 **Show Results Feedback Service**

How to: Navigate to My CC Club Account
Click My Show Results Feedback Service Button

See us on Facebook and Twitter for the latest Show News

Higham Press Ltd., New Street, Higham, Alfreton, Derbyshire DE55 6BP
Tel: 01773 832390   Fax: 01773 520794
Email: mail@highampress.co.uk   admin@dog.biz

THE Lifestyle Zone
THE online insurance portal for pet owners

 Also you can follow us on Facebook and Twitter

Websites: www.highampress.co.uk   www.dog.biz   www.thelifestylezone.co.uk

Debbeacol Bearded Collies
Debbeacol Harmony In Motion JW ShCM
'Hannah'

W&PBAS 2013 – CC & BOB
Judge – A. Wight
Group 1 & Best in Show
Judge – C. Reed

Driffield Agricultural Soc. 2013 – CC
Judge – W. Knowles

BPIS & BIS at Open Shows

Ch Debbeacol Pride And Joy JW
'Elsa'

Elsa is my homebred champion and dam of Hannah

Eastern Bearded Collie Association (EBCA) 2012 - CC
Judge - M. Harkin

National Dog Show 2012 - CC
Judge - A. Pedder

City of Birmingham 2012 - CC & BOB
Judge - B. Harcourt-Brown

W&PBAS 2012 - RCC
Judge - W. Smith

Scottish Breeds 2013 - RCC
Judge - I. Copus

Owned by
DEBORAH WEIGHTMAN
debbeacol@yahoo.com
www.debbeacol.co.uk
01609 881047 / 07787 505428

Catalogues - Schedules - Year Books
Newsletters - Judge's Books - Binding
Prize Cards - Ring Numbers - Steward's
Cards - Award Boards - Show Results
Greetings Cards - Calendars - Printing
Online Entries - Posters - Tickets

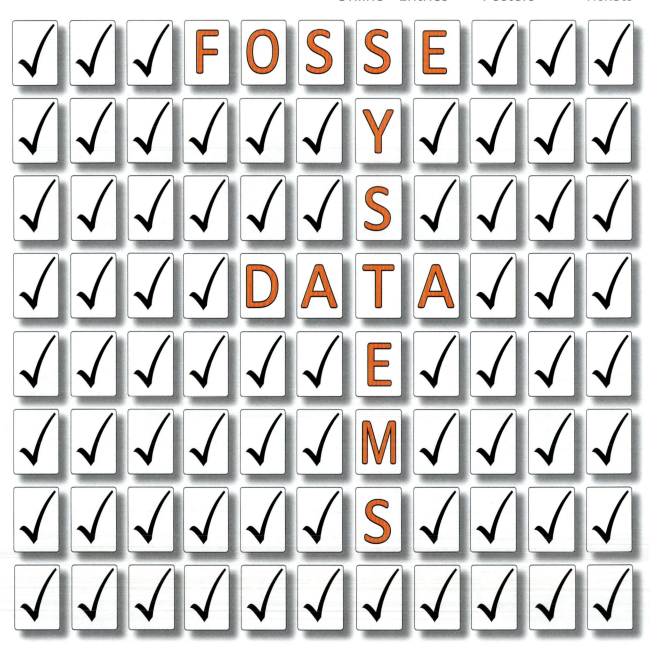

Quality printing services, one company ticking ALL the boxes

Fosse Data Systems Limited
Tripontium Business Centre, Newton,
Rugby, Warwickshire CV23 0TB

Tel: 01788 860960 Fax 01788 860969
enquiries@fossedata.co.uk ~ www.fossedata.co.uk

SCALLYWAGS R AUSSIES
COMBINING THE VERY BEST OF ITALIAN AND AMERICAN BLOODLINES

Their dad is GB CH Allmark Indecent Proposal JW ShCM – 'Sunni' is top male '13 & litter brother to Breed Record Holder, Ch Allmark Fifth Avenue, 'Tiff'. Their mum is Irish & International Ch Hop Scotch Del Whymper Delle G. Jorasses, An Ch '10 '11 '12, Celtic Winner 2010, 11, 12. 'Gab' is Ireland's Top Group and all breeds ch BIS winning Aussie.

At just over 6 months old, those who have made their debut in the show ring have already made their mark...

pictured @ 3½ mths

Congratulations to 'Dixie'
SCALLYWAG MY BLUE HEAVEN IN CASTLEAVERY
rules the house in Comber, County Down, and is owned & loved by Karen & James Gilliland. 'Dixie' won Res Green Star on her official show debut at 6½ months old after taking BBPIB at the IKC International at just 5 mths. Pics by James Gilliland

And 'Wallace'
SCALLYWAG THE HIGHLANDER WITH ALLMARK

'Wallace' lives with Paul Routledge, partner Mandy & son Bradley in Cumbria, where his main pastime as a puppy was gardening (like the rest of his siblings). Paul recently handled him to BPIB and third in the Pastoral Puppy Group at Working & Pastoral Breeds of Scotland Ch show, under judge, Richard C Kinsey; he is co-owned with Angie Allan & Robert Harlow. Pics by Keith Robinson & Kirsty Benton

And 'Brody'
SCALLYWAG STARS N STRIPES WITH ZARACLE

Sarah McCusker and 'Brody' have formed a close partnership since he was 8 weeks and at his show debut at the STCI show in Dublin, he won BOB and 2nd in Group 1 at just 6½ months. Photo by Patrick Fortune

And staying at Scallywag 'Twink' & 'Jason' -
SCALLYWAG SINGIN THE BLUES

AND HER BROTHER
SCALLYWAG TENNESSEE WALTZ

And 'Fonzi'
SCALLYWAG ONE DIRECTION TO JUROVI

'Fonzi' has made himself indispensable to his much loved owner, Helen Flanagan. BBPDIB at 5 mths, 'Fonzi' was 4th from 50 entries, in the Puppy Stakes at Cloghran Ch show at just 6½ months old. Photo by Noel Beggs

Are real Scallywags, and if there were Green Stars for pruning, digging, demolishing sofas and general naughtiness, they would both be Champions already!!
'Twink' was BBPIB at Carlow all breed ch show at five mths. Her brother, 'Jason' looks forward to getting enough manners to be allowed to join his sisters and brothers in the showring shortly...

Not forgetting Scallywag You'll Never Walk Alone, 'Loki' and Scallywag Viva Las Vegas 'Sam' – now living in super homes by the ocean in Kilkeel (NI) and the North West tip of Scotland.

Thank you to all the judges who like the Scallywags as much as we do – we are very proud of this litter – our first in Aussies. Thank you also to the owners of the pups, we are fortunate they are in such caring homes.
We wish them every success for the future.

JOYCE AND DES MANTON – International All Breeds Ch Show Judges (FCI, AKC & KUSA)
irishcaninepress@btinternet.com   Tel: +44 (0) 28 9181 9351

Gayteckels

Adrian, Chris and Russell Marett
www.zidoutceskys.co.uk

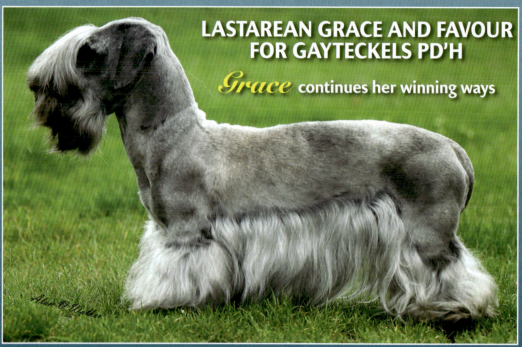

LASTAREAN GRACE AND FAVOUR FOR GAYTECKELS PD'H

Grace continues her winning ways

2013 highlights

Reserve Channel Islands Dog of the Year
Best of Breed – National Terrier
Best of Breed – City of Birmingham
Reserve Best Bitch – Leeds
Reserve Best Bitch – South Wales
Reserve Best in Show winner
Guernsey Kennel Club Prix d'Honneur

And not forgetting...

LASTAREAN KRAL OF ZIDOUT (Taj)

Best of Breed – Three Counties
Reserve Best Dog – Crufts
Reserve Best Dog – South Wales
Channel Island Agility Dog of the Year finalist
and still active at ten years old!

LIMIER DIDIER AT GAYTECKELS PD'H (Didi)

Multiple Group Winner
Channel Island
Dog of the Year finalist

Dog World Annual 2014

FORTHCOMING SHOWS
Make a note of the dates NOW

See Dog World Weekly for more details of these and other shows throughout the coming year

NATIONAL DOG SHOW
'The Society that listens to the exhibitor'

Thursday 8th May 2014 – Utility & Toy
Friday 9th May 2014 – Hound & Terrier
Saturday 10th May 2014 – Gundog
Sunday 11th May 2014 – Working & Pastoral

- Overseas Breed Specialists
- 27 first CC appointments
- Veteran Classes in all CC Breeds
- First Championship Show Puppy Groups of 2014
- Best Puppy in Show
- Good Prize Money - £25 for winners of Veteran Stakes, Champion Stakes, Puppy Stakes, Special Beginners Stakes, and Post Graduate Stakes - £40 for winner of Good Citizens Stakes
- YKC Members and Handling Classes
- Free Car Park
- Daily 'Ring Craft' Training
- Catering unit for outside rings
- Daily Canine Seminars
- Dedicated Grooming Areas
- No increase in entry fees

For further information, please contact the Secretary, Angela Mitchell, Church Clerk's Cottage, Church Hill, Lawford, Essex CO11 2JX Tel: 01206 391984 email thenational@btinternet.com

---

The world famous BLACKPOOL
CHAMPIONSHIP DOG SHOW
Friday 20, Saturday 21, Sunday 22 June, 2014

Friday — Toys, Terriers & Utility   Saturday — Hounds & Gundogs   Sunday — Pastoral & Working

Secretary, Mr Steve Hall, Shenedene, Gregson Lane, Hoghton, Nr Preston, PR5 ODP
Tel 01254 853526   email: secretary@blackpooldogshow.com   www.blackpooldogshow.com

---

THE CITY OF BIRMINGHAM CHAMPIONSHIP SHOW
(Web site: www.birminghamcitydogshow.co.uk)   *Sends Best Wishes for Christmas & the New Year*

2014 show will be held at STONELEIGH PARK, WARWICKSHIRE CV8 2LZ

**Friday August 29 – Hounds & Toys   Saturday August 30 – Working, Pastoral & Terriers
Sunday August 31 – Gundogs & Utility**

Closing date: 7th July, 2014   Online closing: Noon 21st July, 2014

Secretary: Mr Keith A W Young, 17 Riversleigh Road, Leamington Spa, Warwickshire CV32 6BG Tel: (01926) 336480

Dog World Annual 2014

WINDSOR CHAMPIONSHIP SHOW

Held alongside to the historic River Thames in **Home Park, Windsor SL4 6HX**
SINCERE GREETINGS FOR CHRISTMAS AND THE NEW YEAR TO ALL OUR FRIENDS

BOOK FOUR DAYS FOR OUR GREAT SUMMER SHOW IN 2014

THURSDAY 26th June – HOUNDS & TOYS **FRIDAY 27th June — TERRIERS & UTILITY**
SATURDAY 28th June — WORKING & PASTORAL **SUNDAY 29th June — GUNDOGS**

HON SECRETARY: MRS IRENE TERRY, 13 RENNETS CLOSE, ELTHAM, LONDON SE9 2NQ
TELEPHONE 020 8850 5321   FAX 020 8850 5205

 ## MANCHESTER DOG SHOW SOCIETY

Welcomes you and your dogs to
THE CLASSIC 2014
STAFFORD COUNTY SHOWGROUND, BINGLEY HALL

THURSDAY JANUARY 16 – HOUND & TERRIER   **FRIDAY JANUARY 17 – TOY & UTILITY**
SATURDAY JANUARY 18 – WORKING & PASTORAL   **SUNDAY JANUARY 19 – GUNDOG**

Dates for 2015 are January 15–18

Seasonal greetings from the Committee and Members

Hon Secretary: PAUL HARDING, Pringham House, 324 Warrington Road, Rainhill, Merseyside L35 9JA, 0151 430 7698
you can download the schedule and enter on-line at www.highampress.co.uk or www.dog.biz

---

MIDLAND CANINE  COUNTIES SOCIETY

GENERAL CHAMPIONSHIP SHOW 2014

A Quality Affordable Show

Bingley Hall, Stafford County Showground ST18 0BD

THURSDAY OCTOBER 23: GUNDOGS
FRIDAY OCTOBER 24: HOUNDS & PASTORAL
SATURDAY OCTOBER 25: WORKING & TERRIER
SUNDAY OCTOBER 26: TOYS & UTILITY

CLOSING DATE MONDAY SEPTEMBER 1, 2014
Online Monday September 8, 2014

Secretary Mr Rodney Price, Pen Bryn Llech, Llanrhaeadr, Denbigh LL16 4PH
Tel/Fax 01745 890368
Web site: www.fossedata.co.uk   Email: pricerodney1@gmail.com